EDITED BY J.M.S. CARELESS

The Pre-Confederation Premiers: Ontario Government Leaders, 1841-1867

Published by University of Toronto Press
Toronto   Buffalo   London
for the Ontario Historical Studies Series

Canadian Cataloguing in Publication Data

Main entry under title:

The Pre-Confederation premiers
(Ontario historical studies series ISSN 0380-9188)

Includes index.
ISBN 0-8020-3363-6

1. Prime ministers – Ontario – Biography.
2. Ontario – Biography.   I. Careless, J.M.S., 1919-
II. Series.

FC3071.1.A1P74   971.3'02'0922   c79-094772-2
F1056.8.P74

Acknowledgment for permission to reproduce illustrations in this book is hereby
given to the Public Archives of Canada, except for the following: Metropolitan
Toronto Library Board: William Baldwin, George Brown, Spadina house, King St.
Toronto, Weller Stagecoach, St Paul's Yorkville, Macdonald's Hotel, Red Lion Inn;
Osgoode Hall: William Draper; R.S. Longley, *Sir Francis Hincks* (Toronto, Univer-
sity of Toronto Press, 1943): Francis Hincks.

This book has been published with funds provided by the Government of Ontario
through the Ministry of Culture and Recreation.

Contents

The Ontario Historical Studies Series

When discussions about this series of books first arose, it was immediately apparent that very little work had been done on the history of Ontario. Ontario has many fine historians, but much of their work has been focused on national themes, despite the fact that the locus of many of the important developments in the history of Canada – as recent events remind us – was, and is, in the provinces. While other provinces have recognized this reality and have recorded their histories in permanent form, Ontario is singularly lacking in definitive works about its own distinctive history.

Thus, when the Ontario Historical Studies Series was formally established by Order-in-Council on 14 April 1971, the Board of Trustees was instructed not only to produce authoritative and readable biographies of Ontario premiers but also 'to ensure that a comprehensive program of research and writing in Ontario history is carried out.'

From the outset the Board has included both professional historians and interested and knowledgeable citizens. The present members are: Margaret Angus, Kingston; J.M.S. Careless, Toronto; Floyd S. Chalmers, Toronto; R.E.G. Davis, Toronto; Gaetan Gervais, Sudbury; D.F. McOuat, Toronto; Jacqueline Neatby, Ottawa; J. Keith Reynolds, Toronto; and J.J. Talman, London. E.E. Stewart and Raymond Labarge served as valued members of the Board in its formative period. The combination of varied interests and skills of Board members has proven useful. A consensus was soon reached on the need for research in neglected areas of Ontario history and for scholarly and well-written works that would be of interest and value to the people of Ontario. We trust our work will satisfy these criteria.

After much careful deliberation the Board settled on six major areas in which to pursue its objectives: biographies of premiers; a bibliography; a historical atlas; a group of theme studies on major developments (social, economic, and cultural as well as political) in the province; the recording on tape of the attitudes, opinions, and memories of many important leaders in

Ontario; and, as a culmination of these studies, a definitive history of Ontario.

The first edition of the bibliography was published in 1973. As it was well received, the Board has sponsored the preparation of a second, comprehensive edition which will apear in 1980. Our first major publication was the biography of G. Howard Ferguson by Peter N. Oliver (1977). This was followed in 1978 by *Ontario Since 1867*, a general history of the province by Joseph Schull. *The Pre-Confederation Premiers: Ontario Government Leaders, 1841-1867*, edited by J.M.S. Careless, is the second volume to be published in the group of biographies of the premiers. We hope it will find a large and interested reading audience and that it will be followed each year by one or more equally interesting books, the total of which will inform and illuminate Ontario history in a new and lasting way.

The Board has been heavily dependent upon its two editors, Goldwin S. French, Editor-in-Chief, and Peter N. Oliver, Associate Editor. Both men have served the Board with diligence and devotion and we are greatly indebted to them for the refinement of topics and the selection of authors for the many projects we have undertaken.

MURRAY G. ROSS
Chairman, Board of Trustees
Ontario Historical Studies Series

16 August 1979

For many years the principal theme in English-Canadian historical writing has been the emergence and the consolidation of the Canadian nation. This theme has been developed in uneasy awareness of the persistence and importance of regional interests and identities, but because of the central role of Ontario in the growth of Canada, Ontario has not been seen as a region. Almost unconsciously, historians have equated the history of the province with that of the nation and have depicted the interests of other regions as obstacles to the unity and welfare of Canada.

The creation of the province of Ontario in 1867 was the visible embodiment of a formidable reality, the existence at the core of the new nation of a powerful if disjointed society whose traditions and characteristics differed in many respects from those of the other British North American colonies. The intervening century has not witnessed the assimilation of Ontario to the other regions in Canada; on the contrary, it has become a more clearly articulated entity. Within the formal geographical and institutional framework defined so assiduously by Ontario's political leaders, an increasingly intricate web of economic and social interests has been woven and shaped by the dynamic interplay between Toronto and its hinterland. The character of this regional community has been formed in the tension between a rapid adaptation to the processes of modernization and industrialization in modern Western society and a reluctance to modify or discard traditional attitudes and values. Not surprisingly, the Ontario outlook is a compound of aggressiveness, conservatism, and the conviction that its values should be the model for the rest of Canada.

The purpose of the Ontario Historical Studies Series is to describe and analyse the historical development of Ontario as a distinct region within Canada. The series as planned will include approximately thirty-five volumes covering many aspects of the life and work of the province from its original establishment in 1791 as Upper Canada to our own time. Among these will be biographies of several prominent political figures, a three-volume economic history, numerous works on such topics as social structure, education, minority groups, labour, political and administrative institutions, literature, theatre, and the arts, and a comprehensive synthesis of the history of Ontario, based upon the detailed contributions of the biographies and thematic studies.

In planning this project, the Editors have endeavoured to maintain a reasonable balance between different kinds and areas of historical research, and to appoint authors ready to ask new kinds of questions about the past and to answer them in accordance with the canons of contemporary scholarship. Ten biographical studies have been included, if only because through biography the past comes alive most readily for the general reader as well as the historian. The historian must be sensitive to today's concerns and standards as he engages in the imaginative recreation of the interplay between human beings and circumstances in time. He should seek to be the mediator between all the dead and the living, but in the end the humanity and the artistry of his account will determine the extent of its usefulness.

The Pre-Confederation Premiers: Ontario Government Leaders, 1841-1867 is the second volume to be published in the group of biographies of the premiers. In this work Maurice Careless and his associates, George Metcalf, William Ormsby, Keith Johnson, and Bruce Hodgins, have described and assessed the careers of William Draper, Robert Baldwin, Francis Hincks, John A. Macdonald, and John Sandfield Macdonald in the years preceding Confederation. These five men held office as 'co-premiers' of the Province of Canada for significant periods of time. In this capacity they helped to shape and were shaped by the rapidly changing conditions of Canada West, the future Ontario. We hope that these essays will illuminate the parts they played in the politics of Canada West and thereby enlarge our understanding of the foundations on which future premiers from Mowat to Robarts would build.

GOLDWIN FRENCH
Editor-in-Chief
PETER OLIVER
Associate Editor

Toronto
16 August 1979

Contributors

J. MAURICE S. CARELESS is University Professor in History at the University of Toronto, where for over twenty years he has been particularly engaged in teaching Ontario history. Trained at Toronto and Harvard universities, he has written *Canada: a Story of Challenge*, *Brown of the Globe* (two volumes), and *The Union of the Canadas, 1841-1857*, among numerous other books and articles.

BRUCE W. HODGINS, professor in the Department of History of Trent University, was educated at the University of Western Ontario, Queen's University, and Duke University. He is the author of a biography, *John Sandfield Macdonald*, articles on federalism and Canadian politics, and has edited collective volumes in Canadian history.

J. KEITH JOHNSON, professor of history at Carleton University, was educated at the University of Toronto, and was with the Public Archives of Canada in his earlier career. He has written widely in Ontario history, and his publications notably include *The Letters of Sir John A. Macdonald* (two volumes) and *Affectionately Yours: the Letters of Sir John A. Macdonald and his Family, 1842-1891*.

GEORGE METCALF is associate professor of history at the University of Western Ontario, after some years of teaching at the University of London. Trained at Toronto and London, he has worked and published in British imperial history; but also in Canadian history, with which he began, and in which he is now engaged on a major study of William Draper.

WILLIAM G. ORMSBY, formerly professor of history at Brock University and now archivist of Ontario, was educated at Toronto and Carleton, then served with the Public Archives of Canada before going to Brock and more recently to head the Archives of Ontario. Among his publications are *Crisis in the Canadas, 1838-1839* and *The Emergence of the Federal Concept in Canada, 1839-1845.*

William Henry Draper

Allan Napier MacNab

William Warren Baldwin

Robert Baldwin

George Brown

Francis Hincks

John Alexander Macdonald

John Sandfield Macdonald

Louis Hippolyte LaFontaine   George Etienne Cartier

Antoine-Aimé Dorion   William McDougall

Toronto from inland, late 1840s

Toronto Bay and fort, late 1840s

Louis Hippolyte LaFontaine

George Etienne Cartier

Antoine-Aimé Dorion

William McDougall

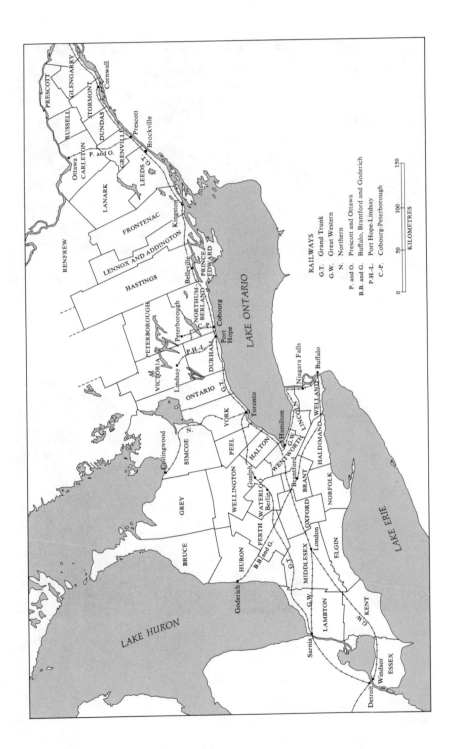

LAKE ONTARIO

LAKE ERIE

LAKE HURON

PRESCOTT
GLENGARRY
RUSSELL
STORMONT
DUNDAS
CARLETON
Ottawa
P. and O.
GRENVILLE
Prescott
Brockville
Cornwall
LANARK
LEEDS
RENFREW
FRONTENAC
Kingston
LENNOX AND ADDINGTON
HASTINGS
PETERBOROUGH
Belleville
PRINCE EDWARD
NORTHUMBERLAND
Peterborough
Cobourg
C.-P.
Port Hope
VICTORIA
Lindsay
P.H.-L.
DURHAM
ONTARIO
G.T.
Toronto
YORK
Collingwood
N.
SIMCOE
PEEL
HALTON
Hamilton
Niagara Falls
Buffalo
WENTWORTH
G.W.
LINCOLN
WELLAND
WELLINGTON
Guelph
Berlin
WATERLOO
Branford
BRANT
HALDIMAND
NORFOLK
GREY
PERTH
P. and G.
B.B. and G.
OXFORD
London
HURON
Goderich
MIDDLESEX
ELGIN
BRUCE
G.W.
LAMBTON
KENT
G.W.
Sarnia
Windsor
Detroit
ESSEX

RAILWAYS

G.T.   Grand Trunk
G.W.   Great Western
N.   Northern
P. and O. Prescott and Ottawa
B.B. and G. Buffalo, Brantford and Goderich
P.H.-L.   Port Hope-Lindsay
C.-P.   Cobourg-Peterborough

0   50   100   150
KILOMETRES

Spadina house, built for the Baldwin family in 1818

Bellevue, Kingston home of John A. Macdonald in the 1840s

opposite Upper Canada or Canada West in 1860

Toronto from inland, late 1840s

Toronto Bay and fort, late 1840s

King Street, Toronto, in the 1860s

Upper Canada Parliament Buildings, Toronto, periodically used in the 1850s and 60s

House of Assembly chamber in Upper Canada Parliament Buildings

Land travel by Weller Stagecoach before the railway age

St Paul's in the village of Yorkville, 1848

Downtown Kingston in the 1860s

Hamilton railway station in the 1850s

City hotel and shops, Toronto

Red Lion Inn, north of the city

Scots Catholic settlers' church at St Andrew's, burial place of Sandfield Macdonald

Rideau Canal and new Parliament Buildings under construction at Ottawa, early 1860s

THE PRE-CONFEDERATION PREMIERS:
ONTARIO GOVERNMENT LEADERS, 1841-67

clearly recognized as well. Still earlier William Henry Draper had left his own mark on the emerging pattern of Ontario leadership. Although no advocate of responsible government, Draper had virtually found that system growing up around him, and in practice had acted as premier and government leader in the mid-1840s even before that role had gained official sanction.

It is indeed worth stressing that just as Ontario was developing long before it was constitutionally proclaimed at Confederation, so the office of premier was evolving well before it was accepted as part of the formal constitition. Of course, a constitution is more broadly viewed not as a set, structural document put into authorized use at some specific moment, but as a continually developing pattern of governmental institutions and political procedures wherein effective practices settle into recognized rules and conventions. So, at least, has largely been the case for the British and Canadian parliamentary constitutions. And so it was for those early government leaders who may be termed Ontario's pre-Confederation premiers. It cannot properly be said that their office, the premiership, began at one fixed point – it was not initiated by any statute – any more than it could even be said that Ontario itself began precisely with the formation of Upper Canada in 1791. For certainly there had been historic growth in that region long prior to that date; during the French period before 1763, for instance, not to mention the preceding Indian era of Huron-Iroquois occupation. The best thing that can be done, then, is to choose the most significant times to mark beginnings: for Ontario, undoubtedly the birth of Upper Canada; for its premiers, the start of the Union of the Canadas in 1841.

This present work thus centres on the government leaders of pre-Confederation Ontario in the years from 1841 to 1867. On occasion, and particularly for the earlier figures of this period, the examination must reach well back into the preceding days of Upper Canada, in order to explain the development of their careers and the forces which shaped them. Yet the emphasis remains essentially on the mid-century decades after 1840. Before that time one can generally contend that there were not in the old province of Upper Canada men who could be termed leaders of government, and unquestionably nothing like the position of premier had yet come into being. Governmental leadership, both officially and practically, still rested in the hands of the British-appointed lieutenant-governors of Upper Canada. True, there were powerful colonial officials who exercised wide influence within the administration, and frequently on governors themselves: men like John Beverley Robinson and John Strachan, for example. Yet they could not openly lead, and their position of authority, entrenched as it might be within the long-enduring Upper Canadian oligarchy called the Family Compact, did not stem from the colonial parliament or people. They were not 'Ontario leaders' in that sense, even though they often had a far wider popular following than modern popular assumptions allow. They ultimately depended for their governmental place on the governor's authority and on imperial policy; and they could be bypassed or removed, and finally were, without recourse to the Upper Canadian populace.

At the same time, there were as well undoubted popular leaders in the original province who were not to be found in government: that was the very crux of the protest of Reform politicians against a governing circle which they could not control. A prominent Reform champion like William Lyon Mackenzie might win himself wide public backing, though its recurrently transient nature and the strength of Tory popular sentiment against him are too often underestimated. Another, like Robert Baldwin, might briefly be drawn into a place in government in the 1830s, only to find that he was effectively powerless there, in a provincial régime that thus far did not even accept the view that governing authority should rest with the spokesman of the popular will. No, in Upper Canada before the Union, government did not turn on the support of representatives of the people. Political parties themselves were but loosely organized. The position of established party leader thus did not yet exist, so that there was no one who as the party head of victorious parliamentary forces could have effectively become premier, as was the later practice – even had that office then been conceived.

Still further, in the days of Upper Canada the provincial administration was scarcely organized itself. Under the leadership of the governor there was an Executive Council for him to consult and a veritable jumble of officials with varied administrative assignments; but there was no collective group of departmental ministers who could have composed a cabinet or ministry headed by a first, or 'prime', minister – that is, by a premier. It was simply too soon. Though men like Robert Baldwin and his father, Dr William Warren Baldwin, were already advocating a true provincial ministry responsible to parliament, it did not then come to pass. Certainly radical Reformers like William Lyon Mackenzie did not press for it, and Mackenzie's abortive rebellion in 1837 had more sweeping aims. When Upper Canada ended as a separate province in 1841, its pattern of government still had not been changed.

Things would work out very differently thereafter, under the Canadian Union. Partly this was true, admittedly, because underlying conditions really were in process of altering: once more, it would be foolish to imagine that a wholly new age began overnight, with the proclamation of the United Province in February 1841. Events in train in the old Canadas – the influence of the rising concept of responsible government and the reforming imperial policies in Great Britain, all running well back before 1841 – meant that governmental patterns would alter with growing rapidity within the Union. In any event the executive now became tied to parliament, well-knit parties developed under recognized leaders the executive officers were moulded into a coherent provincial ministry – and, finally, the premier arose as political head of the administration as well as leader of the party that held the confidence of parliament. Altogether, there is much good reason for treating the Union period as the vital era that produced Ontario's pre-Confederation premiers.

There is more to the story than this, however. Changing imperial policy was already signalized by Lord Durham's famed report of 1839, when as governor general and high commissioner he had investigated the problems of British North America that had produced rebellions in the two Canadas. As a result he had recommended both their union and the granting of responsible government, which had been urged upon him by the Baldwins. British imperial authority proceeded to implement union as quickly as possible. It was reluctant to go as far as colonial responsible rule, although Lord John Russell as colonial secretary and Lord Sydenham as first governor general of the new United Province effected administrative reforms meant to head it off, which, all unintentionally, helped instead to bring it on within the decade. Beyond that, the Union itself, by enabling Lower Canadian and Upper Canadian Reformers to work together within one provincial parliament, gave them a combined party strength there which rendered it increasingly difficult to resist their demands for an executive dependent on the legislature. And further than this, Britain's own continuing shift towards policies of free trade made the imperial power willing at length to let leading colonies manage their own affairs. In brief, by 1848 responsible government could be recognized officially for Canada, where by this time – in practice – it was already far advanced.

The 1850s saw the enlargement of this self-government in Canada, especially in regard to full control of provincial fiscal policy. External aspects such as the conduct of foreign affairs, defence, and the negotiation of treaties still lay with Great Britain; yet this was what Canadians themselves desired, for they were not yet ready to push further. But as far as the Ontario community was concerned, the governing powers that it would hold after 1867 as a province of federal Canada were largely in its hands already. In other words, the functions of the premiers and their cabinets had been well established by the time of Confederation. Those Ontario leaders who afterwards went on into the politics of the new province would work with parliamentary practices and constitutional forms of cabinet rule which continued much the same.

Nevertheless, in two ways there were important differences thenceforth. First, the post-Confederation province was a unit in a federal system, and powers of government were thus divided between the federal and provincial levels of authority. In this respect Ontario government after 1867 had a more limited range of action than the Union government before it. Second, however, the people of Ontario had now gained a political jurisdiction of their own, one not limited by the need always to co-ordinate policy-making with the differing views and interests of French Canada. Hitherto the two sections of Canada had been yoked in often troubled partnership, expecially troubled on issues like education where each community had divergent outlooks to maintain. Politics under the Union had inevitably become a matter of trying to secure a sectional balance of interests. Indeed, from the moment the premiership fully appeared with responsible government in Canada, it had been sectionally divided. Premiers under the Union were really co-premiers, each leading his own half of the government and the country. Hence there was a succession of double-headed ministries: LaFontaine-Baldwin, Hincks-Morin, John A. Macdonald-Cartier, Sandfield Macdonald-Sicotte, and so on. Officially one co-premier took precedence, was actually the 'prime' minister who had charge of composing the cabinet, but the political necessities that stemmed from sectional differences produced the practical reality of dualism in that cabinet's operation.

Dualism, of course, reflected the very difficulties that led to the old Canadian Union's final breakdown and to the greater federal union of 1867. Nonetheless, it also meant that practically speaking there were 'Ontario' premiers in the pre-Confederation era. Men like Baldwin, Hincks, and John A. Macdonald *were* leaders for the Ontario community in government, just as their counterparts were for the Lower Canadian or Quebec half of the United Province. This affords still further reason to study premiers of the Union era within an Ontario frame; for while they had to deal, and continued to deal, with issues and policies affecting the whole province, they equally had a special base and interest in its Ontario segment. As direct forebears and lineal predecessors of the premiers of the province after Confederation, they belong in any biographical treatment of the chief figures in Ontario government.

In the treatment given here, Draper, Baldwin, Hincks, John A. Macdonald, and Sandfield Macdonald are each examined in a separate study, although these at times may overlap and interrelate, since their subjects' interests and careers did also. Still, the different perspectives afforded on developments as they affected these very distinctive politicians should only provide a richer picture. Not every significant Ontario leader of their period is thus covered in this group of essays. Some were simply less significant. These lesser figures are rather dealt with in passing and where relevant to the outstanding who hold the focus of attention. Two prominent pre-Confederation Ontario personages, however, are not awarded chapters in the text below – Allan MacNab and George Brown – and that deserves some words of explanation.

Sir Allan Napier MacNab, the veteran warrior and pugnacious Tory magnate from Hamilton, had an active, long, and far from undistinguished career in Upper Canadian and Union politics, being first elected in 1830 and serving as speaker of the assembly from 1837 to 1840 and again from 1844 to 1848. After leading Tory opposition forces between 1841 and 1844, and once more between 1850 and 1854, he finally became premier of the Union in September 1854, only to be forced from office by discontent within his own cabinet in May 1856. Following this he withdrew from public life, except for a brief return not long before his death in 1862. There is no question of MacNab's significance. He enters many times into the chapters that follow. Nevertheless, he does not qualify strongly as a *government* leader. Much of his career was spent in opposition; even as Speaker he was often not in the innermost governing circles. And though he did attain the premiership, he held it for only a year and nine months, during which time he was increasingly overshadowed by the rising Conservative power within his cabinet who replaced him, John A. Macdonald. Furthermore, Sir Allan was past his prime, elderly and gout-ridden while he held the premiership, and he did not mark it notably with his own accomplishments. In fact, he seemed chiefly happy just to enjoy office at last, and looked like a hoary hangover from the vanished Family Compact to the disgruntled younger Conservative members of his own party. Only in his eager concern for railway promotion did the Tory veteran appear to strike the mood of the expansive 1850s, especially with the classic remark with which he is perhaps best identified: 'All my politics are railroads.'[1]

As for George Brown, proprietor and editor of the forceful Toronto *Globe*, builder and leader of the potent Clear Grit Liberal party (which virtually became the instrument whereby Liberalism ruled Ontario after Confederation until 1905), not even his most ardent enemies could deny his towering presence during the pre-Confederation years. A strenuous, assertive Edinburgh Scot, Brown arrived in Canada as a journalist in 1843 after several years spent in New York. The *Globe*, which he founded the next year, became the powerful organ of the Upper Canada Reformers under Robert Baldwin in their campaign for responsible government. In 1851, however, on Baldwin's retirement from office, Brown split with his successor, Francis Hincks, and entered parliament himself as an independent Liberal. Then after 1854, when the collapse of the old Reform party under Hincks brought MacNab and John A. Macdonald's Conservatives to power, George Brown gradually rebuilt a Reform party by allying with the Upper Canadian Clear Grit radical movement – which indeed became far less radical under his direction. This new Brownite Liberal party won growing support across the western half of the Union by agitating for the annexation of the Northwest beyond the

Great Lakes and by demanding representation by population in order to give Upper Canada a preponderance of seats in the Union parliament and thus overcome its alleged domination by French-Canadian sectional interests.

In consequence, Brownite-Grit forces swept Upper Canada in the election of 1857, and the next year Brown even briefly became premier in the Brown-Dorion government, which lasted two whole days. The trouble was that the forces of sectionalism had become altogether too well balanced in the Union legislature. No government could be strong or last very long: Macdonald Conservative and Sandfield Macdonald Liberal-Moderate régimes followed and fell in turn. Meanwhile, Brown at the crowded Toronto Reform Convention of 1859 had swung his party to federal union as their remedy – but a federation only of the two Canadas, the other colonies being left to join in later. In 1864, when John A. Macdonald's latest attempt to form a viable ministry collapsed after less than three months, Brown himself proposed to sink party differences in joint support of a new government that would solve the troubles of the Union once and for all by adopting the federal principle. The consequent negotiations with his old adversaries, John A. Macdonald and George Etienne Cartier, produced a powerful new coalition cabinet with a commanding majority behind it, dedicated not just to federating the two Canadas but to obtaining a confederation of all the British North American colonies. The initiative of this Great Coalition led, of course, to the Charlottetown and Quebec conferences with representatives of the other provinces, at both of which Brown played a major part in drawing up the scheme of Confederation that was ultimately to go into effect in 1867.

By that date George Brown had left the Canadian ministry, resigning late in 1865 over the cabinet's proposed offer of reciprocity in trade with the United States on terms which he held to be too hastily conceived and easy. Defeated in campaigning for a difficult seat in the first federal election of September 1867, Brown did not seek a safe one but withdrew from the political career he now was anxious to abandon. After Confederation, until his death in 1880, he remained an influential figure behind the scenes in the Ontario and federal Liberal parties. But aside from an unsuccessful endeavour to negotiate a new reciprocity treaty with the United States in 1874, and brief appearances in the federal Senate to which he had been appointed in 1873, he stayed out of public life, gladly devoting himself again to the *Globe*, which, under him, had become the leading journal in British North America.

Even thus encapsulated, Brown's was plainly an imposing career in Ontario leadership. Aside from his ascendancy in political journalism and his role in building Grit Liberalism, he had been the effective initiator of the Confederation movement that won ultimate success: '*the* man' who made British North American union feasible, according to Lord Monck, who was well aware himself of the inner political workings as governor general of the time.[2] Yet further, during the late 1850s and again in the mid-60s, George Brown was conceivably the strongest leader in Ontario – that is, the politician with the strongest popular following. John A. Macdonald with astute clarity affirmed as much when he told a Conservative partisan in 1866 that if he had not entered coalition with the Brownite Liberals in 1864 he would have been 'handing over the administration of affairs to the Grit party for the next ten years.'[3] In fact, Brown was the voice of Ontario sectionalism at its worst and best: embattled to defend Upper Canadian rights against sinister, outside (and notably French) forces, supremely confident of Upper Canada's moral superiority and mission to lead, yet ultimately willing to come to terms and recognize other sectional or regional interests – able, moreover, to initiate a practical search for terms that would promote the broader benefit of all.

It should accordingly be evident that George Brown must constantly come into the accounts presented of the pre-Confederation premiers – as an ally, an agent, a rival, or a formidable opposing force. Nevertheless, he does not receive a chapter of his own here for two major reasons. First, he was premier of the briefest Canadian government of all – the so-called Short Administration of 1858 – and hardly had time to accomplish much as a government leader. Second, he scarcely ever held a ministerial post. Except for his period in the Great Coalition as president of the Council, during 1864-5, he spent his active political years out of office and more usually on the opposition side of parliament. This does not negate his pervasive influence or his vital importance for Ontario and Canada. But it means that he does not fit in the company of government leaders and major holders of the premiership. His was a commanding popular role that could make and unmake governments. He did not sit in them. He belongs in the mainstream of Ontario political development, but not in the genealogy of pre-Confederation premiers.

But what, exactly, was a 'premier'? What did the term signify before Confederation, and was it to be distinguished from the position of prime minister? Today the usage has broadly been established in Canada that 'prime minister' refers to the leader of a federal government and 'premier' to that of the provincial; it is important to recognize that this is indeed a matter of usage hardening perhaps into a convenient rule of distinction, but is not based on any clear-cut constitutional decision. Again one is dealing with a gradual evolution through history, and in looking for meanings should start historically with the original emergence of the prime ministership in Great Britain.

While in eighteenth-century Britain the term 'prime minister' became accepted for the political head of a government based on parliamentary support, it could quite readily be interchanged with 'first minister,' '*premier ministre*' in French – or 'premier' for short. There was no essential distinction made. Even in the early twentieth century British prime ministers were frequently referred to as 'Premier Asquith' or 'Mr. Lloyd George, the premier,' while their counterparts in the self-governing British overseas dominions might be termed either colonial ministers or premiers. Within Canada, similarly, one might speak variously of 'Premier Mackenzie King' or of the 'Prime Minister of Prince Edward Island' at federal-provincial conferences of the interwar years. There, too, there was no inherent distinction.

And yet, there was perhaps a tendency to treat the name 'prime minister' as the more dignified appellation. At any rate, within the British empire of the nineteenth century the 'prime minister' generally meant that superior personage who ruled the dominant motherland, while in a colonial domain like Canada, even after 1867, Sir John A. Macdonald as head of its federal régime was usually to be termed 'premier.' That was certainly true of pre-Confederation Canada. Once responsible ministries had emerged there, their heads were widely called 'premiers' – although a governor, writing in despatches about the government still under his formal charge, might on occasion refer to 'my prime minister.' This latter fact, however, merely points up the original interchangeability of the terms. The more general usage in Canada was to speak of the premiership. In sum, during the pre-Confederation years it became normal to recognize the name and post of premier in the Canadian union, and not to see it as differing in essence from the prime ministership of Great Britain on which it was modelled; except, of course, that its scope was more limited in what was still a British colony, though with its own internal self-government.

There were recognized premiers under the Union, then; but it is also worth remarking that they were not paid as such. The individual who operated as a premier held a specific ministerial office also, for which he received his salary, most usually as attorney-general – in the case of Draper, Baldwin, MacNab, John A., or Sandfield Macdonald – or as inspector-general (minister of finance) in the case of Hincks or Brown. That is to say, the position of premier as head of the cabinet and leader of the majority parliamentary party was politically controlling, but, in administrative parlance, this premier was simply one of the ministers of the crown who supervised some major departmental office. His main function and his power came as 'premier'; but his official title in the government was most often that of 'attorney-general.' Even after Confederation, the first premier of the province of Ontario, Sandfield Macdonald, was still thus formally titled merely as attorney-general; and a specific premier's or prime minister's department would not be set up in the province until 1906. Yet again this points to the fact that the premiership gradually evolved as did the constitution itself, and was not officially erected in full panoply at any one particular date.

The place, the office, and the men all tie together. Like Ontario itself, the premiership was a functioning reality in the pre-Confederation era, even though its status was still incomplete. And the men who rose as premiers helped to build both the office and the province. As moulders, they were moulded, however, conditioned by their material and cultural environments, by the setting and way of life, the aspirations, attitudes, and interests of the community to which they belonged. Hence the society and circumstances of Upper Canada within the Union demand a closer glance, since no man lives an island life outside his times.

The Union period was not only a time of transforming political change, witnessed by growth of responsible government and the rise of the movement for British North American federation. It also saw the passing of the frontier stage of settlement in Upper Canada, the emergence of a prosperous commercial agricultural society, the rise of towns and cities with an increasing industrial component, and a shift from simple pioneer expansion based on the influx of immigrants to the intensive development of a consolidating, maturing provincial community. In short, social transformation was taking place as well. Still further, profound economic and technological changes equally went on. In the forties the building of canals along the great water route to the Atlantic produced the first St Lawrence seaway. In the fifties came the impact of the railway age. Iron rails providing year-round, all-weather transport linked up inland Canada as never before. By the early sixties the Grand Trunk Railway in itself gave the Union the world's longest rail line, leading also to visions and projects for extension eastward by an Intercolonial Railway to ice-free Maritime ports, and, still more spectacularly, for an out-thrust across the empty northwestern expanses to take the locomotive through the Rockies to the far Pacific.

Canadian economic development was thus pointing to a future of continental dimensions; but, within the existing limits of the Union, it was featured by a fevered railway-building boom that made business fortunes, brought labour high wages and to everyone inflation and a heavy load of public debt. Yet, though many a promotional scheme collapsed, many a line was overbuilt, and many an over-hopeful young municipality was left encumbered with worthless railway bonds, the impact of steam and rail technology deeply affected the whole pace and outlook of the Upper Canadian community. During the days of the Union, along with all the other changes, Upper Canada in fact experienced the crucial nineteenth-century industrial revolution in land transport.

Population growth was another factor integrally involved with the major alterations in Upper Canadian society. In 1841, when the Union began, there were approximately 480,000 people in Upper Canada to 670,000 in Lower Canada. In 1867 there were over a million-and-a-half in the new province of Ontario. The rate of growth throughout the period was markedly greater in the Upper Canadian portion of the Union, so that by the census of 1851 this western section already had passed the older eastern community in numbers (952,000 to 890,000), while by the census of 1861 its lead had lengthened (1,396,000 to 1,111,000). The explanation lay chiefly in the long-continuing and highly-consequential flow of immigrants from Great Britain. The bulk of them had regularly moved to the broad, fertile wildlands of Upper Canada, not to the more restricted domains of Lower Canada where, apart from the limited area of the Eastern Townships, rough and uninviting terrain hemmed in the French-occupied St Lawrence valley. British immigration, checked temporarily in the late 1830s by economic depression and the political turmoil in Canada accompanying the rebellions, rose to new peaks in the 1840s. Over the decade of the fifties it gradually fell away, as improved conditions in Britain and the attractions of rich new American prairie lands meant that fewer migrants came to Canada or stayed if they did. Nevertheless, the great inflow of settlers down to that time, and the natural increase as their families soon expanded, ensured that Upper Canada, or Canada West within the Union, would maintain its ascendant population curve throughout the period as a whole.

Indeed, though its annual rate of increase lessened in the sixties with the virtual disappearance of British immigration as a major demographic factor, Canada West kept its population lead down to Confederation (and after) for various other reasons. In the first place, it still tended to attract more of those immigrants who did come, including Americans and some continental Europeans. In the second, its relatively good resources, opportunities, and advancing economic development served to hold as well as attract proportionately more inhabitants than Canada East, which instead suffered from a chronic outflow of native *Canadiens* to New England's countryside and towns. And in the third place, a somewhat better picture of life expectancy in the western half of the Union suggests that it also had a larger net natural increase of population. In both Canadas birth rates were high, and early marriages and large families were the rule. But infant mortality was greater and death rates from major epidemic diseases more severe in the poorer eastern society as a whole. In sum – as the census figures for the Union indicate – not only the comparative flows of in- and out-migration but also the presumably better conditions of health and nutrition in the western section bear on the insistent population advance of the Upper Canadian community across the pre-Confederation years.[4]

It does not seem surprising that such a consistently growing community would soon display a spirit of assertiveness, assurance, even of self-righteousness within the Union, in sharp contrast with the defensive, guarded stance of French Canadians as they saw themselves slipping increasingly into a minority position. Moreover, the emerging sense of a veritable 'Ontario' destiny, to be the heart and focus of a new nation that would gain the North-west and span the continent, surely had some basis in a kind of demographic self-confidence. This sanguine, expansive spirit appeared in Ontario's pre-Confederation leaders themselves, to be well exemplified by Brown, but also in many respects by Hincks and John A. Macdonald. Progress, expansion, beckoning destiny – whether Liberal or Conservative, the leading politicians came to share these terms of aspiration with the buoyant, burgeoning society about them.

Other demographic aspects of Upper Canada's growth were no less signifi-cant. When it entered Union in 1841, thanks to the tide of immigration nearly half its population had been born in Britain; and ten years later, despite the high birth rate (actually then higher in Canada West than Can-ada East), the continued immigrant waves of the 1840s still left more than 40 per cent of its people British-born. The dwindling away of immigration in the fifties then had its consequence, so that by Confederation some three-fifths of Ontario's inhabitants were of Canadian birth. Many of these, of course, were nevertheless the children of immigrants from the British Isles; and in any case the British stamp on the Ontario community re-mained preponderant throughout the entire Union era. In outline, it was a remarkably homogeneous society, largely British in origin and overwhelm-ingly English-speaking, apart from the small French-Canadian element chiefly in the Ottawa valley, some long-established German communities in Waterloo who still maintained their language, and the scant numbers of non-British immigrants as yet to be found.

The Ontario leaders of the pre-Confederation era themselves exhibited the dominant British strain in their society. William Draper was an English immigrant and Francis Hincks from Ireland; John A. Macdonald (and George Brown) had come with their parents from Scotland; Sandfield Mac-donald (like Allan MacNab) was a Canadian-born son of Scottish settlers. Robert Baldwin's grandfather was an Anglo-Irish immigrant and his father had himself been born and educated in Britain. Accordingly, it seems quite probable that public policy guided by such men would show strongly British leanings, to be approved and echoed by the populace who followed them. This was the case. The search for self-government during the Union of the Canadas predominantly sought to realize it within the empire, upon the Brit-ish model of cabinet rule and the parliamentary system; not to achieve American-style republicanism, independence, and a written, congressional constitution. In pressing thus for responsible government, Baldwin and Hincks were no less concerned to maintain the British link than were Draper or MacNab in seeking to block their efforts. As for Confederation, the aim espoused by both John A. Macdonald and Brown was to build a broad new nation on the continent based on British institutions, under British auspices, upholding the imperial connection against American encroachments. In this again they were heavily backed by the Ontario populace. And while Sandfield Macdonald held out for the existing Canadian Union till the end, opposing the 'American' idea of federalism, one of his very contentions was that Confederation would promote annexation to the United States while he himself was 'standing by the British flag.'[5] From start to finish of the Union era, Upper Canadians and their leaders remained all but unanimous in endorsing British symbols, sentiments, and precedents for their community.

This assuredly is not to deny the ever-present American contacts and influences that affected Upper Canada during the same period, or before it and afterwards. That colony was set in the North American world of the Great Lakes basin, and Americanizing forces operated on British immigrants themselves as they increasingly adapted to their surroundings. The point is really that British sanctions, forms, and ideology were especially potent at the time of the Union, as an inherent result of Upper Canadian demography. And, at the same time, defensive power and governorship, much valued British markets and investments, and the high prestige of British culture all operated from the outside to keep the colonial community looking constantly towards Great Britain. But if Upper Canadians displayed a largely undivided response in that regard, there still were strong internal differences among them. In fact, their apparent British homogeneity really cloaked a variety of divisions that again were largely a result of the demographic pattern.

Leaving aside British Americans of Loyalist or post-Loyalist descent, the British population of Upper Canada basically comprehended three different national elements – English, Scots, and Irish, not to mention the Welsh. Furthermore, there was the deep communal separation of Catholic Irish and Protestant Ulstermen, and wide divergences still between Scots Highlanders and Lowlanders. Still further, across the lands of Upper Canada there were distinct 'Scotch blocks' or markedly Irish townships, whether Orange or Green, and compact Catholic Irish groups in the rising towns. The pattern, then, was actually far from homogeneous. Beyond those matters broadly concerning Britain or the United States on which Upper Canadians spoke with notable accord, there was ample room for differences and disagreements among them.

While, moreover, settlement in many neighbourhoods had taken place more on an individual basis than that of interrelated families, immigrants of the same ethnic background still tended to look to each other for social support and common opinions in a strange new land. Thus the Orange Order, to loom large and long in Ontario politics, first emerged as such a mutually supportive society for Ulster Irish newcomers to Upper Canada. Similarly, the national societies of St George, St Andrew, and St Patrick offered association and benevolent aid to their own compatriot groups. Yet the churches, above all, served as a focus for local group life, not only in meeting spiritual needs but also in sustaining inherited values and established modes of conduct for different varieties of Upper Canadians, old as well as new. Indeed, while in time ethnic affiliations might lessen, as newcomers grew acclimated (or moved and removed in a remarkably mobile society), religious distinctions continued to be upheld with both firm devotion and sharp animosity.

Of the component British groups in Upper Canada under the Union, the Irish were the largest, the English the next, and the Scots the smallest. The Irish element was considerably swelled in the later forties by the great and tragic outpouring from a famine-stricken homeland, even though many diseased and half-starved migrants died on the Atlantic passage or in miserably crowded quarantine stations and immigrant sheds soon after their arrival. In any event, a lasting Irish imprint was left on the Ontario community, for it was not until a new wave of British migration in the early twentieth century that English immigrants took a definite lead. It must be borne in mind, however, that among the Irish settlers of the nineteenth century the Protestant and keenly pro-British Ulstermen were much in the majority. They settled everywhere – in towns as artisans and merchants, on country farms, or in backwoods clearings. The Catholic Irish more largely moved into urban settings (often huddling through poverty into growing slums), worked as labourers on the canals and railroads, or went into lumbering, especially up the Ottawa valley.

The English did not usually settle in closely identifiable groups but tended to be more numerous in towns as businessmen or skilled workers, particularly in Toronto; and they were also well ensconced in the upper classes of society, thereby giving cultivated circles a noteworthy 'English' cast. Those of them who had emigrated as gentry or half-pay officers often gained local standing as country magistrates and officials. Others had entered the colonial hierarchy in church or state, in law or education. Moreover, they fairly easily merged in with the older, originally American elements of Loyalist and post-Loyalist descent (the last-named having come through the War of 1812 to an assured British loyalty, after any open adherents of the United States had necessarily departed). The English were a widespread but not clearly distinguishable element outside the élites of town or countryside; but there were also many of them by no means rich scattered all across settled Upper Canada.

The Scots might well have been the smallest group, coming as they did from the least populous realm in the British Isles, but they nevertheless formed a far larger proportion of the colonial people than of Great Britain itself. Besides, through education, enterprise, and strong kinship loyalties, they built up a powerful position in the commercial and professional world of Upper Canada, from banking to wholesaling, and from the Presbyterian and

Anglican clergy to journalism and public life. In the countryside, moreover, they formed the dominant local group in many areas, as among the Highlanders of Glengarry in the east or the Lowlanders of Oxford and the Huron Tract in the west. They held to their clan, religious, and cultural heritage with due tenacity; in fact, the Scottish mark on Ontario still seems almost as evident today as it did in the days of the Union.

At any rate, by Confederation the population of Ontario stood at more than 35 per cent of Ulster Irish origin, 25 per cent English, including those of American background claiming that descent, and 20 per cent Scots.[6] The remainder, less than 20 per cent, comprised mostly Catholic Irish, plus Germans, French Canadians, and very small contingents of other ethnic groups, including Jews from Britain. The result, therefore, was also an overwhelming Protestant dominance – and religious multiplicity as well.

The Church of England, which when the Union began still upheld its claim to be the official church of Upper Canada, remained in a minority position, although it was large and had gained adherents from English, Anglo-Irish, and Episcopalian Scots newcomers. The main Presbyterian body split in the 1840s between the continuing supporters of the Church of Scotland, the state church of the homeland, and the new evangelical Free Church of Scotland, which opposed any state 'intrusion' into religion. Methodism, the denomination most deeply rooted in earlier Upper Canada, had itself divided between the main group of Canadian-based Methodists and the British Wesleyan element which had grown with immigration; and though this breach was closed in 1847, other Methodist sectarian groups remained. Beyond these major Protestant communities there were Baptists, Congregationalists, and minor Presbyterian sects, often of American origin, but attracting Ulster Irish and some Scots or English as well. There were German Lutherans and Mennonites, English and American Quakers. And finally there was the Roman Catholic church, which was notably enlarged by the southern Irish immigration of the 1840s but which also held the allegiance of many Scots Highlanders, along with French Canadians and some Germans too.

In this setting of contending religious loyalties, questions of church and state relations inevitably bulked large; and, as inevitably, religious issues much affected the lives and careers of the Upper Canadian leaders under the Union. William Draper as a loyal state church Anglican sought throughout the long disputed 'university question' of the 1840s to sustain the Church of England's control of the provincially endowed King's College. Robert Baldwin, also an Anglican but of an Anglo-Irish variety, worked instead for a secular provincial university to replace it and free his church from hampering state ties. Francis Hincks, of Irish Presbyterian background, early took up the cause of the 'voluntary principle' as well as responsible government –

that is, that churches should be wholly voluntary bodies without state connection or support. Hence he espoused the movement to secularize the clergy reserves, the rich endowment of public lands held chiefly by the Church of England. George Brown, an ardent Free Church voluntarist, took up the battle that ended in the abolition of the reserves in the 1854 – and carried on a longer, hotter struggle against the separate school laws, which in the fifties built up a state-supported system of Catholic education in Upper Canada.

John A. Macdonald, in contrast, as an adherent of the Church of Scotland which upheld ties of church and state tried for a time to secure the provincial university funds for denominational colleges and to defend the clergy reserves of which his own church had gained a lesser but significant share. As for Sandfield Macdonald, a Glengarry Highland Catholic in descent, he was actually the least concerned with religious issues; indeed, was often looked on with suspicion by zealous leaders of his own church. Nevertheless, during his administration in the sixties, a separate school bill brought in by one of his supporters gravely affected his government's policy and its very chance of survival. All in all, it is hard to overestimate the importance of religion in politics or politics in religion for the leaders of a society that took both so centrally and vehemently.

In similar fashion these leaders had regularly to cope with the ethnic particularism in Upper Canada under the Union. The Catholic Irish vote here, the Highland vote there, the Orangemen virtually everywhere, the English Loyalists of Toronto or the Canadian-American Methodists of the Ontario front – all could repeatedly affect the fortunes of the uncertain agglomerations called parties. Of course, there were some firm power bases like Sandfield's Glengarry Highlander fiefdom, John A's Presbyterian Conservative stronghold of Kingston, or George Brown's Scottish Lowland Grit domain in the heart of the southwestern peninsula. Of course, as well, economic interests or class feelings might overrun ethnic lines to shape broader fields of support. But, generally, the particularist groupings had to be taken carefully into account. Nor did it follow that Scottish, Catholic Irish, Methodist, or Ulster elements would vote on the one side or the other consistently all across Upper Canada. Again the individual locality and those who constituted its majority and minority factions could be critically significant. Such problems are not wholly lacking to the politics of later day. Yet they were far more prevalent in a young community still but recently settled by a mosaic of immigrants, and in its localism and relative isolation still much closer to the frontier world than to modern conditions of ready intercommunication.

Nonetheless, the times were changing steadily during the Union era, as the expanding population filled in the backwoods and the frontiers ebbed away. In the 1840s the remaining gaps in settlement were closed south of a line from Arnprior on the Ottawa across to Lake Simcoe and on to Lake Huron. In the 1850s the Bruce and the southern side of Georgian Bay were occupied, while the last wild land in the western peninsula was auctioned off in 1855.[7] The good agricultural lands of southern Ontario had now been taken up and settlement had reached the hard, inhospitable mass of the Precambrian Shield. Consequently, in the latter fifties and on through the sixties a series of colonization roads was built northward into the rugged Shield country to open new farming districts, in ignorance of the vast extent of this stern barrier. But these access routes chiefly came to serve the extension of lumbering, and the thin settlements that did grow up along them largely survived on the indifferent soils by supplying the needs of local lumber camps. Agricultural Upper Canada had reached its limits; Ontario's mining North would not develop until well after Confederation. The frontier had indeed closed down; its constant expansion was over.

One manifest result was the movement that emerged in Upper Canada in the later fifties and pointed towards Confederation – the movement to gain new lands for settlement beyond the Great Lakes by the acquisition of the Northwest, then the immense and lonely fur trade domain of the Hudson's Bay Company. And there were other less clear-cut but much more widespread consequences, as Upper Canada turned from extensive to intensive growth within its existing confines. Year by year rough bush clearings merged into sweeps of cultivated farmlands, log cabins were replaced with sawn-lumber or brick houses, forest trails became graded or planked roads, and lonely hamlets with mill, tavern, and little more developed into thriving village service-centres. From the forties onward mixed farming spread out from older areas to replace the frontier wheat-raising that exhausted the soil and produced but one staple crop. With the rise of this more complex, costly, and higher-yielding commercial agriculture, the amorphous pioneer agrarian community gradually became a coherent rural society headed by substantial farmers, local merchants, and professional men. Farming Ontario of nostalgic tradition – solid, secure, wealth-producing – really took shape under the Union.

At the same time, accompanying the advances in the settled countryside, came the rise of the towns that supplied and serviced its village market centres. The network of urban places grew particularly fast in the 1850s during the first great railway boom; but that growth was already under way in the forties as roads were improved, canals were built, and steamers increasingly plied the lakes and rivers. Through this mounting trade and traffic the chief towns developed as wholesaling and banking centres for sizeable hinterland areas. Kingston and Hamilton were incorporated as cities in 1846, London in 1854; and Bytown became the city of Ottawa the next year. The process of urbanization in Ontario, so much still with us, emerged very plainly in the

Union period. The urban proportion of the Upper Canadian population increased by 4.5 per cent in the fifties, 4.1 in the sixties; so that shortly after Confederation a fifth of the people already lived in urban communities.[8] The urban segment was thus already growing faster than the rural population, which in some areas had its peak by the early 1860s.[9]

The greatest gainer was Toronto. A city since 1834, it had ceased to be the provincial capital when Upper Canada entered Union, and when Kingston first, then Montreal, replaced it. But thanks to Toronto's large and fertile hinterland, its excellent access to outside markets both by the St Lawrence system and the American Erie canal, and the railway building of the fifties that made it the strategic hub of a radiating set of lines, the Lake Ontario port became the rapidly advancing metropolis of Canada West. Its population, 14,000 in 1841, had doubled and nearly redoubled by Confederation. Then it became a provincial capital again; indeed, it had intermittently been one from 1850 on, when the practice was adopted of alternating the Union's seat of government periodically between Toronto and Quebec. Yet whatever the value of being the political capital, the governmental decision-making centre, it is clear that Toronto's striking advance in size, wealth, buildings, and facilities from 1841 to 1867 stemmed largely from its trade and transportation advantages.

Toronto and the other principal Ontario towns were as yet, however, commercial rather than industrial entities. The rise of manufacturing on a large scale came mainly after Confederation. Nevertheless, there was a considerable development of industries in Upper Canadian urban places from the forties forward. Milling operations grew steadily, both in size and in concentration at favoured sites, from the lumber mills of Ottawa to the flour mills of Galt or Brantford. Steam came into increasing use at many points where the supply of water power was no longer adequate for demands. Cabinet and carriage factories, textile mills, iron foundries, and soon farm-machinery, clothing, leather-working and food-processing plants, sprang widely into being, to diversify the employment of labour and enlarge the range of Upper Canadian urban-centred enterprise. Then came the impact of the railway. Not only did it foster greater industrial activity by opening ways to wide markets; it also brought locomotive and car factories, rail-rolling mills and machine shops to meet its own needs. Hamilton in particular grew with railway-based industry. In short, the new technology of transport laid foundations for heavy industry in Ontario well before the days of the Union were over.

Meanwhile, in towns and cities a flourishing municipal life appeared. The structure of Ontario municipal government was, in fact, erected in this era, culminating in the Municipal Corporations Act of 1849, framed by Robert Baldwin, which provided a complete series of elected local governing authorities for both urban and rural areas. Local or civic politics gained new interest, especially as municipal activities expanded in scope and outlay to meet the demands of the enlarging communities, conspicuously in the field of public education. The city press expanded also with the civic arena, and its influence extended over more widely into the countryside, as communications by road and rail improved. Powerful journalistic empires arose like that of George Brown's *Globe*. The main towns functioned as the focal points of public opinion and debate, as well as of educational, literary, and social activity. And so they became predominant sources of leadership for pre-Confederation Ontario – politically and culturally as well as economically.

Certainly, the leading figures with whom we have to deal were all essentially townsmen. They well might have had rural connections or sometimes roots, but they made their livelihoods, found their social environments, and shaped their personal interests mainly in the town communities. These were obviously not great, dense-packed cities at that time. Yet their life was distinctively urban, as was that of the professional and business men who emerged out of them to become the contemporary leaders of government. No country farmers or village store-keepers were they.

William Draper, son of an Anglican clergyman in the imperial metropolis of London, came to the fore as a talented, successful Toronto lawyer who was well connected with the city's social and political élite. In parliament he sat for Toronto, except for his final years in politics when he represented another rising urban centre, the younger London, Canada West; and throughout his later career on the judicial bench he remained centred in Toronto where the Upper Canadian high courts met. In that same place Robert Baldwin was born and raised when it was still the little town of York. He too became a prominent, prosperous city lawyer; yet particularly so because he was endowed with valuable property and sure social standing as a scion of one of Toronto's leading families. In the legislature, it is true, Baldwin chiefly represented North York in Toronto's farming hinterland. But of course, there were far fewer urban than rural constituencies in a largely agrarian provincial society, so that leading urban politicians often ran for country seats remote from their own place of residence – although they might have to face recurrent rural groundswells against non-resident 'interlopers,' which took careful handling by their local party agents to overcome.

Francis Hincks, very much a 'business' voice in politics, also came essentially from a Toronto setting, although he took readily to Montreal during the period he spent there in the later forties; and he regularly sat for the western county of Oxford throughout his pre-Confederation years in parliament. Brought up in Cork and apprenticed to a Belfast shipping firm, Hincks came directly to another urban mercantile environment when he opened a wholesale house in York in 1832. Then in succession he became a bank manager, an insurance company organizer, and launched the Toronto *Examiner*, as a vigorous Reform journal. Journalism and party purposes combined sent him to Montreal to establish a new Liberal paper, until government duties as a finance minister, and as premier thereafter, demanded most of his time. In office, aside from banking questions and financial policies, Hincks was pre-eminently involved with railway development, most notably the building of the heavily capitalized trans-provincial line, the Grand Trunk. And as a railway politician *par excellence*, he no less became involved in the speculative land deals and alleged financial scandals that clouded his reputation. In any event, his public career plainly belonged to the emergent Ontario of towns, steam, and iron, of entrepreneurship and large capital investment, not to the fast vanishing realm of the agrarian frontier.

With regard to the Macdonalds, both John A. and Sandfield were pre-eminently lawyers and businessmen, at the core of the business and social élites of their home towns, Kingston and Cornwall, respectively. Nor were these eastern centres of minor significance in the Upper Canada of the Union era. Kingston, once the old province's largest town and briefly capital of the union, remained a commanding junction point for the Lake Ontario-St Lawrence water traffic and Rideau Canal from the Ottawa. Cornwall, one of the chief urban places in earlier Upper Canada, was still a busy St Lawrence canal port, the focus of mercantile and milling activities. The business communities of both places, therefore, were of considerable weight – as was each of the two Macdonalds as a member of their respective inner circles. John A. is well and truly described as a large-scale 'corporation lawyer.'[10] He soon acquired directorships, moreover, in Kingston bank, insurance, utilities, road, and railway companies; he invested in railway promotion and lake shipping; he speculated widely in land and became a major Kingston city developer. In fact, it is largely the very extent and interest of his political career that has overshadowed his significant financial and commercial enterprises – which even in pre-Confederation years came to reach well beyond Kingston to Toronto and far into the fast developing western districts of Upper Canada. As for Sandfield Macdonald, he became the leading lawyer of Stormont and Glengarry (having, incidentally, articled for a time under William Draper in Toronto); he bought much land, a mill, and set up a newspaper in Cornwall in his support. Beyond that, he gained social primacy as a veritable laird of his strongly Highland local community. The basis of Sandfield's political strength lay partly in his complex clan and family interconnections, but also in his economic prowess besides.

Allan MacNab and George Brown also fall within the same pattern of urban business leadership: the former was the ambitious Hamilton lawyer, promoter, developer, and railway enthusiast whose lordly, monumental mansion, Dundurn Castle, still stands in his city as a testament to his financial and social attainments. The latter was one of the first to make journalism big business in Canada, and, as a Toronto newspaper magnate, was whole-heartedly concerned to spread the city's influence across Canada West and into the great Northwest beyond. Taken as a group, then, these pre-Confed-eration public men all show significant similarities in their social setting and private interests, however different their political or religious affiliations might have been. They were truly bourgeois, representatives of fast emerg-ing, town-based, capitalist society. At the same time in politics they dealt with wide popular forces that were steadily moving Upper Canada towards the full state of democratic government. Yet they remained part of a provincial middle-class élite, scarcely members of the general multitude of farmers, lumbermen, artisans, and householders on whose votes they depended.

Class divisions were less clearly evident then, however, although older distinctions of social rank still existed in Upper Canada, buttressed by a widespread engrained social conservatism that rejected egalitarianism as un-British and dangerously smacking of Yankee democracy and mob rule. The aristocratic tradition of the Family Compact officialdom, the deep-rooted sense of hierarchy in church, state, and society, did not disappear overnight. There was still an upper class, into which a Baldwin could be admitted, while a Draper or a MacNab might be regarded as a bit of a par-venu; a class against which Hincks or Brown might enveigh as selfish, obso-lete, and a barrier to liberal rights – though one which the Macdonalds could recognize as the crown and keystone of the conservative arch of property. Nevertheless, this upper class of old ruling families and landed gentility had but ever-decreasing power in Canada West under the Union, as the new middle-class popular leadership replaced it. And in any case, a large part of provincial society was spread across a broad, middle ground, as working farm-owners and proprietors of small businesses, shops, and workshops.

These were the 'respectable classes,' a good Victorian usage conveying both 'self-respecting' and 'worthy of respect,' who were held to produce, in duly British terms, a sturdy self-reliant 'yeomanry.' This widely attained indi-vidual proprietorship was both the generalized ideal in mid nineteenth-century Ontario and the basis on which popular politics and parliamentary rule operated – for surely such a social order could judge well and responsibly for itself? It was on this basis, in fact, that the political leaders of the day appealed to the people. They might have formed an upper middle-class élite themselves, but there was no great social distance perceived or felt between them and the 'respectable' mass of the populace below.

At this period there were as yet no manifestly great concentrations of wealth and propertied power at one end of the social scale, nor of crowded labour and widespread permanent poor at the other. That degree of social separation would only become evident with the spreading impact of industrialism in the later nineteenth-century and with the rising differential costs of good farmlands. In the mid-century the rich were not much more than gentry with superior country estates or distinguished citizens with opulent new town mansions. They were not yet captains of industry or lords of high finance. And lower-class poverty was chiefly apparent in the slums of the larger towns, where, in any case, it was still popularly associated with transient immigrants, passing misfortunes or the evils of drink – which presumably could be dealt with by private philanthropy and Christian endeavour. Hence there were few strong outcries raised against malign social conditions, and certainly few from the political leaders of the day. Egerton Ryerson, the Methodist parson turned architect of Ontario public education, might assuredly have been convinced by the 1850s that public schooling was the answer to social misery bred through ignorance; and had become concerned by the sixties to raise the lower social levels by education so as to protect the respectable classes from crime and violence. But any such awareness of social problems, or needs, did not greatly affect the politicians of the time. They took a conservative view of their notably middle-class world, even the political liberals among them. There was accordingly no great difference between the social perceptions of the leading group, from Draper and Baldwin to the Macdonalds.

None of them, moreover, upheld 'democracy' as such, even George Brown. To them, that meant the fallacious principle of universal suffrage – one man, one vote – that gave power to the most ignorant and irresponsible lower elements of society or, worse, to the corrupt and cynical demagogues who manipulated them. It meant elective offices on every level, from judge to dogcatcher, and American machine politics under bosses, instead of responsible appointment from above under the British parliamentary system. And it meant the endangering of minority interests and the rights of property through the 'tyranny of the majority' of the electorate. Of course, these judgments largely expressed the anti-American criticism and pro-British sentiment to be found in the Upper Canadian community. But down to Confederation, at least, 'democracy' was not a good word in British North America generally. In Upper Canada it was still associated with radicalism which made no lasting headway in the Union era. Under Willian Lyon Mackenzie, it had produced violent rebellion in 1837 and raised subsequent threats along the American border still felt as the forties opened. At the turn of the fifties, early Clear Grits had revived the call for elective, universal-suffrage democracy on the American pattern; and Brown in particular had fought hard to subdue their radicalism within Reform ranks. As late as Confederation, moreover, he made clear that the establishment of his pet principle, representation by population, did not involve universal suffrage, which he still rejected.[11]

Indeed, none of these men could be termed democrats in the later accepted sense of the term in Ontario and Canada, though all upheld parliamentary freedom under law. Their responses did vary somewhat. Hincks or Baldwin were naturally more likely to talk of popular liberties and the rights of parliamentary self-government; Draper or MacNab to see dangerous democratic tendencies and radical leanings behind such contentions. Still, MacNab and Draper both were basically men of parliament, and neither was part of the old authoritarian Toronto Compact group among the Tory-Conservatives. John A. Macdonald rightly deemed himself a liberal or progressive Conservative; Sandfield Macdonald might best be called a fairly conservative Reformer. None of them was either a reactionary or a radical; all became, in various shadings, conservative or moderate liberals, moderate or liberal conservatives. The point is that they themselves represented a broad middle ground in Union politics; and even MacNab on the right in Toryism or Brown on the left in Liberalism were still within a range of essentially centrist political behaviour. This moderate pattern in leadership produced no wide variety; there were few unyielding doctrinaires of left or right, all were potential compromisers. But evidently it was what pre-Confederation Ontario wanted (and still would thereafter), and it nevertheless allowed for a good deal of excitement, clash, and fervour in public affairs.

These men, in consequence, were middle road as well as middle class. What they looked to and upheld was the broad proprietorship of Upper Canada; where there were still property qualifications for voters, but they were relatively low; and so many could meet them that the electorate was large and popular. They believed that electors should have a stake in the country in order to be responsible; but that a worthy individual could in due course achieve that stake. They spoke not of democracy but of the just apportionment of liberty under the parliamentary system; not of the rights of man, but of the rights of Upper Canadian freeholders. They were British bourgeois Victorians in their ideology, although they necessarily operated in the practical context of North American popular politics, given the nature of Upper Canada in their day. Like their society, they were largely individualist in outlook, though well aware of ethnic and communal ties. They were also pragmatic materialists, at least in their recurrent emphasis on material progress and economic development; but this, as also in their society, was considerably qualified by their repeated involvement in emotional issues concerning religious or cultural loyalties.

Such were the leaders, and such was the world they inhabited. It remains only to conclude their introduction by taking a closer look at conditions in Upper Canada at the time of Union – that staging point from which their subsequent paths as premiers took their departure.

On 4 January 1841, as the year of union began, Sir George Arthur, the last lieutenant-governor of the old Province of Upper Canada, wrote to his superior, Governor General Lord Sydenham, an estimate of the state of the colony, still under his direction until the new United Province should be proclaimed in the following month:

In reviewing the past, and contemplating the prospects of the year that has just opened, I think I may safely say they are cheering. There are some bitter men at the extremes of both parties – and two or three who have acquired influence during the past year, in whom I continue to place no confidence, but I am certain the moderate party has gained ground very much, and I entertain a confident hope that its ascendancy will be secured. The mercantile and agricultural interests have thriven during the past year exceedingly, and are in good heart. Our exports, exclusive of the Lumber Trade, have exceeded £600,000 during the year 1840; and extensive improvements have been made both in the towns and in the country upon real Capital – I mean surplus Capital, the profits of Trade, not borrowed; and what, at this particular juncture, is more important than all, the feeling in favour of the Union of the Provinces is, in my opinion, extended and strengthened ...[12]

It had not long been so. Neither party moderation nor trade prosperity, capital investments nor belief in the project of Union had been much in evidence in the recent years since the Rebellion of 1837 and during the severe economic storms that had helped to bring it on. Financial panics in London and New York had ushered in bad times in Britain and America after 1836. Upper Canada's markets had slumped drastically; land speculation had collapsed in ruin, banks tottered, and creditors foreclosed on debt-ridden farms. After the angry but ill-starred rising by Mackenzie radicals late in 1837, which had mainly involved several hundred insurgents close to Toronto, conditions if anything had grown worse. A series of armed attacks from the United States by radical sympathizers and would-be American expansionists kept the border in a turmoil for the following year and, more seriously, threatened a new war between Britain and the Republic. Despondent farmers and Reformers made plans to move west to the American prairies; and some did emigrate. Money remained tight, towns and business in the doldrums. Only very slowly did the local and world economic depression lift; and hence Sir George Arthur did not observe clear improvement until the close of 1840.

Meanwhile, through the strained and gloomy post-rebellion period, political problems had been equally acute. Though the sporadic, badly-organized raids were successfully checked, as troops patrolled the border – and sometimes fought sharp little engagements – the relations between the empire and the Republic were not fully eased until the Webster-Ashburton Treaty of 1842 disposed of outstanding issues between them. Following the rebellion, moreover, a mood of vengeful reaction swept a Tory-dominated government and legislature, heightened by the continuing menace along the border. Reform adherents were harrassed; radicals among them were highly suspect. Arthur, who had replaced an inept Sir Francis Bond Head as lieutenant-governor, followed a rigorous legal line of policy in safeguarding order and prosecuting rebels, although if anything his treatment was less repressive and punitive than more impassioned Tory partisans in council or assembly would have desired.

Then, however, the five-month mission of Lord Durham in 1838 to investigate the troubles of both Canadas began to brighten the Reformers' prospects. Durham's sweeping presentation of the wrongs that needed to be remedied in Canada and his recommendation of responsible government injected a different note – as did his proposal for a union of the Canadas that would realize the unity of the great St Lawrence water system and secure its effective economic development. More moderate men moved to the fore in Upper Canada, Conservatives like William Draper, Liberals like Baldwin and Hincks. Prominent Tories such as Allan MacNab, Christopher Hagerman, and even the more circumspect and highly able John Beverley Robinson no longer held the field; any more than radicals like Mackenzie and John Rolph, now watching from exile over the American border.

Attention focussed on the project of Union: recommended in Durham's report of 1839, taken up by his successor Poulett Thomson, later Lord Sydenham, as governor general, and thereinafter implemented by imperial authority in the Act of Union of 1840. This Union scheme, however much it would affect Upper Canada, was assuredly shaped far more by considerations regarding the lower, largely French-Canadian province. Both Durham and the British government had come to the conclusion that the much more serious discords apparent in Lower Canada could only be settled by the absorption of the French Canadians in a broader English-dominated community. Durham would have left representation in the parliament of such a new united province simply on the basis of population, expecting that continued British immigration to Canada would ensure a growing English-speaking majority. But to guarantee an English-speaking ascendancy from the start, the imperial act was drafted to give both halves of the Union equal representation in its legislature. The less populated Upper Canadian section, as it still was in 1840, thus would hold as many seats as Lower Canada; and this western half in conjunction with the eastern English-speaking minority would provide an unassailable English dominance over all. The Act of Union accordingly put the equal sectional division of the two Canadas right into the constitution of the United Province, resulting in the subsequent pattern of dual cabinets and co-premierships, and leading later to the agitation by a now more populous Upper Canadian section for representation by population.

But at the time the act was passed in June 1840, it roused other responses. Upper Canadians were calmed in their fears of being swamped by Lower Canada through the provision for equal representation in the Union. French Canadians, in contrast, saw that the very purpose of the measure lay in swamping them. They could scarcely hail a Union that was intended ulti- mately to assimilate their distinctive society, language, and institutions, and which underrepresented them at the outset, and, still further, would burden the new province with the assumption of the heavy Upper Canadian public debt. Only in the thought that, if responsible government should become established, they, the French, might share in the control of provincial affairs, was there any cause for hope. And that seemed a dubious prospect to downcast French Canadians as they waited for the Union Act to go into effect.

The act itself, apart from its provision for equal representation, largely continued the governmental structure for the United Province which the two old Canadas had known separately under the Canada Act, or Constitutional Act, of 1791. Hence, as in Upper Canada under the constitution of 1791, there was to be a parliament with two chambers, an appointed Legislative Council, and an elected Legislative Assembly, where the control over taxes resided. Similarly, the governor general (there would no longer be lieutenant governors) would have his appointed body of advisers, the Executive Coun- cil, which was increasingly to become a regular body of government minis- ters, especially as reformed by Sydenham – who also established that these ministers should henceforth hold parliamentary seats. Beyond that, counties and a few borough or town constituencies would continue to elect the repre- sentatives from Upper Canada for the new united Legislative Assembly.

The counties, in actuality, were then still not much more than electoral divisions. The real unit of local government was the district, which might contain several counties, wherein the appointed magistrates, or justices of the peace, met in the Court of Quarter Sessions to carry on both administra- tive and judicial functions; and there was a district grammar school as well as a district courthouse and jail in each of the district capital towns. This old Upper Canadian local system was soon to change under the Union, however. In 1841, pushed by Sydenham, the Elective District Councils Act established a series of representative local bodies. But it was not until Baldwin's Munici- pal Corporations Act of 1849 that local government came fully under the control of the elected local representatives – when, incidentally, the county replaced the district as the main rural administrative unit.

The reform of central and local government machinery had been among Durham's recommendations in his report, and among Sydenham's promises in his efforts to win approval for the Union scheme in Upper Canada. He had come to Canada in 1839 charged with gaining public assent for the Union project which the imperial government wished to put into effect. In Lower Canada this caused him little problem, on the surface at least. Representative government had been suspended there because of much more extensive rebellion disturbances, so that he only had to deal with a small, appointed Special Council. But in Upper Canada where the uprising had plainly been very limited, and pro-British sentiments were in loud ascendancy, the legislature elected in 1836 was still in being; and Sydenham had to use his considerable political skills to ensure that the assembly would voice consent. Moreover, while the loyalty of Upper Canadian Tories in government posts or in parliament posts or in parliament could scarcely be doubted, they could no less be reluctant to see themselves linked with 'disloyal' French Canadians, or to face the ending of their own Upper Canada domain where they had been well established in places of power. Nor was this just self-interest. They also felt a sense of Upper Canadian patriotism, and a fear that their young western realm would fall under eastern domination and the spreading power of Montreal, the commercial metropolis of the St Lawrence system.

On the other side, Reformers looked to Union not only for promised specific improvements but beyond them, also, to the hope that it would bring what Durham had forcefully linked with it – responsible government. Business men, besides, whether Conservative or Liberal in their leaning, counted on the economic impetus that Union would provide; the removal of any commercial barriers on the St Lawrence route; the completion of the chain of upper St Lawrence canals which two separate provinces had not been able to effect, and for which Upper Canada had gone deeply into debt. Thanks to such feelings Sydenham was able to build a strong central following of moderate Conservatives and Reformers behind the projected Union. The promise of the principle of equal representation, the projected transfer of Upper Canada's debt to a bigger province with more revenues, and a compromise settlement of the clergy reserves question that would share some of the income from the reserves among churches other than the Anglican – all served to create majority political support in Upper Canada. The governor general gained his popular approval; the imperial act went forward.

Thus it was that Upper Canada was ended – and yet continued – when the United Province of Canada was proclaimed in 1841: just when trade was on the upswing, immigration reviving, and a great era of intensive growth was about to get under way. At this time the names of Draper, Baldwin, and MacNab were already well known in Upper Canadian public life. Hincks and Sandfield Macdonald would both enter the new Union parliament at its first session in 1841. John A. Macdonald was not to do so until 1844, the same

year that George Brown founded his Toronto *Globe*. But all these men would
have their lives shaped by the events that produced the Canadian Union in
1841. The stage was set on which they would play out their parts as leaders in
Ontario's pre-Confederation years.

NOTES

1 This remark is sometimes given as 'Railways are my politics,' and in other
   related forms, but is widely attributed to MacNab. See *Dictionary of Canadian
   Biography*, IX; *1861-1870* (Toronto 1976), 524; and D.G. Creighton, *John A.
   Macdonald: The Young Politician* (Toronto 1952), 176.
2 Monck to Brown, 13 Nov. 1868, quoted in J.M.S. Careless, *Brown of the Globe*,
   II (Toronto 1963), 253
3 Macdonald to S.I. Lynn, 10 April 1866, quoted in ibid., 132
4 See *Census of Canada, 1870-1871*, IV: *Censuses of Canada, 1665 to 1871*
   (Ottawa 1876), for relevant abridged tables from censuses of 1841 (Upper
   Canada), 1844 (Lower Canada), 1851-2 and 1860-1 (the Canadas) on population growth, and especially Appendices 9 and 10 of *Census of the Canadas,
   1851-2* (Quebec 1852) on mortality and its causes.
5 John Sandfield Macdonald, speech in Legislative Assembly, 7 March 1865,
   *Parliamentary Debates on the Subject of the Confederation of the British North
   American Provinces* (Quebec 1865), 736
6 R.C. Harris and J. Warkentin, *Canada before Confederation* (Toronto 1974),
   118
7 Toronto *Weekly Globe*, 14 Sept. 1855
8 L.O. Stone, *Urban Development in Canada* (Ottawa 1967), 29
9 A.R.M. Lower, *Canadians in the Making* (Toronto 1962), 260
10 See below, 200.
11 Careless, *Brown of the Globe*, II, 141
12 Arthur to Sydenham, 4 Jan. 1841, C.R. Sanderson, ed., *The Arthur Papers*
   (Toronto 1959), III, 233

GEORGE METCALF

William Henry Draper

William Draper was the first colonial statesman who could correctly be styled prime minister or premier in the whole history of the British empire-commonwealth – though the role was not of his seeking but was virtually thrust upon him. This came about because the years of his political career as a leading Upper Canadian Conservative, 1836-47, coincided with a phenomenally rapid transmutation of the colonial constitution. Draper preferred the older constitution embodied in the Canada Act of 1791 and wished to promote none of the changes involved. But the structure established by the Canada Act was eroded and ultimately destroyed by colonial pressures and British concessions. Draper stayed in the forefront of politics in the 1840s neither to advance such unwelcome changes nor vainly to obstruct the inevitable, but rather to salvage what could be saved from the point of view of his conservative ideology. In this he was quite successful, and the political forces set in motion by what he saw as the desires of his enemies and the follies of his friends were to some extent harnessed and controlled by the political astuteness and capacity of a leader who knew enough to drift with the current or swim obliquely against it, rather than to perish by opposing it directly.[1]

He was born near London, England, on 11 March 1801. His father, the Reverend Henry Draper, was a Church of England clergyman and rector of St Anthony's in the city itself. Educated at home by private tuition, Draper ran away to sea at the age of fifteen. Finding employment as a cadet aboard an East Indiaman, he made two voyages to India in the next three years. Then, after a brief interval in England, he sailed for North America in the spring of 1820, at nineteen years of age. He appears to have pushed on immediately from Quebec to Upper Canada where he settled in Hamilton Township, boarding at the home of John Covert, a prominent Orangeman of the Cobourg area.[2]

Whatever adolescent rebelliousness led Draper to leave his family so early in life did not take the form of a permanent reaction against his father's religion or social status. He remained a devout Anglican and quickly sought employment in a profession. Nor did he become a political radical. Rather, the romanticism in his nature would appear to have identified itself with Britain's great world empire. He had grown up in the heart of that empire when it was fighting for its life against Napoleonic France; he had travelled to India when a remarkable era of expansion had spread British control of the sub-continent up to the Punjab.

Compared with the portions of empire Draper had already seen, Upper Canada in 1820 was in most ways a tiny and insignificant backwater, but it had its virtues. At the time, British North America comprised almost the only part of the globe where British civilization was extending itself in a settlement pattern. True, the Upper Canadian area was still primitive, and its settlers mostly of American origin. Yet the worst of pioneering was over, a ribbon of cultivated land ran along the upper St Lawrence River and the fronts of the lower Great Lakes, and immigration from Britain was increasing. Above all, the fact that the colony *was* part of the empire saved it from the overwhelming influence of the American frontier. Already an agricultural surplus of wheat and potash was making its way to England via Montreal. Local newspapers were filled with British news and were avidly read. The rawness of pioneer society was leavened by a small but strongly British-oriented élite scattered through every town and hamlet of the province. Some of the members of this group were 'birds of passage,' soldiers, administrators and officials – including of course the pinnacle of Upper Canadian society, the lieutenant-governor himself. Others were British-born who had come to stay, including many half-pay army officers. Others were of American or Loyalist origin, but they had been blooded in defence of the empire in the War of 1812 and still saw the mother country as the centre of their political universe. Draper was drawn towards this influential group of people from both inclination and self-interest. With their assistance a young man of talent and social grace, but without wealth and influence, could have aspirations far beyond what seemed possible in England.

Draper reached the inner circles of this élite gradually. His first employment in Upper Canada was as a schoolteacher in Port Hope. Inspired by Thomas Ward, a local barrister, he began to study law in 1821. After articling at the offices of Ward and of George Strange Boulton, he was called to the bar in 1828. Two years earlier he had married Mary White, the daughter of a retired captain of the Royal Navy.

When the young barrister first began to speak in the courtroom, his listeners were exposed to an oratorical style that would ultimately become famous throughout the province. Both his manner of speaking and the content of his speeches were carefully structured. His voice was full and pleasing, and a typical performance would begin blandly, philosophically, discursively. All pertinent points of view would be covered, all arguments opposed to his own would be advanced and apparently given their proper weight. Then the pace would quicken slightly, as Draper moved to demonstrate that though the ground on which his adversaries stood was unquestionably good, his own position was much better. Having advanced his case gradually and unassumingly, he would sum up his arguments with striking eloquence, replete with classical allusions and, for the first time, with a good degree of emotion. It was later said: 'no man in Parliament ... could so readily enforce a dogma or turn a period as Mr. Draper.'[3] Not everyone liked his style, and his opponents would often comment sarcastically on 'that suavity so peculiar to his nature.'[4] But his calculated appeal to reason was a powerful tool. The sobriquet of 'sweet William' that he gained early was both inevitable and apt.

Draper, therefore, soon acquired a reputation as an especially able lawyer. In 1829 he prepared a brief for the attorney-general, John Beverley Robinson, at the Cobourg assizes. Robinson was impressed and gave Draper a position in the attorney-general's law offices in York.[5] Once there, the new recruit quickly proved that he had the wit and ability to find his way into the inner recesses of the local hierarchy. His connection with the masterful and sophisticated Robinson, close associate of the powerful Anglican Archdeacon of York, John Strachan, meant that Draper was firmly engaged with the orthodox élite. He was also soon fast friends with Christopher Hagerman, a tough Kingstonian whose energy, abrasive oratory, and local connections had enabled him to become solicitor-general. And it was with Hagerman that Draper formed a legal partnership in 1835.[6]

The political leaders of the élite to which Draper attached himself were called by their enemies 'the Family Compact,' and the name has stuck. There has, however, been little agreement then or since as to who was in the Compact, whether the group was large or small, whether it was basically evil or benevolent.[7] Indeed its very existence has been called into question, and by none more so than by its reputed members. There remains, nevertheless, a certain amount of general agreement. An Upper Canadian élite certainly existed. It arose originally from lands and offices granted to his favourites by Lieutenant-Governor John Graves Simcoe,[8] and its supporters came to be entrenched in the Executive and Legislative councils of the province where appointments were usually held for life. Its attitudes were strongly monarchical and anti-American, and it was deeply attached to the constitution bestowed by the Canada Act of 1791 which was the basis of its political power. Although the élite never controlled British governors in the manner that its enemies imagined, its dominance of the Executive Council meant that automatically it had the ear of the monarch's representative. More often than not, it had his sympathy as well. This gave the group the opportunity to influence patronage, and it used this tool to create or co-opt local élites throughout the colony. The members and supporters of this group were frequently termed 'Tories.' They did not shrink from this appellation,[9] though normally they did not think of themselves as an organized political party. It is therefore a convenient label to apply to them. Lastly, it should be mentioned that these Tories, for all their avowed élitism, often commanded much support from the mass of the electorate, especially on 'patriotic' issues.

The political enemies of the Tories usually called themselves Reformers and increasingly saw 'responsible government' as a cure for the ills of the colony. Like 'Family Compact,' the term 'responsible government' has meant many different things. There were, however, at least one or two points of general agreement amongst its proponents – that somehow government should be made more responsive to the wishes of the electorate as a whole and that the hold of the Tory oligarchy on the Executive Council in particular and over patronage in general should be broken.

In the 1830s the Reformers were increasing their power. Organizing themselves more effectively, they began to gain control of the assembly in Upper Canada, while in England Whig colonial secretaries proved willing at least to listen to their point of view. In 1835 this provoked a quarrel between the Colonial Office and Lieutenant-Governor Sir John Colborne that led to the latter's dismissal. Colborne's successor, the eccentric Sir Francis Bond Head, actually appointed some Reformers to the Executive Council when he arrived in the colony early in 1836.

Then events took a new and unexpected turn. When Robert Baldwin, one of Head's new appointments, demanded more consultation, the governor angrily ejected the Reformers from the council, damned them as the 'Republican Party,' dissolved the House of Assembly, and himself took the lead in campaigning for the Tories in elections set for the summer of 1836.

It was against this stormy background that John Beverley Robinson, now chief justice of Upper Canada, began to press William Draper to enter politics.[10] Draper was not enthusiastic. His partnership with Hagerman, established only a year before, was proving remarkably successful, and the swelling clientele meant much work while Hagerman was perforce often absent on his duties as solicitor-general. For the galvanized Tories, now calling themselves the Constitutional party, however, the election was little short of a loyal crusade, and Robinson was able to appeal to Draper's sense of duty and self-interest. The young lawyer had made no secret of the fact that his ultimate goal was the judiciary: politics and government service had long been a road to the bench in Upper Canada, and this was a time when virtue was needed and would no doubt gain its ultimate reward. Draper acceded and was nominated to stand for Toronto.

The election of 1836, which saw most of the leading Reformers defeated, was a victory far beyond the expectations of the 'Constitutionalists.' Draper himself easily won against James Small in Toronto. The loyalty appeal of the governor had been remarkably effective, especially on the immigrants from Britain who were finally coming in numbers sufficient to swamp the earlier influx from the United States. It was therefore a congenially Tory assembly that began its session on 8 November 1836. Within it, Draper soon emerged as a leading spokesman for the government, and his rise in Head's administration was swift. In January 1837 he was appointed to the Executive Council; in April he was nominated solicitor-general. A few weeks after that he was travelling to England as Head's personal representative to deal with the ominous financial crisis that had suddenly beset the colony.[11]

The smooth course of Draper's advance into the Tory hierarchy was broken by the traumatic events of the next three years. The Rebellion of 1837 and its aftermath of alarms along the US border took him from active politics for long periods while he served in such capacities as colonel of militia, judge advocate at courts martial, and aide-de-camp to Bond Head's successor, Sir George Arthur. Then came Lord Durham's whirlwind visit to the colony and the subsequent publication of that governor's famous report which condemned the Tory élite, recommended the unification of Upper and Lower Canada, and suggested the introduction of a form of responsible government. Finally, Charles Poulett Thomson, later Lord Sydenham, arrived as governor to implement the proposed union. In the Colonial Office Lord John Russell declined any formal concession of responsible government but issued a despatch enabling a governor to change the personnel of his Executive Council at will, thus destroying one of the chief bastions of Tory political power. Such events caused Draper much anxious confusion, and began to push him apart from his erstwhile friends and supporters.

It was the question of the union of the Canadas that first split the Tory ranks. Most of the old leaders and some of their younger adherents were strongly against it. Robinson, Hagerman, Strachan, and Henry Sherwood all saw a dubious future in a union that would be less likely to achieve its aim of assimilating the French of Lower Canada than to give the radicals in both provinces a chance to combine. Economically, however, there was much to be said for a measure that would restore the old commercial unity of the St Lawrence-Great Lakes area, eradicate inter-colonial customs duties, and link the Upper Canadian agricultural hinterland more closely with the vital seaport of Montreal.

It was Draper who soon emerged as the leading parliamentary spokesman for those who took this commercial viewpoint. He himself was a director of the Bank of Upper Canada; although he does not appear to have speculated widely personally,[12] he was close to many who were so involved – men such as Hagerman, the Kingston banker John S. Cartwright, and William Hamilton Merritt, the founder of the Welland Canal, and a man whose mind was filled with schemes for the economic development of Upper Canada. Thus the solicitor-general came forward as a staunch supporter of business interests – even when the logic of this pointed in the direction of the merging of Upper Canada itself within a wider province.

Draper could see additional arguments in favour of a union. If, for instance, the imperial government was determined on the measure and the Tories opposed it unconditionally, they would likely have little say in its terms, whereas by supporting union in principle they could also hope to control it to some extent. Lastly, of course, as Draper clearly realized, there remained the stubborn fact that the French Canadians *were* a real problem. Restoring any measure of actual power to them as the majority in Lower Canada would mean that they could again pursue their traditional anti-commercial policy to the detriment of the upper province. At worst, they might seek independence or annexation to the United States, thus sundering Upper Canada's lifeline completely. Yet to continue to rule the French Canadians autocratically, as had been done since the rebellion, was to court further disaffection and perhaps revolution. Thus Durham's proposal of attempted French assimilation through union might not be a good solution to the problem, but it might well be the least bad.

Under the circumstances, Draper accepted Thomson's request to introduce the union bill and pilot it through Upper Canadian assembly. Aided by tremendous pressure from the masterful governor and by the promise of a munificent imperial loan to the new colony, the solicitor-general had secured the house's acceptance of the measure by 9 December 1839. Yet this particular battle was won at a terrible cost. The Tory ranks had separated so widely on the issue that many thought the breach irreparable. Draper himself was particularly reviled as a man who had sold his political principles for the pottage of the governor's table; when he was promoted to attorney-general the Tory press commented that he had been 'advanced for conduct the very reverse of every principle on which he was *supported by the friends he has deceived and the constituents he has betrayed.*'[13]

Yet Draper was no convert to the liberalism of Thomson, now ennobled as Lord Sydenham. Rather, his earnest desire was to remould the right-wing element in Canadian politics into a shape that was more acceptable to the electorate. He had been moving in this direction even before the rebellion. The aspect of Tory policy then most decried in the colony was the support of the privileges of the Church of England. In his first session in the assembly, Draper, supported by Bond Head, had attempted to ease grievances such as the Anglican hold on the clergy reserves and the endowment of King's College.[14] He had accomplished little that was final, but his performance had gained him goodwill amongst Methodists and Presbyterians that would be a significant feature of his future political career.

If the question of increasing the popular appeal of the Tory party had seemed important in the halcyon days of early 1837, it was surely one of acute urgency when elections were about to be held for the first parliament of united Canada. Yet the majority of the Upper Canadian Tory leaders did not seem willing even to begin to rise to the new situation. Draper's old mentor, John Beverley Robinson, had by now simply lapsed into making gloomy Cassandra-like prophesies. The test of the union, wrote the chief justice, 'will be made when the Assembly contains a clear majority against the Government, prepared to act under the ruling demagogue of the day – an event that is as certain to happen ... as the return of seedtime and harvest.'[15]

There were several reasons for the political rigidity of the Tories. They had idealized the little colony in which they comprised the élite of the citizenry and they had cherished the old constitution which had preserved their power. They could scarcely believe that both were disappearing. Above all, perhaps, they had participated in the crowning traumatic experience of early Upper Canada – the War of 1812. Most of the older Compact members had fought in the conflict and they had passed on their fierce prejudices to their children. The hatred and contempt they felt for the invaders was easily extended to 'Yankee democracy' and to popular political institutions in general. In response, they had idealized the 'British' constitution of 1791 as something almost holy. They had held to it tenaciously, ignoring the fact that in intervening years the constitution of Great Britain itself had substantially altered. And when the British had proved willing to listen to those colonists who did demand change, the Tories reacted with a feeling of massive betrayal. To Robinson, Lord Durham was not merely misguided, he was actually evil.[16]

But William Draper had not arrived in Upper Canada until 1820. Although he too viewed popular rule with alarm and distaste, he lacked the fervour of those who had fought the war. Equally, he was more able to view the English for what they were, rather than as what Upper Canadian Tories wished them to be. Indeed, he never fully appreciated the depths of Tory political intransigence and was somewhat baffled when the swift changes after 1837 left so many of his colleagues numb and frozen in an archaic stance. They would thaw in time. But the process would take over a decade, and meanwhile there was work to be done. If much that Tories and more moderate conservatives cherished was gone or was going, much remained. And what remained was worth struggling for.

Under the circumstances, Draper felt the times called not for Robinson's weary Jeremiads but for constructive action. In the mother country like-minded people had responded to broadly similar circumstances when the Great Reform bill of 1832 had appeared to shatter the Tories there. Yet, working patiently, Sir Robert Peel had built up 'conservative associations,' issued a call-to-arms in the Tamworth Manifesto, and ultimately had produced the British Conservative party out of the wreck of Torydom. Surely the Canadian situation called for the same sort of flexible response. It was from this point of view that Draper wrote to J.S. Cartwright in November 1840 in order to 'settle the basis of a party on what are called Conservative principles.'[17] Cartwright, an eminently successful lawyer and banker, had acquired a reputation for prudence, sobriety, and integrity remarkable for a young man in his mid-thirties. So greatly was he respected that the Compact Tories viewed his support as absolutely essential.[18] But he, too, favoured the union, and unlike his friends trusted Draper's political honesty.

The main party platform that Draper now proposed would stress the single issue of maintaining the British connection. By this, he did not mean simply a principle that everybody talked the usual 'claptrap' about; rather, conservative spokesmen should clearly interpret the impact of every specific issue on the British link. This was a popular approach (as the existing complexion of the Upper Canada assembly indicated), and if the Conservatives were well enough organized and conveyed their views clearly enough through the press, they could hope to sweep Upper Canada. With the help of the 'British party' of Lower Canada, they might command a majority in the future united legislature.

'The connexion with Great Britain.' What did it really mean to Draper? As his letter to Cartwright implies, clearly much more than sentimental or patriotic platitudes. Since it was the heart of his politics, it invites some investigation. No comprehensive dissertation of his on the subject exists; nevertheless, occasional remarks, his actions, his interests, the very way he lived his life, all provide solid clues.

Unquestionably of high importance was the fact that it made him and all Canadians part of a cosmopolitan world-empire. Draper himself had seen the Union Jack flying on four continents. One did not have to be a crude race-patriot to believe that British expansion was part of a grand design of Providence. But this expansion was much more than the mere flexing of imperial sinews; it also meant the spread of civilization. In Canada this latter was a precious commodity that might perish only too easily. The frontier was the enemy of civilization and the neighbouring United States was the embodiment of the frontier. Whatever Draper may have thought of the American constitution and of the sober republican virtues of the first presidents, he would have seen all his doubts of the American system fulfilled following the election of Andrew Jackson and the concomitant victory of the frontier. The frontier had its virtues – incarnate perhaps in Jackson himself. It also had its vices. In understanding the political attitudes not only of Draper but of many Canadians in the 1840s, some reference must be made to the fact that American politics in the same period were plumbing one of their periodic depths of inanity. 'Rumpsey dumpsey, rumpsey dumpsey, Colonel Johnson killed Tecumseh,' was the slogan under which Richard M. Johnson, alleged slayer of the great Amerindian, became vice-president of the United States in 1836. In 1840 Tecumseh's other nemesis, 'Tippecanoe' Harrison, was elected president, campaigning that he drank hard cider, dressed in home-spun, and lived in a log cabin while his incumbent opponent was so effete as to sleep on a Louis XV bedstead and enjoy French wine. Since Americans talked loudly of their democratic system, it is little wonder that 'democracy' was a pejorative word to so many Canadians of Draper's generation.

In purely physical terms the Canadian frontier was even more raw and overwhelming than the American. If it did not dominate society in the same way, this was surely owing to the salutary weight of British institutions. The rule of an ancient legal system kept lynch-law and vigilantism at bay. Political institutions were something of a problem. In common with the Tories, Draper had believed in the desirability of a constitutionally entrenched élite in Upper Canada. But if that cherished dream was fading, neither had matters sunk to the American level; nor would they so long as the British connection remained. To his mind, 'Rumpsey dumpsey' politics might exist at the municipal and constituency stages, but Queen Victoria would be head of state, governors would be British gentlemen, Canadian political leaders would be responsible to the crown and/or a parliamentary assembly and would not be elected directly by the voice of the frontier as was General Harrison.

The British connection also stood for more than things purely British. Draper believed profoundly in the potentialities of Canada. Yet whatever unique merits Canada itself possessed owed their existence to British military protection. This was true even for the French. Nothing threatened their culture more starkly than the United States. Moreover, British justice should also protect the French from undue exploitation by Anglo-Canadians. In Draper's eyes, it was a regrettable lapse in this respect that had provoked the rebellions in Lower Canada. Lastly, the ties with Britain provided the access to British capital and investment that would build railways, develop industry, and ultimately vanquish the frontier entirely.

Yet even as Draper wrote to Cartwright about the formation of a party whose watchword would be 'the British connection,' he may have felt a sort of living spectre peering over his shoulder. Did not Robert Baldwin, fast rising as the champion of responsible government, claim to value British institutions as much as anyone? Did he not maintain (as had Durham) that to divide the functions of government so as to give Canadians internal self-rule would cement links with the mother-country by erasing areas of differ-ence, and would bring the colonial constitution into a closer approximation of the British? Draper obviously felt it essential to raise this point: 'I can-not agree with those who think the principle [responsible government] can be applied here to local measures ... Who shall decide what is a local measure?... Take for instance the question of importing produce from the United States – Its direct consequence would be local but it would in its remoter consequence affect the carrying trade of the Mother Country.'[19]

Draper's 'refutation' of Baldwin's principle was one that could hardly be termed crushing. Indeed, his strained example possibly illustrates how small a gap now remained between Draper's constitutional position and that of the Reformers. If the attorney-general felt uncomfortable about this problem, however, it was at least one that could be evaded for the time being. Whatever else Lord John Russell had conceded, he had repudiated full responsible government. Given that fact of imperial policy, Baldwin's insistence on the theory seemed in itself a threat to the ties with Britain.

Meanwhile, Draper's move to reunite and reshape his group of supporters was warmly aided by Sir George Arthur before he left Upper Canada; Arthur saw Draper as the only hope of the Conservatives and as a leader who might 'marshall all moderate men.' Yet this, too, came to nothing. Cartwright was disposed to help Draper, but under pressure from other more unbending Tory leaders, such as Sir Allan MacNab and Chief Justice Robinson, he eventually drew back.[20] Worse still, Governor General Sydenham was about to turn all of his remarkable energy and talents in a different direction. He, in fact, had no wish to work with the Compact Tories and preferred to have them in opposition. About to break with Baldwin's Reform group, he was determined to 'make a middle Reforming party I am sure which can put down both [Tories and Baldwin Reformers].'[21] And, as leader of such a party, the governor had hand-picked Samuel Bealey Harrison, Arthur's civil secretary – an English lawyer and a recent immigrant to Upper Canada.

Having made his decision, the governor general moved with speed and skill. As soon as the Union of the Canadas was proclaimed in February 1841, he formed a coalition Executive Council from as many political groups as he could, and went to the polls that spring, clearly leading the government himself. The result to a high degree was a triumph of his political manipulation. In Lower Canada the French – opposed both to the governor and a union meant to swamp them – were reduced to twenty out of forty-two seats. In Upper Canada both Sir Allan MacNab's Tories and Baldwin's 'Ultra' Reformers mustered little more than half a dozen supporters each. In the middle was the body of moderates – both Conservatives and Reformers – pledged to support the governor. Sydenham had his victory and the assembly in his pocket. Draper and Harrison emerged as the principal spokesmen of the government in the parliament that met in the new capital, Kingston, in June 1841.

In fact, Draper's power was more apparent than real. His support was not critical to the ministry – the moderate Conservatives that he led numbered only about five.[22] Also, the governor himself could not have cared less about

Draper's credibility with the Tories or his desire to build a broader base for Conservatism. Draper's oratorical abilities still made him useful, but rather as a sort of government 'whipping boy'; he became the chief focus for the resentment of the Baldwin Reformers and usually parried their attacks. But important legislation was increasingly introduced and piloted by Harrison, and by August 1841 the latter was virtually accepted as sole government leader.

The general trend of events during Sydenham's administration was therefore little to Draper's liking. Yet, as he watched matters proceed, a new possibility began to form in his mind. This was the result of a major development which had been going on gradually and without fanfare – the 'taming' of the French Canadians. The union had been designed to extinguish their nationality; yet, though protesting, most had reluctantly accepted it. Their parliamentary representation had been reduced by Sydenham through gerrymandering and sharp practices at the elections; but those who were elected had peacefully taken their seats in the house. They had hoped through a party alliance with Baldwin to command a majority in the united assembly; when this failed they had behaved in exemplary fashion as a constitutional opposition. In short, Baldwin's eastern counterpart, Louis LaFontaine, had accomplished what Lord Durham had thought was beyond human expectation – within a few years of the rebellion, he had apparently turned the French into loyal British subjects.

Yet, was not their alliance with Baldwin an unnatural one? Behind the French Canadians lay the great conservative forces of the Roman church and an agricultural way of life. Surely their league with Baldwin did not betoken a real commitment to the impractical concept of responsible government, but simply an understandable desire to achieve their fair share of power and patronage? So Draper surmised, so some of the French themselves hinted to him.[23] They were allied with Baldwin, therefore, because they had expected a great Reform victory in the election. With that hope dashed, surely the promise of positions in government would lure them from the 'ultras' into an alliance with the moderates. Paradoxically, then, that section of the new united province which was most feared for its rebellious tendencies might be transformed into the greater force for stability. When Draper raised this possibility with Sydenham, however, the governor was not interested.[24] His majority in the assembly would last out his administration; he would not woo again those who had rejected him. The French Canadians were left with Baldwin, and tied to responsible government.

Towards the end of the parliamentary session new developments occurred which discouraged Draper even further. In September 1841 Robert Baldwin, hoping to split the moderate Reformers that Harrison managed, gave notice of a series of resolutions calling explicitly for responsible government. The administration had had due warning and Sydenham parried them by having Harrison move a set of counter-resolutions which were accepted by the assembly.[25] Although the Harrison resolutions in no way limited the powers of the governor, they did distinctly imply that executive councillors must have the confidence of the assembly. Worse still, the colonial press was soon claiming that the 'Magna Carta'[26] of responsible government was now on the statute books. Though he voted with the government, Draper was dubious. He knew well how little had been conceded legally; but a situation where the Canadian public had been deceived into thinking it had responsible government when it actually did not could be unstable and even dangerous.

Worse followed. The capable 'ultra,' Francis Hincks, now claiming that Sydenham had indeed introduced responsible government and desiring to participate, broke with his close associate, Baldwin. The governor, considering this a great coup, offered Hincks the inspector-generalship. But *could* a government that was acceptable to Hincks, the fiercest of Reformers, be also acceptable to Draper? As a general rule Conservatives surely should support British governors; but in Sydenham's case it appeared that they could do so only if they were prepared entirely to swallow their conservatism. The attorney-general considered for twenty-four hours and submitted his resignation. The governor, now dying after a fall from his horse, refused to accept it on the day before he expired.[27] The offer to Hincks lapsed. Once again Draper waited on events.

Perhaps to his surprise, events appeared to develop in the most gratifying way imaginable. After all, from the point of view of an Upper Canadian Conservative whose main political watchword was 'the British connection,' the past decade had been disastrous; and not the least disastrous aspect of it had been the intervention of the imperial government and its agents. Ever since 1832 a series of Whig colonial secretaries had pursued a policy for Canada apparently based on ignorance and indecision.[28] They had simultaneously encouraged the colonial radicals while denying them their ultimate desires. This was surely calculated to produce nothing but rebellion and unrest. As for the governors themselves, after Bond Head's uncontrolled Toryism, Durham's autocratic radicalism, and Sydenham's steel-hard liberalism, one scarcely knew what strange sort of apparition would next appear from the mother country. But soon after Sydenham's death the news arrived that the Whig ministry in Britain had fallen. The Conservatives under Sir Robert Peel had assumed office with a strong majority. Perhaps a new era in colonial policy had begun at last.

The arrival of Sir Charles Bagot as governor general in January 1842 confirmed such hopes. Though an urbane and talented diplomat, Bagot refreshingly made no claim to political wizardry. The instructions and advice that he brought with him from Lord Stanley, the Conservative colonial secretary, were the same as Sydenham's. Responsible government was to be resisted; all-party government was to be pursued; the co-operation of the French was to be sought. But could Sydenham's all-party system work without Sydenham himself? From England Sir John Colborne, now Lord Seaton, gave an astonishingly accurate prediction of what was to come: 'I conceive therefore that Sir C. Bagot will be supported by the Unionists and their opponents and that he will endeavour to steer clear of every party and to distribute favours to French and British with an impartial hand: 'till he finds that the Responsible Government which has been set up and carried out by an unexampled system of corruption, must have the effect of leaving the Governor in a minority *bientôt* unless the machine is constantly worked by an artist as clever and unscrupulous as the one that contrived to secure the majority of the first session.'[29]

On the new governor general's arrival, however, such troubles were in the future. Bagot, by both political conviction and by temperament, was a moderate Conservative of the same mould as Draper himself. The two men became fast friends, and Draper rapidly replaced the enigmatic Harrison as the governor's chief adviser. They worked well together. With Bagot's full support, Draper hurried to Toronto to accomplish a favourite project – that of putting King's College on an operational basis. The cornerstone of the institution itself was laid by Bagot in April in the midst of a triumphal all-party reception for the governor, organized by Draper. Soon after, Bagot was treated to an equally splendid reception in Montreal, and he expressed his goodwill towards the French in a series of practical concessions. A new list of government appointments included for the first time a large number of French Canadians, and prominent French-Canadian figures were invited to join the Executive Council. The latter refused for political reasons, but the gestures were well noted.[30]

All this goodwill, however important, did not alter one hard fact. The French as a group would not enter Bagot's government because they remained tied in a political alliance to Robert Baldwin, and Baldwin remained inflexibly committed to the principle of responsible government. Moreover, matters had gone too far for British governments or governors to turn back quietly the clock of Canadian political evolution.

The problem began to become apparent to the governor and his advisers in the spring of 1842, some months before parliament was scheduled to meet in September. With Sydenham dead and Harrison's influence waning, the moderate Reformers whose support was critical for the government began to drift towards Baldwin. Bagot, still believing in the necessity of multi-party government – 'I am convinced that the country is to be held on no other terms'[31] – attempted to bolster the sagging centre with support from the extreme left and right. Francis Hincks was still willing to join the administration; Bagot proposed to accept him but to balance the appointment with that of a leading Tory such as J.S. Cartwright. Draper, whose sentiments about Hincks had not changed, was nonetheless willing to work with him if Cartwright was. And Harrison would swallow Cartwright if Hincks came in.[32]

But Cartwright, the key figure, declined. Having long suspected such an invitation might be in the offing, he had corresponded earnestly about it with virtually every leading Compact Tory. Their advice was unanimous. Great as his duty was to support the governor (of whom they all thought highly), he must never associate himself with Hincks, 'the apologist of traitors.'[33] Cartwright not only declined to serve in the council, he almost certainly showed Draper the correspondence to warn him that he too would lose all Tory and Conservative support if he accepted the *ci-devant* Reform leader. Certainly Draper was convinced that he could not take Hincks without an influential Tory as well. Otherwise, as he wrote to Bagot, 'not only should I be useless to the Government but even an encumbrance. I should bring no party – command no respect – influence nobody.'[34] Under these circumstances Bagot might fare better with a more 'harmoniously Liberal' council. In effect, Draper was being forced to an unpleasant conclusion. The ideal of all-party government, so earnestly desired by Bagot and himself and so imperatively recommended by the Colonial Office, was proving hard indeed to work. More and more, party politics seemed the order of the day. The Baldwin and LaFontaine Reformers espoused them; the Tories reprobated them in theory and followed them in practice. Men closer to the centre – Draper, Harrison, and their respective followers – might try hard to work together, but their coalitions were clearly shaky affairs.

For a moment it seemed the immediate problem might be solved when, under Draper's urgings, the rising Toronto Tory, Henry Sherwood, whose ambition was said to be notorious,[35] proved willing to enter the council. But second thoughts came quickly. Draper became convinced that even this reconstruction of the government would not save it from being defeated in the assembly. If that happened, as the attorney-general wrote to Bagot in a crucially important letter, the Harrison resolutions would oblige him and the rest of the council to resign. In that case, the governor would either have to call on the opposition to form a ministry or to fight an election himself as Sydenham had done. The second course was dangerous and would likely achieve nothing; the first might be unacceptable to the Colonial Office. The only way to avoid either would be a radical reconstruction of the council by the governor before a defeat came in the house.

French support would save the day; but the French would not be had without Baldwin, and Baldwin would not sit with any Conservative councillors. In this case Draper declared himself willing to resign and added that the other Conservatives or British party members should do likewise.[36] Bagot, already thinking in this direction but somewhat afraid of French demands,[37] now rapidly made up his mind. Harrison and others had given him precisely the same advice as Draper. The governor wrote to Colonial Secretary Stanley that securing the accession of the French as a party was the only solution he could see, but added that he would not take such a step without the 'entire concurrence' of the imperial government.[38]

The concurrence of the imperial government was not forthcoming. Stanley wasted time consulting Peel and Wellington, and his dispatch forbidding Bagot to make his move came too late to help or hinder the governor general. Once parliament met on 8 September Bagot was forced to act to avoid a government defeat. On 10 September he asked LaFontaine if the French would enter the council, bringing the support of their entire people. LaFontaine was grateful but insisted on coming in with Baldwin. This was agreed, but negotiations appeared to founder when Bagot felt he could not accept LaFontaine's demand of four seats.[39]

With the crisis reaching a point of desperation, the Executive Council itself now took decisive action. Meeting on 12 September in the office of Dominick Daly, Draper and Harrison led the councillors in drafting an ultimatum to the governor. Basing their position on the Harrison resolutions, they advised that LaFontaine's full demands be met. One seat was vacant. Draper would retire. Sherwood and one other Tory must do likewise or be forced out. This would provide four places and the Reformers could be offered two other positions outside the council. If the governor failed to act on this advice, the councillors 'after great deliberation' felt they must all resign.[40]

There was now little room for Bagot to manoeuvre, and the next day he offered LaFontaine the precise terms stated by the council. One final obstacle remained. Robert Baldwin had indeed been hoping to establish the principle of responsible government by bringing down the ministry in the house. He therefore made further difficulties and LaFontaine again rejected the governor's offer.

But now it was Bagot who was not to be denied. Even as he brushed off complaints from outraged Tories like MacNab and Sherwood, he empowered Draper to read out the details of the negotiations in the assembly on the apparently correct assumption that most of the French members did not know the full extent of his offer. It was a bold course, and the following day in the house Draper carried out his critical task superbly. Justifying his own past conduct and stating his belief that the French were entitled by justice to play a full role in government, he gradually revealed the extent of the governor's offer and the story of its refusal, ending: 'it is not for me to say why these proposals have been rejected, why the hand of reconciliation has been refused and the olive branch of peace dashed to the earth by the Honourable

Gentlemen opposite; I will leave them to explain their own views and motives.'[41]

The speech had the desired effect. Baldwin, unprepared, gave a witty but somewhat contradictory reply. The French members appeared 'quite electrified' by Bagot's offer and astonished at how little stood between themselves and power. After rumours that LaFontaine might be thrown over by his own followers; the Reform attack was broken off.[42] On 16 September LaFontaine accepted Bagot's offer. The ministry was then reconstructed with five Baldwin-LaFontaine Reformers taking office. The governor had not only avoided having this forced upon him by a defeat in the house, he had still apparently preserved 'all-party' government. The new council contained one Tory, R.B. Sullivan, two 'non-political' members, Daly and H.H. Killaly, and the independent moderate Reformers, Harrison and J.H. Dunn. And Harrison, rather than Baldwin or LaFontaine, was acknowledged as government leader.

Thus Draper could depart from the administration with the feeling that matters had been resolved as well as could be expected, while he himself had played a significant part in avoiding a major political breakdown. There were, however, some unpleasant legacies – such as the undying enmity of Henry Sherwood. Sherwood had been seduced into the ministry by Draper, ridiculed by his Tory friends for taking the position, then unceremoniously ejected on the advice of the attorney-general a few months later! He had a reasonable grievance, and Henry Sherwood cherished grievances very well.

More important was the fact that from Draper's point of view his success had been basically a rearguard victory and aspects of his own actions carried ominous portents. In particular, the action of the Executive Council in delivering a virtual ultimatum to a governor, backed by a unanimous threat of resignation, was without precedent in colonial history. It was not, of course, actually done in order to coerce the governor, but rather to push him into a ministerial reconstruction he himself desired, and perhaps to provide him with justification for his act before the Colonial Office. From this point of view it worked well, and indeed proved to be Bagot's strongest defence with the home authorities.

The news of the governor's action reached England during a political lull there and caused a great air 'for want of something better' to occupy public opinion.[43] Though it was decided ultimately to accept Bagot's measures as a temporary *fait accompli*, Stanley left the former in little doubt as to how strongly the imperial government disapproved of them.[44] The colonial secretary admitted that the council's decision 'placed you in a position in which you had little choice of your course of action,'[45] and credited its members, Draper in particular, with entire disinterestedness in the matter. Yet Stanley still felt 'the advice itself was injudicious and that in giving it, the council went beyond their proper function.'[46]

This was true. If the ministers' action had provided Bagot with some needed justification, it had also made more clear how heavily a governor had to rely on their advice. His position was therefore, willy-nilly, becoming more analogous to that of a constitutional monarch. But whereas British monarchs, formally responsible only to God and the law, could gracefully withdraw from the field of real executive action, a colonial governor's prime responsibility was still to the Colonial Office. The position of governor, and with it the peace of the Canadas, might yet be ground to pieces between the millstones of imperial authority and the power of the colonial assembly.

Such a possibility would arise in a little over a year. But at the moment Draper was glad to retire to Toronto to devote himself to his legal practice. He was not, however, entirely divorced from politics. In early 1843 he was created a member of the Legislative Council – an appointment Bagot had stipulated as part of the terms on which he was willing to admit Baldwin and LaFontaine to his government. Draper, though accepting the position, was not greatly interested in it. Meanwhile, politics ran smoothly enough. The gratitude of the Reformers, especially the French, towards Sir Charles Bagot held them back from embarrassing the governor with further demands in the succeeding months, when he lay ill and dying. Besides, the tide seemed to be quietly flowing in their direction. The ministry gradually became a harmonious Baldwin-LaFontaine affair. The Tory, Sullivan, the moderate, Dunn, and the 'non-political' Killaly soon merged as good Reform party men. Only Harrison, the nominal government leader, and Dominick Daly retained their independence of party, and Harrison was soon to resign.

With the arrival of Bagot's successor, Sir Charles Metcalfe, in March 1843, the high hopes originally held by the Reform leaders that the new governor would be a firm supporter of their cause were dispelled rapidly. Still, Metcalfe gave his ministers 'correct' if somewhat frosty support on most issues, including the potentially explosive change of the seat of government from Kingston to Montreal. This move, introduced in October 1843, was exceedingly unpopular in Upper Canada and brought some dissension in the Reform cabinet, including Harrison's resignation (he sat for Kingston). It and other Reform measures also briefly reunited the sundered Tories and Conservatives. In Toronto the Constitutional Society was reformed, with Draper as president and MacNab as vice-president.[47] In the Legislative Council, where the Reformers were still in a minority, Draper indeed pushed through a resolution to block the change of capital. A new spate of appointments, however, soon produced a Reform majority in the upper house which repealed the earlier resolutions and led Draper and thirteen other Upper Canadian members to stalk out of the chamber in protest. After this rather empty gesture, he resolved never to return to politics again.[48]

Yet he was soon back before the bar of the assembly, acting as counsel for King's College in opposition to Baldwin's proposed bill to secularize the university. Here his masterful speech against 'the University Spoliation Bill' electrified the Anglicans, and Bishop Strachan had numbers of copies of it printed and circulated.[49] For Draper, however, this was to prove yet another in a series of ludicrous accidents that damaged his credit with the Tories when unexpected circumstances ultimately gave him the responsibility for settling that question. For the time being, Baldwin's bill was lost not through Draper's eloquence but through the eruption of a dangerous political crisis.

On 26 November Metcalfe's entire Executive Council resigned, except for Dominick Daly, apparently over a minor appointment that the governor had made. In the assembly on 1 December, however, the ex-ministers claimed that Metcalfe had contravened the Harrison resolutions and that the whole principle of responsible government was at stake. Resolutions supporting them were passed by the house, and on 9 December parliament was prorogued.[50] A few days earlier Draper had been summoned to appear at the governor's residence.

If Draper expected the governor general to be a man beleaguered, he discovered instead that Sir Charles was about to launch what had every appearance of being a devastating counter-attack. It was no less than the project of forming another all-party ministry, but on a much broader basis than ever Sydenham or Bagot had dreamed. Besides Draper, Metcalfe had summoned Samuel Harrison, J.S. Cartwright, and the prominent French leader, Denis-Benjamin Viger. It was a shrewd plan. In Upper Canada many moderate Reformers were already feeling that Baldwin had pressed his principle too far; Tories and Conservatives had never doubted it. In Lower Canada the British party would unquestionably support the governor, and now the opportunity had emerged to break LaFontaine's hold on the French. Viger was willing to work for Metcalfe, precisely because he was more radical and nationalistic than LaFontaine. Believing responsible government to be constitutionally impossible, his ultimate goal was an independent French Canada.

Independence, Viger felt, would come in the fullness of time – it was natural and 'inevitable' for colonies to grow up and sever links with the mother country, an opinion then shared by many in Great Britain. Until that happy sequel, however, French Canadians should strive to avoid another rebellion with its futile bloodshed, and to promote and guard French institutions by making the most of any governor who was sympathetic to them as a people. Viger had applauded Bagot's 'great measure' of bringing the French into the council. Now, with horror, he saw LaFontaine apparently throwing away that hard-gained influence for the sake of Robert Baldwin's impractical constitutional convictions; convictions which were dangerous because they could lead to the type of direct confrontation with British power that had caused the rebellions in 1837.[51]

Hence, though Viger's ultimate aim – separation – was completely opposed to the views of Draper and Metcalfe, they all had good common grounds to work together for the time being. Nor was Viger an ordinary individual. At the time of Union he had been unquestionably senior to LaFontaine both in length of service and in the hearts of his countrymen. Moreover, Viger's influence on both personal and political levels reached into the Papineau family, and it was widely believed that the august *patriote* leader of the Rebellion of 1837, Louis-Joseph Papineau, shared Viger's views. Indeed, it seemed not impossible that once his pardon had been granted the unquestioned hero of French Canada might return to take a place beside Viger in Metcalfe's administration. Thus, the odds seemed fair that the governor might win a crushing victory that would reduce Baldwin and LaFontaine to isolated individuals with small rump followings. The war cry would be 'loyalty.' Loyalty to the crown in Upper Canada; loyalty to Viger, Papineau, and the *patriotes* of old in Lower Canada.

The possibilities of this grand coalition appear to have captivated Draper so quickly that he advised the governor to appeal to the electorate immediately.[52] Soon, however, the first flush of optimism was muted. In Lower Canada there were ominous indications that the support of the French as a whole had not shifted automatically to Viger and might have to be torn from LaFontaine's capable hands. Viger felt confident of ultimate triumph but asked for a few weeks to consolidate his position. In Upper Canada both the moderate Reformers and Tories, represented by Harrison and Cartwright, declined to give the governor immediate support. This meant that a carefully managed campaign might have to be waged. In the meantime, of course, the queen's government had to be carried on. But only Viger and Draper were sworn into the council to take their places beside Daly. Both refused any specific ministerial office or emoluments until a proper government could be formed. This strange ministry, popularly nicknamed 'the triumvirate,' was designed to be very temporary – but was to last nearly a year.

It was a period of intense strain for Draper. He was the workhorse of the administration. Governor Metcalfe, though by no means *hors de combat*, was already dying of cancer. The ageing Viger had much more enthusiasm than energy, and all the energy he possessed was needed for the purely political struggle developing in Lower Canada. Daly, a cautious though efficient bureaucrat, had no practical experience regarding Upper Canada. To Draper, therefore, fell much of the responsibility for the whole province, and almost the entire burden of its Upper Canadian half. Metcalfe praised him handsomely and wrote to Stanley that he did the work of six men,[53] but it was hard, unpaid work that Draper could ill sustain either emotionally or financially. A protracted struggle, ultimately unsuccessful, would likely leave him with neither a political nor a judicial career and with a legal practice ruined through neglect.

If back-breaking work and a sound business acumen sufficed for routine administration, the political side of Draper's duties needed a delicate and diplomatic hand. The stakes were high. If he *could* unite Upper Canadian Tories with moderates, both Reformers and Conservatives, and link them all with the French, then from the wreck of the Family Compact he would indeed have created a new Conservative party, and one that would have even wider support than that which he had envisaged in his letter to Cartwright in 1840.

To win over the mass of the moderates, Draper singled out three men he wished to acquire for his government – William Hamilton Merritt, Samuel Harrison, and Egerton Ryerson, the influential Methodist leader then principal of Victoria College. Merritt, '*the* man as relates to popular influence in the Western section of the province,'[54] was a Reformer who had disagreed with Baldwin over the resignation of the ministers in 1843. His acceptance of office would be a great political coup. Even more important was the expertise in business and economics he would bring. Although best known as founder of the Welland Canal, Merritt was an intelligent enthusiast regarding all types of communications.[55] At the moment his mind was filled with schemes for slashing government expenditures while increasing revenue through tariff and tax reforms[56] – preoccupations extremely close to those of Draper himself. For the attorney-general, who so ardently wished to promote business interests and to develop public works, the acquisition of Merritt as inspector-general would be invaluable to a development-oriented Conservative party.

Draper's efforts were all frustrated. Merritt and Harrison ultimately declined, while Metcalfe vetoed Ryerson on the grounds that the grant of a political position to a clergyman was a dangerous precedent. Instead, Ryerson was to obtain the non-political post of assistant superintendent of education for Canada West. Yet this first, unsuccessful round of cabinet-making was not without its positive effects. It was soon popular currency that both Harrison and Merritt leaned towards the governor rather than to Baldwin. Indeed, Merritt privately supported Draper, claiming that his actions 'will merit a Civil Crown.'[57] Ryerson, though not joining the ministry, plunged into print, writing long articles praising the provisional administration and claiming that Draper, who had 'thrown himself into the breach and defended and supported the Government in no less than three emergencies when others have abandoned and even sought to overthrow it,' should be supported at all costs.[58]

If Draper could feel that he was at least making some headway in Upper Canada, the picture which was taking shape in Lower Canada was decidedly bleak. To the vast majority of French Canadians the basic issue, as always, was the *survivance* of their culture, and essential to this was the unity of the French political bloc. After some weeks of paralysed indecision, a consensus began to form in French Canada that it was Viger in breaking with LaFontaine, rather than LaFontaine in breaking with the governor, who had most jeopardized that unity. And once the ageing patriot was decisively cast as a *vendu*, he was spared no abuse nor invective from the French politicians and the press. Only in Montreal itself did Viger hold some ground. And he did score one coup. In August 1844 Denis-Benjamin Papineau, brother of the great *patriote* and a man whose political opinions matched those of Viger, entered the council as commissioner of crown lands. But from his European exile Louis-Joseph Papineau critically refused to endorse the administration, even with his brother in it, while outside Montreal Lower Canada rallied defiantly and solidly behind LaFontaine.

Draper was becoming exasperated. Though Viger remained maddeningly optimistic about eventually winning French support, and in the meantime claimed that a cabinet of three was not a bad size for the colony, the Upper Canadian leader was already determined by the spring of 1844 to form a real government and meet the electorate as quickly as possible. In the western section his patient work at last bore modest fruit. William Morris, an influential moderate and lay leader of the Church of Scotland, accepted the position of receiver-general, and some Tory support was gained when Henry Sherwood became solicitor-general west, though without a seat in the council. Draper himself now took the portfolio of attorney-general west; the Upper Canadian half of the ministry was complete. Hurrying to Montreal to investigate the Lower Canadian situation personally, however, Draper was shaken. He soon informed Metcalfe that little support was to be had there and none would be gained by further delay.[59] Draper hastily added as attorney-general east the undistinguished Montreal lawyer, James Smith, and asked the governor to dissolve parliament and call a general election. Metcalfe agreed, 'not,' as he wrote to Stanley, 'with any great confidence, but as the least of all evils.'[60]

The campaign of September 1844 was waged with violent invective and polemic, and the ensuing elections were held amidst riots and tumults, especially in Upper Canada. In Lower Canada two French supporters of Viger were elected – Papineau and Sabrevois DeBleury. Nine British party members were returned in predominantly English-speaking ridings. All the rest of the eastern section solidly backed LaFontaine; Viger lost in two constituencies. In Upper Canada, however, the situation was the reverse. While Baldwin himself was easily elected, his followers were reduced to about eleven.

Elsewhere Tories and moderates carried the day in the West. On an overall basis, it appeared that the government supporters might have a slight majority in the Union's parliament.

The reasons for the outcome of the election are clear for the eastern section, more complex for the western. Although most of the measures of the previous Baldwin-LaFontaine administration affecting Lower Canada pleased the majority of the electorate there, the same could not be said of the performance of the Reformers regarding the western section of the Union. For example, the removal of the capital from Kingston and Hincks' Upper Canada Assessment bill, introducing much higher taxes, had scarcely been widely palatable. Yet most historians are probably correct in seeing the key to the Reform defeat in Upper Canada in 1844 in terms of the active and vociferous intervention of Sir Charles Metcalfe in the campaign in support of his ministers. But Metcalfe's victory was not based simply on a glandular response to his appeal for 'loyalty.' In urging loyalty on the Tories and Conservatives, the governor would have been preaching to the converted. Equally, such an appeal would have little effect on staunch ultra Reformers, who had had it used unfairly against them before and regarded it as cant. The really crucial sector of the Upper Canadian electorate in 1844 was almost certainly 'the minor host of Moderates,'[61] who were not likely to give their support automatically to a British governor, right or wrong. If they had been, there would have been no political crisis under Sir Charles Bagot. For the moderates the loyalty cry made sense because of the constitutional issue.

Constitutional questions often appear so theoretical that it is difficult to imagine them having a wide impact on an electorate. Certainly Viger's long and polished articles on the subject did not significantly move the voters of Lower Canada. But in Upper Canada the constitutional problem was clear, was well publicized – and Sir Charles Metcalfe quite certainly had the best of the argument. In the first place, the debate centred around the Harrison resolutions of 1841, and the fact that Harrison, though he did not forthrightly condemn the Reform ex-ministers, had signally failed to support them and had accepted a judicial appointment from the governor did not go unnoticed. Second, when Metcalfe replied to the district councillors of Gore: 'you speak of the Resolutions of September, 1841 ... but in no Administration have they been so thoroughly carried into operation as in mine ...'[62] he was stating the plain truth. Whereas Sydenham and Bagot had both taken a lead in making or reconstructing their Executive Councils, Metcalfe, by his lights, had duly supported his councillors until they had deserted him. In contending for independent control of patronage – the particular question that had caused the rupture – he was not only acting under explicit orders from the Colonial Office, but was doing nothing that all his predecessors had not done before him.

Even the governor's performance of campaigning in person was not beyond the bounds of responsible government as outlined by Lord Durham himself, who had written: 'the Governor if he wished to retain advisers not possessing the confidence of the existing Assembly, might rely on the effect of an appeal to the people.'[63] Against this, the ex-ministers implicitly were arguing for a principle that Baldwin had already stated explicitly: 'that the representative of the Sovereign ... is *necessarily obliged* [author's italics] to make use of the advice and assistance of subordinate officers in the administration of his Government.'[64] Time would ultimately justify the political logic of this proposition. In 1844, however, it was in advance not only of the colonial constitution, but indeed of the British constitution itself.[65] Moderates feared that the imperial government would not and could not accede to it, and that insistence on it would lead only to a severing of connections with the mother country. Thus Baldwin was pressing too far too fast, not only from the point of view of the Colonial Office and of both Whigs and Tories in Great Britain, but also from that of the majority of the Upper Canadian electorate. Quite correctly, that electorate had bade him halt.

On 28 November 1844 the second Parliament of United Canada met in spacious new quarters in Montreal. As the total outcome of the election was still somewhat in doubt, it was with a good deal of anxiety that Draper, in the Legislative Council, awaited news from the assembly. However, on the first day, Sir Allan MacNab edged out A.N. Morin, LaFontaine's leading supporter, for Speaker by three votes. Then, on 6 December Baldwin's amendment to the Speech from the Throne was defeated by forty-two votes to thirty-six. The government therefore had a slight majority. Draper was thus able to launch a political programme designed ultimately to realize the same broad ends towards which he had worked since he first took office under Metcalfe – the formation of a strong and popular party and government comprised of Tory-Conservatives from Upper Canada linked with the majority of the Lower Canadian French.

At first glance, the chances of attaining such goals, given the parliamentary situation of the time, must have seemed remote. The French had decisively rejected Viger. The Upper Canadian Tories were as prickly as ever and their dislike and distrust of Draper himself had not abated. Though willing to support the governor with their votes, they were still extremely wary of attaching themselves to the government itself. Indeed, Sherwood had probably accepted the position of solicitor-general because it no longer entailed a seat in the Executive Council, rather than in spite of that fact. Moreover, if the Tories insisted on using their power to promote really Tory causes – such as the defence of Anglican privileges – they would almost certainly lose the support of the moderates which had won them their seats. William Morris, on the eve of the election, felt the divisions within the Conservative ranks were so strong that the party might fall apart at any moment.[66]

It was possible, however, to see matters in a more optimistic light. For instance, one could interpret the action of the French electorate simply as a bid for power that had failed. If the French had still backed LaFontaine, then was it not because they had expected the Baldwin Reformers to sweep Upper Canada and that an alliance with that group would thus be the best way to maintain French influence? If so, now that their gamble was lost, would they not reappraise their position, become weary of opposition, and move toward the government?

As for the Tories, it was mainly a matter of 'civilizing' them. They represented the core of unshakeable loyalty to the British connection that Draper valued so highly, but they still maintained political principles and postures that were unacceptable to the majority of the Upper Canadian electorate. The trick would be to keep them, use them, and at last coerce and cajole them into a type of Conservatism that would be attractive to the community at large. Indeed, this process had already begun. Metcalfe, after all, had not repudiated the Harrison resolutions in his campaign. He had embraced them, and the Tories elected on his coat-tails had accepted them as well. Whereas, as recently as 1842, Hagerman had written to Cartwright, 'the Duty of the Conservative Party is to repudiate Responsible Government,' in the election of 1844 so staunch a Tory as William Benjamin Robinson (John Beverley's brother) had run on the promise to uphold 'the pure principles of Responsible Government.'[67] If the Tories had thus accepted ministerial responsibility against their deepest convictions, they might move yet further in the directions in which Draper wished to lead them.

His own position rested on three stout legs: the support of the governor, the lack of alternative leadership, and time. The Tories, or at least the more intelligent of them, realized that their electoral triumph of 1844 did not represent a swing of the voters towards the Family Compact position of the past. They had won only because moderates had turned to them as the least of all evils in the constitutional crisis. Their mandate was simply to support the governor, and the governor supported Draper with all his heart and soul. Even setting aside Metcalfe's championing of his attorney-general, the Tories as yet had no one to challenge Draper as government leader. Their two most prominent spokesmen in the House, MacNab and Sherwood, disliked each other, and both were considered erratic and arrogant even by their fellow Tories. Moreover, Sir Allan, at least, had placed himself out of harm's way for the moment by accepting the position of Speaker. Although, as Metcalfe reported to Stanley, Draper, while 'universally admitted to be the most talented man in either House in the Legislature,' had scarcely a single real follower, nevertheless – as LaFontaine was later to write – 'they [the Tories] may hate Draper as much as they please; still without his talents, their party ... would be no party at all.'[68]

In the long run, however, time seemed likely to prove most decisive in enabling Draper to gain his ends. A desire for some of the rewards of power would surely lead the Tories eventually to support the administration actively, while the responsibilities of power would push them toward more realistic policies. The trick, then, would be to ride the twin horses of Toryism and moderatism until they gradually ceased to strain in opposite directions and became a unified Conservative team.

Such then were Draper's hopes as he watched the assembly from his remote position in the Legislative Council. The beginning was somewhat shaky. The two government leaders in the house, James Smith and Denis-Benjamin Papineau, managed to contradict each other ludicrously during the debate on the Speech from the Throne.[69] In fact, with both Draper and Morris in the Legislative Council, and Papineau too deaf to hear the debates, the government was decidedly weak on its front benches. Most measures were introduced by Smith, and he at least revealed some hitherto unsuspected capacities for parliamentary leadership. Indeed, the fact that Smith was soon publicly styling himself as 'head of the Administration'[70] indicates that the attorney-general west hoped that his own role might be confined gradually to the background, and that, if things went well, he might leave politics entirely and accept a promotion to the bench.

For Upper Canada, Draper planned a quiet and unexceptional programme that would cut expenses in all departments, remit taxation, extend internal improvements, regulate trade and commerce more sensibly, and would be accompanied only by 'measures of minor importance comparatively.'[71] Such sound and mildly progressive government might calm matters for the moment and realize his own ideal of a time when 'public consideration will prevail over party feeling, and sound constitutional principles ... will be carried out in full operation without stopping the machine of government every now and then to test the proper form of any of its different parts as a matter of speculative demonstration.'[72]

While Draper's approach to Upper Canadian affairs was one of cautious retrenchment, the government's policy towards Lower Canada showed remarkable panache and daring. Its ultimate aim, of course, was to win the support of the whole French bloc or at least a substantial part of it for the administration. The campaign began with some notable successes. Among those things most dear to the hearts of all French Canadians was the fate of those *patriotes* exiled since the Rebellion of 1837. Metcalfe had long been advocating an amnesty, and even before parliament met a series of individual pardons had been obtained. This work was then crowned when the governor transmitted to the assembly in February 1845 the news that a complete amnesty had been granted.

Earlier in the same month an even more spectacular coup had occurred when, forestalling a motion of LaFontaine's, Draper had persuaded the governor to abrogate that part of his instructions which restricted the use of French as an official language. On 21 February the Reformers were stunned when Papineau moved the address to that effect on behalf of the government. Finally, as if to lay entirely the spectre of 1837, a Rebellion Losses bill was brought in by Papineau to indemnify citizens of Upper Canada who had had property destroyed during the rebellion. A committee was then set up to tackle the same question in the thornier area of Lower Canada, where damage had been much greater and where it was more difficult to distinguish between rebel and loyalist. All in all, no one could claim that Draper's ministry had not done its best by the French Canadians. What fruit this might bring remained to be seen.

Ironically enough, it was an Upper Canadian crisis that was to dash Draper's dreams of a broadly based Conservative party, and was also to drag him back to the 'vortex' where, as he put it, 'I must swim – if I can.'[73] So far as the western section of the province was concerned, the ministry had been careful to introduce nothing but the most unexceptionable measures such as relieving insolvent debtors and establishing full public ownership of the Welland Canal. The Reform press had gleefully satirized the apparent do-nothingness of the administration with a series of headlines such as: 'THE GREAT GOVERNMENT MEASURE OF THE SESSION, THE DOG BILL, CARRIED – THE MUSKRAT BILL LOST.'[74] Yet this cautious course had paid its dividends. Moderate sentiment had not been outraged and the Tories were warily but predictably moving towards the government. In December 1844 William Benjamin Robinson had entered the cabinet, to take the vacant portfolio of inspector-general. But in the spring of 1845 the attorney-general was forced to risk all such modest gains.

One of the most disastrous effects of the Metcalfe crisis for Draper was that it had aborted Baldwin's University bill of 1843 and left that question still to be dealt with. Here was Scylla and Charybdis indeed. A narrow settlement on strict Anglican terms (those terms Draper himself had pleaded for when employed as counsel for King's College) would alienate the Methodists, Presbyterians, and moderates generally, assuring a government defeat in the next elections. A liberal solution might well throw enough Tories into opposition to bring down the government in the house. Yet a liberal solution was virtually imperative if the Conservatives were to gain that broad credibility with the electorate that Draper knew was so necessary. Almost certainly it was a promise to this effect that had drawn William Morris into the cabinet, and as one of Morris's Presbyterian supporters put it, if a good University Act did not pass, 'it is all up with you.'[75] And after the election of 1844 the rumours had rapidly begun to spread that such a measure would indeed be '*the bill of the session.*'[76]

Yet Draper moved with extreme care. As circumstances developed, the University bill was his greatest battle, greatest defeat, and his most remarkable performance as an 'artful dodger.' Almost as soon as the full cabinet was formed, Morris had been put to work secretly drafting the measure that would finally be presented. In the meantime Draper began to circulate a skeleton bill drawn up by Metcalfe himself after correspondence with leading religious and secular authorities throughout Upper Canada. This measure was totally unacceptable to the Anglicans and, after fierce opposition from William Robinson, Henry Sherwood, and Bishop Strachan, the attorney-general promised to do his best to prevent it going any further.[77] From Draper's point of view, the Metcalfe 'skeleton' was almost certainly a softening up measure – designed to persuade the Tories that the governor himself was determined on *some* solution, and to make the less objectionable measure Draper and Morris were drafting appear as the best bargain that could be had. The new bill itself was a neat compromise. The proposed university would take over the endowment of Anglican King's College but the Anglican, Presbyterian, and Methodist colleges of King's, Queen's, and Victoria, respectively, would become affiliated residential colleges receiving a generous share of the endowment while maintaining their own religious instruction. Thus, while being the least bad measure so far brought forward from the Anglican point of view, it was close enough to Baldwin's old bill that it might draw some Reform support.

The pace began to quicken. It was soon clear that no measure could pass the house without Draper to guide it. Consequently, in late January 1845 Lawrence Lawrason, the assembly member for London, gave up his seat, while a change in the Act of Union was effected to allow Draper to resign from the Legislative Council. Duly elected for London, the 'great magician from the Lords' was reintroduced to the house on 25 February with 'public opinion elevated to the very tip toe of expectations.'[78]

At the same time, the attorney-general began to tighten the screw on the Tories. Previously it had been assumed that a University bill would be introduced as an open question; now the ministry made it a firm government measure, thus raising the spectre that its defeat might not only mean another Baldwin-LaFontaine administration, but probably a worse University bill from the Anglican point of view as well. In the cabinet, William Robinson wavered and was uncertain of what to do.[79] In the assembly Draper introduced the bill briefly on 4 March, and prepared for the great struggle on the second reading six days later. On 10 March he announced that the bill would be a government measure and that the ministry would 'stand or fall by it.'

Then in a graceful, three-hour speech, his oratorical powers at their best, he guided the house clause by clause through a measure which he pleaded for as one that would reconcile freedom of conscience with the 'great interests of religion.'[80] It was a magnificent performance; but at the end of it a Tory motion was carried to postpone the vote on the second reading until counsel for King's College could be heard.

In the intervening week Tory resistance crystalized. Bishop Strachan, now 'quite rabid,'[81] leaked the news that he would use all his influence to defeat the government if necessary, claiming that he could always get a University bill of Baldwin's disallowed in England, but that the British Parliament would not do this to a measure passed by a loyal Conservative administration. He gained his point. In the cabinet Robinson now firmly tendered his resignation, while Henry Sherwood led a block of Tories in promising they would vote for the second reading only if there would be no third. Metcalfe himself, who had always been in favour of making the bill an open question, was now is despair about the fall of the government and pressed the ministry for a compromise.[82]

Draper hung on until the last moment, perhaps hoping for some Reform support; but when the debate which resumed on 18 March made it clear that this was not forthcoming, he announced that he would postpone the bill for the session if it passed the second reading. He claimed this would at least confirm that the university question was a proper subject for legislation – a point which the Anglicans had hitherto denied. Sherwood accepted this, and the reading passed. Robinson still insisted on voting against it, however, and Draper, even with the battle lost, forced his own inspector-general's resignation on the floor of the house.[83]

The retreat from the University bill was a bitter and nearly complete rout that left Draper's Upper Canadian policy in ruins. In terms of popular support the Tories, by rejecting the measure, had destroyed both their own constituency amongst the moderates and Draper's credibility as a leader who could forge a progressive party of Conservatism. People such as Ryerson might still support and eulogize him, but there were limits to what the attorney-general alone could do. In parliamentary terms, Draper's manoeuvring over the bill had merely confirmed the Tories in their distrust and hatred of him and of a ministry made up of 'moderates, trimmers and dishonest politicians.'[84] Once again it was only Metcalfe's support and Tory disunity that left Draper in office.

Under these circumstances, it is not surprising that the attorney-general now moved decidedly towards the one area where popular backing might yet materialize. He began to investigate whether the strongly pro-French policy of his administration might be ready to pay some political dividends. True,

LaFontaine's hold over his parliamentary party was as strong as ever. Outside the legislature, however, large sections of the French Canadians were becoming restive at being kept in opposition, to which position the Baldwin alliance appeared to bind them. This feeling was becoming particularly noticeable in the area around Quebec City itself, where LaFontaine's Montreal leadership increasingly seemed both aloof and incapable of realizing any tangible political gains. It was at this point, with discontent on the rise, that one of Viger's constitutional assertions – hitherto ignored – began to gain adherents.

This was the double majority principle, which affirmed, in brief, that the Executive Council should be divided equally into Upper and Lower Canadian segments, with the ministers from each part drawn from whichever party had gained a majority in that particular section of the United Province. Whatever practical difficulties it might entail, it assured that the French would always directly control half the ministry; it was a policy that even LaFontaine could hardly condemn. Viger had bruited it in his own newspapers just after the election of 1844. Pro-Lafontaine editors had at first ignored it, but independent papers, including the prestigious *le Canadien* of Quebec, took it up. It caught on throughout Lower Canada, and by the spring of 1845 even pro-LaFontaine organs accepted it in principle.[85] It soon brought more substantial returns. Viger's victory in July 1845 at a by-election in Tory Three Rivers was scarcely a surprise; more to the point was the by-election at Dorchester in September. Here André-Joseph Taschereau came out in favour of Viger and the double majority. On 1 September Viger named Taschereau solicitor-general east, and eight days later the largest riding in Lower Canada (significantly near Quebec) gave the new government supporter a thundering victory.

In the midst of these improving circumstances Draper made a determined effort to split LaFontaine's hold on the French. Somewhat earlier he had confided to René-Edouard Caron, the highly respected mayor of Quebec and Speaker of the Legislative Council, his own desire to bring the French into the ministry. Caron's interested response confirmed Draper in his feeling that not all in the French party were indissolubly committed to the alliance with Robert Baldwin. A month later in Montreal, Draper made a definite proposal to Caron. Viger and Papineau could be prevailed upon to retire. Morin and any other French Canadian except LaFontaine (who could be promoted to the judiciary) could replace them. Once in office the French could no doubt gain a more considerable share of cabinet positions. Caron seemed eager, but stressed that he would have to consult his 'friends.'

In fact, the mayor found wide sympathy for such views in the Quebec area. In Montreal, however, LaFontaine was both angered and dismayed by the readiness of his compatriots to abandon Baldwin. But in his reply the French leader astutely avoided this point, suggesting that Draper was trying only to multiply the *vendus*, and that a serious offer should involve reconstructing the whole Lower Canadian wing of the ministry. It was a telling point which Caron quickly communicated to Draper.[86] After a delay of nearly two months, while he was absent on circuit duty, Draper finally responded on 19 November that Daly, too, was willing to resign and that Smith, though not as yet consulted, was unlikely to raise difficulties. He added, somewhat curiously, that the whole Upper Canadian wing of the council, himself included, was also willing to retire if need be; and ended by asking Caron what the French desired as a *sine qua non*.[87]

The development of the Draper-Caron negotiations to this point leaves several questions still difficult to answer. The smallness of Draper's initial offer was probably owing simply to normal bargaining practice; but why was he so willing to sacrifice Viger and Papineau just when their ideas finally appeared to be gaining support from the public? Did he actually accept the double majority principle, and was he sincerely willing to contemplate so total a reconstruction of the ministry as his letter of 19 November seemed to indicate?

The decision to let Viger and Papineau go certainly appeared indefensibly callous, given the services these men had rendered to the governor. LaFontaine saw it in this light, writing to Baldwin: 'His Excellency is willing to give them a kick out!! What a reward!!'[88] Yet both of the French ministers were privy to the negotiations and in agreement as to the ends.[89] The problem was that the reaction in favour of Viger symbolized by the recent Lower Canadian by-elections had done little to solve the government's immediate difficulties. Even if the whole of the French electorate were finally to swing behind the administration, this would not affect the parliamentary situation until the next general election. And though Draper might in different circumstances have been willing to wait that long, the failure of the University bill had rendered it dubious that he could carry Upper Canada in a new election. Thus the attorney-general's immediate need to strengthen his position could only be met by gaining the support of those French members of the assembly itself. But while it might have been possible to detach that group from Baldwin or even from LaFontaine, there is no evidence that the French-Canadian assemblymen were themselves any more willing to embrace Viger. However disillusioning such a situation must have been to the ageing *patriote*, he does appear to have understood and accepted it. As for D.-B. Papineau, he was entirely without personal political ambition, and would have been well-satisfied with any solution that brought the French back into the Executive Council.

What, then, of the double majority idea? It has usually been written off as impractical, and indeed it was most unlikely to work under a system of full responsible government. What would happen if different parties triumphed in each section on diametrically opposed political platforms? Yet, under Draper's more limited conception of responsibility, where the governor retained much independent power, it was less objectionable. In the case of an intra-cabinet stalemate, the governor could presumably act as an honest broker between the two sections of his ministry; indeed, his position of real power might be increased. Though Draper never formally accepted the principle, this possibly reflects his dislike of all hard and fast constitutional formulae. Thus, by stressing in his last letter that all the Lower Canadian ministers, indeed the whole cabinet, were willing to resign for the 'public good,' he was implying that the French could have all they wished so long as they did not insist upon having it as a constitutional principle. At any rate his important offer of 19 November 1845 was the most generous one he made, and might well have achieved success if the negotiations had continued. Instead they were dropped, when a new circumstance entirely changed the Canadian political scene.

The governor, now Lord Metcalfe, his life being cruelly devoured by the cancer that had at last rendered him blind, and nearly unable to eat or speak, wished to go home to die. He had stayed on only to support the ministers who had so generously come to his aid in 1843. He was prepared to die at his post if they needed him, but they accepted his pathetic request unanimously. Nonetheless, much ground was cut from under their feet. Viger and Papineau who had so identified themselves with Metcalfe's generous policy and personality had now lost most of their remaining political *raison d'être*. Draper too was immeasurably weakened. The Tories elected to support the governor were now released from their tacit pledge to uphold the minister he had so stoutly defended. Moreover, it was Metcalfe's departure that terminated Draper's negotiations with the French, just when his apparent offer to reconstruct the whole Lower Canadian section of the council gave them some chance of success. Neither the attorney-general nor Lord Cathcart, the commander of the forces who now took over the administration temporarily, wished to inaugurate any radical changes that might embarrass whoever succeeded Metcalfe.

This same awkward transitional period, however, also dulled any Tory desire to overthrow Draper immediately. So did the outbreak of the Oregon crisis in the winter of 1845-6, which drew interest away from domestic struggles because of the looming threat of war with the United States. The attorney-general continued on, therefore, as head of the ministry, and prepared for the parliamentary session of 1846 – which was deliberately designed to be as devoid as possible of all controversial measures.

As might be expected, much of the session was, in fact, crushingly dull, marked by a spate of bills regarding the establishment of agricultural societies, municipal improvements, and penitentiary reorganization. Some of these, such as the incorporation of ten new railways and of Hamilton and Kingston as cities, at least had symbolic importance in pointing to the growth and prosperity of the colony. Despite the fact that scarcely anyone could object to such measures as these, the Tories used their own position of strength ruthlessly to strip from the legislative programme anything that *did* upset them. A series of defeats on issues that were not tests of confidence left the government's weakness clear for all to see. Nevertheless, Draper did manage to pilot through the house some really sound and useful legislation. William Cayley as inspector-general brought in the first real 'budget' in Canadian parliamentary history,[90] and the possibility of war necessitated an important Militia bill. Another prominent measure was the provision for transferring the permanent civil list into Canadian hands. The Act of Union of 1841 had left provisions for the salaries of the principal officers of state to be fixed permanently by the imperial government. Draper and Metcalfe prepared a measure that left the salaries the same but transferred the control of them to the Canadian parliament. Ultimately accepted by the British government, the principle that Canadians should control the whole of their own revenue was now established.

Also important was the Upper Canada Common Schools Act of 1846, drafted at Draper's behest by Egerton Ryerson. Besides ironing out some unmanageable areas of Baldwin's School Act of 1843, the new bill took education from the Provincial Secretary's Department and placed it under the aegis of a chief superintendent of common schools for Upper Canada, appointed by the governor, and assisted by a Board of Education. The superintendent, who would be responsible for the maintenance of common standards, uniform textbooks, and teacher training, was given control of the Upper Canadian share of the legislative grant to education. A rate-bill clause required all property holders and not just those sending children to the public schools to share in the taxation. This latter provision – so dear to Ryerson as the 'poor man's clause' – was ultimately removed from the bill by the opposition of both Tories and Reformers despite a stubborn parliamentary defence by Draper.[91] The debate on this issue revealed that a noticeable split between Tories and Conservatives existed in the field of school as well as university education. Draper and Ryerson argued that the education of the lower classes was not only the duty of the rich and privileged but also an act of self-interest. Even so rural a province as Upper Canada contained by the 1840s a noticeable and unruly urban proletariat whose offspring held few prospects of betterment. Unless education provided the latter with a stake in the community, they would ultimately threaten all social order.[92] The Tories could hardly cavil at the logic of such arguments. They could and did take a more short-sighted class stance when it came to the immediate issue. Among them, Edward Ermatinger maintained that since the rich already provided most of the money for the provincial grant to education, to tax them again at the municipal level would be unfair. And John Tucker Williams spoke up for the 'industrious yeoman' striving to send his children to a good private school, who might be unable to afford it if faced with additional taxes for the presumably inferior public institutions.[93] Although the rate clause was lost, the act itself and the appointment of Ryerson, named under it as first chief superintendent, were important milestones in the evolution of the Upper Canadian educational system.

This same period also saw an event of immense importance for the political development of the colony. This was nothing less than the gradual acceptance of the full principle of responsible government for Canada by the Colonial Office and the consequent emergence of William Henry Draper as the first colonial prime minister. This change in policy occurred unheralded and indeed was totally unknown in Canada – especially to Draper himself. The attorney-general had been Sir Charles Metcalfe's chief adviser from the moment he took office in December 1843, and he had become government leader in the assembly as well in 1845. Constitutionally, however, his position had differed little from that which he and Harrison had shared under Sydenham and Bagot. Taking a slightly inexact English analogy, he had played Lord North to Metcalfe's George III. True, Metcalfe's illness had placed virtually all political responsibility in Draper's hands after the election of 1844, but that situation too had its precedents – notably in the roles taken by Baldwin and LaFontaine while Sir Charles Bagot was dying. Yet the acquisition of power, even when accidental and undesired, often creates its own precedents.

For instance, the question of patronage over which the whole Metcalfe crisis had erupted was quietly solved during Draper's administration when pragmatic logic began to prevail over theoretical principles. When Baldwin and LaFontaine, backed by a large majority in the assembly, had tried to assert their control over that issue, it had appeared as an arrogant usurpation of the governor's power to Metcalfe, to the imperial government, and to the Upper Canadian electorate alike. But Draper's ministry with a majority of only four or five clearly had to use patronage to its utmost extent if it were to survive at all. And if Metcalfe conceded this, as he did, could it ever be denied again to any ministry? Metcalfe himself had dimly perceived the logic several weeks before his break with Baldwin and LaFontaine, when he had written to Stanley: 'I see no prospect of any cessation of this almost unavailing struggle until the principle for which the present Executive Council ... are practically contending, namely Democratic and Party Government is fully admitted ... were the power of the majority in the hands of a Party thoroughly attached to the British interest and connection there would be grounds for mutual cordiality and confidence which would render real co-operation more probable, concession more easy, and even submission more tolerable.'[94]

Of course, Metcalfe was not advising that responsible government be 'fully admitted.' His instructions were clear and he was determined to carry them out whatever the consequences rather than 'to surrender the Queen's Government into the hands of rebels and to become myself their ignominious tool.'[95] But if Metcalfe's duty 'was not to reason why,' others whose duty lay in precisely that sphere perceived the logic of events. In England Lord John Russell's Whigs, though now in opposition, had quietly dropped their stance that responsible government was an impossibility. Furthermore, James Stephen, the great colonial under-secretary, was a positive advocate of it behind the scenes, as a civil servant. Such views, however, could not prevail while Stanley, brilliant and imperious, held sway at the Colonial Office. But when Stanley resigned a month before Metcalfe's departure from Canada, the new ideas surfaced. William Gladstone, who became colonial secretary, was now advised by Stephen: 'Canada appears to me to have shaken off or laid aside the Colonial Relation to this Country and to have become in everything but name, a distinct State, receiving, indeed, its Governor from hence and submitting to our general laws of Trade and Navigation but otherwise self-governed so completely, as to render almost superfluous and unnecessary any attempt to prescribe to the Governor any line of policy on any internal question whatever.'[96] Later, Stephen assured Gladstone that 'such is the point of self-assertion already obtained, that if Canada requests to have the nomination of her own Governor it must be given.'[97] Stephen's strong statement of Canada's quasi-independence may have surprised Gladstone, but it accorded well with the latter's general view of colonial affairs. Under the circumstances it is not surprising that it was decided to renew an offer, already tentatively made by Stanley, to entrust the governorship of Canada to Lord Elgin, a moderate Peelite Conservative. However, Elgin 'could not be had' at the time, and the outbreak of the Oregon crisis led to the decision to promote the soldier Cathcart from acting to full governor.[98] This, however, produced a curious misunderstanding which clouded in Canada itself the change of attitudes that had occurred in the Colonial Office. When Gladstone wrote instructions for Cathcart he followed Stephen's advice and gave few specific directions regarding internal colonial affairs, save that Metcalfe's administration might 'justly be regarded as a model for his successor.'[99] The latter advice probably reflected Stephen's respect for Metcalfe as a governor who had solved his own problems in Canada and had not called for help to the Colonial Office. To Cathcart and to Draper in the Canadian context, however, such a phrase would imply an admonition to continue resisting further constitutional encroachments and to avoid a Baldwin ministry.

The effect was paradoxical. Had Draper realized, as the Stephen-Gladstone interpretation of the constitution implied, that he was now in effect a premier and that even the choice of a governor general might well lie in the hands of his ministry, he would not only have been stupified, he would probably have thought of resigning. Instead, following the confirmation of Cathcart in office in April 1846, Draper began to act as a real prime minister. Since the new governor was uninterested in civil affairs and had been instructed to follow in Metcalfe's path, he did so by leaving civil administration almost entirely to his attorney-general. And Draper, once more backed by the authority of a full governor, now rallied in another great effort to produce a strong and stable government.

Perhaps the first indication of the premier's renewed confidence was the resurrection of his University bill on 5 May, when it was introduced as a private members' measure by George Barker Hall, a moderate Conservative.[100] Draper appears to have hoped that a private member's bill at the end of the session might catch the Tories off guard, and also might draw support from the Reformers since they could not defeat the administration. But nobody rose to the bait. Baldwin again attacked the bill as too illiberal; the Tories, inside the cabinet and out, freely opposed it, and it was soundly defeated 39 votes to 20.[101]

Undismayed by the loss of this measure, Draper now took decisive action to reconstruct his ministry. On the day after the parliamentary session ended he moved to force both Viger and Sherwood out of office. The latter had long been using his positions both as solicitor-general and as member of the legislature to obstruct the leader he detested and whose position he desired. Acting virtually as a spy and agent for Bishop Strachan, Sherwood had produced no support but much opposition.[102] He refused to resign, and an ultimatum from Cathcart was necessary to remove him.[103] Viger, in contrast, resigned with dignity. Now a nearly complete liability to the ministry, he wished to depart; and Draper was glad to have him go.

Indeed, once the retirement was secured, the attorney-general again began negotiations with the French. Matters on this front had improved considerably during the fallow period between Metcalfe's departure and the confirmation of Cathcart as full governor general. The growing disenchantment of the Quebec French with their Montreal leaders was greatly bolstered in the spring of 1846 when LaFontaine backed the idea that the proposed railway to the seaboard should run from Montreal to Portland, Maine, instead of through Quebec to Halifax. This created great bitterness in the Quebec area. In February 1846 Caron resigned as mayor to lead the movement for a Quebec line. Then came the parliamentary session of 1846. The most sensational event of this otherwise dull meeting of the assembly was the reading out and publication of the secret Draper-Caron correspondence of the previous year.

LaFontaine, who had seen copies of Draper's letters to Caron confidentially, believed that the attorney-general's references to the possible retirement of Viger and Papineau might be excellent political capital if these two gentlemen were, as he suspected, unaware that they might be 'retired.' Accordingly, disregarding protests from an outraged Caron, he announced in the house on 7 April that he was going to lay the documents before parliament prior to publishing them. But he miscalculated. Since Viger and Papineau had been aware of the negotiations, the ministry did not split. Draper replied by reading out those parts of the letters which most favoured his own position, and Caron eventually published his share of the correspondence, accompanied by an introduction strongly condemning LaFontaine. Even Viger scored a few points off his opponents, claiming the correspondence had proved false the picture they had drawn of him as 'an ambitious, avaricious, office loving old man.'[104] Thus there were few gains from the incident for the Reformers. At the same time, it was clear for all to see that an apparently generous offer to the French by the ministry had not been even seriously considered by LaFontaine and had been used only for a cheap political manoeuvre.

As an extraordinarily bitter newspaper warfare now arose amongst the French factions in Quebec and Montreal, Draper attempted to turn the 'sad blundering of the opposition'[105] to real account. In July he invited Caron to Montreal, offering him seats on the council for three French Canadians. Caron agreed to help, and he and Denis-Benjamin Papineau sounded out Morin. Morin, second in importance amongst the French only to LaFontaine himself, began to waver. Much desperate politicking ultimately forced him to break off negotiations with Draper, but in doing so he stated publicly that he had acted 'without, although not against' LaFontaine. There now seemed a definite possibility that the monolithic French wall was beginning to crumble.[106] Perhaps time would yet bring them into the fold.

At this critical juncture, however, Draper found himself in serious trouble with the Upper Canadian wing of his ministry. Henry Sherwood and his followers were clearly at odds with the attorney-general, but otherwise Draper had moved with great dexterity in balancing Tories and moderates. Two key appointments were those of William Cayley as inspector-general and of John Hillyard Cameron as solicitor-general. Both of these men had earned glowing credentials with the high Tories as a result of their attacks on the University bill, yet otherwise they inclined towards the type of conservatism espoused by Draper. In the brilliant young Cameron, in particular, Draper appears to have seen a possible future leader of the party he was trying to create.[107] Another such possibility was John A. Macdonald, the twenty-nine-year-old lawyer who had succeeded Samuel Harrison as member for Kingston. Draper soon slated Macdonald as a ministerial possibility, and Macdonald rapidly became one of the premier's most outspoken followers.[108] Matters were thus evolving well, when what appeared like a political coup brought disaster instead.

Draper's Militia Act of 1846 had established the permanent position of adjutant-general for the entire province. This officer would direct the separate militias of Upper and Lower Canada, would receive the handsome salary of £1000, and be precluded from sitting in the House of Assembly. Sir Allan MacNab, the greatest focus for Tory discontent other than Sherwood, by his military repute was clearly the best man for the job, would be immensely gratified by both the position and the salary, and would be removed from active politics if he accepted it. Therefore, three admirable ends could be satisfied. Cathcart approached MacNab regarding the office in the session of 1846 and Sir Allan eagerly accepted in principle. Then complications developed. A ludicrous dispute over one of the proposed deputies to the adjutant-generalship resulted in Sir Allan returning his commission. But then he discovered that as his own appointment had been officially gazetted, his refusal of office was really a resignation, and that by his prior 'acceptance' of it he had forfeited his position as Speaker of the house! Draper, who apparently had not expected MacNab to go so far as to resign over the issue, hastily attempted through intermediaries to patch things up. But Sir Allan, now understandably in a forbidding rage, refused to be placated and went off to England on railway business, swearing dire vengeance against the attorney-general.[109]

Since parliament was not sitting, there was no immediate threat to the ministry, but with both MacNab and Sherwood alienated there seemed little chance the government would survive the next meeting of the house. Although the better part of a year would pass before that event, during which reconciliation could be attempted, Draper now learned in August 1846 that Cathcart had been superseded as governor general. There was also a new Whig ministry in England, and what all of this portended no man could say. The attorney-general might well be the 'artful dodger' that Hincks had christened him, but his resources were nearing their end.

During the period between Cathcart's departure and the arrival of his successor, Lord Elgin, in January 1847, Draper appears to have done little more than carry on routine administration. Following the new governor's arrival, the remaining few months of Draper's ministry saw a great deal of hectic but confusing activity. This period included his last determined attempt to stave off the Tories and rally the moderates; it also witnessed Draper's apparent abandonment of negotiations with the French, only to have them taken up and brought within an ace of success by Elgin himself. Finally, the whole span was marked by the premier's increasingly imminent retirement. This last event revolved around the circumstances of Draper's old friend and partner, Judge Christopher Hagerman. For several long months, Hagerman's resignation from the bench seemed daily forthcoming, first through the judge's illness, then through his remarriage and desire to retire to England, then through illness again. In any event, Draper was determined to have the judicial position as soon as it became vacant.

Yet the question remains as to whether the premier willingly retired or was forced out. Certainly he was eager to go. 'Le jeu ne vaut pas la Chandelle,' he wrote to Ryerson in March of 1844, 'while it burns the candle at both ends.' He also maintained that his own departure from office was the sole way of healing the split in the Tory-Conservative ranks.[110] But was this simply high-sounding rationalization of a desire to grasp his longed-for judicial career at any price? Elgin thought so, and deemed the premier's desertion of his moderate Conservative cabinet 'shabby' and the 'reverse of magnanimous.'[111] Other evidence makes it clear that the attorney-general's moderate friends were in fact finding it difficult to retain him in the face of strong pressure from the Tories.[112] Likely the truth is a combination of the two circumstances. Though Draper did not in fact have to resign quite as early as he did, this was only because the warring MacNab and Sherwood factions had not yet made up their differences. Indeed, there is proof that MacNab, in an excessively vindictive mood, wished to keep Draper in office just long enough to deprive him of Hagerman's position and then to have the satisfaction of defeating him in the house.[113] If he was thus bound to go in any case, it is hardly surprising that the attorney-general chose to depart at a time of his own choosing rather than that of his enemies.

There was also another very potent reason for Draper's wishing to retire as soon as it suited him. The new direction in colonial policy that had surfaced at Stanley's resignation had now reached its culmination, and in so doing removed almost totally what had been Draper's political *raison d'être* in his own eyes. In England, Peel's Conservative party had shattered over the repeal of the Corn Laws that marked the decisive adoption of free trade, and the Whigs under Lord John Russell were in office. Russell no longer objected to responsible government; Lord Grey, colonial secretary and brother-in-law of the late Lord Durham, was determined to implement it. Elgin, whom Grey sent to Canada, had recently married Durham's daughter and was determined that his own career should be 'the real and effectual vindication of Lord Durham's memory.'[114]

Draper realized only gradually what had happened. Initially he imagined his own role would remain what it had been since 1843 – to help the British governor of the day in 'governing the country without the necessity of asking Mr. Baldwin's assistance.'[115] Moreover, the new governor was of necessity very circumspect in his early meetings with the ministry. Draper's bare majority, after all, had been elected in 1844 in order to oppose the extreme interpretation of responsible government; for Elgin to force that principle down its throat would have been an abrogation of responsible government itself. Instead, the governor correctly saw his duty lying in giving his ministry all the support that he constitutionally could. Moreover, Elgin was impartial in fact as well as in theory. Nothing in the documents suggests that he felt any special affinity towards Baldwin, and he agreed with Draper that the French were ideologically closer to the Conservatives than to the Reformers.[116] Nevertheless, the governor eventually made it clear that if the present ministry were defeated, he would have no qualms in sending for the leaders of the opposition.[117] This fact must certainly have strengthened Draper's desire to retire. He had re-entered the hated field of politics in 1843, expressly because a British governor had asked him to help defend the British connection from the iniquitous doctrines of the Reformers. If the Colonial Office could now stomach Baldwin and LaFontaine, the existing attorney-general's tour of duty had clearly come to an end.

Despite Lord Elgin's impartiality, a certain awkwardness did arise between the governor and his prime minister almost from their first meeting. It was over the French. Draper, who had been so insistent to Metcalfe and Cathcart about the necessity of French adherence to the government, began by counselling Elgin to turn his back on them completely. They had refused to join the ministry, he claimed, because its internal strife and slim majority convinced them it would soon fall. Better then to strengthen the government and so force them eventually to court it, rather than vice versa. To this end Draper asked Elgin to write to the Colonial Office requesting eight appointments to the Legislative Council for six Tories, together with Viger and a follower that would firmly secure the ministry's control of that body. Yet another seat in the upper house should be made available to MacNab, and indeed Sir Allan, if he accepted, might be made its Speaker – though Caron would have to be ejected from the position for that purpose.

Elgin was taken aback. Convinced that the removal of Caron as one of his first official duties would brand him as being anti-French, he proposed instead that he himself should first make one more effort to bring the French into the ministry. Draper agreed wholeheartedly. The baffled governor was then unable to ascertain whether Draper's original proposal had simply been a ploy to get Elgin himself to initiate negotiations, or whether the attorney-general had hoped to brand the governor publicly as anti-Gallic.[118] The first surmise was no doubt correct. Though as eager as ever to gain French adherence to his government, Draper had by now exhausted his own credit in that question. Many Tories had constantly disliked such 'negotiations with the opposition,'[119] while the French themselves had ended the last talks with a blank refusal. However, no one could object if Elgin himself took the initiative.

The governor's first approaches to Morin and Taché met with the same polite refusal on grounds of 'lack of confidence in the present Ministry.' But in Quebec Caron again took up the cudgels, hoping to end the 'intolerable tyranny' of the Montreal leadership.[120] Ultimately, Denis-Benjamin Papineau wrote to Caron offering three council positions for the French party. Caron now came to Montreal to get further details from William Cayley, representing the ministry. Cayley reaffirmed Papineau's offer, adding that employment would soon be found elsewhere for Dominick Daly, and both wings of the new Executive Council could jointly decide on who would fill that position.[121]

Caron hurriedly returned to Quebec and a crucial meeting of the French leaders was held. LaFontaine was enraged; but finally, after much wrangling, it was decided that if Caron could form an administration on the double majority principle he should do so, but that no less should be accepted.[122] Accordingly, Caron wrote that if Daly were removed from office as a parliamentary measure, he, LaFontaine, Morin, and one other Lower Canadian Reformer would take office and form an 'Administration for Lower Canada.' This proposal, calling for the public sacrifice of one individual and giving the French four out of seven seats on the council, was deemed too high a price to pay both by the ministry and by Lord Elgin. It was accordingly rejected.[123]

Thus foundered negotiations which might have produced the Conservative-French alliance that actually took form nine years later. In fact, the outcome was a decisive victory for LaFontaine. With his own party quite prepared to throw over Baldwin and to embrace the double majority, he had, for the sake of its unity, at last given way – yet managed to raise the price just that amount too high to be acceptable.

Though no doubt taking an active part in council deliberations on the subject, Draper's tactic had been to leave the actual French negotiations in the hands of others – Elgin, Papineau, Cayley. But on the Upper Canadian front he was deeply involved in the final political struggle of his ministry. Strange to say, it was in these same last months of his political career that his old hope of somehow creating a Conservative party from the wreckage of intransigent Toryism began to show unmistakeable signs of germinating. Both within the assembly and without it, moderate voices were increasingly being heard. Indeed, of the government supporters from Upper Canada who sat in the house during the sessions of 1845 and 1846, only eleven were steadfast Tories, while twenty could realistically be called Conservatives.[124] In addition, two others held a special position and can be best described as 'intermediaries.' These latter individuals – William Cayley and John Hillyard Cameron – were 'Tory' on the University question and in terms of their social and business connections. Otherwise, they loyally supported Draper and indeed used their Tory credentials to assist him. The Tories thus did not have the advantage of numbers. However, they could count on some assistance from those members of the 'British party' of Lower Canada who were disenchanted with Draper's dealings with the French, while the slight edge the combined pro-government forces enjoyed over the Reformers left the Tory element holding the balance of power.

What made the difference between the Tory and Conservative groups? (See p. 80 below.) Age, at any rate, was not very important. In 1846 the average age of both groups would appear to have been in the low forties. Moreover, the two oldest individuals whose age is identifiable were both Conservatives – James Cummings, who was fifty-seven, and 'Tiger' Dunlop at fifty-four. Occupational disparities were somewhat wider. Six of the eleven Tories were lawyers, as were both of the intermediaries, but only five of the twenty Conservatives. Four of the remaining Tories were businessmen, as were most of the remaining Conservatives, but the activities of the latter group covered a broader spectrum. The Conservative ranks also contained two medical doctors and a journalist, Ogle Gowan.

More significant as a differentiating factor was place of birth. Of the nine Tories whose origin has been identified, six were born in Upper Canada, while one, Edward Ermatinger, was the son of a Canadian though himself born in Europe. Only five of the twenty Conservatives were from explicit records born in Upper Canada. At least nine, as well as both intermediaries, were immigrants. Of the latter, Draper and Henry Smith, as well as Cayley and Cameron, were of English origin. Ogle Gowan was a Protestant Irishman. Six Conservatives definitely emigrated from Scotland and three more were of Scottish ancestry if not immigrants themselves. This was an important factor, not only ethnically but religiously. Of the nine Tories whose religious affiliation has been discovered, all were Church of England. The church connections of the Conservatives have proved more difficult to ascertain, but Presbyterians would appear to have comprised the largest element. Anglicans were well represented, and at least one Conservative was a Roman Catholic.

The remaining differences between the two groups can be summarized in terms of social status, political prominence, and affiliation with the city of Toronto. Eight of the Tories and both intermediaries were intimately, though not exclusively, connected with Toronto through ties of residence, representation, or business. Of the Conservatives, only Draper himself was a man of the metropolis. Again, nine of the Tories and each of the intermediaries had a widespread political reputation in 1846.[125] Virtually all of the Conservatives were men of substance, but mainly on a very local basis. Only Draper, 'Tiger' Dunlop, and Ogle Gowan, grand master of the Orange Lodge, were widely known by that year. Surprisingly, of the remaining seventeen Conservatives, only two would ever attain more than a very modest prominence on the national scene. These were Henry Smith, who would become well-known in the later Conservative party under John A. Macdonald, and Macdonald himself.

Political prominence and social status were connected. After all, it was the 'name,' earned by their forebears, that gave a number of Tories their political start. Since the Family Compact had been a social élite as well as a political oligarchy, it is no surprise that the Tories dominated in this sphere. Seven of their number as well as the intermediaries (who had both married Boulton girls) were connected by family or friendship to the old Compact. Of the Conservatives, only Draper himself had once moved in such exalted company. These were the two groups. They were both factions of young men, and in terms of talent neither was particularly strong as a whole. The Conservatives were manifestly far more varied in origin, religious affiliation, occupation, and the areas of Upper Canada they represented. The Tories' strength was much more concentrated in Toronto, but in other ways they represented a very parochial Upper Canadian social élite. In a word, they clearly were what their contemporaries claimed – the remnants of the Family Compact.

Was there a significant ideological difference between the two sections? Obviously, many Tories regarded the Church of England as the one true church of God in the wilderness of Upper Canada. Even that view was passing, however, and apart from it few real issues stood between the two factions in 1846. Albeit with infinite ill-grace, all politically active Tories had finally accepted the Union, the Harrison resolutions, the necessity of building a party with popular appeal. But though issues had faded, personal bitterness remained. Draper had sinned the great sin of adapting to the new order too quickly. Worse still, he had apparently profited from it, and even preempted the Tories' once unquestioned right to lead conservative Canadians. They would not forgive him for having made the best of unwelcome change while they had nobly and nihilistically stood fast.

But at least Draper was no longer fighting a lone battle. Moderate newspapers like the *British Colonist* supported him, religious leaders like Ryerson and Morris stood by his side. Within the assembly, men such as John A. Macdonald were increasingly eager for a show-down with 'the Family Compact Party, who with little ability, no political principle, and no strength from numbers, contrive by their union and active bigotry to override the Conservatives and to make us and our whole party *stink* in the nostrils of all liberal minded people.'[126]

Macdonald, who was sanguine about getting the University question solved in a satisfactory manner in the forthcoming session of 1847, clearly underestimated Tory strength. Draper himself now deemed it necessary to placate MacNab with a seat on the council and even made pleasant noises towards his arch-enemy, Henry Sherwood, and his 'Toronto Clique.'[127] Yet the moderates were, after all, his political heirs, and he would do his best for them before he went. Still hoping for active support from the governor, the premier urgently summoned Macdonald and Gowan to meet Elgin and discuss politics with him, thus allaying any distrust the governor might have developed by 'mistaking ultra Toryism for Conservatism (i.e., selfishness for patriotism).'[128] A month later, the moderate solicitor-general, John Hillyard Cameron, was given a seat on the council. In May Macdonald was offered and accepted the position of receiver-general with cabinet rank, William Morris writing to him that 'if you will not put shoulder to the wheel, you assist those who ... desire to regain the power which you and I hope to deprive them of; I mean the "Family."'[129]

An attempt to bring the able Conservative, Gowan, into the ministry broke down. MacNab, hurt at Gowan's newspaper attacks on him, refused to sit with the Orange leader. The latter, needless to say, was angry about the possibility of being excluded from the administration because of his earlier support of it.[130] This produced a stalemate and neither joined the council for the moment. But time had now run out. On 14 May Christopher Hagerman at last expired. Two weeks later, Draper resigned as attorney-general and was named judge of the Court of Queen's Bench. A last-minute effort to keep a moderate ministry by making Cameron attorney-general and effective premier failed.[131] Morris, deftly manoeuvring with the aid of Macdonald, blocked a bid for power by MacNab[132] – but the price was the ascendancy of Henry Sherwood. The moderates were not ousted from the re-made ministry, yet pristine Toryism flourished there for one last fling. William Badgley succeeded Smith as attorney-general east. Caron was unceremoniously removed from the speakership of the Legislative Council and replaced by Peter McGill, a relic of old Lower Canadian Toryism. The attorney-generalship and position of effective leader of the ministry were assumed by Sherwood himself. William Draper's leadership was over, his efforts for conservatism apparently defeated.

Apart from the few significant legislative measures that reached the statute books, the importance of Draper's ministry was never so dubious as at its end. He had fought against both the Compact Tories and the Reformers; both had defeated him. Sherwood succeeded him in mid-1847 and the 'Great Ministry' of Baldwin and LaFontaine would overwhelm Sherwood only a few months later. Draper had made three manful efforts to link the moderate Conservatives with the French; three times he had utterly failed. Finally, the political evolution which would see the Executive Council transformed into a cabinet and Draper himself 'emerge' as premier was one he had generally resisted. Almost certainly the satisfaction with which he accepted his judicial position was compounded by a sense of personal failure regarding his political career. Nevertheless, he could hardly have pursued a different course, given his own beliefs. The core of Draper's political philosophy had always been the tie with the mother country. He believed in 'the firm maintenance of the connexion between this colony and Great Britain as the basis or foundation of all political principles.'[133] Yet if this were true it naturally followed that 'the Government shall be administered under and according to the constitution granted to this country by the Imperial Government.'[134] This meant to Draper that he had no option but to accept the British concessions embodied in Lord John Russell's despatches and the Harrison resolutions.[135] Between 1841 and 1846 such a position placed him, however, in inevitable opposition both to the Reformers who wanted more and to the Tories who yearned for the old constitution. He believed both were wrong. 'Responsible Government' – in the abstract the principle is right – In England its practical result is to give the popular branch of the legislature the power to eject a ministry – But if the same power to the same extent were lodged here it would virtually abrogate the Imperial authority.'[136] Thus, to Draper, Baldwin and his reformers, in continuing to insist upon responsible government, could only cause trouble that at the very least resulted in 'stopping the machine of government every now and then to test the proper form of ... its different parts, as a matter of speculative demonstration.'[137]

But, in his view, the Tories could be equally futile. After the British concessions, 'I felt that with all I could do, to carry on the Government of the country upon old notions, was utterly out of the question.'[138] Draper counselled Sherwood that the Tories 'ought to embrace the opportunity of rallying around to assist the [governor-general] in going forward instead of perpetually looking back.'[139] When they had signally failed in this, he saw them as putting class interests above the national welfare, or in his own words, placing 'selfishness' ahead of 'patriotism.'[140] Yet there could be no doubt of Draper's deep conservatism. Never did his own élitist position shine more clearly than when advocating a 'democratic' measure. Thus, on the rate clause in the Common School Act of 1846 he said: 'Nothing is more important to a community than ... that those who possess property should assist and pay for the education of their poorer neighbours; and thus raise the lower classes on the scale of moral and intellectual beings.'[141] Progressive legislation was championed not from the point of view of 'the rights of man' but from that of *noblesse oblige* and because of its contribution to the stability and tranquility of society.

After the Union, the stability of society also necessitated the participation of the French in government. 'The administration ... can only be made strong in the support of the Province generally by a due infusion of gentlemen of the French Canadian Party.'[142] Thus, the Conservatives must proffer their hand to the French and forget the rebellions. The situation necessitated 'the administration of Government, without distinction of races or origin, and an entire oblivion of the past.'[143]

The culmination of all Draper's policies would have been the creation of a strong, Conservative 'consensus' party. As he said in his parliamentary swan-song: 'My purpose was, Sir, to found a party on a larger basis than ever had been formed before; I tried to do so for the advantage of our common country.'[144] As the word 'tried' implies, Draper was aware that he had not succeeded. Writing to Ryerson before he resigned, he said that when speaking of the Conservative party, 'I am forced to use a name as representative of an idea.'[145]

Time, however, would justify much of Draper's political ideology and political instincts. Toryism indeed was virtually dead; Conservatism was not. The brief and unlamented Sherwood administration amply proved the bankruptcy of the former. But the country did not then dissolve into the welter of demagoguery that John Beverley Robinson had so gloomily predicted; instead, by 1854 the Conservatives were back in power and in the longed-for alliance with the French. Two years later, with the ousting of MacNab and the assumption of leadership by John A. Macdonald, the moderates were in firm command of the party, and launched on a long career of government and growth.

Although some claim might thus be made for Draper as a harbinger of the modern Conservative party in Ontario and Canada, his greatest role was unquestionably in acting as a buffer in his day, between the course of Canadian politics and the policies of the imperial government. By the Union of 1841, through Lord John Russell's dispatches and Lord Sydenham's actions and concessions, the Melbourne Whig ministry had diverted the flow of Canadian politics into a new channel. But it had done so in its last days in office, and Peel's Conservative government had suddenly bade the waters halt in 1842. Sir Charles Bagot's coming to terms, though grudgingly accepted, had only confirmed them in this determination. The British Conservative ministers prepared to stand their ground more firmly in the future, and instructed Sir Charles Metcalfe to that effect. What they threatened the Canadians with was not fire and sword, but premature independence. As Peel himself put it: 'It is a hard bargain enough to have to give every advantage of connection with the Mother Country and to undertake serious responsibility and charge of providing for internal tranquility and for defence from external attack. But at the same time ... to be met at every turn by a captious and quibbling spirit – and above all to be denied the means of well-governing the Province – of insuring the independent and respectable administration of justice and the employment of honest and efficient civil servants, will make the connection too onerous a burden to be borne. We shall soon have to tell the factious people that there is one limit to our concessions – we will not govern you in a manner discreditable to us and injurious to you.'[146]

There is, of course, no evidence that Peel and Stanley would not have retreated from this position if faced, for instance, with a strong Reform victory in the elections of 1844. Equally, there is no evidence that they would have. But, even had a separation taken place peacefully, such a new Canadian nation would then have been still-born. Unable to support itself politically or economically, it would soon have succumbed to either the blandishments or the force of its great neighbour to the south. Certainly, virtually everybody in the 1840s saw independence as equivalent to annexation to the United States.

The critical danger point for producing such an eventuality was the resignation of the Reform ministers in November 1843. Whoever had done the most to cause that event, it was clearly Metcalfe himself and the Upper Canadian electorate who did most to avert the dangers it brought by securing a Conservative victory in the elections of 1844. But the governor needed a government, especially when his own physical powers began to fail; and it was here that Draper proved to be a mainstay. It was no easy task. Working desperately both before and after the election, first to construct the ministry, then to hold it together from such unlikely material, Draper performed a feat that virtually all, friendly or hostile, acknowledged could have been accomplished by no other politician of the day. As the unfriendly *Toronto Examiner* put it: 'He was the great star of the Conservative firmament, the soul, the whole soul of the party. If his talent did not atone for his faults ... it did much to keep a contemptible ministry above contempt: but this is a task which no earthly power could altogether accomplish.'[147]

Indeed, Draper's performance was a *tour de force* ultimately beyond his power. Yet it lasted just long enough. Stanley's resignation in 1845 and Peel's free-trade policy, which significantly lessened the benefits Canada received from the empire, led to a reappraisal of the situation whereby British statesmen now looked more indulgently on colonial aspirations to local self-government. Finally, 1846 saw the advent of a British Whig ministry willing, even eager, to concede full responsible government. If the achievement of this principle was an overdue vindication of Robert Baldwin's logic, the fact that it was achieved peacefully and within the context of the British connection was a tribute to Draper's unceasing efforts.

Yet, if an earlier generation of historians, concentrating solely on the achievement of responsible government, virtually ignored Draper, it is now perhaps equally easy to be too uncritical of his merits. A man who dislikes politics but engages in them out of duty or principle, whether it be Draper himself, his great example, Sir Robert Peel, or his great rival, Robert Baldwin, often receives more than his fair share of credit. Such individuals are usually thrown up by exceptional circumstances and often accomplish much through their disregard of normal political commitments or debts. But they are rarely popular with their parties, and this in itself sets limitations to their achievements. In the end, Draper and Peel were unable to contain unrepentant Toryism, just as Baldwin subsequently failed to contain an unrepentant populist radicalism.

Politics requires politicians. Draper, for all his 'hatred' of politics, actually had much to offer as a party leader. Political courage, administrative talent, oratorical eloquence he possessed in abundance. Moreover, in terms of what he was striving for in a broad sense, his political instinct was sound and his ideas were good. But there were also deep flaws. Despite that 'suavity so peculiar to his nature,'[148] he did not handle men well. He himself easily shrugged off personal taunts and political reverses as part of the game; he does not appear to have understood in the least the degree of humiliation he visited upon men such as Sherwood and MacNab or the amount of enmity this aroused. Though his letter to J.S. Cartwright in 1840 shows that he early understood the importance of party organization at the grass-roots level, he did little to further this end himself. Perhaps he considered this would be wasted effort until the various factions of the party could unite on a common policy; but this was in many ways putting the cart before the horse. Indeed, he sometimes betrayed an aristocratic fastidiousness far beyond that felt by most Tories. To Ryerson he once wrote: 'I frankly confess to you I do not like the public press as a mode of addressing the public. It seems to [be] giving your antagonist his own dunghill to fight upon. As a public man I prefer to defend myself in the more fitting arena of the Legislative Halls.'[149] How Sir Allan MacNab would have laughed at such *hauteur*!

Finally, for all his fabled 'dodging' and apparently sophisticated manoeuvring, Draper lacked a sure touch in handling specific issues. No man can win all his political battles, and each of Draper's major defeats can be written off as owing to circumstances beyond his control. Yet, taken together, they clearly suggest that something was missing. Here the contrast between Draper and his ultimate successor as party and government leader – John A. Macdonald – is instructive. Impossible though it might seem to achieve such tasks as overcoming the Conservative split on the university question, or of removing an albatross of the size of Sir Allan MacNab without destroying the party, both and much else were accomplished by Macdonald with a minimum of political damage. Of course, the future premier was working in different times and circumstances (circumstances in some ways rendered easier by what Draper had already done); but the discrepancy in the two careers in terms of consistency of success is hard to overlook.

It would be unwise to push such criticism too far. If Draper suffered many needless defeats, he also won some remarkable victories, important in their consequences to all his countrymen. Nor should a catalogue of his inadequacies suggest that some other individual might have done his work better at the time he did it. On the contrary, when the dangerous circumstances of the 1840s provided a constructive Conservative leader with so important a role to play, there was no one else to do the job at all.

As to the aftermath, Draper's departure from politics to the bench was for the former premier not a retirement but the very beginning of his chosen career. If the thirty years of this latter phase of his life appear stately and quiet, this was entirely consonant with his own wishes. After a decade of such rapid and often unwelcome constitutional changes, it was a clear relief for him to move in areas where the law altered only in a gradual and ordered fashion and where decisions could be carefully made within the quiet of his chambers. A study of these decisions suggests a man with a tremendous respect for the letter of the law, and it was from this position that he handed down most of his judgments.

Two events brought him back prominently, though briefly, to the political scene. In 1857 John A. Macdonald, then co-premier of the province, chose Draper for a task well suited to the latter's legal and diplomatic talents: to attend the imperial inquiry by a select committee of the House of Commons into the Hudson's Bay Company's rule over the great Northwest. Macdonald, then under heavy pressure from George Brown and his supporters to do something before western British North America was lost to the United States, was nevertheless worried about the danger that might be created by a premature Canadian occupation of that area. Draper accordingly was sent to London to represent Canada's interests, with wide latitude for discussion but no powers of decision. He did his work well, arguing that only settlement could save the west from American occupation, that the Bay Company was inimical to settlement, and that its chartered rights should be tested legally. The committee was deeply impressed by his testimony, and the outcome was precisely what Macdonald desired. Nothing was done for the present, but the principle that Canada should be the ultimate legatee of the company's territorial rights was more clearly established.

A year later Draper was involved in a much more unpleasant affair that certainly strained the appearance if not the substance of his beloved judicial impartiality. The legality of the famous 'double shuffle' of the Cartier-Macdonald government, the dubious device by which it took office following the defeat of the two-day Brown-Dorion administration of 1858, was tested when legal proceedings were begun against Macdonald and two of his colleagues. The case was heard before Draper who, with his associates, gave judgment for the defendants on 18 December.[150] Stressing once again the

Tory and Conservative members of the 1840s

member	principal alignment	constituency represented	own residence
William Henry Boulton	Tory	Toronto	Toronto
John Hillyard Cameron	Intermediary	Cornwall	Toronto
William Cayley	Intermediary	Huron	Toronto
George Chalmers	Conservative	Halton East	?
James Cummings	Conservative	Lincoln South	Chippewa Welland
Walter Hamilton Dickson	Conservative	Niagara	Niagara
William Henry Draper	Conservative	London	Toronto
George R. Duggan	Tory	York Second	Toronto
William Dunlop	Conservative	Huron	Goderich
Edward Ermatinger	Tory	Middlesex	St Thomas
Ogle R. Gowan	Conservative	Leeds	Brockville
George Barker Hall	Conservative	Northumberland South	Peterborough
Hamilton Dibble Jessup	Conservative	Grenville	Prescott
James Johnston	Tory	Carleton	Bytown
John Alexander Macdonald	Conservative	Kingston	Kingston
Rolland McDonnell	Conservative	Cornwall	Cornwall
George McDonnell	Conservative	Dundas	Cornwall
Sir A.N. MacNab	Tory	Hamilton	Hamilton
Adam Henry Meyers	Conservative	Northumberland	?
George Monro	Tory	York Third	Toronto
Edmund Murney	Tory	Hastings	Belleville
Archibald Petrie	Conservative	Russell	?
Robert Riddell	Conservative	Oxford	East Zorra
William Benjamin Robinson	Tory	Simcoe	Holland Landing St Catharines Toronto
Benjamin Seymour	Conservative	Lennox and Addington	Fredricksburg, Bath
George Sherwood	Tory	Brockville	Brockville
Henry Sherwood	Tory	Toronto	Toronto
Henry Smith	Conservative	Frontenac	Kingston
Neil Stewart	Conservative	Prescott	Hawkesbury
William Stewart	Conservative	Bytown	Bytown
James Webster	Conservative	Halton West	Fergus
John Tucker Williams	Tory	Durham	Port Hope
Joseph Woods	Conservative	Kent	Sandwich

The information for this table is drawn from a wide variety of sources: newspapers, assembly debates, and many local histories, as well as standard biographical works. Readers interested in the data for particular individuals should consult the author.

age in 1846	religion	occupation	place of birth	had some relationship with Family Compact	widely-known in UC in 1846
34	C of E	lawyer	UC	x	x
29	C of E	lawyer	France*	x	x
39	C of E	lawyer	Russia*	x	x
?	?	?	England (?)		
57	?	businessman tanner, distiller	UC		
40	C of E	?	UC		
45	C of E	lawyer	England	x	x
33	C of E	lawyer	UC	x	x
54	none	Canada Co Agent Author, MP	Scotland		x
49	C of E	businessman banker, fur-trader newspaper-owner	Elba**		x
43	C of E	journalist	Ireland		x
?	?	sawmill operator	?		
40	RC	medical doctor	UC		
?	?	businessman auctioneer newspaper-owner	?		x
31	Pres.	lawyer	Scotland		
37	Pres. (?)	financier	?		
c 40	Pres. (?)	lawyer	?		
48	C of E	lawyer speculator	UC	x	x
?	C of E	lawyer	?		
45	C of E	businessman	Scotland	x	x
c 40	C of E	lawyer	?		
?	Pres. (?)	Paymaster R. Navy	?		
?	C of E (?)	money-lender (?)	Scotland		
49	C of E	fur-trader	UC	x	x
41	?	merchant money-lender	UC		
35	C of E	lawyer	UC	x	x
39	C of E	lawyer	UC	x	x
34	C of E	lawyer	England		
?	Pres. (?)	merchant	Scotland		
?	Pres. (?)	timber merchant	Scotland		
38	Pres.	merchant	Scotland		
?	C of E	Naval Officer	England (?)		
46	?	miller	UC		

* of British parents
** of Canadian parents

letter of the law, Draper's ruling was entirely consonant with the whole cor-
pus of his judicial decisions. Nevertheless, since Macdonald had so egre-
giously offended against the spirit of the law, the bitterness of George Brown
was entirely understandable, even if his descriptions of Draper as a 'pliant
tool,' a 'servile judge,' and a 'very fair Jeffreys' who 'might have served
even for the Bloody Assize' were somewhat overdrawn.[151]

The necessity of sitting in judgment on his political heir with all the taunts
a favourable verdict was likely to bring was the last of those awkward
incidents that had so dogged Draper's career. On the whole his judicial performance was praised by former enemies as well as by friends, and his
advancement in that sphere was easy and gratifying. After nine years on the
Court of Queen's Bench, he was created chief justice of the Court of Common
Pleas in Upper Canada in 1856. In 1863 he was named chief justice of the Court
of Queen's Bench and in 1869 of the Court of Error and Appeal in Ontario.

Draper settled in Toronto on Wellington Street, and also built a summer
cottage overlooking Rosedale ravine. Throughout the remainder of his life
he was active in diverse civic and religious organizations. In his latter years,
therefore, he moved through the community as a man of weight and fame at
the apex of his career and with his political legacy safely in the hands of John
A. Macdonald. He enhanced dinner parties, indulged to the full his layman's
interests in the affairs of arts and sport, of science and religion, and was at
last one of the chief adornments of that social and professional élite to
which he had so earnestly aspired from afar when a young law student. It was
with all such dreams of success fully consummated that he died at Yorkville
on 3 November 1877.

NOTES

1 For his contemporaries' views of Draper see J.C. Dent, *The Last Forty Years*
   (Toronto 1881), I, 70; A.E. Ryerson, *The Story of my Life* (Toronto 1883),
   334-45; letter of 'Uncle Ben,' quoted in *Globe*, 11 Nov. 1845.
2 *Dictionary of Canadian Biography*, X: *1871-1880* (Toronto 1972), 253 [hereafter
   DCB]
3 D.B. Read, *Lives of the Judges of Upper Canada and Ontario* (Toronto 1888),
   224
4 See speech of T.C. Aylwin in *Debates of the Legislative Assembly of United
   Canada*, ed. Elizabeth Nish (Montreal 1970-), I, 90. [hereafter *Debates*]
5 DCB, 253
6 Read, *Lives of the Judges*, 205
7 For the general confusion regarding such well-known terms as 'Family Compact' and 'responsible government' see Graeme Patterson, 'An enduring Cana-

dian myth: Responsible Government and the Family Compact,' *Journal of Canadian Studies*, XII, 2, 1977, 3-14.

8 On this point see Robert J. Burns, 'The First Elite of Toronto: an examination of the genesis, consolidation and duration of power in an emerging colonial society' (unpublished PHD thesis, University of Western Ontario, 1974).

9 Read, *Lives of the Judges*, 205

10 Public Archives of Canada [PAC], Merritt Papers, Draper to Merritt, 20 June 1844

11 For accounts of this curious affair see John Ireland, 'John H. Dunn and the Bankers,' *Ontario History*, LXII 1971, 83-100, and George Metcalf, 'The Political Career of William Henry Draper, 1836-47' (unpublished MA thesis, University of Toronto, 1959), 23-30.

12 In the early 1840s he owned two Toronto properties besides his personal residence. This would appear to have been the extent of his 'speculating.'

13 *Commercial Herald*, quoted in *Examiner*, 19 Feb. 1840

14 See *Journals of the Legislative Assembly of Upper Canada, 1836-7*, 16 Dec. 1836; Ryerson, *Story of my Life*, 179.

15 Queen's University Archives [QUA], Cartwright Papers, J.B. Robinson to J.S. Cartwright, 16 April 1841

16 John Beverley Robinson's political credo is to be found in his book, *Canada and the Canada Bill* (London 1840). It is analysed by Terry Cook in 'John Beverley Robinson and the Conservative Blueprint for the Upper Canadian Community,' *Ontario History*, LXIV, 2, June 1972, 79-94. See also C.R. Sanderson, ed., *The Arthur Papers* (Toronto 1957), II, Robinson to Arthur, 19 Feb. 1839.

17 QUA, Cartwright Papers, Draper to Cartwright, 18 Nov. 1840

18 Ibid., MacNab to Cartwright, 5 April 1841

19 Ibid., Draper to Cartwright, 18 Nov. 1840

20 D.R. Beer, 'W.H. Draper and the Formation of the Conservative Party,' Notes and Comments, *Canadian Historical Review* [CHR], LIV, 2, 1973, 230

21 G.P. Scrope, *Life of Lord Sydenham* (London 1884), 164

22 In *The Alignment of Political Groups in Canada, 1841-67* (Toronto 1962), P.G. Cornell (see Table I) lists E.C. Campbell, W. Dunlop, A. McLean, and Henry Smith in this category.

23 From the beginning of the Union, many French Canadians kept open communications with the Conservatives, if only in hopes of repealing the Union itself.

24 See Draper's speech in *Debates*, II, 28-31.

25 Ibid., I, 790-2

26 *Montreal Gazette*, 9 Sept. 1841; see also *Globe*, 16 Sept. and 25 Nov. 1845.

27 PAC, MG 24, A 13, Bagot Papers, Draper to Bagot, 9 June 1842, private

28 Actually the Colonial Office gave Canadian affairs a much closer and more careful scrutiny than was evident to the colonists themselves. The problem was that

concessions (especially regarding colonial autonomy) made to Upper Canada would be difficult to withhold from Lower Canada and in the latter colony the anti-commercial attitude of the French-speaking majority was dubiously regarded by the imperial authorities. For a fuller appreciation of the Colonial Office dilemma of this period see Peter Burroughs, *The Canadian Crisis and British Colonial Policy, 1828-1841* (Toronto 1972).

29 Ontario Archives [OA], Robinson Papers, Lord Seaton to J.B. Robinson, 27 March 1842
30 Jacques Monet, *The Last Cannon Shot: A Study of French-Canadian Nationalism, 1837-1850* (Toronto 1969), 97-102
31 Bagot Papers, Bagot to Stanley, 26 Jan. 1842
32 Ibid., Bagot to Stanley, 8 Feb. 1842; OA, S.B. Harrison Papers, Bagot to Harrison, 2 July 1842
33 Bagot Papers, Cartwright to Bagot, 6 June 1842; OA, Cartwright Papers, Hagerman to Cartwright, 29 Jan. 1842, private; John Macaulay to Cartwright, 4 Feb. 1842; MacNab to Cartwright, 16 Feb. 1842
34 Bagot Papers, Draper to Bagot, 9 June 1842, private
35 See Cartwright Papers, J.B. Robinson to J.S. Cartwright, 14 July 1842.
36 Bagot Papers, Draper to Bagot, 16 July 1842, private and confidential
37 Ibid., Bagot to Stanley, 10 July 1842
38 Ibid., Bagot to Stanley, 28 July 1842, private and confidential
39 Ibid., Bagot to Stanley, 26 Sept. 1842, confidential
40 Public Record Office, CO 537/140, Memorandum, 12 Sept. 1842
41 For this speech and the Reform replies see *Debates*, II, 28-47.
42 Sir Francis Hincks, *Reminiscences of his Public Life* (Montreal 1884), 87
43 Lytton Strachey and Roger Fulford, eds., *The Greville Memoirs, 1814-1860*, 8 vols. (London 1938), V, 46
44 Bagot Papers, Stanley to Bagot, 3 Nov. 1842; 3 Dec. 1842; PAC, RG7, 65/32, Stanley to Bagot, 2 Nov. 1842
45 Bagot Papers, Stanley to Bagot, 16 Oct. 1842, confidential
46 CO 537/40, Stanley to Bagot, 2 Nov. 1842
47 D.L. Beer, 'The Political Career of Sir Allan MacNab, 1839-49' (unpublished MA thesis, Queen's University, 1963)
48 S.B. Leacock, *Baldwin, LaFontaine and Hincks* (Toronto 1926), 183; Merritt Papers, Draper to Merritt, 20 June 1844; *Examiner*, 15 Nov. 1843
49 Metropolitan Toronto Central Library [MTCL], Speech of the Honourable W.H. Draper, QC, at the Bar of the Legislative Assembly of Canada; Friday, December 21, 1843; OA, Strachan Letter Book, Strachan to Draper, 11 Dec. 1843
50 *Debates*, III, 1072-1102, 1111-29, 1189-91, 1211-12
51 Monet, *Last Cannon Shot*, 150-1
52 Merritt Papers, Draper to Merritt, 20 June 1844
53 J.W. Kaye, *Life of Lord Metcalfe* (London 1854), II, 550

54 OA, Hodgins Papers, Ryerson to Draper, 19 Sept. 1844
55 Typescript of J.J. Talman, 'William Hamilton Merritt,' for volume IX of DCB
56 William Hamilton Merritt, *A Brief Review of the Revenue, Resources and Expenditures of Canada, Compared with those of the Neighbouring State of New York* (St Catharines 1845)
57 Merritt Papers, Merritt to Draper, 20 July 1844
58 Ryerson, *Story of my Life*, 334-5
59 Merritt Papers, Draper to Merritt, 20 June 1844; Kaye, *Lord Metcalfe*, II, 552-4
60 CO 537/143, Metcalfe to Stanley, 17 Sept. 1844
61 The words are the *Globe*'s, 14 Jan. 1845
62 Kaye, *Lord Metcalfe*, 533-5
63 Gerald Craig, ed., *Lord Durham's Report* (Toronto 1963), 141
64 *Journals of the Legislative Assembly of Canada, 1841*, 3 Sept. 1841
65 Although the major constitutional principles were also established in England in the 1840s, it was not until the writing of the third Earl Grey and Nassau Senior in the 1850s and 60s that they were fully understood. See J.M. Ward, *Colonial Self-Government: The British Experience* (Toronto 1976), 207-8.
66 QUA, William Morris Papers, W. Morris to A. Morris, 15 Nov. 1844
67 OA, Cartwright Papers, Hagerman to J.S. Cartwright, 29 Jan. 1842, private; *Debates*, IV, 2387-91
68 CO 537/143, Metcalfe to Stanley, 13 May 1845; MTCL, Baldwin Papers, LaFontaine to Baldwin, 2 Dec. 1845
69 *Debates*, IV, 143, 173
70 Ibid., 248
71 Merritt Papers, Draper to Merritt, 26 Dec. 1844
72 Hodgins Papers, Draper to Ryerson, 26 Jan. 1844, private and confidential
73 Merritt Papers, Draper to Merritt, 26 Dec. 1844
74 *Examiner*, 5 March 1845
75 Morris Papers, Buchanan to Morris, 3 March 1845
76 *Debates*, IV, 2387
77 Ibid., 2387-8; Robinson Papers, J.B. Robinson to Strachan, 31 Dec. 1844
78 *Examiner*, 12 March 1845
79 This is my conclusion from the conflicting evidence. See Morris Papers, W.B. Robinson to Morris, 12 July 1845; Morris to Robinson, July 1845; see also speeches of Robinson and Draper in *Debates*, IV, 2387-92.
80 *Debates*, IV, 2052-3, 2064-94
81 Morris Papers, Hugh Scobie to Morris, 7 March 1845
82 CO 531/143, Metcalfe to Stanley, 4 April 1845, Confidential Despatch, No 52
83 *Debates*, IV, 2249-69. Robinson's resignation was accepted by Metcalfe only under great pressure from Draper and the ministry.
84 MTCL, Baldwin Papers, J.H. Dunn to Baldwin, 14 Dec. 1844
85 Ibid., 204-8

86 *Correspondence between the Hon. W.H. Draper and the Hon. R.E. Caron* (Montreal 1846), 1-11
87 Ibid., 12-13
88 Baldwin Papers, LaFontaine to Baldwin, 23 Sept. 1845, confidential
89 See the debate on the reading of the correspondence in 1846 in *Debates*, V, 338-435, especially Viger's speech on 424.
90 Ibid., 318-30
91 Ibid., 593; C.B. Sissons, *Egerton Ryerson* (Toronto 1937), II, 101
92 This aspect of the education question has been well analysed by Susan E. Houston in 'Politics, Schools, and Social Change in Upper Canada,' CHR, LIII, 3, 1972, 249-71.
93 *Debates*, VI, 593
94 CO 537/142, Metcalfe to Stanley, 9 Oct. 1843, confidential
95 Kaye, *Lord Metcalfe*, II, 528n
96 CO 42/531, Stephen to Gladstone, 12 Jan. 1846
97 Gladstone to Kimberley, 8 Dec. 1881, quoted in Paul Knaplund, 'Sir James Stephen and British North American Problems,' CHR, V, 1, 1924, 29, footnote 1
98 British Library [BL], Gladstone Papers, Add. Mss 44735, f 280
99 PAC, RG 7, G 5/34, Gladstone to Cathcart, 3 Feb. 1846
100 *Mirror of Parliament*, 1846, 5 May 1846
101 Ibid., 28 May 1846
102 PAC, Macdonald Papers, vol. 209, Draper to Cathcart, 10 June 1846
103 MTCL, J.H. Cameron Papers, Draper to Cameron, 22 June 1846; Daly to Sherwood, 12 June 1846; Sherwood to Daly, 17 June 1846
104 See *Debates*, V, 388-435, for the whole debate. Viger's speech is on 424.
105 Hodgins Papers, Ryerson to Draper, 20 April 1846
106 For more details of this episode see Monet, *Last Cannon Shot*, 238-40; Baldwin Papers, Hincks to Baldwin, 16 Aug. 1846; R.B. Sullivan to Baldwin, 29 Aug. 1846.
107 Draper appears to have been considering the possibility that Cameron might succeed him as attorney-general at least as early as November 1846. See Cameron Papers, Draper to Cameron, 20 Nov. 1846.
108 Sir A. Doughty, ed., *The Elgin-Grey Papers, 1846-1852* (Ottawa 1937), I, 19; D.G. Creighton, *John A. Macdonald: The Young Politician* (Toronto 1952), 105
109 For a comprehensive discussion of this issue see D.R. Beer, 'Sir Allan MacNab and the Adjutant-Generalship of the Militia, 1846-47,' in *Ontario History*, LXI, March 1969, 19-32.
110 Hodgins Papers, Draper to Ryerson, 3 and 23 March 1846
111 *Elgin-Grey Papers*, I, 45-7, 50
112 Hodgins Papers, Ryerson to Draper, 16 Feb. 1847; 29 March 1847, private; Macdonald Papers, vol. 336, Cayley to Macdonald, 22 May 1847
113 Beer, 'Sir Allan MacNab,' 26

114 W.P.M. Kennedy, *Documents of the Canadian Constitution, 1759-1915* (Toronto 1918), 501
115 Hodgins Papers, Draper to Ryerson, 1 Jan. 1847
116 *Elgin-Grey Papers*, I, 14
117 Ibid., 38
118 Ibid., 12-18
119 See John Macdonald to Ogle Gowan, 26 March 1847, in F.H. Armstrong, 'The Macdonald-Gowan Letters, 1847,' *Ontario History*, LXIII, 1971, 5-6
120 *Elgin-Grey Papers*, I, 20-4
121 Ibid., 27-33
122 Baldwin Papers, Hincks to Baldwin, 25 March 1847, private; 29 March 1847; 18 April 1847; LaFontaine to Baldwin, 11 April 1847, private
123 *Elgin-Grey Papers*, I, 27-33
124 For basic information regarding the Tory-Conservative analysis that follows see Appendix.
125 It could be argued that G.R. Duggan and George Monro did not have a 'widespread' reputation in 1846. However, both were extremely well-known in Toronto which seems to me a special enough case to warrant including them here.
126 Armstrong, 'Macdonald-Gowan Letters,' 6-7, Macdonald to Gowan, 30 April 1847
127 Ibid.
128 Macdonald Papers, vol. 209, Draper to Macdonald, 4 March 1847
129 Ibid., vol. 336, Morris to Macdonald, 6 May 1847, private and confidential
130 Ibid., Macdonald to Morris, 9 May 1847, private
131 Cameron Papers, Cameron to Daly, 22 May 1847
132 Armstrong, 'Macdonald-Gowan Letters,' 9-10, Macdonald to Gowan, 14 May 1847
133 *Debates*, II, 30
134 Ibid.
135 See ibid., 29, for Draper's appreciation of the importance of Russell's despatches. For the Harrison resolutions see Bagot Papers, Draper to Bagot, 16 July 1842, private and confidential.
136 Cartwright Papers, Draper to Cartwright, 18 Nov. 1840
137 Hodgins Papers, Draper to Ryerson, 26 Jan. 1844, private and confidential
138 *Debates*, VI, 221
139 Bagot Papers, Draper to Bagot, 18 June 1842, private
140 Macdonald Papers, vol. 209, Draper to Macdonald, 4 March 1847
141 *Debates*, V, 593
142 Macdonald Papers, vol. 209, Draper to Cathcart, 10 June 1846
143 *Debates*, II, 30
144 Ibid., VII, 221-2

145 Hodgins Papers, Draper to Ryerson, 22 Feb. 1847
146 BL, Peel Papers, Peel to Stanley, 2 Feb. 1844, Add. Mss 40468, f 124. See also Peel to Aberdeen, 16 May 1842, in C.S. Parker, *Sir Robert Peel*, III, 389.
147 *Examiner*, 23 June 1847
148 Speech by T.C. Aylwin. See *Debates*, I, 90.
149 Hodgins Papers, Draper to Ryerson, 26 Jan. 1844
150 *Globe*, 20 Dec. 1858
151 Ibid.

J.M.S. CARELESS

Robert Baldwin

Robert Baldwin, revered as Father of Responsible Government, architect of the Ontario municipal system, unblemished statesman who followed his political principles unswervingly to their realization: can any leader in Ontario's past sound nobler – or duller? Not for him the rash, romantic failure of rebellion like the radical Mackenzie, nor the fine, resounding Tory fury of a Sir Allan MacNab. Here instead was the cautious, constitutional Reformer, pushing on through long successions of parliamentary manoeuvres and debates, cold-eyed if clear-headed, patiently expounding his doctrine of responsible cabinet rule, carefully guarding his political virtue. He lacked Draper's smooth, attractive manner, Hinck's tough political realism, the shrewd, manipulative mastery of John A. Macdonald, or the earthy wit and lively temper of Sandfield Macdonald. In many respects Baldwin was almost un-Canadian as a successful political leader. But succeed he did in the life task he set himself. When he entered politics in 1829 in Upper Canada, responsible self-government for a colony was only a vaguely formulated notion. When he retired from the cabinet of United Canada in 1851, it was an established fact – and no one individual had had more to do with it than the Honourable Robert Baldwin.

His career should only look dull, indeed, if one holds that abortive extremes are inevitably more engrossing than middle-way achievements, that sharp practice in politics is more fun than integrity, or that the events and tactics by which Canadians gained the crucial freedom to run their own affairs are only bourgeois constitutional trivia, of small significance for the lives of the mass of the people. But was Robert Baldwin, the man, as grey and colourless a person as his symbolic role in history might yet make him seem? Far from it. The private, personal Robert was an emotional, sometimes agonized being. A public stance of cool reserve and sober dignity masked sensitive shyness, dark times of anguish, a happy warmth of family feeling, and a passionate devotion to his wife. It also hid the cordial generosity of friendship shown to those he trusted, such as his great political partner of the 1840s, the Lower Canadian Liberal leader, Louis Hippolyte LaFontaine.

There was in Baldwin, too, a tenaciously logical intellect that probed into and brought forth the meaning of political concepts beyond most of his contemporaries in public life. In many respects he was one of the most rationally reflective politicians that Canada, or certainly Ontario, has ever had. Still, he was never wholly a theorist, nor a doctrinaire, but could display a judicious practicality which more dogmatic zealots might denounce as timorous over-caution, yet which seemed largely to work out as sound common sense. Above all, however, his whole personality was ruled by a moral imperative that repeatedly drove him on to difficult decisions which his inherent sensitivity shrank from making. Here realists would condemn him as absurdly, if not morbidly, worried about principles; but to him appeals to rectitude, honour, duty were sovereign commands. A later age indeed might deem these rather pious and excessively Victorian protestations. Yet to Robert Baldwin the concern for an unstained public reputation was as real and compelling as his strong religious faith. Proud, prudent and deliberate, withdrawn, anxious and compulsive, he was a person of no ordinary calibre or complexity.

His social circumstances were not ordinary either. A well-off, well-connected member of Toronto's 'best' society, he was less a man of the people than any of the other Reform leaders of his era; and while some of the older Tories might share a background similar to his, to be men of the people was hardly their earnest desire. On the one hand, Baldwin could not readily develop a cameraderie with his party followers and rural constituents, though he long held their deep respect and confidence for his ideas and integrity. On the other, his reforming brand of politics worked to mark him off from Toronto's would-be aristocratic and largely Tory little urban world, although his social and business contacts within this close community did not disappear at any time. Furthermore, as a member of the influential and socially notable Baldwin family he shared its aspirations (or those unquestionably held by his father, Doctor William Warren Baldwin) to maintain a due dynastic eminence, backed by property holdings and graced with a fine family seat in town or country. Though he led popular and democratic forces of Reform, Robert was something of a colonial or Canadian Whig in social conditioning, the kind who would believe in government for the people by the best of the people: self-government under the leadership of a dedicated political élite.

The divergences between this sort of élitist, affluent Whiggism and the concerns of a largely agrarian popular electorate were, perhaps, less significant or evident in his own day, when egalitarianism was still a dubious Yankee or radical conception, when class distinctions were considerably blurred in the broad Upper Canadian middle mass of 'respectable' proprietors, and when strong ethnic and religious allegiances cut across class patterns as well. Nevertheless, the very degree of difference between Baldwin's own social surroundings and those of the bulk of his supporters undoubtedly represented a further complication throughout his seemingly direct and even-tenored course in public affairs.

Probably the single most important circumstance affecting his career, however, was the family bond with his father that ran as a strong connecting thread through both his private and public life. The very idea of colonial self-government effected through 'a provincial ministry ... responsible to the provincial parliament' came to him from his father.[1] Robert always acknowledged the source of his basic principle; and in a sense his whole political endeavour was to realize and complete the doctrine that had thus been taught to him. Moreover, he began his legal career in William Baldwin's law office, entered politics under the auspices of his father (already a leading Reformer), and continued to work steadfastly with him. In later years, when Robert had taken over the mantle from the elder Baldwin, the latter strove as wholeheartedly for his son – assisting in local elections, acting as his agent, offering counsel, but readily and proudly supporting Robert's decisions. Their private correspondence is marked by free discussion and exchange of views, yet equally by entire confidence and warm affection. And they had much to deal with together regarding family and business matters as well as political concerns.

In any event, there was a veritable firm of Baldwin and Son in the Upper Canadian Reform movement that was ended only in 1844 by William's death at sixty-eight when responsible government was not yet attained but was well on its way, and but seven years from Robert's own political retirement. In short, the intimate tie between the Grandfather and the Father of Responsible Government needs constantly to be kept in mind in assessing the younger man's career. Their close relationship seems to have been essentially positive in character, and there is little basis for a detailed psycho-historical inquiry into neurotic fixations or deep Freudian complexes. Family feelings most generally were strong and open among the Baldwins, as witnessed by the letters between Robert and his own children, full of family chatter and affectionate banter on either side. Yet there was close regard in William for his first-born, depicted when he thus began a letter to young Robert as a boy: 'When I folded my paper to write to you, I did not anticipate the warm emotion I felt upon writing "My dear Robert" dear, indeed, to my heart as all your brothers are ...'[2] In any case, whatever the father felt, the way in which the son faithfully took forward what his parent had begun suggests that for him the bond was powerful indeed.

It is in this respect that their relations must be emphasized, for their effect on a sensitive Robert Baldwin, acutely aware of his father's teachings and ambitions for the family's standing, and of his own filial duty. In comparison, the senior Baldwin was a much more outgoing, urbane individual; ambitious beyond doubt, resourceful and adaptable, capable of turning from his early training in medicine to a highly successful legal career; and of gaining valuable family alliances and influential patrons, thereby considerably advancing the Baldwin fortunes. At one stage or another William Warren Baldwin directed a school for the sons of the gentry of little York, designed and built houses with some evidence of architectural talent, read his way into the legal profession and became a judge, sat in the legislature as one of the most respected of leaders of Reform protest, and took up his pen to the great Duke of Wellington on his own key answer to colonial troubles. To his reserved, more introverted son, who did not shine in school or social drawing rooms, William must have seemed a figure of masterful accomplishments, whose aims and desires had to be taken up fervently – if they could not be brilliantly – and carried onward for the family name and honour, not to mention the liberty and welfare of Upper Canada itself.

Robert Baldwin has often been termed the man of one idea – responsible government; but perhaps his idea and mission went deeper into his inmost feelings: to be worthy of the father he so looked to and admired. In fact, he might otherwise conceivably have stayed a distinguished lawyer or a gentleman of means. Instead he went into politics, came out again, and went back in again, until his duty was done and the task was complete. Thereafter he retired, aged only forty-seven, to a private life of family retreat – fulfilled at last in his mission as William Baldwin's eldest son. Much of this can only remain as speculation; but it does convey the same fundamental point: that behind the good grey symbol of 'Robert Responsible Government' there was a complex and imperiously-driven human personality.

Robert Baldwin's grandfather, another Robert, arrived in Canada in 1799 from southern Ireland as a widower of fifty-eight, accompanied by two sons and four daughters, and leaving behind a married daughter, and two boys in naval and merchant-shipping service. Sprung from sixteenth-century English origins, the Baldwins had been a solidly established family in Cork and its surrounding area, Protestants and Anglicans, members of the established Church of Ireland. In their background were substantial merchants and county gentlemen, not great aristocratic landowners but local notables, who included a mayor and alderman of Cork. Robert Baldwin the Emigrant, as he became known in family history, had himself controlled a sizeable estate, Summer Hill, outside Cork, until a burden of debts, Irish disorders, and the lure of Upper Canada – to which some of his Cork associates had already moved – brought his decision to leave Ireland. In Upper Canada he quickly bought a thousand acres in the thinly settled township of Clarke, Durham

County, some forty miles east of the capital village of York along the Lake Ontario shore. He thus acted with typical impetuosity, without waiting for a 1200-acre grant which an old friend from Cork, Peter Russell, the influential president of the council in the provincial government, was arranging for him, along with another 1200 for his twenty-four year old eldest son, William Warren Baldwin.[3] In any event, the early years were arduous for the emigrant Baldwins at their new home in Clarke, living not in a well-appointed stone mansion surrounded by tenanted farms, but in a crude log cabin in a wilderness of forest and isolated clearings.

Nonetheless, the clearings enlarged and an agricultural neighbourhood gradually emerged. As a mark of Robert the Emigrant's standing with the powers at York, moreover, he was named a magistrate in 1800, lieutenant of the County of Durham (a largely honorific post, soon to lapse), and colonel of militia. He became a substantial figure in the local official establishment, though he never was a very successful farmer. Meanwhile, his son William Warren began to chafe at the limitations of backwoods country life. He had worked long and hard in settling the family and starting up the farm, putting aside his talents and his training to do so. For William had taken his medical degree at the University of Edinburgh, where he had also been admitted to the distinguished circle of the Speculative Society.[4] He resolved to move to York, since there would be more opportunity for a medical practice at the capital than among the poor and scattered homesteads of Clarke. He was settled in the town by June 1802, living in the home of another family friend from Ireland, William Willcocks, a cousin of Peter Russell, a former mayor of Cork himself, and a large property-owner with a remarkable penchant for land speculation.

Young Dr Baldwin, still only twenty-seven, soon found, however, that there was not much business for him even in the tiny capital, although the Russells and the Willcockses duly came as patients. Hence, he decided to take up law as a supplementary or alternative profession. To help make ends meet while he pursued this new field of study, he opened his small school at the beginning of 1803, to instruct twelve boys (at eight guineas and one cord of wood each, *per annum*) in 'Writing, Reading, the Classics and Arithmetic.'[5] That same year he married Phoebe, daughter of William Willcocks, to begin a long and devoted domestic life. Still further, he was admitted to the Law Society of Upper Canada and licensed to practice as a barrister and attorney.

The young couple acquired a house on Palace (Front) Street, and here on 12 May 1804 their first child, Robert, was born. The father jubilantly gave his school a holiday to signalize the occasion.[6] In the next few years four other sons were born to William and Phoebe Baldwin, of whom one died in infancy, two in their teens, and one (William Augustus) long outlived

Robert Baldwin himself. During these years before the War of 1812, Dr Baldwin effectively established himself as a well-known lawyer, with a growing practice, a business as well as a social intimate of some of the leading men of York. His advance was considerably aided by a close link with Peter Russell and the latter's unmarried sister, Elizabeth, who presided over the house of her bachelor brother. From Peter he purchased a prime Front Street property on which he would later build a handsome town house.[7] More important, when Peter Russell died in 1808, leaving all his wide accumulation of Upper Canada lands to his sister, William Baldwin helped settle the estate for her; and when Elizabeth drew up her own will in 1811, William was made sole executor and trustee.[8]

There is no reason to look for sinister machinations in this regard. In the close-knit gentry society of York, organized about family ties and friendships, privileged patrons and dutiful clients, it was wholly natural that the highly acceptable and obviously able young doctor-lawyer, a constant companion at dinners, teas, and church services, should gain such a valuable position of trust. In any event, however, it made William a power in his own right, renting, selling, and developing a range of town or country properties. Elizabeth Russell did not finally die for eleven years more, but then she left the bulk of her holdings to her cousins, Maria Willcocks and Phoebe Willcocks Baldwin, so that Dr William continued to manage the great estate on behalf of his wife and her sister.[9]

Still further, old William Willcocks himself had died in 1813, leaving to his son-in-law, William Baldwin, two hundred acres of his own adjoining the Russell tract to the northwest of York, where the land rises suddenly from the lake plain.[10] Here the doctor would develop a spacious surburban estate, to be called Spadina, and lay out a splendidly broad thoroughfare, Spadina Avenue, downward to the western fringes of the town. He now also had his late father-in-law's other extensive properties to deal with, bequeathed as they had been to Phoebe and Maria Willcocks – 'Aunt Maria,' who came to live with the Baldwin family. William's fortunes were rapidly expanding; yet it should be made clear that this was by no means simply a matter of good luck and good connections but equally involved his own hard work and strong capabilities. He went out on circuit with the courts – though he might take time out from arguing a case to deliver a baby. He managed the financial affairs of Quetton St George, York's leading merchant, who took William's younger brother, John Spread Baldwin, into the business. And he began trying his hand successfully at architecture, when in 1809 he designed and supervised the construction of a large new house for St George, one of the earliest brick private residences in York.[11]

It was in this atmosphere of advancing family wealth and position that Robert Baldwin grew up. He was apparently rather indulged by fond parents in his early years, but in any case he lived in a large, warm household of relatives, which came to include his elderly grandfather Robert after he retired from the rigorous life in Clarke. Before the boy turned nine, he gained an eventful memory of the War of 1812 when, in April 1813, an American fleet attacked and briefly seized York. The Baldwin women and children and old Robert the Emigrant were hurriedly packed off northward up Yonge Street to the safety of a distant cabin at the present Eglinton Avenue. Young Robert trudged behind Elizabeth Russell's carriage packed with valuables and supplies, while his father laboured in town among the wounded and dying left from the American assault.[12] But the rest of his youthful memories were less stirring: family gatherings and trips to country properties, including a stay on a Willcocks farm at Millbrook well inland from York until the war was over, a winter sleigh excursion to New York with his parents and brother Henry in 1816, but, mostly, school.[13]

Back in York, Robert went to the Home District Grammar School, which had replaced earlier little private academies like his father's, and which was now directed by the Reverend John Strachan, the Anglican rector of York, a first-rate teacher if a fiercely combative politician. Strachan, of course, was well known to the Baldwins, for they regularly attended his church of St James. Robert, studying with the other sons of the town's élite, proved an attentive and thorough pupil rather than a brilliant one, but he at length was made head boy, and presented the prologue in Latin at the school's closing exercises. The bond between Strachan and his pupils often became enduring. It certainly affected Robert in later years, although political differences spread between them.

In 1820 he entered his father's law office as a clerk, to begin studying for the bar. Dr Baldwin (as he continued to be called, though he had ceased to practice medicine) was now embarking on the most vigorous years of his career. His legal activities continued to expand; he had already served as a judge of the Home District Court, was master in chancery and repeatedly treasurer of the Upper Canada Law Society. His properties were only gaining in value as the waves of British immigration began to flow into the province, and as York started its climb towards the City of Toronto. He was designing and erecting buildings both public and private, including, as he described it, 'a very commodious house in the country' for his own family on his hillside tract some three miles beyond the town – 'I have called the place Spadina, the Indian word for Hill – or Mont.'[14] And he had turned to active politics, being first elected to the provincial assembly as member for the County of York and Simcoe in the summer of 1820, at that time as an evident supporter of the government.

His young law-clerk son was increasingly caught up in these brisk developments. In the growing office, where his father was often away, Robert's responsibilities soon mounted. He worked there with James Small, a senior clerk shortly to be called to the bar and a parliamentary associate in time to come. He also struck up a keen friendship with a junior clerk, his cousin, Irish-born Robert Baldwin Sullivan, who joined the office in 1823. The Sullivan connection sprang from Barbara Baldwin Sullivan, William's married sister who had remained in Ireland during the original family migration. But after the war the Sullivans, too, had settled in York; and among their other children was young Augusta Elizabeth, Robert Baldwin's future wife. Still further, William's brother, Captain Augustus Baldwin, had retired from the Royal Navy on half pay following the Napoleonic conflict and likewise came to York, where he had purchased the Russell land adjoining Spadina and built a home called Russell Hill.[15] By 1820 both these Baldwin neighbours were comfortably established in their large new residences on the farmed and wooded hill-crest estates that reached southward from the present St Clair Avenue to Bloor Street. Here Robert Baldwin spent much of his time with the family group, roaming the pleasant setting that looked down on the town below – when he was not busy in the law office or helping his father with parliamentary campaigns. He gradually became, in fact, William's competent and trusted aide in dealing with political affairs. Then in 1825, at twenty-one, he was admitted to the bar and was made a partner in the law firm, henceforth to be known as W.W. Baldwin and Son.

By that date his father had fully committed himself to the cause of Reform in politics. This crucial development needs explaining. One might otherwise presume that William's place in society and own extensive property interests would have kept him a supporter of the powers that be, of the firm-fixed government forces and the York-based côterie of powerful officials, men of wealth and social notability which was to be branded for all time as the Family Compact of Upper Canada. Any such presumption, however, would ignore several important factors that inevitably affected William Baldwin's outlook: his Irish background, the political experience of his own father, and his dynastic ambitions for his family's standing in the colonial community.

As an Irishman (and the Anglo-Irish of the time certainly believed they were Irishmen), Dr Baldwin resented 'the clannishness ... and alleged favoritism' of the strongly Scottish element which had exercised wide influence in government circles at York, ever since the passing of Peter Russell's early days of dominance.[16] John Strachan, William Allan, a wealthy merchant, and other Scots seemed almost abrasively ascendant in local cliques of power in the period after the War of 1812. But even before the war protests had been voiced against the maladministration of the 'Scotch party,' particularly by Robert Thorpe, chief figure in a largely Irish group of critics of the government. And William Baldwin had acquired a lasting sympathy for the Thorpe faction. His father-in-law, William Willcocks, had become associated with them, as had a Willcocks cousin, and onetime close friend, Joseph Willcocks – who, however, went on from being a popular agitator to joining the American invaders during the War of 1812, while William unshakeably upheld British loyalty against republican violence. The latter was in his own view of loyalty really an Irish Whig: a thorough believer in the constitutional monarchy set up in Britain by the Glorious Revolution of 1688, which had preserved the crown yet placed it under the lawful supremacy of parliament. William stood by loyalty, but to a principle – that of constitutional govern-ment based on representative institutions. By background and ethnic feeling he was not likely to give long support to an Upper Canadian government that came to appear in his eyes as an arbitrary set of official cronies operating with scant heed to the duly elected representatives of the people.

That attitude was only enhanced by the political traditions of his own father. Back in Ireland in his younger years, Robert the Emigrant had been an ardent member of the Volunteers, the patriotic militia force which sprang almost spontaneously into being to defend the Irish homeland from French attack during the wars of the American Revolution, but which went on to become a powerful popular support for a free Irish parliament within the British empire. More than that, during the exciting period at the close of the revolution, when it seemed that Britain might move far ahead with much-needed parliamentary reform, this Robert and a brother had published a widely circulated reformist newspaper in Cork, called the *Volunteer Journal*. Its pages had reported and expounded on the rights of parliament and people, the responsibilities of ministers of the crown. William Baldwin was later to claim that his father's paper had been approvingly spoken of by the great Liberal champion of its day, Charles James Fox.[17] In a sense, then, his own commitment to reform was transferred on from his father. What one Baldwin had commenced in Ireland, another would press forward in Can-ada – just as William's own son, in turn, would take up the liberal political tradition for a third Baldwin generation.

And finally, there was William's assertive sense of his own worth and his aspirations for the Baldwin family. He may have been disappointed in efforts at personal political preferment, though on the whole he had not done badly at government hands in gaining official duties and appointments. But why, in any event, should he seek to curry favour with an official clique to whose members he felt quite equal in wealth and social position, if not superior? A Baldwin could stand on his own name and family, appealing to and supported by the people, making good his right to leadership by championing their rights in turn. This, indeed, was a traditional Whig attitude, and incidentally one which had been well expressed by the English branch of the Russells as a great Whig aristocratic family. As William Baldwin's fortunes rose and the family stature grew, he displayed an ambitious confidence, if not arrogance, which scarcely endeared him to members of the ruling provincial oligarchy and only widened the growing breach between them.

Thus it was that after entering the legislature in 1820, 'the doctor' soon found himself associating with critics of the government, the advance guard of an emerging Reform movement that was voicing popular grievances across the province. These concerned such issues as the control of patronage and revenue, Anglican dominance of education and the clergy reserves, land policy and absentee proprietorship, the rights of non-Loyalist American settlers, and the mounting need for schools, roads, and general public improvements (without increased taxation, of course). This varied set of issues was not the simple consequence of an ill-intentioned, corrupt, or apathetic government, which in fact was striving hard and honestly to cope. Instead, the problems arose far more because Upper Canada was now undergoing rapid and continuing expansion, bringing with it strains and friction, making existing institutional machinery inadequate, and rousing discontents and partisan prejudices that fluctuated back and forth, but in general swelled with the very growth of the province. In such circumstances it was all too natural to blame the provincial administration; yet not always incorrectly, seeing that it remained associated with favouritism and entrenched privilege, had little means of altering, and showed less desire to do so. In fact, it tended to treat expressions of discontent as disloyalty, and usually over-reacted harshly to its adversaries.

Among Reform-minded opponents, a Baldwin hardly had to face imputations of disloyalty, and William was too firmly rooted in York society to be repressed as an upstart troublemaker, as was the case with a number of other outspoken antagonists of the provincial régime. Self-interest and thwarted governmental ambitions were perhaps more effective-sounding charges against him; and, whether true or not, there is no question that self-seeking and ambition for power were not only to be found on the government side in politics. In any event, William Baldwin to some extent became a figure of importance in the early Reform movement because he was far from being a demagogue, and added a decided note of respectability and social worth to the rising cause. His secure status, apart from his undoubted talent, energy, and debating ability, worked to make him a leader in a Reform party that was taking shape by the parliament of 1824.

He was not and never became *the* leader. The party itself was for some time to come not much more than a label, having no organization to speak of and an uncertain, shifting membership both in parliament and country. Nonetheless, during the 1820s a permanent core of Reformers developed in the assembly; newspapers sprang up to deal in Reform policies and principles, and local constituency groups organized themselves to fight elections for candidates regarded as members of a Reform comradeship. Party evolution was assuredly under way; and, on the other side, it would similarly produce a recognized Tory party in support of the existing establishment, the ruling Family Compact.

In the Reform ranks of the mid-twenties William Baldwin was but one of several party worthies to arise, along with the coolly capable Marshall Spring Bidwell and Dr John Rolph, another combined physician-lawyer, of English birth, whose keen intellect and shrewd political skill made him a formidable opponent. And soon that invincibly indignant Scot, William Lyon Mackenzie, would start his own rise to party prominence, though not till after hot-headed scions of the Compact in York had won him much public notoriety and sympathy by their mob assault on the printing office of his vituperative *Colonial Advocate* in 1826. Undoubtedly, too, young Robert Baldwin through his father became associated with the developing Reform leadership element at the capital. Indeed, within a few years John Rolph would refer to the central guiding group as a party 'cabinet' or caucus, while insisting that the junior Baldwin should be deemed a member, 'for he is often in consultation with us in the Session as well as out of it.'[18]

At the same time, Robert was pursuing a deep private concern of his own. He had fallen utterly in love with his cousin Eliza – that is, Augusta Elizabeth Sullivan. They had known each other since childhood; but by 1825, when he was twenty-one and she was seventeen, he was sending her cherishing letters such as this (written at four in the morning): '... every day increases my affection. Every account which we hear either of you or from you makes me more proud of the *choice* of my heart ... When you write do tell me always how your health is, particularly your cough – how often you cough in the course of the day, if at all. You do not know how anxious it makes me ... therefore, for your *own*, for *my* sake, do take care of yourself.'[19] Two years later, in May 1827, Robert and Eliza were married at St James, and went to live at Spadina in his parent's roomy household.

The next year he came into full political view on his own, during the tangled Judge Willis affair and the libel trials of Francis Collins. Reform sentiments were closely involved with these stormy episodes, and Robert Baldwin made his own clear by the prominent part he took. John Walpole Willis was an English jurist of some distinction, and more social pretension, who had come to Upper Canada in 1827 as a justice in the court of King's Bench. Collins was a radical Irish journalist who since 1825 had been publishing the *Canadian Freeman* in York, no less vitriolic than the *Colonial Advocate* in its attacks on the Family Compact. The careers of these two very different individuals became intertwined in a common clash with the ruling provincial authorities. The lofty, dictatorial Willis had soon fallen out with his fellow officials, who gained a jealous dislike of this lordly import from the great world outside. Accordingly, he virtually became a government opponent within officialdom itself, an associate of Dr Baldwin, and a rallying-point for Reformers. Events came to a head in February 1828, when Francis Collins was brought up for libellous utterances in his newspaper by the attorney-general, John Beverley Robinson, and tried before Mr Justice Willis. Collins, however, boldly countercharged Robinson with failing to do his full duty in prosecuting a fatal duelling case of some years previous, in which the solicitor-general, H.J. Boulton, had been a second. It was all decidedly irregular; and the trial degenerated further into irregularity – or chaos – when Willis himself took up the accusation against Robinson. He compelled the dropping of the Collins case and ordered the trial of solicitor-general Boulton instead.

In this latter trial young Robert Baldwin served as prosecutor. It was almost to be expected that his case would fail, since the prime figure in the duel, the winner himself, Samuel Jarvis, had long before been cleared.[20] Robert still did what he could with an abortive cause, and consequently was thrust into the centre of the mounting partisan dispute. Willis, feuding with his fellow justice in the court of King's Bench, next argued that the very operation of the court was illegal in the absence of its chief justice, who was on leave in England seeking his retirement. Robert and John Rolph ceremoniously removed their legal gowns at the court's next meeting in support of Willis's opinion. The attorney-general and solicitor-general gave strong contrary opinions – as might be expected. And so, late in June 1828, an exasperated lieutenant-governor, Sir Peregrine Maitland, dismissed the factious Willis from the bench.

A loud Reform outcry burst forth against this executive assault on the independence of the judiciary. The imperious Willis became a party hero martyred by the government. At a public meeting held in York early in July, chaired by Dr Baldwin, a subscription was launched to present the departing hero with testimonial silverware, while a committee was established to look after his wife's interests till she should follow him, consisting of William and Robert Baldwin and another Willis associate, John Galt, the novelist and founder of the Canada Land Company, himself no friend to Maitland.[21] Moreover, a lengthy petition to the imperial parliament was launched, largely drafted by William Baldwin, which set forth the grievances in Upper Canada, proposed remedies (among which might be found a germ of the idea of responsible government), and urged the recall of Governor Maitland.[22] In forwarding a copy of this document to the colonial secretary in September, Maitland testily declared of its main author, 'with the exception of his son, he is the only person throughout this Province, in the character of a gentleman' associated with such an odious radical scheme.[23] The imperial authorities upheld the dismissal of Willis, however; nor had Maitland really exceeded his authority by his action. Nevertheless, a widespread impression was left that the provincial government had moved despotically and remorselessly to crush an opponent, a view that was reinforced when it again took up a libel charge against Francis Collins.

In October Collins went on trial once more, and Robert Baldwin joined John Rolph in defending him. They argued forcefully and capably; the jury was out five hours, but reached a verdict of guilty.[24] Again the Reformers had only the limited satisfaction of having secured another popular martyr. Still, these highly visible proceedings, however lawfully handled by authority, could well be presented to the public as a contest between free speech and official persecution. Reform sentiment rose further. Moreover, even in defeat, Robert Baldwin had been making a name for himself in the process among the partisans of Reform: as a youthful but robust defender of popular freedom, a true chip off the old block in his dignified stand for liberal, constitutional rights.

It was highly significant, also, that these excited clashes that so held public attention occurred in the midst of the campaigns to elect a new parliament of Upper Canada. It was no less significant that Robert Baldwin should decide to run as well as his father, the former in the County of York, the latter for Norfolk County. Reformers readily carried the elections to the assembly, borne along by the anti-government popular wave, and William Baldwin won Norfolk in a vigorous campaign of stump oratory. Robert, however, failed in York. His inexperience had much to do with it. There was also the fact that one of the four candidates for the county's two seats was William Lyon Mackenzie, and another the well-known wealthy York tanner, philanthropist, and Reformer, Jesse Ketchum: these two took York in the Reform sweep. It should be noted that there was little co-ordination or control as yet in bringing forward party candidates. They might well compete and contend against each other. Furthermore, Mackenzie was himself reported as saying that he would oppose Robert Baldwin's candidacy, because 'I do not like the family.'[25]

Yet there was perhaps another factor in Robert's defeat as well, one noted in friendly criticism by Robert Baldwin Sullivan, his cousin and brother-in-law, who had been helping Dr Baldwin in the battle in Norfolk. Sullivan wrote: 'You were entirely too late [to stand] for your County [Robert's decision had not been taken until the Collins trial in October, and probably with Collins helping to urge it] – and your reserved manner almost the opposite to your favorite Mr. Foxe's way with the people caused you to be comparatively little acquainted with them personally – I do not mean merely as to knowing their names – or having them entered in the docket, but that familiar acquaintance which the people of this country require ... Now I have no doubt of your having public favour and confidence at your command – but it requires time with you, as it will be from real value and worth you will be prized.'[26]

It was a sound judgment from an astute friend. Robert indeed had to learn by experience to deal with his natural reserve and cautious deliberation, which could make him respond too sluggishly in political affairs. Nevertheless, he did learn from this lesson, when the next year he found a chance to try again for parliament. The appointment of John Beverley Robinson to the chief justiceship had opened up a seat for the town of York. Robert announced his candidacy in August 1829, this time well ahead of the polls to be held in November. Campaigning as a known Reformer in home surroundings, and now supported by Mackenzie in the *Colonial Advocate*, he handily defeated his only opponent, his former law-office associate James Small, who ran as an independent. In his victory speech the triumphant candidate declared himself 'a Whig in principle.'[27] Yet his triumph was brief, for the election was declared void, on the ground that the writ calling it had been improperly issued. Determinedly, Robert Baldwin tried again, in a new by-election held on 3 January 1830, against a substantial member of the York official element, Sheriff William Jarvis. Once more he was returned, though by a narrow majority.[28]

Thus on 5 January he formally took his seat in the assembly, introduced and conducted to it by Dr Baldwin and Jesse Ketchum. His apprenticeship years were over; now he was manifestly launched on his own political career. Still, it was symbolic that his father led him to his parliamentary seat. William's lead and sponsorship would yet greatly influence the evolution of Robert's own political position in the days ahead.

He learned his way in the assembly; but through events beyond him Robert Baldwin was only to sit in this house for a single session. In the summer of 1830 George IV died, and as was then the practice at the death of the reigning monarch, parliament had to be dissolved and new elections called. Both Baldwins ran again; yet both were defeated, since now the tide had turned against Reform in one of the repeated fluctuations of that era. One must recall how rudimentary party formations still were in Upper Canada, and that a large mass of voters and many members remained shifting and uncommitted to them. Moreover, to many electors it simply seemed the correct course of action to back the duly constituted government; both as a matter of loyalty, for most abhorred the thought of damaging British allegiance, and as a matter of common-sense, for the government had the money and the patronage to develop the country and make local appointments. Still further, if 1828 had seen an anti-government swing in public feeling, the victorious Reformers had been able thereafter to do little but talk in an assembly with only limited power; and the more unbridled in their parliamentary ranks had lost them sufficient sympathy and raised sufficient doubts to help turn opinion back in the other direction. Finally, a new and more judicious governor,

Sir John Colborne, had taken over from Maitland in 1829. Colborne's own moderating moves had raised popular hopes, while intemperate attacks upon him by Reform intransigents had done the party's cause more harm than good. Accordingly, the assembly that was newly elected in 1830 was decidedly pro-government or Tory-led in character, even though some Reform stalwarts, including Bidwell and the vociferous Mackenzie, had been returned.

It was, nevertheless, a heavy disappointment for the Baldwins, after their intensive political efforts since 1828. They certainly did not lose their connections henceforth with Reform, and remained influential in party circles at York. Still, they were now outside the active political arena, and more largely concerned again with business and family affairs. Both father and son found no lack of legal and property-management duties to attend to over the next few years. William was busy as well with his architectural pursuits, sharing in drawing up the plans of Osgoode Hall, York's handsome new home for the law courts and the Law Society, finished in 1832. He was joint designer of a large town market building on the site of the present St Lawrence Market, which also housed the civic government of Toronto once York became a city under that name in 1834. Furthermore, when in 1834 William's own home of Spadina was destroyed by fire, he planned and built a stately brick mansion on his original Front Street property, in the city's best residential district, and rebuilt Spadina as a smaller country house – completing the former in 1835, the latter in 1836. Nor was this the total of the doctor's 'extra' activities. He helped found the town's Mechanics Institute; and during the severe cholera epidemic at York in the summer of 1832 he worked to the point of illness himself as president of the newly appointed Board of Health.[29]

Robert Baldwin was still the junior partner, transacting legal business, appearing in court, and generally looking after property interests on his father's behalf. Or rather, on their joint behalf, since he was equally involved with the family estate, much of which would ultimately come to him. Moreover, when Aunt Maria Willcocks died in 1834, he became a major inheritor as well as a trustee of her large estate, Dr Baldwin and his wife holding only a life interest.[30] At the age of thirty, in short, Robert was already an affluent lawyer in his own right, with the prospect of much greater affluence ahead. By that date, too, his own family was complete. He and Eliza Baldwin had had four children; Phoebe Maria, born in 1828, William Willcocks in 1830, Augusta Elizabeth in 1831, and another Robert, born in 1834. This new Baldwin clan continued to live at Spadina, until the big house was burned, then moved to the city mansion, with many subsequent returns to the second, smaller country house on the Spadina estate. As well, the Baldwin firm had built an office at the corner of King and Yonge[31] – a promising area – and there Robert became well acquainted with their neighbour and tenant, Francis Hincks, an alert, agreeable young Irishman from Cork, three years his junior, who had settled in York in 1832.

Hincks had set up as a wholesale merchant and rented a Baldwin-owned warehouse. Well trained in business, of a cultivated family background, and a Cork Irish Protestant at that, he was also a convinced liberal in his political views. Clearly, he would go down well with the Baldwins, and they soon gained a strong respect for his intellectual capacities besides. Their ties were further strengthened when he left wholesaling in 1835 to manage the newly formed Bank of the People, a Reform-oriented enterprise of which William Baldwin was a director.[32] The powerful Bank of Upper Canada centred at York had always been closely linked with the government and the dominant Tory oligarchy, though Robert Baldwin was also a substantial shareholder.[33] The new venture was a Reform response, with Rolph and many other party notables on its board. Hincks gave it sound direction. The Baldwins' respect for him only grew, as did the close relations between Robert and Francis, both of whom were essentially moderates in their outlook on Reform party affairs.

By now there had been another parliamentary election, and this time, in 1834, the pendulum swing had put Reform again in a majority position in Upper Canada's assembly. Neither Baldwin ran, however; in fact, the *Colonial Advocate* accused them of having 'left the reformers in the lurch.'[34] They really did not welcome the radical trend in the party, most evident in the growing ascendancy of Mackenzie, which was carrying Reform in directions they could not approve. Mackenzie and his associates seemed to be more concerned with agitation and grievance-mongering than with finding a parliamentary way to remedies. And those remedies they did put forward sounded far too sweeping, endangering the British tie and the very British nature of the constitution, both of which the Baldwins so earnestly upheld.

There was, for instance, the popular Reform demand for an elected Legislative Council, to break the barrier imposed by the appointed upper house, which rejected many assembly bills or amended them out of meaning. To the Baldwins an 'elective senate' was not only foreign to the British constitution, it was unnecessary. The real crux of the matter to them lay in the Executive Council, the core of government: if it could be brought under popular control, one need not worry about the government's dominance of the appointed Legislative Council. Many other radical proposals, moreover, were aimed at adopting American practices – not the least, a written constitution – all at wide variance with the British parliamentary system. In fact, Mackenzie had gone so far by the close of 1833 as to declare that he no longer found the British constitution suitable for the country, but preferred 'a cheap elective, representative government, including both an elected Legislative Council and an elected governor.'[35] That way lay republicanism and a break from Britain. William and Robert Baldwin stood wholly aloof from being associated with such alarming developments.

Instead, they pinned their hopes to the idea of responsible cabinet government on the British model, an outgrowth of the parliamentary system itself. William had been building up that concept for some years past. In the petition he had worked to frame in 1828, following Judge Willis's dismissal, one of the remedies sought for Upper Canada had been the removal of the government's 'advisers from office, when they lose the confidence of the people.'[36] And early in 1829 he had sent the petition to the Duke of Wellington, then prime minister of Great Britain, enclosed with a letter which was much more specific: '... the principle alluded to is this, the presence of a provincial ministry (if I may use the term) responsible to the provincial parliament, and removable from office by his majesty's representative ... especially when they lose the confidence of the people as expressed by the voice of their representatives in the assembly; and that all acts of the king's representative should have the character of local responsibility by the signature of some member of this ministry ...'[37] The next year the doctor drafted further letters to leading British statesmen concerned with colonial affairs on the nature of the local ministerial responsibility required, and the means of extending this British constitutional practice to Canada.[38] In this respect he took Robert's suggestions and advice, so that by now the responsible government doctrine was being formulated by both men.[39] The younger Baldwin came to concentrate on it more and more.

This is not to assert that the Baldwins produced the idea on their own, *de novo*. The notion of local ministerial responsibility was evident in Ireland in the late eighteenth century – and notably in the *Volunteer Journal* produced by Dr Baldwin's own father.[40] The concept was also expressed in Lower Canada before the War of 1812. After all, it was based on a fairly obvious assumption – that what was considered to be the basic pattern of the parliament at Westminster, where governments manifestly rested on majorities in the House of Commons, could some day be extended to British daughter legislatures across the seas. Moreover, by the 1830s in Upper Canada, Reformers were repeatedly talking of responsible rule and a responsible Executive Council.[41] In none of this did William or Robert Baldwin stand alone.

Their fundamental contribution lay rather in their emphasis on the principle of responsible government as *the* great solution, and in their insistent belief that it could and indeed should be applied in a colony as the very means of maintaining the British tie. Unlike other Upper Canadian Reformers, the Baldwins did not spread themselves on a heterogeneous collection of sometimes conflicting remedies. A responsible Executive Council was not just one more thing to be urged (and less so than an elected Legislative

Council), but the prime end to be pursued, which, if gained, could make the rest redundant. For a responsibly-governed Canada, freed from the old unchanging oligarchy, could in due course reform itself in all the ways that the popular will required. And while contemporary British statesmen, from the Duke of Wellington on the Tory right to Lord John Russell on the Whig left, held that a responsible ministry was not feasible in a subordinate colonial legislature – that the ministers of the crown in England were not at all in the same position as the advisers of a Canadian governor dependent on imperial instructions – the Baldwins instead regularly contended that local ministers could be fully responsible for local concerns, advising the representative of the crown and standing or falling by that advice in parliament in the same way that the king's ministers at Westminster were made or unmade by the voice of the House of Commons.

Furthermore, the introduction of their 'great principle' seemed simplicity itself. It involved no drafting of new written constitutions, no complex legislative machinery, no importation of republican and non-British forms, but merely the adoption of the precept that when the Executive Council could not maintain a parliamentary majority behind it, it must resign in a body and let another group take office that could do so. The acknowledgment of this customary British practice would effectively transform an immovable official oligarchy into a responsible political cabinet. It would thus permit colonial self-government without a break in structure or imperial connection, since the people of the province would henceforth control their own affairs through a colonial ministry dependent on the representatives they had elected. No wonder Robert Baldwin became the man of one idea as he strove to put this single basic doctrine into effect; 'imbibed,' as he said of it, from his father, yet in its fully defined and most coherently expressed form, very much his own.[42]

He gained a chance to try to apply his doctrine when, in 1836, a new lieutenant-governor, Sir Francis Bond Head, offered him a place in a remade Executive Council. Late in 1835 the Colonial Office had recalled Governor Colborne, shocked into believing that more must be wrong in Upper Canada than Colborne had reported because of the Seventh Report on Grievances, the giant catalogue of woes which Mackenzie and his radical friends in the assembly had compiled after a rampaging parliamentary inquiry. The newly-appointed governor was a largely unknown quantity, but reputed to have reformist sympathies. Actually, Bond Head's most noteworthy characteristics were endless enthusiasm, for his own opinions, and an energetic busy-ness that had carried him into a variety of pursuits and made him a facile writer of periodical articles and popular travel books. He arrived in Upper Canada, however, supremely confident that he could put matters to right. Though he took a hasty dislike to Mackenzie and his associates as 'implacable' republicans, he sought to widen his Executive Council in order to bring it public support beyond the Compact Tories.[43] To that end he offered seats to John Rolph, J.H. Dunn, a moderate Conservative not closely linked to the Compact, and to Robert Baldwin.

Such an offer no doubt reflected the standing of the Baldwins as prominent Reformers – and as moderates and 'gentlemen' besides. It also indicated Robert's own recognized public stature, despite being out of active politics for several years. The proposal came, however, at a bitterly tragic time for him. His wife Eliza had died on 11 January 1836, just twelve days before Bond Head descended on the province. Robert Baldwin was caught up in a consuming grief that never wholly lifted throughout the rest of his days. He had been married only nine years. They would always seem the happiest of his life. The lively yet delicate Eliza had returned his deep affection, given him the children he delighted in, and been his staunch, confiding companion. She had offset his tendencies to reserve and lethargy, brought out the bright wit and humour that underlay his shyness, warmly understood his sensitivity. He in turn had fussed happily over her health, her interests, her wishes; made his personal life revolve about hers. Now he was a widower before he was thirty-two. He was not to re-marry. He held always to her memory, with emotions that endured.

It might look easy to dismiss such feelings as overdone Victorian romanticism, sentimental role-playing with lockets and locks of the loved one's hair, brooding at appropriate intervals in darkened rooms amid the cherished mementos. of the departed. All this Robert often did; and here one might rather see a sentimentality that merged into morbidity.[44] Yet morbid or not, the emotions ran deep. In a marked degree Robert Baldwin's consciousness continued to revolve about his dead wife. In fact, it was wholly in keeping with his introspective, withdrawn nature that he should constantly thereafter seek refuge in her memory, and maintain his outward appearance of calm composure while inwardly affirming with all the force of his religious convictions that Robert and Eliza would at last be reunited in a better world to come.

In any event, the immediate effect of her death in early 1836 was to bring him to a state of gloomy apathy – and then came Bond Head's invitation. Everything in Robert's make-up sought to be left alone in passive solitude, except for that driving demand of principle and duty that impelled him so often, almost against his will. At first he held out, asserting that his well-known position on government meant that he could not enter the Executive Council unless it became a truly responsible body.[45] But Head, initially a convincing man with his hopeful proposals, argued that Baldwin could more effectively put forward his concept from within the council. The governor's real desire was just to add new names, by no means to open the way for an unworkable, dangerous doctrine. Still, he seldom looked beyond immediate circumstances – thus tending to bounce from crisis to crisis, which he did much to bring upon himself.

Robert was still disinclined. But after earnest consultation with his father, Bidwell, and John Rolph, he finally agreed that the opportunity to make a mark for Reform from within the government was too important to let pass.[46] No one could say what might come from pressing the principle of collective ministerial responsibility from inside the circle of the governor's advisers themselves. Hence, in February 1836, setting aside his own doubts, he took his place in the Executive Council, for the sake of the doctrine and the country.

In office, he proceeded to put forward his own view – that the council was, or should be, a cabinet; should act as one and so be treated. Accordingly, in March he managed to convince the whole group to issue a unanimous request to the governor that they be consulted on all general questions of government policy. This the Tory members of the council were willing to support because they were concerned over Head's failure to seek advice on matters for which the public still might blame them – though they assuredly did not accept the Baldwin concept of responsible rule.[47] Indeed, when Head flatly refused the council's request as beyond their legal powers, its members except for Robert and John Rolph were ready to retract. Seeing a chance for a quick, admonitory victory, the governor insisted, however, that all must retract or resign; and so the executive had forthwith to depart in a body. As a result, they gave the very appearance that Robert had sought, of acting in concert, as a cabinet. They had collectively taken a stand and collectively resigned when it had not been accepted. It was only a beginning step, taken in a defeat; yet it was a useful precedent for the future.

The Reform-led assembly now took the logical next step by passing a motion of no confidence in the newly-appointed Executive Council. Then in mid-April, after a select committee had investigated and truculently reported that the governor had engaged in 'a deceitful manœuvre,' the House took the next successive – if drastic – step of refusing to grant supplies.[48] Head responded to this outright challenge, dissolved parliament and called elections, preparing to put his case before the country as the Reformers did their own. The issue now was running well beyond a matter of responsible government by orderly parliamentary process. Tempers were too high; the extremes on either side were pressing the pace. There would be an all-out battle at the polls, between the claim on one hand that loyalty and the British connection were imperilled by republicans, and the charge on the other that a sinister despotism was destroying the rights of free-born colonists. From the standpoint of Robert and William Baldwin, neither position represented the reality of the question. They had made a little progress with their doctrine, but the times were not right for making more. They would have to wait for more suitable occasions.

They would have to wait, in fact, until the angry storm now rising had reached its peak in the violence of rebellion and exhausted itself in futility. Meanwhile, neither ran in the election of 1836, although Dr Baldwin did head the Constitutional Reform Society, formed to promote responsible government in the campaign, with Francis Hincks as its secretary. But Robert instead left for a prolonged visit to Great Britain, in an effort to overcome the profound depression that had seized him with renewed power once his brief flurry of activity in the government had ended. Moreover, he was to visit the Colonial Office and interview influential British political figures, to impress upon them the critical state of Upper Canada and the one true answer to its problems. Anxious for his son's health, William was no less counting on the mission to win British support for their principle. Robert's children would remain with his parents, where his mother watched over them. At the end of April he left for New York, to take ship for England. He embarked in early May, and after a month's voyage under sail reached Liverpool on 5 June.[49]

The new modern miracle of transport, the railway, took the traveller as far as Manchester. Then it was on by stage coach to London, where he remained until late August. Throughout this time, however, he failed in his main mission. Lord Glenelg, the colonial secretary, would not grant him a personal interview, for Bond Head had urged the danger of recognizing such a prejudicial emissary. Nevertheless, Robert sent letters to Glenelg, setting forth the case and the solution with forceful clarity. The one he dated 13 July 1836 was to prove of crucial significance. It presented a virtual blueprint for responsible government: '... to put the Executive Council permanently upon the footing of a local Provincial Cabinet, holding the same relative position with reference to the representative of the King and the Provincial Parliament, as that on which the King's Imperial Cabinet stands with respect to the King and the Parliament of the Empire.' And it noted that this concept, far from introducing alien, disruptive, or revolutionary influences, 'being an English principle, it would strengthen the attachment of the people to the connexion with the Mother Country; and would place the Provincial Government at the head of public opinion, instead of occupying its present invidious position of being always in direct opposition to it.'[50]

He could do little more than transmit his letters and hope they would be taken seriously at the Colonial Office. But he also met the chief radical or Whig-Liberal sympathizers with the cause of Colonial Reform, such as Joseph Hume and John Roebuck. The former he found cordial in his support and understanding of responsible government. As for the latter, who had close connections with Mackenzie radicalism, he reported, however: 'Mr. Roebuck seems to think the making of the Legislative Council elective

ought to be the great object of Canadian Politicians. An absurdity – if I may
be allowed to say so ... But I was never more satisfied of anything than that
this is merely grasping at the shadow and losing the substance.'⁵¹ Robert
made all the political contacts he could, though he found the widespread lack
of any awareness of Canada a problem. 'At Mr. Hume's, of course, there was
more acquaintance with colonial affairs. At all events they seemed all of
them to know there was such a place as Canada and that it was not in the
Southern Hemisphere.'⁵²

Following his political mission, he went on to Ireland in a private pilgrim-
age to his family's place of origin. He went to Dublin and Belfast, spent two
months at Cork, visited his father's old friends and relations, and was
warmly received by the relatives of Francis Hincks. He did not leave Ireland
till late autumn, in fact, for the country pulled strongly upon him. 'From the
moment I set foot in it I felt at home – The faces seemed more familiar – the
Children seemed more like my own – the accent so soft and agreeable – the
voice of everyone I met sounded like the voice of a friend ... I am prejudiced
and hope I always will be so in favour of this dear land of my parents and of
my own Eliza and if it makes me a worse philosopher I shall be satisfied if it
makes me a better Irishman.'⁵³

Sailing homeward finally in mid-December, Robert reached New York on
27 January 1837, after a violently rough passage; but was not back in
Toronto until 10 February, having visited more connections in up-state New
York.⁵⁴ He soon found conditions in Upper Canada were if anything more
disturbing than when he had left. Tory and Conservative forces had triumphed at the elections of 1836 in another pendulum swing. Bond Head's
fervent calls to defend the government and the British connection from their
rabid foes had won response from an electorate dismayed by the wordy extravagance and radical propositions of Mackenzie and his Reform comrades.
The large Methodist element had apparently swung over, led by their influential spokesman, Egerton Ryerson. Orangemen and the mounting mass of
recent British immigrants had also rallied to the governor against the presumed threat of Yankee-style democracy. The mood had been and remained
impassioned and hotly prejudiced. The administration had pulled out all the
stops to win success. The old and temperate Reform leader, M.S. Bidwell,
himself defeated, wrote bitterly to Robert Baldwin of its 'denouncing every
man as disloyal, a revolutionist, a secret traitor, etc., who happens to differ
with the Provincial government ...'⁵⁵

With Bond Head and Toryism securely in control and making the most of
it, moderate Reformers like Bidwell and the Baldwins standing by perplexed
but powerless, the defeated radical faction of Reform was left in sullen isolation. Condemned as disloyal revolutionaries, some of them as the months
went by took up the part. Sure that they had been wronged, convinced that

the constitution had failed them, they took up the resolve to re-make the constitution and remove the wrongs by non-parliamentary means – by force if need be. Only a portion of what was, in truth, a radical minority seriously entered into the effort. But led by William Lyon Mackenzie, whose over-weening confidence and faulty judgment were about on a par with Bond Head's, an ardent left-wing campaign of agitation was unleashed through the spring and summer of 1837.

Robert Baldwin and his father could only watch uneasily and unhappily, as the state of affairs in neighbouring Lower Canada and the onset of severe economic depression gave new weight and danger to the Mackenzie move-ment. In the lower province a clash was coming to a head between the governing régime and the far more powerful radical forces there led by Louis Joseph Papineau. Radicals in both provinces might well make their thrust in unison, the Upper Canadian element being much encouraged by the existence of seemingly strong allies at their side. Moreover, the depres-sion, which brought a bank crisis to shake Upper Canada, could lead farmers hard hit by low prices and large debts to take out their resentment against the 'money power' upon the government they saw behind it. That fall the situa-tion degenerated steadily. Mackenzie openly called for a display of force, and men drilled in the countryside. In November fighting broke out in Lower Canada, while in secret conclave radicals at Toronto planned a co-ordinate uprising, to be launched in a march on the Upper Canadian capital.

On 4 December several hundred semi-armed insurgents gathered uncer-tainly at Montgomery's Tavern on Yonge Street above Toronto, in a milling confusion of mismanagement. In the city, alarm bells rang out late that night as their presence was made known. Governor Head, only somewhat less well organized than his adversary Mackenzie for armed confrontation, feverishly decided to parley under a flag of truce, to offer the rebels amnesty if they would disperse. Robert Baldwin seemed the obvious person to make the offer, a man clearly not involved with the radicals under arms, but one whose role in Reform would hold their respect. Urgent persuasions brought his reluctant consent, if a trustworthy partner like Bidwell would accompany him.[56] But Bidwell refused, whereupon John Rolph was prevailed upon to join him. What Robert did not know was that the often-devious Rolph was himself involved in planning the rebellion – one of the few mistakes in back-ing a hopeless venture which that acute individual ever made.

In the early afternoon of 5 December Baldwin and Rolph rode forth under a white flag to meet Mackenzie's advancing forces about half-way between the rebel headquarters and Toronto. In a brief, tense discussion, the insur-gents insisted on a written guarantee of amnesty and agreed to halt before reaching the city until a reply had been received. When this was reported to Head, however, he simply withdrew the offered amnesty, for now there was news that loyal militia were gathering.[57] Baldwin and Rolph went out again to the rebels with this decision – and Rolph contrived a quiet word for Mackenzie telling him to go on and attack, since the city was still all but defenceless and unprepared. The attack went forward that evening, but resulted only in a disordered skirmish and the rebels' hasty retreat back up Yonge Street. The next day they were scattered in a counter-thrust at Montgomery's Tavern by strong loyalist forces that had been assembling on the capital. The little Yonge Street rising was over, Mackenzie and his men fleeing for the border, although the repercussions would go on. In any event, Robert Baldwin was left with a dark sense of having been exploited, both by Head and John Rolph. It appeared that duty and honour were not enough. One had to be very careful, too.

In the next few months Tory reaction rose to a peak, as rebels were hunted down and imprisoned, suspected dissidents were seized for trial, and as American sympathizers rallied to Mackenzie's 'patriot' cause across the border. It was a black time for Reformers, even moderates like the Baldwins. They were beyond official attack, but they were still subject to suspicions about their connections. Bidwell was virtually forced into leaving for the United States. Other party leaders prepared to do so; Rolph had wisely fled already. At least there was one gain: Sir Francis Bond Head soon himself departed. In truth, he had already forwarded his resignation even before the rebellion, as clashes over policy steadily mounted between the Colonial Office and himself.

Robert Baldwin might have been out of politics, but as a lawyer he took a conspicuous and self-possessed part in the ensuing political trials, serving as a defending attorney for Reformers brought before the courts, including Dr Morrison, one of the radical leaders in the conspiracy to revolt. March of 1838 brought a new lieutenant-governor, Sir George Arthur, to Upper Canada, whose chief objective was to ensure order and not to change the system. He at least was orderly and experienced, unlike his erratic predecessor. Two months later, however, there was a much more significant arrival, the Earl of Durham, who as governor-general and high commissioner was to investigate the problems which had produced rebellions in the two Canadian provinces. That in Lower Canada had plainly been the more serious and extensive. Durham accordingly spent most of his five-month's stay in the lower province. But his prominent career as an advanced British Liberal gave the Reformers in Upper Canada new reason to hope. When he finally came on to the upper colony in July, they were eager to present their views to him, the Baldwins not the least. Father and son could secure only a brief interview in the great man's crowded schedule.[58] Yet they made their mark upon him, and he invited them to submit their ideas more fully in writing.

William did so in a long screed setting forth twenty-one grievances with four points of solution, one of them his version of responsible government.

But Robert put forward a much briefer, concentrated document, arguing that Upper Canada's problems could be settled by that one principle alone.[59] With this, moreover, he enclosed a copy of the letter of 13 July 1836, which he had sent to Glenelg, and which had been lying at the Colonial Office ever since. This time it reached its proper destination. The lucid, succinct description which his letter gave of responsible government and its operation had a telling effect. Durham till then had been thinking in terms of a federation of all the British provinces as a key solution to colonial troubles. Now he set that aside, and saw responsible government, coupled with a union of the two Canadas, as a necessary answer to the involved colonial question.[60]

In Lord Durham's monumental report which he issued the next year, responsible government stood forth as a leading recommendation. In presenting that idea, moreover, his report so closely echoed passages of Robert's letter of 1836 as to make plain its debt to that document.[61] Yet Durham added his own contribution. He dealt with the question which the Baldwins had never plainly tackled, of how to cope with the problem of having a colonial governor act through locally responsible ministers yet still fulfil his own responsibility to the imperial government. They had relied mostly on faith in the flexibility of British institutions and on mutual good will between colony and Motherland to settle any differences that arose. Durham made a practical division of authority, whereby certain areas such as defence, external relations, and constitutional enactments would still remain under imperial control, whereas in internal colonial matters responsibility would rest with the local ministry. This was a practical solution indeed, since at that time internal affairs were all that the colonists were popularly concerned to manage.

But Durham did more. He gave the powerful endorsement of a leading British statesman and an imperial governor to the idea of responsible government. Henceforth it could scarcely be thrust aside as disloyal or alien. Henceforth not just two local colonial notables, who were not even in the assembly or the government, would stand as sponsors to the concept: it would come under debate in the parliament of the empire with Lord Durham's name upon it, would affect imperial cabinet policy, and certainly the proceedings of the Colonial Office. He effectively put the Baldwin's 'great principle' on a new level, in a whole new sphere of action. Still, nothing alters the fact that behind Durham's advocacy in the report of 1839 lay Robert Baldwin's convincing statement of 1836. If Durham was the Fairy Godfather, Robert remained the Father of Responsible Government.

Meanwhile, before the report was even in the drafting, Robert and his father were roused to new activity in the Reform resurgence that had accompanied the Durham mission in Canada. To raise a strong party voice for the idea of responsible government (and thus help to impress Durham with its popularity), the Baldwins, Francis Hincks, and other leading moderate Reformers of the Toronto circle toured the areas north of the city in the summer of 1838. They had almost a clear field for their concept among party adherents, the radicals, of course, being in retreat, disgrace, or exile. But further to spread understanding and support of the principle, Hincks undertook to establish a newspaper in its behalf in Toronto, where the Reform press had disappeared. In July he began the *Examiner*, the first journal in the province to identify itself with responsible government.[62]

It is clear that Hincks worked closely with his friend Robert Baldwin, both in the decision to launch the *Examiner* and in that paper's campaign, after Durham visited Upper Canada, to convince the populace that 'Mr. Baldwin's principle' was not only right but would probably be adopted. When it did appear in the report of 1839, the Baldwins and Hincks again journeyed to 'Durham Meetings' in the countryside that summer, to applaud the vital recommendation and build party enthusiasm behind it. In consequence, responsible government became a widely popular doctrine, and Robert Baldwin the dominant figure in Reform. His father, growing elderly, was still active, but in a supporting role. It was Robert who had most powerfully presented the doctrine, and who now stood forth as the advocate who would carry it to achievement.

In Britain, the Melbourne government that received Durham's report still denied the feasibility of colonial responsible rule, but was prepared to effect many of his other recommendations for change, and, above all, to carry out a union of the Canadas. To undertake the work of remedy and win acceptance of the union project, they chose a first-rank politician as governor-general, Charles Poulett Thomson, later Lord Sydenham, while at the Colonial Office Lord John Russell amply backed up his endeavours. Thus Thomson came to Canada furnished with despatches from Russell which, firstly, rejected responsible government in principle yet promised to establish harmony between government and assembly, and, secondly, declared that henceforth a governor could change his officials as often as need be for reasons of 'public policy.'[63] This freed the governor's hand from any entrenched oligarchy. It meant the final end of the Family Compact, already fast disintegrating. Accordingly, even though responsible government was not officially to be granted, the new policies spelled a big step forward. And quite possibly Robert Baldwin and his allies could use this more flexible pattern of government, under a politically sensitive governor in search of 'harmony,' to press their principle further forward still.

In November 1839 Governor General Thomson moved on from Lower Canada to the upper province. He made a good impression among Reformers and more moderate Conservatives, intent as he was on beginning a new era in government and economic development. His personal charm and eloquence also had much to do with it. Thomson managed to convince

Reformers that he accepted the responsible system for practical purposes while merely rejecting its formal acknowledgment. What he really wanted was wide support from both parties for the union scheme, but he was prepared to make gestures to suit the occasion, and certainly to effect many long-delayed specific reforms. Moreover, he presented his dispatches as proof that he was empowered to choose for his Executive Council men who would hold the confidence of a majority in parliament, and who in all local affairs would govern in accord with the wishes of the legislature.

In these terms Thomson approached Robert Baldwin in February 1840, offering him the post of solicitor-general in Upper Canada's government. That Reform champion again was full of apprehensions, but again was driven to accept for the sake of his own objective. He felt no confidence in his Tory-Conservative colleagues to be, and told Thomson as much, but the hope of promoting responsible rule under a seemingly favourable governor was too tempting to refuse.[64] On the governor's part, in writing confidentially to Lord John Russell, Thomson showed his own keen appreciation of this new-won appointment: 'the greatest possible *coup*,' 'the best Lawyer in the province,' 'the man most esteemed and looked up to by the whole of the Reformers of Upper Canada, and [who] carries that party with him altogether.'[65]

Having gained the broad endorsement of both moderate Reformers and Conservatives, leaving only right-wing Tories and hard-core radicals aside, Thomson had successfully completed his immediate tasks in Upper Canada. The union project was accepted by the legislature; even a new compromise clergy reserve settlement was carried. The governor general returned to the lower province to await the imperial measure which would now proceed to establish a United Province of Canada. The Union Act was accordingly passed by the British parliament in June 1840, to be proclaimed early the following year. An age indeed was ending for Upper Canadians. And in general, like Robert Baldwin, they looked with mingled doubts and apprehension, but still more hope, to the new era that was opening.

By now he was thirty-six, a tall man, but round-shouldered and heavily built, so that the impression he gave was more of steady solidity than of imposing height. His eyes were hooded, his countenance gravely impassive, his manner sedate and dignified. His style of speaking was intricate, though carefully thought out – at times wittily perceptive, but seldom eloquent. He would not play to a crowd. And in his constant concern for rationality unshaded by emotion he guarded himself jealously, as he said, 'lest my judgement be misled by my wishes.'[66] How could such an individual as Robert Baldwin gain and hold wide public support, become a leader in the rough-and-ready politics of a turbulent North American colony? The only answer is force of character and the power and clarity of his principle. He inspired trust:

his conviction and his purpose seemed beyond question. In the shift and turmoil of Upper Canadian political tides Baldwin was an unmoved rock. Plainly he did not seek office for office's sake and needed no personal favours. Besides, if he was cautious and essentially conservative in temperament – seeking to build on precedents, not overturn them – Upper Canada, for all the passing effusions of radicalism, was just as basically cautious and conservative in its broadest attitudes. Baldwin, after all, was the right Ontario leader for the right moment, to carry through a revolution to responsible rule in the most ordered and non-revolutionary way possible.

Now he held a place in government again, and might expect to retain it once a united administration was set up for both Canadas, when the Union Act had taken effect. Yet now, as well, he had to raise his eyes to enlarged horizons, embracing the eastern half of the projected union, old Lower Canada. As the 1840s commenced he began to look in that direction, towards French-Canadian Reform allies with whom he could work in the political life of a united province. As Canada was itself, Robert Baldwin was entering a new phase – and for him, it was to be the climactic period of his career.

Francis Hincks showed the way. As early as April 1839 he had opened correspondence with the prominent and powerful Lower Canadian Liberal, Louis Hippolyte LaFontaine, to promote joint action by the Reformers of both Canadas within a united parliament. There, he pointed out, the combined Reform forces would be in a strong majority that could press for responsible government. Once this was gained, French Canadians would share in ruling, and would be able to overcome features of the union scheme they deeply disliked, whereas any efforts to block it or to create a separate French state were bound to fail. LaFontaine listened. A former supporter of Papineau, he had not participated in the latter's abortive rebellion. Yet he was a wholehearted defender of the rights of French Canadians and understood their detestation of a union that was intended to submerge and ultimately assimilate them as a people. At the same time, discerningly realistic in his outlook, he recognized that if union could not be prevented by constitutional means (and it could not), it must be endured and worked with. Hincks' approach offered a way by which it might be utilized to advantage by a firm French-Canadian block co-operating with western allies. Without as yet clearly comprehending all the implications and requirements of a stand on responsible government – and naturally always first devoted to the interests of French Canada – LaFontaine grew ready to accept the principle and to shape a party alliance for the future.

His correspondence with Hincks expanded in volume and depth; gradually Robert Baldwin was drawn into it as the leading Upper Canadian exponent of the responsible principle. By November 1840 Baldwin himself was writing earnestly to his future Lower Canadian colleagues about the objectives of a Reform alliance: 'There is and *must be no question of races* – It were madness on one side and guilt, deep guilt, on both, to make such a question. But, my dear Sir, while the Reformers of Upper Canada ... are resolved, as I believe them to be, to unite with their L.C. Brethren cordially as friends and to afford them every assistance in achieving Justice *upon precisely the same footing* in *every* particular *as ourselves*, it is to be assured not by the adoption of a course of proceeding leading necessarily to collision and tending to stop unavoidably the whole machinery of the Constitution ... but on the contrary [by looking] to the harmonious working of the Constitution itself, by means of the new principle ...'[67]

By this time campaigns were already getting under way for the parliamentary elections to be held once Union came into operation. In his own constituency of Terrebonne in Lower Canada LaFontaine declared his support for 'this English principle of responsible government.'[68] In Upper Canada Robert Baldwin was asked to run in several constituencies, but finally decided to stand for two, the North, or Fourth, Riding of York, a secure Reform stronghold, and a more challenging one, Hastings, where his chief opponent was actually a cousin by marriage. Indeed, a number of the Baldwin connections were often to be found in the Tory-Conservative camp, including both his uncles, Captain Augustus Baldwin and John Spread Baldwin.

In the ensuing elections, after the Union of the Canadas was proclaimed in February 1841, Baldwin took Fourth York handily and Hastings after a hard battle. Francis Hincks was himself elected for Oxford, while Reformers and government supporters generally swept Canada West, the Upper Canadian half of the Union, with only a handful of Tory oppositionists gaining seats. In Canada East the French-Canadian Reformers inevitably composed the largest parliamentary contingent, but LaFontaine was not among them. He had retired from the elections in the face of threatened violence, the result of the governor's flagrant efforts to keep down the number of French Canadians returned, since they remained his most inveterate opponents. Lord Sydenham (for such Thomson now was) had indeed sought previously to win LaFontaine over, as a key to the support of the French-Canadian political bloc, and to that end had offered him a place in the Union government. LaFontaine had rejected the offer, lest he appear as a *vendu*, a sell-out to his *Canadien* compatriots.[69] It was a problem, of course, that Baldwin had not faced on his own entrance to Sydenham's administration, since the same strong racial overtones and implications were absent in the Upper Canadian case. Nevertheless, Baldwin's hopes rested first on the 'harmonious working of the Constitution' by the new principle, not on an outright anti-government position 'leading necessarily to collision' against which he had counselled LaFontaine, but which course the latter had apparently still adopted.

In the enlarged council that was named in February when the Union began, Robert Baldwin still sat as solicitor-general for the western section, while the attorney-general west continued to be William Draper, the capable Conservative whom Sydenham had used to good effect in carrying his union programme through the old Upper Canadian legislature. Robert Baldwin Sullivan also held a council seat, though as a Conservative; for this Baldwin's brother-in-law had made his own resourceful way in law and politics since leaving Dr Baldwin's legal office, and had risen on the Tory side. In sum, it was a 'mixed ministry' that contained three western Reformers and two western Conservatives, along with eastern British Tories and non-partisan civil servants. Such a ministry – as now it might well be called, since the old loosely organized Executive Council had been formed into a definite group of departmental heads or ministers – was designed by the governor general to give him the widest possible popular backing. Drawn from various party elements, it could provide him with a moderate, middle-ground majority in parliament that left out only the right-wing Upper Canadian Tories and the Lower Canadian French. For Sydenham's aim was to be his own prime minister, conducting a coalition, all-party government with broad support in the assembly, thus assuring harmony between executive policies and the votes of the elected representatives.

It was not Baldwin's aim, however. He looked for a Reform majority in parliament, and thus, in keeping with his principle, for an all-Reform government in office. Once the new Union administration was formed, and even before the elections had been held, he therefore sounded out the way. He protested to Sydenham his 'entire lack of confidence' in the freshly appointed ministry, except for its Reform members, and his 'almost nervous anxiety' lest his own position seated beside former party foes be misunderstood.[70] The governor general brushed the protest aside, telling Baldwin that there would be time enough to discuss conflicting opinions in the council when they arose there. Obviously, Sydenham had no desire to yield a coalition he could control to a party cabinet he could not – nor to recognize the principle of responsible rule implicit in Baldwin's plea. Equally, the latter had found by his probing that the governor was not inclined after all to go further towards the responsible principle and that perhaps the working of the constitution might yet have to become inharmonious. For the time being the matter remained in abeyance, since Sydenham needed the Baldwin Reform support at the elections, and Baldwin did not want to risk a rupture that might throw the governor towards the Tories, allowing them again to claim at the polls that they were the only true defenders of the crown.[71] But trouble was laid up for the future, once the composition of parliament had been determined.

It was to meet at Kingston, new capital of the United Province, in June 1841. That spring, as the preparations were made, Baldwin and Hincks conferred closely about the prospects of the desired Reform alliance in the assembly. There was the problem that the French were scarcely likely to work in effective unison with Baldwin as long as he continued in the administration of a governor whom they deeply distrusted. The time had come, then, for a showdown. But it was only after racked and sleepless nights that Robert faced the prospect (as he told his father), since all his sensitivity recoiled from facing an open break with the politically adroit and ruthless Sydenham.[72] He had as well his ingrained respect for the office of the crown's representative, and his inherent hope of harmony in colonial dealings with imperial authority. Still, the demands of principle were inexorable. On 12 June, just before parliament met, he pronounced to the governor general that since the 'United Reform Party' clearly held the bulk of parliamentary support, the Conservative members of the government had necessarily to be replaced, and, above all, by Lower Canadian French Reform representatives.[73]

This was not only a call to admit the French-Canadian bloc to office; it was a plain demand for a party cabinet and the operation of the responsible system. Sydenham responded decisively, reprimanded Baldwin for 'dictating to the Crown' in a most unconstitutional way, and accepted his resignation 'without the slightest regret.'[74] The battle lines were drawn. Baldwin was out of office after some fifteen months; but in so retiring he had forced Sydenham to declare himself, and had confirmed to the French Canadians that he stood by the alliance and the doctrine. His father wrote to him: 'Your dear Mother rejoices in the honest part that you have taken, and why should not I? Be assured, my dear Robert, I heartily approve of your resignation, and the consolation you feel in doing your duty is a reward beyond price ... Your dear child, Maria, read your letter with great emotion. They are all endearing children ... and join your Mother and myself in love and anxiety for you.'[75]

On his side the governor general counted on the wide degree of popularity he had assuredly won for himself as a constructive, energetic leader eager to get on with concrete problems of development: ready to govern in practice through the assembly's support, without a finicky insistence on a theoretical principle. Many moderate Reformers as well as Conservatives were in fact quite satisfied with Sydenham's version of responsible government. Moreover, in his speech at parliament's opening, the governor set forth a tantalizing programme of specific reforms and improvements, and backed this up with the glowing announcement of an imperial guaranteed loan which would lift the burden of public debt and allow work on the canalization of the St Lawrence route to go forward. Sydenham proved right in counting on his well-prepared position. When the votes were taken in the house, it was clear that the bulk of Upper Canadian Reformers had departed from Baldwin and endorsed the government, leaving only Hincks and a few other so-called 'ultras' standing with him and the French Canadians in a Reform opposition to Sydenham's ministry. The party alliance had failed in its first test – at the Upper Canadian end.

As the session went on, it also became apparent that Francis Hincks was in danger of being captured by the governor general. A keenly practical politician himself, and strongly interested in economic growth and efficient government, Francis was ready to treat Sydenham's measures on their merit, since Reform unity had broken down in any case. As he spoke and voted increasingly on the other side from Robert Baldwin, a rift grew between them which never fully healed. Despite their later political reconciliation, the man of principle would not wholly depend on the man of strategy again.[76]

In any case, Baldwin kept hard after the ministry, which by no means had things all its own way. Sydenham constantly had to use his best skill in management to keep assembly support behind his government and prevent the Upper Canada Reformers shifting back to Baldwin. In September, moreover, that champion of responsible government found an opportunity to move a series of resolutions on the subject which directly challenged the governor and could bring his ministry to defeat if it openly rejected them. Instead, through Samuel Bealey Harrison, the leading western Reformer in the government, an amended version of the resolutions was put forward which Baldwin accepted as 'substantially the same' and which the house duly passed.[77] Apparently the governor general had won again – as he thought – in staving off the responsible doctrine through a watered-down and vaguer statement. But had he? In actual fact, he had given Reform the claim, to be reiterated in the future with increasing moral fervour, that responsible rule had been solemnly acknowledged as existent in parliament in 1841. When Sydenham died a few weeks later, through a fatal riding accident, his system was already on its way to failure, although in his own optimistic self-confidence he never realized it.

Still further, as the session was drawing to a close, Baldwin made a dramatically effective move to consolidate the Reform alliance with French Canada – by making a place for LaFontaine in the assembly through getting him an Upper Canadian seat. Since Robert had decided to represent Hastings himself, it had been agreed that his father (now in his later sixties) should try for the strongly Reform Fourth York constituency which the son had also won. Robert now wrote from Kingston to his father to suggest that LaFontaine be offered the nomination instead.[78] William readily concurred, undertaking to promote the project in the riding himself. Grateful if uncertain, LaFontaine came to Toronto to stay with the Baldwins, where he proved a most agreeable (and bilingual) guest. He and the doctor toured North York and found conditions favourable. Robert put up fifty pounds towards campaign expenses, and offered more: 'In fact, let it be what it may,' he told

William, 'he must not be defeated.'[79] Later in September the unusual candidate was easily victorious in Fourth York. As William reported to his son, '... not a word of opposition was uttered anywhere – the meetings were generally thin in consequence of getting in the harvest, except at Sharon and Stouffville, at those places the meetings were full ...'[80] In any event, through Robert Baldwin, his essential Lower Canadian partner and co-champion of responsible rule had been given entry to the Union's parliament.

In October it became known that the new Peel Conservative government in England had appointed as Sydenham's successor Sir Charles Bagot, a distinguished veteran diplomat of polished charm and judicious insight. While awaiting his arrival and the reconvening of the legislature under his authority, Baldwin and LaFontaine, now back in Toronto and Montreal respectively, kept up their contacts by letter, developing their partnership and refining its position as they exchanged political views; for one thing, on how to deal with Bagot: 'As to Governors [wrote Baldwin in December] it is I think not only idle but mischievous to ... profess to rely upon or look to them. Upon our own principles they are to look for their advisors from among those possessed of the confidence of Parliament, and if the country requires a change in the Councils of the Crown it is through Parliament that they must look for it. As to the G[overno]r G[enera]l I think it is due to him as the Representative of the Sovereign to pay him all the respect and afford him all the constitutional support in our power – but that I look upon as altogether a different thing from supporting the Provincial administration, which remains and will remain unchanged until Parliament pronounces upon it.'[81]

The provincial administration did continue largely as Sydenham had left it, with Draper and S.B. Harrison as its leading members. But after Sir Charles Bagot arrived early in 1842, he soon set about trying to strengthen it, recognizing how shaky was its hold on an assembly majority which his predecessor had only gained and kept through much manoeuvring. The new governor sought to maintain the Sydenham system. Indeed, he was instructed to do so by the colonial secretary, now Lord Stanley. He was to govern in his own right, through a coalition non-party ministry that had the assembly's backing. Yet Bagot was not prepared to accept Sydenham's methods, as he told Stanley in confidence: 'the unscrupulous personal interference ... combined with practices that I would not use';[82] and he saw spreading defection and reviving opposition that could only be checked by enlarging the basis of government support. In particular, he wanted to win over the French Canadians, realizing how adversely they had been treated under Sydenham and how much abused they felt by the Union that had meant to submerge them as a distinct community. By personal effort and official appointments he considerably mollified *Canadian* feelings and gained their respect. But he could not crack their party front or bring individual French Canadians into the eastern half of his government.

Bagot had better luck in widening its western half. From the Upper Canadian Tories he drew in Henry Sherwood, mayor of Toronto. He did so rather than deal with Sir Allan MacNab, by now the most forceful western Tory politician, who had built a military reputation of strenuous loyalty in putting down the Upper Canada rebellion, but acquired a political taint of demagoguery and double-dealing in his unabashed quests for power and preferment. From the Reform side, moreover, the governor gained Francis Hincks to be inspector-general or finance minister, an office Sydenham had earlier had in mind for him. Hincks declared that he still held to his party principles, but his breach with Robert Baldwin was decisively confirmed.[83] By this time it was June. Parliament was being held off longer than Bagot had intended, as he strove with increasing concern to improve his governmental position. And the session could not be delayed much further.

Throughout this process of ministerial negotiations and delay Baldwin stayed calmly hopeful, offering his carefully reasoned counsels to LaFontaine on the situation before them. 'With respect to Bagot,' he wrote, 'I am glad that he is popular. It indicates a belief that he has personally no prejudices against us and I think it desirable that henceforth under all circumstances we should so act towards the head of the Government as not to excite in him any prejudices ...'[84] As to the French Canadians, he observed that the 'great and constant cry' against them was that they would not give support to any administration, and if any of them did enter a government, they would lose the confidence of their associates, 'who would remain as hostile as ever.' Furthermore, this feeling was strong among the Lower Canadian Reformers themselves, much as he would personally like to see them enter into government as a body. But if they should do so as the supporters of '"The Gr Gl" and not as the supporters of "the Provincial administration," in my opinion more ultimate harm than immediate good will grow out of it. To enable them to become its supporters ... that administration must be placed on a footing to deserve their confidence. The proper and far the most beneficial means of arriving at such a result would be the dissolution of the present Cabinet as a Cabinet and the construction of a new one. Nor would such in my opinion *necessarily* lead to the services of *all* the present ministers being dispensed with. A second course would be the reconstruction of the present Cabinet without a formal dissolution of it.'[85]

As Baldwin projected his own game-plan, the hard realities were increasingly borne in on Bagot. That summer his most percipient ministers, Draper and Harrison, separately advised him that the Executive Council had not been sufficiently rebuilt. The only way they saw to avoid its defeat in parliament was to gain the support of the French-Canadian party. The Conservative ministers might have to resign, if need be, to enable Robert Baldwin to be acquired also; for if French Reform leaders were to join the ministry, they might well be expected to stipulate that their chief western ally should enter it as well. In consequence, an uneasy Bagot warned the colonial secretary that he might have no alternative but to undertake to bring the French Canadians into his ministry as a group, once parliament had finally opened.[86]

When it did so on 8 September, the government's perilous position was immediately apparent, as a vigorous LaFontaine made good his ascendancy over the eastern Reform members, western Reform strength flowed back to Baldwin, and both leaders prepared for a vote of confidence that seemed certain to go against the ministry. Before that issue could come to debate, Bagot acted to head it off. He sent for LaFontaine on 10 September, to ask on what terms French Canadians would agree to enter the Executive Council: not as individuals – as putative *vendus* – but as representatives of their party and people. LaFontaine gave the reply that was necessary to affirm the responsible principle and the Reform alliance. He asked for four government places, in keeping with party strength, one of them for Robert Baldwin.[87] That partnership which Baldwin had worked to build up would thus be sealed by LaFontaine securing his admission to office.

The governor general balked at these strong terms, especially at the admission of the man most fully identified with the responsible system and the least inclined to accept the half-way, all-party system of 'harmony' established under Sydenham. The discussions with LaFontaine see-sawed back and forth in the next few days. But they were decisively renewed, when Bagot's own ministers advised him that if they were defeated in the assembly they felt bound to resign in accord with the Harrison-Baldwin resolutions of 1841, and when Baldwin himself forced on the pace by launching a no-confidence motion in the house. To save what he could of his position, the governor, through Draper, disclosed his final offer in parliament on the night of 13 September. He would accept Baldwin and three Lower Canadian Reformers into the council, but keep the Conservative Sullivan, the Reformers Harrison and Hincks, and other independent non-political members of the ministry still in office.[88]

By this move Bagot won backing for what was in any case a strikingly large concession. He thus avoided the certain parliamentary defeat of his government and its all-but inevitable replacement by a complete Reform administration headed by LaFontaine and Baldwin. There would still be a mixed ministry under the governor, not one imposed on him by outright parliamentary action. He had indeed saved something. Yet his opponents had gained much more. They had secured a commanding Reform presence in the reconstructed government (which the assembly now happily endorsed) and the initiative had really moved into their hands. Above all, they had made the Reform alliance work. Baldwin's counsels and LaFontaine's actions had together given their followers an administration 'placed on a footing to deserve their confidence.'

The new ministers moved into the council, the former Tory-Conservative members moved out, and all was settled by late September. Baldwin was now attorney-general west, as LaFontaine was attorney-general east, and each had to face the by-election then required of a minister on taking office. Robert, however, was beaten in his constituency of Hastings early the next month by an indignant Conservative resurgence, one that ended in a violent battle at the polls in which troops had to be called out. Since the legislature closed shortly afterwards, he had no immediate need to find another seat. But the new one that was subsequently offered to him was another noteworthy demonstration of the workings of Reform alliance. This time LaFontaine (who had been re-elected in Fourth York) returned the favour by opening a seat in Canada East for his colleague, in the thoroughly French constituency of Rimouski. In January 1843 Baldwin was triumphantly acclaimed by a *Canadien* electorate who knew the reputation if not the man. In fact, he soon made a strong impression on Rimouski. LaFontaine was later to tell him, in words that were not just flattery, that not another candidate there, 'nor myself, nor even Papineau himself, could be returned in opposition to you.'[89]

Meanwhile, the reconstructed government under Bagot had taken on a coherent character of its own, which was distinctly Reform in colour. The errant Hincks came back to the party mainstream. He was assuredly too talented and valuable to be left aside, and Baldwin agreed to keep him in office.[90] Harrison, the leading Sydenham Reformer left in the government, shortly thereafter resigned and withdrew from public life. James Small, who had been both Baldwin's ally and opponent in earlier Upper Canadian days, now sat as his reliable supporter in the council. Other surviving ministers, like J.H. Dunn and R.B. Sullivan, gradually moved into the Reform camp, leaving only the Lower Canadian long-term civil servant, Dominick Daly, as a non-party member in the Executive Council. Moreover, the elderly governor general fell seriously ill – in truth, he was exhausted and dying – and his hand was largely removed from the direction of public affairs. His relations with his remade council were excellent: he trusted them; they returned a sincere respect. Yet for all practical purposes, Canada was being governed in Bagot's final months of office by a virtual Reform cabinet under LaFontaine and Baldwin.

In March 1843, however, another governor general took over and faced the ministry: Sir Charles Metcalfe, an experienced colonial administrator with a substantial record of achievement both in India and the West Indies. At first, relations between Metcalfe and his council seemed to run smoothly, but a sense of trouble looming grew on either side. Metcalfe was again under instructions from Stanley to rule through ministers who held a parliamentary majority behind them – but, above all, to be the active head of his own administration and not necessarily to be bound by his ministers' advice. Stanley clearly felt that Bagot had yielded too much; the balance had to be restored. Metcalfe not only agreed, and sought faithfully to fulfil his orders; he also had no affinity for the kind of politics that stemmed from a broadly democratic colonial society. He was used to possessions ruled from above, and viewed Canadian popular parties and their leaders as disruptive factional interests that sought to undermine imperial authority. He set out to halt the drift, as he saw it, to full responsible government, an unwanted system based on the extravagant (or disloyal) assumptions of his Reform ministers. In so doing, Metcalfe wholly believed that he was only defending the governor's just rights, and rising as an impartial arbiter above self-seeking party. But whatever his intentions, he was on a collision course, expecting trouble and soon finding it.[91]

The main issue that emerged concerned patronage. This power to appoint to posts under the government, from low to high, officially rested with the governor, but there was no question that the Reform ministers wanted to see it exercised for party purposes, just as their predecessors had always sought to have public offices filled with political friends. Baldwin might argue that ministers could hardly be responsible in parliament for policies if they could not rely on those who carried them out. LaFontaine would seek to give his *Canadien* compatriots the due share of administrative positions from which previously they had been excluded. But Metcalfe could respond, first, that ministers owed responsibility to him, and, second, that he could not yield the governor's prerogative right of appointment to mere partisan purposes, since his final impartial authority had to be maintained. The issue brewed and bubbled through the spring and summer, while the governor general cast out lines both to Tory-Conservatives and to possible French-Canadian alternatives to LaFontaine, connections which might enable him to escape from the 'domination' of his present Reform advisers.[92]

When the assembly met again that fall, the Baldwin-LaFontaine ministers set forth an active legislative programme, some of which, however, roused considerable objections beyond the house. The capital was moved from Kingston to the broader facilities of Montreal – which brought complaints in Canada West of undue French influence over the ministry. Baldwin carried a Secret Societies bill, essentially aimed at reducing the power of the Orange Order to unleash political violence and influence elections, but it equally did not make him friends among Orangemen in general: Metcalfe made some instead by reserving the bill. And Baldwin also brought forward a University bill that notably angered western Anglicans, even if strong elements in

Upper Canada approved it, including Ryerson and the Methodists. This measure planned to change Upper Canada's provincially-endowed yet Anglican-dominated King's College into a secular University of Toronto, with which religiously based colleges might affiliate, but as little more than divinity schools. The scheme foreshadowed the future, but the bill never came to a final vote, since the gathering clash with Governor Metcalfe over patronage now broke out in the open.

Through the autumn Metcalfe had been dealing with official appointments as he saw fit, on occasion not even informing Baldwin or LaFontaine, and offering the important post of Speaker of the Legislative Council to their party opponents. Hence they protested to him bluntly that he should not propose appointments without the Executive Council's advice, or make any against its interests. He no less bluntly refused this 'virtual surrender into the hands of the Council of the prerogative of the Crown.' On 26 November, in consequence, all the ministry resigned, except for Dominick Daly. Baldwin contended that a governor's use of patronage without or against the council's advice denied the responsible principle accepted in the Harrison-Baldwin resolutions.[93] Metcalfe replied that the only issue was whether the crown's patronage should be used to buy assembly support.[94] (That indeed had been done by Sydenham: the real issue, apparently, was who should do the buying!) At any rate, an assembly still firmly dominated by Reformers west and east passed emphatic resolutions expressing continued confidence in the governor's ex-ministers. In the face of such hostility Metcalfe prorogued parliament, to gain time to reconstruct his ministry before facing the assembly again.

That effort went on through the opening months of 1844, as William Draper rallied to the governor's side and others, too, sought to overcome the political grasp of the Baldwin and LaFontaine forces. But for the moment Robert Baldwin was again caught up in a personal sorrow. On 8 January his father died at sixty-eight, after a year of declining health. Appointed to the Legislative Council a few months before, William had never been able to take his seat; yet he remained cheerful, kindly, and keen-minded even as he failed physically. Robert wrote to Louis LaFontaine at his death: 'I had seen his gradual decay and the certain termination was daily before my eyes but my mind was occupied by the attentions which I was able to pay to him; but when this was over and all I had to dwell on was the past – that past which brings him back to my memory as one of the kindest parents and best of men, it seems as if I could scarcely realize it ... And you, my dear friend, will not, I am sure, be surprised at my feeling little able to return at once to any other subjects and least of all to politics, from which, if I could with honour, I would fly forever.'[95] LaFontaine's reply was warm: 'If you were conversant with my native language, or if I could express myself in your own as well as I can in French, I would not fail, I am sure, in conveying to you the deep and painful feelings which were produced on my mind when ... I heard of your good and venerable father's death. I liked him as if he had been one of my *parents*.'[96]

Shattered by his loss, Robert Baldwin at first tried to retire. But again he was prevailed upon by arguments that this would be ruinous to the party's leadership in a time of continued crisis. He still had his duty – the more so now – to carry on with what his father had begun. Resolutely, he entered into the movement to organize popular sentiment in Canada West once more behind the cause of responsible government. The need was to combat Metcalfe's claim, increasingly taken up by Tories and Conservatives, that the choice lay between scheming partisans greedy for offices and an unbiased upright British governor – who rather seemed to be emerging as the effective head of Tory-Conservative partisans himself. Baldwin accordingly welcomed the vigorous press support of an aggressive young Reform advocate lately come to Canada, George Brown, who in March began his Toronto *Globe* as a party organ. He also backed Francis Hincks's move to Montreal to found a strong Reform journal in English at the new capital – the *Pilot*. Moreover, he spoke widely across the province in the ensuing months denouncing 'the Irresponsible System,' the 'Compact System.'[97] In general, Baldwin counted on the force of popular opinion to defeat the governor's contrivings. 'If the people look to any quarter but themselves for ultimate triumph,' he declared, 'they will be disappointed.'[98]

The contest for public opinion rose to clamorous heights, as Draper strove in Canada West and Denis-Benjamin Viger, a notable old Papineau associate, in Canada East to rebuild a ministry for Metcalfe. Theirs was a strange alliance of opposites. While Draper by deepest conviction sought to uphold the governor and prevent the further erosion of the British tie, Viger ultimately looked for a separate French-Canadian republic. But in the meantime he was willing to work with Metcalfe against the LaFontaine forces who accepted both the alien British responsible principle and an English-French partnership in a common state. Together this odd couple began to put together a government based on anti-LaFontaine, anti-Baldwin reactions, but it was a tortuous endeavour that took until September to complete. Only then did Metcalfe finally dare to dissolve the prorogued parliament and call an election, hopeful that his Draper-Viger ministry could hold a majority in a new assembly.

Actually, in Upper Canada, at least, the Metcalfe forces had made considerable headway. Vehement Reformers had done what Baldwin always counselled against – attacked the person of the governor instead of the failings of his ministers; and so indeed had strengthened the feeling among moderates that the imperial representative and British tie were being dragged down in partisan abuse. Many came to believe with Metcalfe's champions that lust for the spoils of office, not the responsible doctrine, was the real drive behind the Reform campaign. Egerton Ryerson himself came out powerfully in print during the summer in the governor's defence, and R.B. Sullivan's published letters in reply, while often wittily devastating, were perhaps too clever by half. Finally, there was the fact that the late Reform ministers had put forward a number of measures that had aroused considerable animosity in Canada West. All these consequences came home at the elections in the fall of 1844.

They were angrily waged in Upper Canada. Baldwin won Fourth York (LaFontaine had gone back to his old riding of Terrebonne), but only after turbulent encounters, as when he was pursued by a mob of club-wielding Orangemen and barely managed to outdistance them on horseback.[99] Hincks, however, was beaten in Oxford, Dunn in Toronto. The Reformers, in general, did badly in Upper Canada, where a strong pro-Metcalfe majority of Tories and Conservatives was returned against them. Fortunately for the Reform cause, LaFontaine and his followers carried Lower Canada; for here the Viger group could make little progress against the former's clear achievements for the *Canadiens*. Hence Metcalfe, Draper, and Co gained only a small margin in the Union elections as a whole. Nevertheless, it was plain that Baldwin had not yet convinced sufficient middle-ground Upper Canadians that insisting that the governor general take his ministers' advice on all internal matters was inherent in the British doctrine of responsible government, and not a disloyal threat to the British tie itself.

LaFontaine was much disgruntled by the failure of his western allies, though Baldwin was his usual calmly circumspect self.[100] When parliament met in Montreal in November, moreover, it became apparent from the start that the new ministry's majority was decidedly narrow. In the opening test, the selection of the Speaker of the assembly, the ministerial candidate, Sir Allan MacNab, won by only three votes over LaFontaine's chief eastern lieutenant, Augustin-Norbert Morin. As for William Henry Draper, holding only a slim parliamentary majority behind him, with considerable strains between Tory and Conservative factions in his own section, and critically weak in French Canada where Viger was still failing to do much to improve matters, he had to chart a wary course as operative leader of the government. The compromise Upper Canada University bill he brought forward had to be dropped under the threat of revolt by his own western Tory supporters. Displaying a good deal of skill and courage, Draper yet managed to do little more than survive until the session ended in March 1845.

He did, however, have the governor's full confidence as a firm defender of his own views, while Metcalfe himself was succumbing to the relentless spread of cancer which was finally to kill him. Accordingly, Draper was left all but free to become the effective head of the government – a premier in fact, if not in recognition. Of course, this had largely happened to LaFontaine and Baldwin as co-leaders of the administration in Bagot's dying months. Yet now it had happened again; and this time it went on longer, and went further. Above all, to keep his thin parliamentary majority, Draper had to use government patronage to the hilt, while Metcalfe of necessity let him do so. The irony was that what had been refused to Reform champions of the responsible principle had now been conceded to Tory-Conservatives who rejected the theory but carried out its practical application without any imputation of disloyalty. It would be difficult, if not impossible, to reverse the results henceforth.

What had actually occurred by the time Metcalfe went home to die in November 1845 was that a party premier and cabinet were dispensing patronage and maintaining themselves in office, dependent on a parliamentary majority that was controlled (if barely) by the chief minister in the government. In short, responsible government, party rule, and the premiership were all practically in being. Robert Baldwin's opponents had nearly carried the day for him – he might well afford to stay calm. Of course, none of this was yet acknowledged doctrine, and the imperial authorities would not then have accepted it in any case. Yet Baldwin could comment at the time to LaFontaine: 'I have as you know great faith in the ultimate triumph of sound principles ... And however discouraging may have been the result of the last general election, I am always inclined to look further back and compare the present condition of our political principles with that which they occupied ten years ago. And when I do, I am more surprised at what has been accomplished than discouraged at more not having been done.'[101]

The process went still farther. Metcalfe's successor as acting governor, the commander of the forces, Earl Cathcart, was made the next governor general in April 1846, since the danger of war with the United States over the possession of the far western Oregon Country seemed to require a military man in control. Cathcart paid little attention to the internal affairs of the Canadian Union, so that Draper functioned still more fully as a prime minister, virtually directing the civil government by himself. And while this was the situation in the colony, at the centre of empire views on responsible government were undergoing a fundamental change.

In 1846 Britain went through its decisive shift to free trade. If British colonies were no longer to be subordinated to imperial economic policy, but opened to world commerce, there seemed small reason to keep them politically subordinate either. They should be positively encouraged to manage their own affairs, thereby reducing their role as imperial burdens, as they now looked largely to be. The Whig-Liberal government which had gained office in Britain was dedicated to free trade and headed by Lord John Russell, who had already dropped his earlier opposition to colonial responsible rule. The new Whig colonial secretary, Lord Grey, at once took up the task of implementing the responsible principle advocated seven years earlier by his dead brother-in-law, Lord Durham. To do so in Canada, he sent Durham's son-in-law, the Earl of Elgin, as governor general; and supplied him with explicit instructions not only to accept as his ministers those who had the confidence of parliament, but also to change them only in accord with 'the wishes of the people,' whenever power in parliament itself changed hands from one party to another.[102] The governor, that is, was no longer to try to form and head a ministry, but was to rely on that which the dominant party gave him; and to accept its advice, for which it stood wholly responsible to parliament. In brief, what the Baldwins so long had wanted was now established as imperial policy.

It still took time to go fully into effect, and Elgin did not arrive in Canada himself until late January 1847. Meanwhile, in the year preceding, of crucial change in Britain but of little alteration in Canada, Robert Baldwin again had participated in an inconsequential parliamentary session. Draper had just kept his margin of power, but had failed in repeated endeavours to win over the main French-Canadian bloc to the government side. The negotiations still left LaFontaine firmly behind the Reform alliance with Baldwin, although some of his restive followers had been tempted by the alluring prospect of a 'double majority' of French and English segments sharing government power between them. Baldwin himself wholly condemned the idea of a double majority, asserting to LaFontaine: 'The arrangement will be viewed as one based essentially on a national origin distinction wholly irrespective of political principle ... British and French will then become in reality what our opponents have so long wished to make them, the essential distinctions of party, and the final result will scarcely admit of doubt.'[103]

Baldwin, in fact, had clearly striven since the Union against the forces in both Canadas that saw politics in the emotional and explosive terms of 'race.' He had sought to use political organization and principles to bridge the French-English division – through parties that were indeed political and comprehensive, not racist and exclusive. He had made his own personal approaches to the French-Canadian community, not just through his close friendship with LaFontaine or his contacts with Rimouski, but by sending his children to be educated in French, the boys William and Robert to the seminary in Quebec and the girls Maria and Eliza to the Ursuline convent there. At parliamentary sessions in Montreal he had widened his own circle of *Canadien* acquaintances through the hospitable LaFontaines. In every way he had made sincere approaches to the other Canada. In return, he had confirmed the trust in himself and his principles already felt by faithful western Reform followers. That trust was now renewed most fruitfully through Louis

LaFontaine. In holding to his Upper Canadian comrade, the latter took the position that for the French-Canadian group to align with Draper for a temporary share of power would settle nothing. The only way was to secure the recognition of responsible rule through a completely Reform administration, one to be gained by popular victory at the polls. The next election would bring the decisive settlement, without doubt!

Indeed, at least by the close of 1846, Reformers were expectantly considering election prospects, confident that their party opponents were reaching the end of their rope. Baldwin told LaFontaine in December, 'Depend upon it, everything is ripening fast if our friends do but stand firm.'[104] Draper made one last approach to the French in the spring of 1847, furthered by Lord Elgin himself on the valid ground that while the existing councillors held parliamentary backing they were his ministers and deserved his best assistance. The attempt failed again, thanks largely to LaFontaine. Beleaguered as Draper was by malcontent Tories in his own ranks, he was now ready to give up. In May he resigned and departed to the ranks of the judiciary, leaving a still weaker ministry behind him, headed by Henry Sherwood and dominated by the Tory right-wing. With a majority of only two, the Sherwood government struggled through a brief parliamentary session that summer, then faced up to the inevitable in the autumn, when parliament was dissolved and elections called for the end of the year.

By November when the compaigns opened, Baldwin was already hard at work as Western Reform leader, corresponding about party candidates and local organization, as well as shaping up his own campaign for Fourth York. There, after a lively battle, he was victoriously returned in December. In fact, Baldwin's party swept Canada West this time, just as LaFontaine's once more carried the East. The old Tory régime was so obviously played out and demoralized; the issues of the Metcalfe election seemed so dead and empty. There was a new governor and a new imperial policy, to which Reformers could jubilantly point as proof of the validity of their responsible doctrine.[105] It is also fair to add that a new period of depression had struck, for which the government in power as usual suffered.

Parliament met late in February 1848. There was an inescapable sense of a new era about to open, in government and in the life of Canada itself. The Sherwood ministers had remained in office, as they had the right to do, to await the verdict of the assembly. It was a foregone conclusion. On Baldwin's motion, Morin was made Speaker by vote of fifty-four to nineteen. On the Throne speech Baldwin then moved an outright test of confidence, and when the debate had ended, the government was decisively defeated, fifty-four to twenty. The ministry resigned. Elgin duly called on the Reformers headed by LaFontaine and Baldwin to form a new administration.

On 11 March, in orderly fashion, having gone through all the required stages, an all-Reform cabinet took office, thus signalizing the full acknowledgment and implementation of responsible rule in Canada. It was now in constitutional operation beyond all doubt. And the man who had done so much to produce this result stood at the head of the Upper Canadian half of the government. Robert Baldwin was effectively co-premier. He had reached the peak of his political achievement, though he would find little chance to rest on his laurels.

Baldwin had shared with LaFontaine the task of choosing the members of their cabinet, supplying his partner with the list for its western half even back in January 1848, when it was evident that they must soon be called to power.[106] He himself would be attorney-general west again, Hincks the inspector-general, and Sullivan provincial secretary. The other Upper Canadian ministers were to be James Hervey Price and Malcolm Cameron, two veteran Reformers. As for Sullivan, Baldwin told LaFontaine that that legal eminence 'naturally looks for promotion in his profession and could not be expected to take office without an understanding that his doing so was not to interfere with his claims to the first judicial vacancy that presents itself in U.C.'[107] A vacancy did present itself quite soon after the Reform administration took office, whereupon Sullivan retired. The prominent Upper Canadian businessman, William Hamilton Merritt, in due course entered the cabinet instead, a noted apostle of canal-building and reciprocal free trade with the United States.

LaFontaine had the larger parliamentary following in an assembly which was in any case about two-thirds Reform, and the new administration was properly termed the LaFontaine-Baldwin régime. Indeed, Elgin had approached LaFontaine to form the ministry. Baldwin himself always scrupulously deferred to his eastern colleague as the government's ultimate head, and talked of 'your cabinet.' But practically speaking, they remained co-equals and co-premiers, partners who worked easily together, each with particular concern for the leadership of his own half of the United Province. In this sense, then, 'Ontario' had its own government leader in premier Robert Baldwin.

Parliament was adjourned not long after the new government took over, both because its ministers had to face by-elections and because time was needed to plan a major programme of legislation that would give effect to the new era of Reform. Back in Fourth York, Baldwin was easily returned, and then settled down in Montreal again to work on the legislative plans with his chief colleagues. The process took some months. Furthermore, there were time-consuming matters of patronage appointments to be dealt with. As the Reform régime set up in office, scores of place-hunting party faithful gathered to it, in person or by letter: assembly members pressing the claims of constituents to minor local posts, loyal followers of the lean years seeking to have promises redeemed at last, and hopeful newer 'friends,' many of whom inevitably had to be disappointed.

Under the circumstances, it may seem the more significant that many *were* left disappointed. There were no mass discharges, no wholesale replacement of government officials. The American spoils system feared by former Tory opponents was not applied, so that a permanent core of public servants largely remained and grew. The growth of governmental services, in fact, supplied a helpful answer to the problem of place-finding, one to be adopted by many a succeeding régime in Canada. Aside from the filling of official vacancies as they occurred, the very increase in municipal, educational, and developmental activities projected by an energetic new Reform ministry served to provide a considerably increased number of administrative posts over the next few years; and while this expansion assuredly was not designed just to create more places, it did have that helpful effect. Furthermore, the taking over of the Canadian customs system from imperial authority in 1849, and the postal system in 1851, gave still wider areas to domestic political patronage. Along with these, the enlarging dominions of public works and crown lands administration, including road-building and lumber management, were also fruitful realms for appointments, favours, and contracts. Indeed, it would be fair to say that the new LaFontaine-Baldwin administration not only marked the decisive recognition of party cabinet rule but also the full establishment of a party patronage system centred in the responsible ministry. The onset of railway promoting and building, just around the corner, would merely supply the capstone to the 'modern' structure of party political brokerage which was thus emerging for pre-Confederation Canada.

Well before Confederation, indeed by the mid-fifties, some measures of legislative control came to be applied to the generous disposal of government favours; although for long years after Confederation opposition forces could still find ample cause to deplore the widespread 'jobbery,' extravagance, and corrupting influence of patronage. One must, however, make two points about its exercise during Robert Baldwin's own day in government; first, that it did not then result in the manifest excesses that later followed during the free-spending railway-building era; second, that the active use of government patronage was in any case the inevitable concomitant of responsible rule by organized political party. To Robert, indeed, patronage was to be held as an executive responsibility of the party leaders in the cabinet, just as it was in Britain. His thinking did not go far enough to seek parliamentary constraints upon it, or even to recognize clearly the party abuses of patronage that might otherwise develop. That belonged to a post-Baldwin era of experience. Nevertheless, there is no question that he regarded patronage as centrally important, and stood ready to use it to maintain or strengthen his political cause. His papers are full of dealings on patronage matters – just as are those of his great successor, John A. Macdonald, who knew their importance even more.

Yet in this respect there was no necessary clash between principle and practical politics in Baldwin's position. He believed and stated, after all, that the control of official appointments was vital to a government, that it could not make or carry out responsible policy without it. He had resigned on that very issue in 1843. He knew still earlier, from his dealings with Bond Head and from his father's experience with the old oligarchy in Upper Canada, how critical was the executive's power to appoint or remove. There is thus no reason for a kind of debunking delight in finding that the upright Baldwins were perfectly willing to try to place their own friends in offices. Certainly, as Whig élitists they were consistently ready to do so – but always within the frame of a constitution controlled by the people. The most that could be said against them is that they were far more cognizant of the abuses of patronage produced by non-elected or oligarchic authority than of those that might arise within a popularly-based régime itself.

In any event, the Reform ministry that took power in 1848 necessarily turned some of its would-be friends into critics by not exercising the patronage power to the degree of supplying posts in quantity or quality sufficient for all the party suitors. And notably, if naturally, that ministry tended to be more beneficent to party moderates than to erstwhile radical proponents. Self-styled 'Old' Reformers were thereby left disgruntled and restive long before Baldwin's government was at last ready to meet parliament again in January 1849. But by this time, also, there were still more ominous indications that the heralded dawning of a new Reform era might not prove to be bright and rosy, but would rather be lit with the angry, lurid red of an approaching storm.

To begin with, there was the continuing impact of world depression. Trade had nearly dried up along the St Lawrence route, and the completion of its expensive, long-awaited canal system in 1848 had brought few of the golden returns expected. Unemployment was rife; businesses were going to the wall. Tory merchants of the St Lawrence were particularly inclined to blame Britain's adoption of free trade, which had removed the old imperial structure of commercial protection within which they had flourished. Tory-Conservatives generally were bitter over the twin blows of free trade and responsible government, whereby the motherland seemed to have callously abandoned her most devoted colonial defenders. Some disheartened, resentful Tories were even playing with ideas of annexation to the United States as the only answer. In this they could well be joined by reviving left-wing radicals or 'Old Reformers,' who increasingly now looked to the republic as the continental home of true freedom, not to the mere half-way house of British responsible government.

Radicalism assuredly was re-emerging in both English and French Canada, inspired to new vigour by the Reform triumph of 1848, and the hopeful sweep of revolutions that year all across Europe. Former radical figures like Louis Joseph Papineau – and soon William Lyon Mackenzie – reappeared on the political scene. New younger exponents of democratic and republican ideals came forward, to be dubbed Rouges in Canada East, Clear Grits in Canada West. Still further, in French Canada resurgent radicalism was strongly linked with *nationalisme*, with those aspirations for a separate *Canadien* national existence which roused strong emotion in the eastern community. LaFontaine faced a serious threat that his countrymen might turn from the gains he had won under responsible rule and the Anglo-French partnership toward the *patriote* visions of Papineau, who had already issued an eloquent address denouncing responsible government as a delusion, and calling for an end to union and a Lower Canadian state with American-style elective government.

Baldwin expressed his own profound misgivings over Papineau's return to politics, seeing 'nothing but embarrassment from his being in Parliament ...' 'Are we to go back to a system of agitation which nothing could justify but the entire denial to the people of their constitutional influence upon the executive government? If that is what is desired I at least will have no part in it. And depend upon it, let people say what they may about there being a tendency to annexation and American connection in Upper Canada, it is not by any means as extensive as some seem to imagine – and as to its existing in any shape to respond to such an effusion as that of M. Papineau, I do not hesitate to say that there is not a constituency in Upper Canada in which any man could appear with the least chance of success if he made the sentiments of that address the basis on which he claimed the suffrages of the electors.'[108] Hincks, he noted, seemed to think it some advantage to have a radical group in the assembly 'avowing more ultra opinions than those entertained by us,' for in the British parliament left-wing liberals had clearly pushed on the cause of reform. But Baldwin could see no similarity in the situations in the two countries. In short, as his own planning went ahead for the fulfilment of the new era in Canada, he was very much aware of dangers on the left as well as the right. But perhaps he was more prepared and able to deal with Tory-Conservative opponents he had already defeated than with dissent and discord within Reform itself.

When the legislature reassembled on 18 January 1849, an imposing budget of reforms was laid before it. One hundred and ninety-five acts were to be passed before the session ended on 30 May, many of lasting importance. But, in particular, the leading measures brought in by Robert Baldwin would

have made him enduringly important in the history of Ontario, whether or
not he had fathered and fostered responsible government. His work in revis-
ing the Upper Canadian judicial structure was significant in setting up a
Court of Common Pleas and in reorganizing the Court of Chancery into an
efficient institution. Yet besides this, his University Act of 1849 and the
Municipal Corporations Act (often called the Baldwin Act) became veritable
monuments to him in Ontario, and their influence spread far beyond.

The University Act carried out the purpose of Baldwin's abortive bill of
1843 by doing away with Anglican-connected King's College and establishing a non-sectarian University of Toronto in its stead, to which the state
endowment of the college was transferred. Henceforth there would be a
secular, publicly-maintained provincial university in Upper Canada, with
which denominational colleges might affiliate and be represented in its Senate. The system would undergo many revisions and additions in subsequent
periods. Still, the essence remained: a central, secular public institution of
higher learning, and the possibility of denominational colleges becoming
linked with it. From this there subsequently emerged a federative pattern at
Toronto that had widespread influence on university education both within
and without Ontario.

The Municipal Corporations Act was the crowning achievement in the
development of local self-government in Ontario, which had begun even
before the Canadian Union of 1841 but advanced most markedly since that
date. In many respects it was the local counterpart of the movement for
responsible government in the province as a whole. It was fitting, and natural, that Baldwin should have played a commanding role in both of them.
He wholly believed that the art of self-government began in the locality. This
was the training ground for responsible rule, since a people who could not
freely and directly manage their own local affairs through elected representatives would not be adequately prepared for self-government in a broader
setting. Thus his act applied an old Anglo-Saxon term to a key elected local
official, the reeve, reflecting the belief that British traditions of popular government ran back deep into the local assemblies of freemen in Anglo-Saxon
times. In general, the Baldwin Act provided an ascending series of incorporated elected municipal bodies for both rural and urban communities; from
township to county councils on the one hand, from villages to cities on the
other. The complete co-ordinated pattern set up by this 'Municipal Magna
Carta' in its sixty-eight painstaking pages would continue very largely unchanged in Ontario until the 1970s brought the widespread introduction of
larger combined units of regional government. Yet the mark of the original
system remains; and its influence equally remains extensive in newer western provinces that built on the Ontario model laid down by Robert Baldwin.

His two main measures received considerable attention in the assembly of 1849, but they roused nothing like the intensity of concern and controversy produced there by LaFontaine's principal piece of legislation, the Rebellion Losses bill. This undertook to compensate for the damages incurred during the Lower Canadian rebellion of 1837-8 in the same way that claims had already been paid for losses in the Upper Canadian rising. In the western case, however, the destruction had been identifiable as chiefly due to the incursions of a small rebel group against a substantially loyal population. In the east, the damage had often been produced by vengeful loyal forces acting on doubtful grounds of suspicion; and in any case, the identification of loyal or rebel sympathies was a good deal more difficult among the far larger body of Lower Canadian claimants. In consequence, all the underlying antipathies between French and English came into play. To *Canadiens*, the injustices in the repression of rebellion had to be put right, their people's sufferings redeemed. To Lower Canadian British, the bill meant payment for treason, open or secret; sure proof that disloyalty was triumphant and the defenders of the empire cast aside.

In both Canadas Tories and Conservatives rose in outrage to condemn the measure and its party supporters, but the strong Reform majority in parliament carried it steadily through all its stages. Baldwin himself made clear his own support at the outset, arguing that the bill only sought to do what had been done for Upper Canada, and would furnish compensation on the same basis.[109] His hope for equal justice, his loyalty to LaFontaine, no doubt played their part. Yet so did a realization that if the bill did not go forward, the result could be to throw French Canada to Papineau's extremism. For if the *Canadiens* were not shown that responsible government could work for their interests in the Union, they might well agree that it was a delusion after all, and that racial withdrawal and agitation was the only answer. In Toronto a Tory mob replied to Baldwin's stand by burning an effigy of him in the city streets, on 29 March, along with one of William Lyon Mackenzie: the first time they had appeared in company for years.[110]

In Montreal a cool-headed Governor Elgin was quite aware of the incendiary qualities of the Rebellion Losses bill. But this measure had been advised by ministers responsible to parliament and was manifestly supported by the will of that body. On 25 April he gave his assent to it, thus affirming the consistent operation of the responsible principle – but causing a violent eruption among furious Tory adherents. Parliament was invaded while it sat, the building set ablaze as the members escaped. In the three days before order was restored in the city the governor general was attacked, the homes of Baldwin and Hincks assaulted, and LaFontaine's new house ravaged.[111] Yet Elgin steadfastly refused the ruinous step of taking military counter measures; his ministers held firm through the rioting; and the uproar at length exhausted itself. As one consequence, Montreal was seen as too bitterly racially divided to remain the seat of government. Henceforth the capital was to shift periodically between Toronto and Quebec. As a greater consequence, the responsible principle was assured by its ultimate test of force and fire. Though Sir Allan MacNab led a Tory mission to England that summer to seek the disallowance of the Rebellion Losses Act, the imperial authorities refused to interfere with a legitimate constitutional decision of the Canadian legislature and government. The principle and the Reform party alliance behind it came through intact.

Baldwin visited Upper Canada in the summer, and returned to urge that the capital should first be moved to Toronto in order to convince the western population that the talk of 'French domination' of the government was untrue.[112] The ministers assented. Lord Elgin also made a grand public progress through the West, arousing loyal responses and cooling down still-seething Tory indignation there. By autumn, the western leader indeed had other worries than the disappearing threat of French-English clash. In particular, talk of annexation raised a growing threat – not only from darkly despondent Tories of Lower Canada but also from hopeful radical enthusiasts in his own western party ranks. In Montreal there was an active annexation movement. In Upper Canada it was echoed among some newspapers and Reform politicians. In an attempt to check it, by making his own position as party leader emphatically plain, Baldwin addressed a public letter to Peter Perry, once a leading radical associate of William Lyon Mackenzie in parliaments before the Union, who was now deciding whether to stand in a by-election in the Third Riding of York and had expressed an apparent support for annexationism. On 4 October Baldwin wrote to declare his own unaltered 'attachment to the connexion with the Mother Country ... upon this question there remains in my opinion no room for compromise ... All should know therefore that I can look upon only those who are for the Continuance of that Connection as political friends – those who are against it as political opponents.'[113]

The tension mounted when, on 13 October, the annexation movement in Montreal backed by prominent Tory merchants and Rouge associates of Papineau, issued a manifesto calling forthwith for union with the United States. In both sections of the province opposing forces rallied to deluge the signatures on the Annexation Manifesto with their own counter-declarations. In point of fact, the annexationist forces proved decidedly limited and gained little ground in either English or French Canada. Still, at first the appeal looked dangerous, and its attraction for western radical Reformers seemed all too likely. Hence Baldwin fought vigorously against it, as did the editor of the powerful Toronto *Globe*, George Brown, a coming man in the party. In Third York Peter Perry was at least brought to declare that he would not advocate annexation in parliament, if elected – which indeed he was in early December.[114] By the close of year annexationism was plainly dwindling away across the whole province. Moreover, the western harvest had been good, and the eastern trading interests of the St Lawrence were reviving as the cycle of world depression lifted. Canada, in fact, was entering on a rapidly ascending curve of good times, of commercial and agricultural prosperity, and a booming period of railway building. Accordingly, Baldwin might have cause to relax thankfully as the exertions and anxieties of 1849 ended. Elgin paid tribute to his minister's efforts in a private letter to Grey at the Colonial Office: 'I consider him of more importance to the [British] connexion than three regiments.'[115]

Instead of finding time to recuperate, however, the western leader fell seriously ill at the beginning of 1850, brought down by months of worry and fatigue. By now Baldwin had more to worry about, besides, as he watched the continued advance of radicalism in his Upper Canada party. Annexationism had been thwarted, but left-wing elements were resentful of the ministerial pressures used against them. The party leadership seemed to them more concerned to wield power than make fresh departures; it was growing fat and cautious in office, and had to be pushed on. Their feelings were expressed in Perry's return in the York by-election, and in the increasing coalescence of radicals old and young behind a movement to re-make Upper Canada Reform and carry it forward in the path of democratic progress. This, the Clear Grit movement, took strong shape in early 1850, and soon devised a sweeping set of demands, drawn up in local popular conventions, for the election of government officers on every level, a written constitution, universal suffrage, and much more. With none of this was Baldwin in sympathy. It would replace responsible cabinet government and the British constitution with republican-style government and an American congressional system. Yet, while his health recovered, the Clear Grit advance continued. By the time parliament met in May – now in Toronto – it was evident that the radical group would form an aggressive faction in the assembly, including both Perry and Malcolm Cameron, who had left the ministry and become a Clear Grit champion.

In general, the Grit radicals' demands for constitutional reform made small headway in parliament, but they did far better on another theme – the old issue of the Upper Canadian clergy reserves. The reserves question had been dormant during the forties, during the larger struggle for responsible rule; yet now that this was over, increasing numbers of Upper Canadians were demanding that the victorious Reform régime should abolish clergy reserves altogether, and the Clear Grits had wholeheartedly taken up that cause. Baldwin himself, though an Anglican, had recognized the need to remove the dominant privileges of the Church of England in regard to the reserves no less than in regard to the university – both for the good of the state, to free it from embittering religious conflict, and for the good of the church, to free it from prejudicial political associations. Nevertheless, as a moderate Whig-Liberal, he was concerned for the due rights of property, and was not ready to liquidate the reserves by arbitrary action. He meant only to move with his usual deliberate care beyond the compromise redistribution of the clergy reserves income among various Protestant denominations laid down in 1840.[116] LaFontaine, however, was directly opposed to abolishing the reserves, as a Roman Catholic upholder of the principle of church and state connection. In view of the differences among Reformers, no government policy could be put forward. Instead, J.H. Price brought in a broad series of resolutions calling for action on the reserves, but only in his personal capacity, not as a cabinet minister. These passed, with Baldwin and LaFontaine voting on opposite sides. Yet more significantly, Malcolm Cameron's counter resolution on the Grits' behalf, requiring an immediate abolition of the reserves, although defeated, still drew nearly half the support of the Upper Canadian Reform members. Here was an ominous portent for the future.

The party indeed was in increasing disorder, saved perhaps by the continued weakness of their shattered Tory-Conservative opponents, but consequently led into growing internal divisions since there was no real external rival that could drive them back together. Matters became still worse after parliament rose in August. George Brown and his *Globe* zealously took up the voluntary principle – that religious bodies should be wholly divorced from state connections and all public aid.[117] This stand alienated them and their supporters from both Upper Canadian Catholics and the French Catholic Reformers. William Lyon Mackenzie, re-established in Toronto and hovering waspishly around the Grits, now decided it was time to re-enter parliamentary politics. In March 1851 he ran in a by-election, and defeated the presumed candidate of the ministerial Reformers, George Brown himself. Brown, however, felt that the government had let him down, especially Francis Hincks, with whom he had been clashing for some time.[118] Unquestionably, the ministerial side was in disorder.

In the spring of 1851 Baldwin fell ill again. He was overworking himself constantly, as he had for two years past. While he felt duty-bound to attend the parliament that opened on 20 May, he was sick at heart and weak in body, worn by the constant strains of trying to keep the seemingly grand but sadly leaking Reform ship on an even keel. In contrast, Clear Grit raiding craft swept in eagerly to harry the lumbering ministerial vessel. Mackenzie, in particular, was gleefully paying off old scores as he blasted away at this or that failing of the moderate Reformers in government. Finally, on 26 June, he launched a scathing attack on the Court of Chancery, which Baldwin had reformed but two years earlier, calling for its outright abolition. His motion was beaten thirty-four to thirty, but only through Lower Canadian votes. On the Upper Canadian vote itself, Mackenzie carried a majority.

To Robert Baldwin, depressed and dismayed as he was by the state of the party in Upper Canada, this was a devastating blow. The measure which he had drafted with all his legal skill had become, he said, 'the sport of demagog [sic] clamour' in his own community.[119] An intemperate, vindictive leader of Reform from a vanished past, along with some irresponsible radicals, had been able to turn the western half of the house away from the leadership he had given so long and conscientiously. So it appeared to Baldwin, and he was not entirely wrong; unless in being too thin-skinned in a notoriously thankless profession. He brooded, and determined to resign. There was certainly no need for him to do so. The ministry had not lost any test of confidence, or even a vote on the motion; and he did not subscribe to the double majority doctrine that would require a government regularly to hold majority support within both sections. In this case, indeed, it was not a matter of political principle for him, but of personal feeling. Or perhaps it was really a matter of deeper principle that led to his resignation, a belief that the honour and pride he so much cherished would be marred if he held office any longer. A Baldwin should not accept a moral defeat.

Bad health, mounting frustration, and sharp sensitivity led him to withdraw when most others would have stayed. On 30 June 1851 Robert Baldwin left office. The ministry remained in being; he continued to give it his support. But to all intents and purposes he had abandoned his influential political career. In actuality, it was complete in any case. The responsible principle had been gained and sustained, and the rest was postscript. There was no reason to stay on in the party leadership against all his feelings, now that the compelling task was done.

LaFontaine shared his attitude to the degree of announcing his own retirement from office after the session ended. He, too, had had to contend with radicalism in his own section, had no zest for new parliamentary battles, felt he had achieved his main end in politics – and did not seek to continue without his long-accustomed partner. In the autumn of 1851 the cabinet was reconstituted under Hincks and Morin, the party heirs of the two former leaders. What followed under the Hincks-Morin Reform ministry, and, after its fall in 1854, under the new Liberal-Conservative coalition régime of MacNab and Morin which then won power, would not relate to the life of Robert Baldwin, except in a peripheral way.

His ties with Reform certainly continued. When his health improved, he even made a brief attempt to run again for Fourth York as a backbencher in the general elections held at the close of 1851. But he was defeated by a Clear

Grit candidate, Joseph Hartman, and readily accepted the fact that his role was over in the then unfavorable climate of western Reform. Party notables still kept in touch with Baldwin at his Toronto home of Spadina. In fact, through John Ross, a prominent Toronto lawyer who married his daughter Eliza in 1851, he had a line of communication into the ministry itself, for Ross was brought into the government under Hincks and continued in office for some time under the succeeding coalition. Furthermore, an element of moderate Upper Canadian Liberals continued to proclaim themselves 'Baldwin Reformers' for years after his own retirement. Thereby they expressed their distinction from the George Brown-Clear Grit combination that took charge of the next stage in the development of the Reform party – though Brown brought the Grits to an acceptance of British-style responsible government and parliament such as Baldwin would have hoped for.

The former leader essentially stayed in retirement after 1851. He had already given up his legal practice in 1848, because of the heavy demands of government on his time. He did not need to work, of course. He was a wealthy man, having inherited the larger portion of his father's estate, including Spadina, and of his mother's on her death at eighty.[120] With high-yielding urban properties in Toronto, with farm tracts to the north, family and social connections throughout the Toronto business élite, and a son-in-law, John Ross, who became president of the costly new Grand Trunk Railway, Robert Baldwin could easily have lived in a world of directorates and large financial dealings, even with little effort on his part. But he chose not to. He largely withdrew to the peaceful solitude of Spadina, keeping his town house in the city, but building himself a more private cottage on the estate where he could live with his library, his property accounts, and his reflections.[121] He was not a hermit; there were still his many relatives and three of his children, now grown, all close at hand. He saw them regularly, enjoyed visitors and visiting. But nonetheless, this was life in retreat.

Aside from anything else, his health remained shaky and his vitality low. Although he was only forty-seven when he retired, the strain that unremitting political struggles had placed upon an emotionally anxious nature – heightened perhaps by his usual depiction of unruffled composure – had aged him far beyond his years. He suffered renewed bouts of illness, as well as from headaches and fits of giddiness and mental confusion.[122] Thus, in 1853, he 'most affectionately' refused a cordial invitation from LaFontaine – who was beginning a second active career on the judicial bench – to accompany him and his wife on a European holiday, because he had no confidence in his own health: 'I feel life hanging by a most precarious thread and have no wish to have that thread cut in a foreign or distant land far from my family and home.'[123] Doubtless, Baldwin was still rather inclined to be morbid, as he sought to avoid 'stimulating diet and excitement' and 'to preserve mental activity' by resting.[124] He also refused offers of honours and returns to office, because he could not 'interfere with my physical regime and tax my mental application.'[125]

At any rate, he lived tranquilly enough within his limits, looking after his estate, having his children and their children stay at Spadina, rising very early, reading and writing, puttering about the farmlands. But always there was a sombre loneliness about him that had never departed since his wife Eliza had died so many years before. He copied out the letters that had passed between Eliza and himself, to leave with his daughter, Maria, who now kept his house. The originals were to be buried with him: so he instructed Maria in a carefully detailed memorandum which he wrote as he felt the end approaching in the fall of 1858.[126] At his death, his wife's letters were to be laid on his breast: 'I have ever wished to die with one of them near me.'[127] Her handkerchief was to cover his face, as it had covered hers at death. Their coffins were to be placed side by side in the family vault, and bound together with an iron chain. 'These are my last requests, not made in the ebullition of youthful grief, but after years of widowed bereavement, which as they have one after another rolled over have but shewn me still more distinctly the irreparable loss which I have sustained.'[128]

That winter came the final illness, as his heart gave way. The children were with him: William and his wife, Eliza Ross and her husband, Maria and Robert, a ship's captain recently returned from North Atlantic voyages. On 9 December 1858 Robert Baldwin died peacefully, and was buried at Spadina, on his father's land.

NOTES

1 Public Archives of Canada [PAC], CO 42/390 (microfilm), W. Baldwin to the Duke of Wellington, 3 Jan. 1829
2 Metropolitan Toronto Central Library [MTCL], W.W. Baldwin Papers, W. Baldwin to R. Baldwin, undated, but sent to Millbrook, hence c 1813-14
3 R.M. and J. Baldwin, *The Baldwins and the Great Experiment* (Toronto 1969), 46
4 Ibid., 36
5 *The Upper Canada Gazette* (York), 18 Dec. 1802, quoted in E. Firth, *The Town of York, 1793-1815* (Toronto 1962), 196
6 G.E. Wilson, *The Life of Robert Baldwin* (Toronto 1933), 7
7 A.S. Thompson, *Spadina: A Story of Old Toronto* (Toronto 1975), 52-3
8 Ibid., 62-3
9 Ibid., 64-5
10 Ibid., 68
11 Baldwin, *The Baldwins*, 85

12 Ibid., 100
13 Ibid., 76
14 W.W. Baldwin Papers, W. Baldwin to Q. St George, 29 July 1819
15 Thompson, *Spadina*, 75-6
16 G. Patterson, 'Whiggery, Nationality and the Upper Canadian Reform Tradition,' *Canadian Historical Review* [CHR], LVI, 1, March 1975, 30
17 Baldwin, *The Baldwins*, 23
18 W.W. Baldwin Papers, J. Rolph to W. Baldwin, 9 Oct. 1828
19 PAC, Baldwin Papers, Series II, R. Baldwin to Miss Sullivan, 27 June 1825
20 Baldwin, *The Baldwins*, 125
21 A. Dunham, *Political Unrest in Upper Canada, 1815-1836* (London 1927), 116
22 Ibid., 166
23 CO 42/484, Sir Peregrine Maitland to Sir George Murray, 18 Sept. 1828
24 Baldwin, *The Baldwins*, 125
25 *Canadian Freeman* (York), quoted in ibid., 126
26 MTCL, R. Baldwin Papers, R.B. Sullivan to R. Baldwin, undated, but clearly concerning the elections of 1828.
27 *Colonial Advocate* (York), 3 Dec. 1829, quoted in E. Firth *The Town of York, 1815-1834* (Toronto 1966), 125
28 Ibid., 127
29 Baldwin, *The Baldwins*, 123-4, 131-2; Thompson, *Spadina*, 83
30 Thompson, *Spadina*, 83
31 Ibid.
32 Baldwin, *The Baldwins*, 132
33 C.L. Vaughan, 'The Bank of Upper Canada in Politics, 1817-1840,' *Ontario History*, LX, 4, Dec. 1968, 190. William Baldwin had been one of the bank's promoters. Ibid., 187
34 *Colonial Advocate*, 11 April 1833
35 Ibid., 28 Nov. 1833
36 CO 42/390, enclosed in W. Baldwin to Wellington, 3 Jan. 1829
37 Ibid.
38 W.W. Baldwin Papers, undated memorandum by W. Baldwin bound into his copy of Charles Buller, *Responsible Government for Canada* (London 1840)
39 Ibid.
40 Patterson, 'Whiggery,' 37
41 Ibid., 24-44; Dunham, *Political Unrest*, 167-9
42 *Journal of the House of Assembly of Upper Canada, 1836* (Toronto 1836), Appendix 106, *Report on the Executive Council*, R. Baldwin to P. Perry, [hereafter *Journal*] 1836
43 G.M. Craig, *Upper Canada: The Formative Years, 1784-1841* (Toronto 1963), 233
44 Wilson, *Robert Baldwin*, 27, 300

45 *Journal 1836*, Appendix 106, Baldwin to Perry, 16 March 1836
46 Ibid.
47 Dunham, *Political Unrest*, 179
48 *Report of the Select Committee ... Relative to a Responsible Executive Council* (Toronto 1836), 7
49 R. Baldwin Papers, R. Baldwin, 'Memorandum of visit to England, 1836.' Incidentally, Robert carried with him a letter of introduction to the colonial secretary, Glenelg, written by his old schoolmaster, John Strachan.
50 PAC, Durham Papers, R. Baldwin to Glenelg, 13 July 1836
51 R. Baldwin Papers, 'Memorandum of visit'
52 Ibid.
53 W.W. Baldwin Papers, R. Baldwin to W. Baldwin, 24 Sept. 1836
54 R. Baldwin Papers, 'Memorandum of visit'
55 Ibid., M.S. Bidwell to R. Baldwin, 29 July 1836
56 Baldwin, *The Baldwins*, 153
57 Craig, *Upper Canada*, 248
58 Chester New, *Lord Durham* (Oxford 1929), 412
59 PAC, Durham Papers, W. Baldwin to Durham, 1 Aug. 1858; R. Baldwin to Durham, 23 Aug. 1838
60 New, *Lord Durham*, 412-15; Chester Martin, 'Lord Durham's Report and its Consequences,' CHR, XX, 2, June 1939, 188
61 New, *Lord Durham*, 413, footnote
62 *Examiner* (Toronto), 4 July 1838
63 PAC *Report*, 1932, Russell to Thomson, 14 and 16 Oct. 1839
64 PAC, L.H. LaFontaine Papers (copies), Hincks to LaFontaine, 22 Feb. 1840
65 P. Knaplund, ed., *Letters from Lord Sydenham to Lord John Russell* (London 1931), Sydenham to Russell, 13 Feb. 1840, 47-8
66 R. Baldwin Papers, R. Baldwin to Hincks, 27 Jan. 1848
67 LaFontaine Papers, Baldwin to LaFontaine, 26 Nov. 1840
68 *Le Canadien* (Quebec), 18 Oct. 1840
69 Jacques Monet, *The Last Cannon Shot: A Study of French-Canadian Nationalism, 1837-1850* (Toronto 1969), 62
70 R. Baldwin Papers, Baldwin to Sydenham, 18 Feb. 1841
71 J.M.S. Careless, *The Union of the Canadas, 1841-1857* (Toronto 1967), 41
72 R. Baldwin Papers, R. Baldwin to W. Baldwin, 15 June 1841
73 Ibid., Baldwin to Sydenham, 12 June 1841
74 CO 42/479, Sydenham to Russell, 23 June 1841
75 R. Baldwin Papers, W. Baldwin to R. Baldwin, 16 June 1841
76 LaFontaine Papers, Baldwin to LaFontaine, 20 Jan. 1844
77 Elizabeth Nish, ed., *Debates of the Legislative Assembly of United Canada* (Montreal 1970), I, 790, 3 Sept. 1841 [hereafter *Debates*]

78 Robert's aim was to 'greatly cement the union between the Upper and Lower Canadian Reformers.' R. Baldwin Papers, R. Baldwin to W. Baldwin, 10 Aug. 1841
79 Ibid., 20 Aug. 1841
80 Ibid., W. Baldwin to R. Baldwin, 11 Sept. 1841
81 LaFontaine Papers, 4 Dec. 1841
82 PAC, Bagot Papers, Bagot to Stanley, 26 Sept. 1842, confidential
83 R.S. Longley, *Sir Francis Hincks* (Toronto 1943), 106-7
84 LaFontaine Papers, Baldwin to LaFontaine, 28 June 1842
85 Ibid.
86 Careless, *Union of the Canadas*, 65-6
87 Ibid., 67-8
88 Ibid., 68-9
89 R. Baldwin Papers, LaFontaine to Baldwin, 12 Nov. 1844
90 Longley, *Hincks*, 113-14
91 Careless, *Union of the Canadas*, 78-80
92 Ibid., 81-2
93 *Debates*, III, 1087-89, 1 Dec. 1843
94 *Chronicle and Gazette* (Kingston), 2 Dec. 1843
95 LaFontaine Papers, Baldwin to LaFontaine, 20 Jan. 1844
96 R. Baldwin Papers, LaFontaine to Baldwin, 25 Jan. 1844
97 *Proceedings of the First General Meeting of the Reform Association* (Toronto 1844)
98 LaFontaine Papers, Baldwin to LaFontaine, 24 Feb. 1844
99 Ibid., Baldwin to LaFontaine, 15 June 1844
100 Ibid., Baldwin to LaFontaine, 7 Nov. 1844
101 Ibid., 16 Oct. 1845
102 Earl Grey, *The Colonial Administration of Lord John Russell* (London 1853), I, 209-13
103 LaFontaine Papers, Baldwin to LaFontaine, 10 Aug. 1846
104 Ibid., 17 Dec. 1846
105 *Globe* (Toronto), 13 Nov. 1847
106 LaFontaine Papers, Baldwin to LaFontaine, 24 Jan. 1848
107 Ibid.
108 Ibid., 25 Jan. 1848
109 *Montreal Gazette*, 2 March 1849
110 *Globe*, 24 March 1849
111 J.C. Dent, *The Last Forty Years*, 2 vols. (Toronto 1887), II, 162
112 A.G. Doughty, ed., *The Elgin-Grey Papers*, 4 vols. (Ottawa 1937), II, 462, Elgin to Grey, 3 Sept. 1849
113 Ibid., II, 520, Baldwin to P. Perry, 4 Oct. 1849
114 G.M. Jones, 'The Peter Perry Election and the Rise of the Clear Grits,' Ontario Historical Society, *Papers and Records*, 1914, 168-71

115 *Elgin-Grey Papers*, Elgin to Grey, 28 Jan. 1850
116 *Globe*, 22 June 1850
117 J.M.S. Careless, *Brown of the Globe*, 2 vols. (Toronto 1959, 1963), I, 119-20, 126-7
118 *Elgin-Grey Papers*, Elgin to Grey, 28 June 1851
119 PAC, Baldwin Papers, Baldwin to John Ross, 28 June 1851
120 Thompson, *Spadina*, 95
121 PAC, Baldwin Papers, Baldwin to LaFontaine, 21 Aug. 1853
122 Ibid.
123 Ibid.
124 Ibid., Baldwin to Ross, 15 Feb. 1854
125 Ibid., Ante-mortem Instruction by R. Baldwin (undated)
126 Ibid.
127 Ibid.
128 Ibid.

Sir Francis Hincks

When Robert Baldwin resigned as leader of the Reformers from Canada West and co-premier of the United Province of Canada in 1851, Francis Hincks was generally regarded as his logical successor. A powerful, practised politician, aggressive and resourceful, he had earned the right to succeed Baldwin through the prominent role he had played in the Reform movement almost from the time of his arrival in Upper Canada in 1832.

The youngest son of Thomas Hincks, an Irish Presbyterian minister turned school teacher, Francis was born in Cork on 14 December 1807 and grew up in a liberal, academic atmosphere. His brothers chose careers in the church or as scholars and his father assumed young Francis would follow their example. But, when he showed a decided preference for commerce, he was apprenticed to John Martin and Company, a Belfast shipping firm. Upon completion of his apprenticeship he had visited the West Indies and Upper and Lower Canada in 1830-1 to investigate economic prospects with the intention of entering into business for himself. Impressed with the untapped economic potential of Upper Canada, he decided to open a wholesale importing business in York, the capital of the province.

In August 1832 he set sail from Belfast with his bride of two weeks, the former Martha Stewart, for their new home in Upper Canada. Upon their arrival in York he rented warehouse space at 23 Yonge Street from William and Robert Baldwin, whose law office was next door, and the two families became close friends. The Hincks family, moreover, soon started to increase. After staying with them three days in April 1834, William Hutton, Francis' cousin, wrote home: 'Frank Hincks and his lady are truly kind and hospitality itself and have an interesting lovely baby of ten months old.'[1] A daughter, Ellen, was born in 1835, and by 1843 there were three more children.

Although he operated his wholesale business for more than two years, Hincks found it difficult to obtain sufficient credit to carry on under the economic conditions that prevailed in Upper Canada. Consequently, when he was offered the position of cashier (manager) in the new Farmers' Joint Stock Banking Company he readily accepted it. But a rift developed among shareholders when the directors elected Tories as president and solicitor. A number of prominent Reformers withdrew from the company and formed the Bank of the People, with James Lesslie as president and John Rolph and Hervey Price on the board of directors. Hincks' strong liberal bias led him to cast his lot with the Reformers and he was appointed cashier of the new bank.

Hincks had not been greatly influenced by his father's love of learning, but he had thoroughly absorbed the liberal principles of the man who had supported Wilberforce's campaign to abolish slavery, advocated a liberal extension of the franchise, and promoted the application of scientific methods to agriculture as the basis for social and economic reform in Ireland. With this background and his friendship with the Baldwins, he was inevitably drawn into the Reform movement in Upper Canada. By 1834, when York was incorporated as a city and renamed Toronto, he was speaking on behalf of Reform candidates in the civic elections. From the outset, however, he was a moderate Reformer who distrusted the radical wing of the movement. He was delighted with the Reformers' victory in the provincial election of 1834 and received an indirect benefit from it when he and James Young were chosen to audit the Welland Canal Company's books for a select committee of the Legislative Assembly. Like most Reformers he had rejoiced at the appointment of Francis Bond Head as lieutenant-governor and had shared in the disillusionment which followed when Head's true reactionary views became evident in the political crisis of 1836 and the government-influenced election that followed it.

He could appreciate the Reformers' frustration and their conviction that they had been defeated by deception and corrupt practices; he could also understand the desperation born of economic depression and the threat of mortgage foreclosure, but he had no sympathy with those who began to follow William Lyon Mackenzie on the road to rebellion. Rebellion, he was convinced, was not the answer. The chances of success were extremely small and a rebellion would only do further harm to Upper Canada's financial prospects which had already been seriously impaired. He encouraged Robert Baldwin in the alternate course of going to England and making a direct appeal to the colonial secretary, Lord Glenelg, abortive though that attempt turned out to be.

Although the Reform movement occupied an increasing amount of his time, Hincks was kept busy with his banking responsibilities and other enterprises. In 1836 he took an active part in organizing the Mutual Fire Insurance Company of Upper Canada and became its first secretary. It required all of his skill to keep the bank on a sound financial footing during the financial crisis of 1837. Under his guidance the Bank of the People was among the last to suspend and the first to resume specie payments. Rather than forcing the banks to continue specie payments as Bond Head attempted to do, Hincks believed the government should make the banks a loan of £150,000 in small debentures which could be used either as specie or security for bank notes. This would have enabled the banks to resume specie payments and relax their restrictions on credit immediately.

The Rebellion of 1837, which occurred in the midst of the economic crisis, was soon crushed, but the Tories sought to take maximum advantage of it. Erstwhile reformers were indiscriminately accused of being rebels or rebel sympathizers. The Bank of the People was accused of having financed Mackenzie and, although this was denied, financial institutions under Tory influence refused to accept its paper. As accusations and rumours circulated freely, Hincks himself found it advisable to go into hiding until passions cooled.

In the aftermath of the rebellion, moreover, many Reformers lost hope and made plans to depart for the United States. Hincks shared in the general despondency and joined a group of prominent Reformers, including Peter Perry, James Lesslie, and Thomas Parke, to plan for a mass migration to Iowa. The Mississippi Emigration Society was formed and shares were offered to prospective emigrants for £25. Hincks was both a director and secretary of the society and, on its behalf, he made a trip to Washington in the spring of 1838 to investigate the possibility of obtaining a large block grant in the vicinity of Davenport, Iowa.

Upon his return to Toronto he was agreeably surprised to discover that Lord Durham had been appointed to inquire into the causes of the Canadian rebellions. Durham was known by reputation to all Reformers and his appointment awakened new hope among them. If he could be persuaded to recommend responsible government – namely, parliamentary government on the British model – as the basic solution for Canadian problems, all might yet be well. Plans were made to promote the concept of responsible government among the inhabitants in order to increase the possibility of Durham endorsing it as the logical solution. A revitalized Hincks took a prominent part in these activities, travelling through the Reform stronghold in the settlements north of Toronto with James Price and other leading Reformers. They soon realized that though the term responsible government came readily to the lips of Reformers, few had any clear idea of what it actually involved. It was agreed that a newspaper was needed to educate the public on the details and virtues of responsible government and to sustain the hope that Reform leaders had felt upon learning of Durham's appointment. After serious consideration, Hincks decided he would establish the new paper, to be called the *Examiner*. At the age of thirty-one he left his banking career and began a new enterprise that would have a great effect on his future.

By the end of June 1838 he had completed his arrangements and the first issue of the *Examiner* was published on 3 July with the motto 'Responsible Government' at its masthead. Soon, the words 'and the Voluntary Principle' were added. For the four years that Francis Hincks was proprietor and editor the motto was indicative of the *Examiner*'s major editorial themes – parliamentary government, and equal rights for all religious denominations with no official privileges, state grants, or endowments for any of them. Influenced by his father's views on religious equality, Hincks found himself in complete accord with the voluntarist principles held by a majority of the Upper Canadian Reformers; thus secularization of the clergy reserves was a primary objective for him and his newspaper. Furthermore, in its early issues he emphasized the claim made by Simcoe, as Upper Canada's first governor, that the province had not been given a mutilated constitution but one that was 'the very image and transcript' of the British constitution. The *Examiner*'s editor appealed to all Reformers to forget the insults and oppression of the past and to look to the future, giving their confidence and support to Lord Durham.

During Durham's hurried visit to Upper Canada, the Baldwins and Hincks had only a twenty-minute interview in which to present the case for responsible government. Robert Baldwin gave Durham a copy of the memorandum he had left at the Colonial Office for Lord Glenelg two years before; Hincks left a copy of the 11 July issue of his newspaper which asserted: 'It is evident that the great point of difference between our Constitution and that of Great Britain is the want of practical responsibility on the part of the Executive Government to the representatives of the people ...'[2] It was for this reason, the *Examiner* insisted, that the Upper Canadian constitution did not work well and that of Great Britain functioned smoothly. Baldwin and Hincks left Durham feeling that they had been given a good hearing and that they had increased the possibility of responsible government being recommended. In any event, as Hincks continued his editorial campaign throughout 1838 and into 1839, the Reform movement began to revive.

When that spring Lord Durham's report was at length received in Upper Canada, it astounded the Tories and provided a great stimulus for the reviving Reform movement. Durham's endorsement of responsible government restored the Reformers' respectability. No one could accuse Lord Durham of disloyalty; his report substantiated virtually the entire moderate Reform thesis. Durham clubs were formed in almost every community and meetings and rallies were scheduled throughout the summer and autumn. Hincks eagerly participated in as many rallies as possible, seeking to reinforce the influence of the *Examiner* with personal contacts in his determined efforts to mould together a united Reform party. His efforts could be hazardous as well. On one occasion, when an irate gang of Tories tried to break up a

Reform rally, he was forced to flee for his life chased by a man with a drawn sword.

On all sides the busy publicist could mark the Reform movement's growing momentum across the province, but it was not merely an Upper Canadian party that he aspired to build. Lord Durham had recommended a legislative union of the Canadas, and Hincks saw immediately that this would provide an opportunity for Upper Canadian Reformers to join forces with their French-Canadian counterparts. His intense interest in Canadian commercial and economic development led him to regard the proposed union as an excellent idea. He also had a shrewdly calculating cast of mind. If Robert Baldwin was the acknowledged leader of the Reform movement in Upper Canada, Francis Hincks was its major strategist and also, through the *Examiner*, its chief popular spokesman. It was he who immediately recognized the strategic value of an alliance with the Liberals of French Canada, and it was he who took the initiative by entering into correspondence with Louis Hippolyte LaFontaine as one of their most prominent representatives. Having established contact with LaFontaine, Hincks, rather than Baldwin, remained for some considerable time the main link with the Reformers in Lower Canada. This was, in fact, a reflection both of his own role in the Upper Canadian movement and of his close personal ties with Baldwin's leadership.

On 12 April 1839 Hincks wrote his first letter to LaFontaine exploring the possibility of an alliance with French-Canadian Reformers if the proposed union took place. 'Lord Durham ascribes to you national objects,' he observed, 'if he is right, union would be ruin to you, if he is wrong & you are really desirous of liberal institutions & economical government the union would, in my opinion, give you all you desire, as an United Parliament would have an immense Reform Majority.'[3] There could be no basis for an alliance if LaFontaine and his followers were intent on creating a separate French-Canadian state, but if they were not, Hincks assumed that they could have only one other goal – 'liberal institutions & economical government.' His Whig bias blinded him to the idea of *la survivance* – cultural survival – and the concept of the collective rights and liberty of an ethnic group. His contact with LaFontaine would soon provide him with an education in French-Canadian values and objectives.

LaFontaine's reply was encouraging[4] and the two men became regular correspondents. By the time the union of the two provinces was proclaimed on 10 February 1841, Hincks had written twenty-eight letters to the French-Canadian leader. He had established amiable relations with him, and there had been some visiting back and forth between the Reformers of each province; but beyond this he was not certain what had been accomplished. He had sought to impress upon LaFontaine that the Reformers of Upper and

Lower Canada had equal need of each other's support, that it was only through union they could join forces to attain responsible government, and that once a responsible Reform ministry was in office any obnoxious aspect of the union could be eliminated. He repeatedly assured LaFontaine that though the Upper Canadian Reformers found it necessary to adopt somewhat devious tactics, they would prove themselves to be the true friends of French Canada when the united assembly met. He believed he had made some impression, yet he knew that LaFontaine still had reservations and doubts.

The two men had exchanged information on political tactics, possible candidates in various constituencies, and election prospects. It was understood that the Reformers from both provinces would co-operate with each other in the united assembly, but this was much less than the full alliance he sought. The Upper Canadian strategist wanted a commitment that French Canadians would be willing to accept office to form a responsible ministry.[5] At the same time he wished LaFontaine to realize that such a ministry would probably have to contain English-speaking representatives from Lower Canada. But, try as he might, he could obtain no assurance from LaFontaine that he would take office with any English-speaking Lower Canadians who appeared to be likely candidates for the cabinet. It was all very discouraging. 'I really can hardly answer your letter on the subject of the provincial Cabinet,' he wrote. 'Now I think we as a party should be prepared to crush any administration in which we have no confidence & as a necessary consequence to be prepared to take the government into our own hands if strong enough ... I should like to know whether you would consent *to any compromise*, that is would you act with any of your old enemies provided they agree to carry out our policy.'[6]

There must have been times when Hincks felt that LaFontaine had only an imperfect understanding of responsible government, but he could sympathize with the French-Canadian leader and his people. He knew they were alarmed at Lord Sydenham's use of the Special Council to push through legislation intended to facilitate their assimilation; he knew they expected something more tangible from Upper Canadian Reformers than mere promises of future support. Yet when the *Examiner* became critical of the governor, Hincks was reprimanded by Baldwin for abandoning a policy of conciliation and encouraging the French Canadians to think in terms of confrontation.[7] He realized it would be no easy task to unite the Reformers from the two provinces. In the face of LaFontaine's refusal to consider possible compromises in the formation of a cabinet, he decided to wait until after the elections of March 1841, when the character of the first assembly of the new United Province would be known.

Hincks ran successfully for Oxford County. By his analysis, nineteen Reformers were elected in Upper Canada to seventeen supporters of the governor and five Tories. But, in Lower Canada, when LaFontaine's own followers were threatened with violence at the polls in Terrebonne, he abandoned the election. Hincks now feared that indignant French-Canadian members might adopt a rigid anti-union stance and refuse to co-operate with the governor under any circumstances. At the same time he knew that many Upper Canadian Reformers had been closely run, and that they were anxious to avoid a clash with the governor, at least until they had provided for the local improvements expected by their constituents and had passed an election reform act. 'One thing you must make up your minds to ...,' Hincks warned LaFontaine, 'is that if you drive the Upper Canadian Reformers from you now by refusing to co-operate with them & going into determined hostility to the Gov. Genl., they will be thrown upon the Tories of L.C. who I know are ready and anxious to meet their wishes with regard to crushing the Compact and the Orangemen here.'[8]

The first session of the united legislature was a bitter disappointment for Hincks. He had expected that two years of hard work would result in the emergence of a united Reform party, but instead most of the Upper Canadian Reformers soon aligned themselves against the French-Canadian members. He, Baldwin, Price, and a few others might realize that if a united Reform party was to be born some demonstration of good faith must be given to French Canada, but the majority of the Upper Canadian Reformers knew that their constituents wanted the public works Sydenham had promised and they had no intention of letting any obligation to French Canada stand in the way of obtaining them. 'I can hardly be surprised that the L.C. members are disgusted at the conduct of our Reformers,' he wrote to LaFontaine, 'I am so myself ...'[9]

Since party lines were still fluid, Hincks' own basic pragmatism and opportunism soon led him to act independently and to judge each measure on its own merits, regardless of the source from which it came. As the session progressed he began to think that a number of Lower Canadian Tories were more liberal and more progressive than many so-called Reformers in Lower Canada. Baldwin, in contrast, continued to stand by the French Canadians and, in addition, had arranged to have LaFontaine elected for an Upper Canadian constituency. The first session of the legislature was over before the election took place, but when LaFontaine was elected in the Fourth Riding of York on 23 September 1841, the basis had been established at last for the alliance Hincks had worked so hard to achieve.

Ironically, before the session ended a rift had developed between Francis Hincks and his Reform colleagues. The practical Hincks supported the government's bills to create much-needed municipal government in Upper Canada and to establish a bank of issue. Though he believed both measures were capable of improvement, he was critical of Baldwin and the French-Canadian members for opposing them out of hand. Both Hincks and Baldwin regretted the differences that had developed between them during the session, but each felt that he had acted correctly. Hincks believed that it was absurd to join the French Canadians and Tories to defeat liberal measures simply because they emanated from Sydenham's government. Baldwin had indeed once cautioned him that Upper Canadian Reformers would never support the French Canadians in a deliberate attempt to paralyze the government, but it now appeared to Hincks that he was following precisely that course.

Hincks also deeply resented insinuations that he had betrayed the Reform party and French Canada in the hope of gaining an appointment. But when in June 1842 he accepted the office of inspector-general of public accounts from Sydenham's successor, Sir Charles Bagot, and ceased to edit the *Examiner*, many Reformers believed their suspicions to have been confirmed. Some were so incensed that they urged Baldwin to eliminate Hincks politically by running against him in Oxford when he sought re-election after his appointment. Yet though he disapproved of Hincks accepting office, Baldwin did not wish to widen the breach further or impair the possibility of a future reconciliation.

Within three months, however, Hincks and Baldwin were members of the same cabinet. In September, faced with the need to strengthen his government or see it defeated on a vote of no confidence, Bagot entered into negotiations with LaFontaine as the chief Lower Canadian Reform spokesman, and LaFontaine, Morin, Aylwin, Baldwin, and Small thus joined six members of the former council in a coalition ministry. Hincks was now reunited with the Reformers in office; but he had earned a reputation as a political opportunist that would remain with him for the rest of his life. Baldwin readily forgave him, though he did not wholly forget his old comrade's 'desertion' of the Reform cause. For his part Hincks was pleased with the reorganization of the council. He had never ceased to regard himself as a reformer at heart and he looked forward to a reconciliation with Baldwin and his followers. Scarcely had the new council been formed than he was writing to Baldwin suggesting Reform tactics in the assembly. In the ensuing months of office under Bagot, and under Metcalfe into 1843, Hincks again became a key figure in the Reform party élite.

The Metcalfe crisis which occurred in November 1843 was a test of the principles and the tactical skill of Hincks. This time he did believe the Reformers were united as a party and prepared for a fight, and he was convinced that Sir Charles Metcalfe had been sent to Canada as governor general for the express purpose of overthrowing responsible government. The issue, then, seemed far more urgent and decisive than that of merely choosing the best temporary options under Sydenham. And so he readily resigned with his Reform colleagues.

Having thus challenged the governor, it was important for the Reformers to make sure their case was fully presented to the people. In this task Hincks performed yeoman service. He spoke at banquets and rallies, wrote letters for publication in the newspapers, published a pamphlet, toured the countryside, and stood ready to serve in whatever capacity he was needed. When Robert Baldwin, grief-stricken over his father's death, decided to retire from public life, Hincks' persuasive arguments that this would seriously injure the Reformers at a crucial moment caused him to reconsider.

Hincks' own resignation entailed a considerable personal sacrifice. On his salary as inspector-general he and his family had lived quite comfortably in Kingston and they had taken Anna Hutton, the daughter of Francis' cousin William, to live with them as a governess for their four young children, the eldest of whom was eight years old.[10] With the loss of his ministerial income Hincks was anxious to find means to supplement his salary as a member of the assembly. Consequently, he was keenly interested when LaFontaine, for one, suggested that he consider taking over the editorship of the Montreal *Times* to make it the English Reform organ in the lower half of the province. Though Baldwin reminded LaFontaine that 'he certainly went wrong in 1841-42 and we have therefore a right to protect ourselves as far as possible against a similar want of judgment on his part or that of any other,' Hincks was still offered the position.[11] He accepted and moved to Montreal in February 1844, having sold the *Examiner* to James Lesslie. He had hoped to have control of the *Times* but when he was unable to come to satisfactory terms with the owner, he decided, with the promise of financial assistance from Theodore Hart, LaFontaine, and Baldwin, to start a new Reform paper, the Montreal *Pilot*.

Hincks and the *Pilot* plunged with zest into the politics of Canada East and his vigorous, provocative editorials were soon drawing heated replies from Tory journalists. Baldwin and LaFontaine would have preferred him to adopt a more moderate tone, but Hincks thoroughly enjoyed the vituperative journalism of his day. In addition to promoting responsible government, he sought to unite the Irish working class of Montreal with the French Canadians in support of the Reform party. On a number of occasions he had seen Reformers intimidated by Tory mobs in Upper Canada; now when the opportunity presented itself he could not resist organizing a striking force of Irish workers to disrupt Lower Canadian Tory meetings and control the polls.

Despite his efforts and to his surprise, Hincks was defeated in his Oxford constituency by Robert Riddell in the election of 1844. As he analysed the results afterward, it was clear that he had been defeated by the Highland Scots vote in Zorra Township. He believed that the Zorra Scots had been swayed more by his vote in favour of the 'game bill' which permitted hunting on Sunday than by the Metcalfe crisis.[12] To the stern Presbyterian conscience he was supporting desecration of the Sabbath. Quite possibly, too, his wide-ranging criticism of Scottish Tory merchants in Montreal had aroused the ire of his Zorra constituents as Baldwin had feared.[13]

In any event, a year's experience in publishing the *Pilot* revealed that the paper would require a great deal of assistance from Upper Canadian Reformers in order to survive. French Canadians could not be expected to subscribe in large numbers, and as most of the Montreal merchants were Tories, they were unlikely to give Hincks much advertising. But when Robert Baldwin asked Upper Canadian Reformers to subscribe to the *Pilot*, George Brown protested that Hincks' paper was being favoured at the expense of the *Globe* and the *Examiner*. To compete with other English newspapers in Montreal, Hincks set his subscription rate at $2.00, but Brown criticized this as totally unrealistic. He found it particularly galling to be asked repeatedly, 'Why can't you sell as cheap as Hincks?' and, at the same time, to have it intimated that Reformers had a duty to sustain the *Pilot* with their subscriptions.[14]

Hincks had been contemplating raising his rates, but he resented Brown's complaints and his interference. He believed that the *Pilot* performed a special function as the essential link between English- and French-speaking Reformers and was therefore entitled to special treatment. He soon convinced himself that Brown was a political as well as a newspaper rival. 'I have ... been much disgusted,' he wrote to Baldwin, 'at recent information from Oxford. George Brown has been there exerting himself *not only against the Pilot*, but against *me* personally. His object is to unseat me for that Co & as my friends think to substitute *himself*. He proposes also to substitute Blake for you as leader.'[15] All the evidence indicates that Hincks' fears were groundless,[16] but the fears themselves were indicative of his growing sense of insecurity. His relations with the Zorra Scots had deteriorated steadily since he began publishing the *Pilot*. Brown, a Free Church Presbyterian, was highly regarded in Zorra; he and his newspaper appeared to present a challenge to Hincks and the *Pilot*. Isolated as the latter was from the mainstream of Upper Canadian politics, it was all too easy for him to give credence to the wildest rumours. He may also have vaguely connected Brown and the Free Kirk with the militant Protestantism and 'no popery' feelings that were clearly gaining strength in Upper Canada. Such sentiments, he feared, could pose a threat to the alliance with French-Canadian Reformers.

At times Hincks became very discouraged as he endeavoured to serve as the link between Upper and Lower Canadian Reformers. He was critical of the leadership provided by Baldwin and LaFontaine. 'You do not *lead* enough,' he complained to Baldwin, 'you seem rather to follow than to lead.'[17] He was particularly disappointed at LaFontaine's failure to canvass actively among French-Canadian Reformers for funds to support the *Pilot*. On a number of occasions he considered selling the paper and came close to doing so in the spring of 1847 when mining investments yielded him a profit of $4500.00 and gave him an opportunity to pay off his debts. Each time, however, he drew back because he liked editing the paper and he enjoyed the influential position he had attained with Lower Canadian Reformers.

Hincks' advice indeed was frequently sought and his influence was skilfully used during the 'double majority' controversy through which the Lower Canadian Reformers passed in the years following the election of 1844. Many French-Canadian Reformers, especially those from the Quebec District, resented being denied the fruits of victory simply because their Upper Canadian allies had failed to carry their half of the province. They began to talk of a double majority in government and to claim that the Lower Canadian half of the council ought to be replaced by men who had the support of the Lower Canadian members in the assembly. Under the guise of recognizing the equity of the double majority principle, the Conservative leader of the government, William Draper, made attempts in 1845 and 1846 to detach the French Canadians from their alliance with Baldwin and to lead them into an alliance with the Upper Canadian Tories. Each time, at the crucial moment in 1845, 1846, and again in 1847, Hincks' advice and initiative were powerfully directed to keeping the French Canadians united behind LaFontaine and true to the Reform cause.

Hincks regained his seat in Oxford in the Reform victory in the election of 1847-8, but he owed his success largely to the efforts made on his behalf by George Brown. He had gone on a visit to Ireland in the summer of 1847 and, although he arrived back in Montreal just before the election, urgent personal business prevented him from making even a token appearance in his constituency. He owed Brown a debt of gratitude, but this very likely increased, rather than diminished, the latent animosity between the two men. In Hincks' mind Brown was closely connected with his difficulties in Zorra and, while Brown had used his influence with the Zorra Scots on Hincks' behalf, he had, at the same time, enhanced his own reputation in Oxford and with the Reform party. For his part Brown knew he had exerted himself for the sake of the party, and not really because of Hincks; he probably doubted that Hincks was worth all the effort that had been made on his behalf.

When in 1848 LaFontaine offered Hincks his old office of inspector-general of finance in the first responsible ministry to be formed in the Province of Canada, he readily accepted. Upon taking office he was dismayed to discover the extent to which the finances of the province had deteriorated, largely because public works had been authorized without adequate provision being made to retire the growing provincial debt.[18] A firm hand was required and Hincks was determined to provide it. He took immediate steps to restore the province's financial reputation by depositing funds with the Bank of England to pay the interest due on current loans. When Baring Brothers were reluctant to act as financial agents for Canada, he continued to promote Canada's economic prospects until they found that Canadian debentures could be sold at a premium rather than a discount.

As a leading member of the cabinet, Hincks took an active interest in each government measure introduced in the session of 1849, but he was especially concerned with two bills he had prepared that related more to development than to reform. To improve the province's credit he introduced a bill establishing a sinking fund to retire the provincial debt. His major piece of legislation, however, was a Guarantee Act designed to encourage private enterprise to provide the railways Canada needed. Under the terms of the act the government would guarantee 6 per cent interest on half the bonded debt of any railway over seventy-five miles in length after half the line had been constructed. Passed with little opposition, the act reflected both the members' confidence in Canada's economic prospects and the extent to which they had been smitten with the railway mania.

Hincks' measures were well received, but LaFontaine's Rebellion Losses Act produced a violent reaction that culminated in a Tory mob attacking Lord Elgin and burning the parliament building. Convinced of the Reformers' intention to compensate rebels for losses they had incurred, the Tories sent William Cayley and Sir Allan MacNab to England to press for the act's disallowance. Upon learning of this mission the Reformers determined to send Hincks to counteract their influence and also to allay the fears which the recent disturbances had aroused in the minds of British investors.

When Hincks found there was no likelihood of the Rebellion Losses Act being disallowed he concentrated his efforts on the financial aspects of his trip and succeeded in persuading Baring Brothers and Glyn, Mills, and Company to handle jointly the sale of £500,000 in Canadian debentures. Unfortunately, renewed agitation in Canada and increased talk of annexation made the debentures unsaleable. Frustrated and embittered, Hincks returned to Montreal in October 1849 to find a new crisis at hand.

The annexation movement had culminated in a manifesto signed by many prominent Montreal business and professional men calling for an end to the connection with Great Britain and union with the United States. Conscious that his financial mission had been unsuccessful because of the annexation agitation, Hincks was critical of the government for permitting the movement to gain in strength during his absence. 'Had *prompt* measures been taken with the annexationists they would have been down by this time instead of increasing in influence and numbers,' he complained to Baldwin.[19] Even now, after the cabinet had agreed to deprive those who signed the manifesto of any appointments or honours they held, LaFontaine still hesitated to apply the decision to queen's counsel. 'I am strongly of the opinion that unless we dismiss these annexationists we are ruined,' Hincks warned.

He was in a peevish mood and he took no pains to disguise it. 'The whole country cries out against *you all* & I must say against you in particular for vacillating,' he wrote to Baldwin.[20] It was obvious that the cabinet must be reconstructed, but nothing had been done. 'There would be no difficulty about it with any man of decision,' he asserted bluntly. 'I could myself complete the administration on a permanent and satisfactory footing in 24 hours, but I find no disposition to act on your part or Mr. LaFontaine's.' In the cabinet he had argued in favour of a single session in Toronto followed by the return of the capital to Montreal, but his colleagues decided instead to alternate the seat of government between Toronto and Quebec. Disturbed by the unsettled state of affairs, Hincks considered retiring from public life rather than contemplate moving every few years as the capital rotated. His mood changed in the wake of the cabinet reorganization a few days later and the government's revocation of the commissions of those who had signed the annexation manifesto. 'I am sure the effect will be excellent,' he wrote to Baldwin. 'It shows we have some energy.'[21]

By the spring of 1850 the economic picture had greatly improved and towards the end of May Hincks was elated to learn that the balance of the £500,000 loan had been negotiated and the debentures had been sold slightly above par. He had good reason to be well pleased for, in contrast to the dismal situation when he took office, Canadian revenue was increasing significantly; Barings were happy to act as Canadian agents; and Canadian securities were selling at a premium.

At this point, indeed, the province of Canada was entering upon a period of rapid economic growth which would foster optimism, speculation, and the formation of close links between government and certain sectors of the economy. Simultaneously, however, the province was moving into a phase of acute ideological conflict in which the relationship between the churches and state and the two cultures would be the principal centres of concern. The political tensions generated by these developments would expose the Reform party in its true guise as a marriage of convenience between certain groups in Canada East and West to secure a firm grip on the levers of political power and the distribution of patronage, rather than to effect major changes in the social and political order. In the wake of this process of illumination, the Reform party began to disintegrate. Francis Hincks, as a keen practitioner of the art of political management, attempted to adapt the party to the new conditions, but in the end he had to give way to a more adept set of political pragmatists.

Initially, the focal point of controversy in the Reform party was the renewal of agitation for the secularization of the clergy reserves. Hincks feared that extreme voluntarists like the emerging Clear Grit radicals, or even George Brown, could lose the Roman Catholic vote in Upper Canada and threaten the alliance with French Canada. Hincks had always considered himself a voluntarist. He was opposed to special privileges, or state support for any religious denomination, and for that reason he was as staunch an advocate of secularizing the clergy reserves as the Grits or Brown. But, as he explained to Thomas Shenston, his friend and political agent, his voluntarism was tempered by his 'notions of civil and religious liberty.' Believing each denomination should be permitted to conduct its own affairs in its own way, he considered it 'most unfair' of those who did not wish their own churches to have corporate powers 'to deprive others of what they conscientiously believe necessary.'[22] Similarly, state-aided separate schools for religious denominations did not conflict with his voluntarist principles and, though he would have preferred a single state school system, he was willing to make concessions that George Brown deplored in the summer of 1850 as the 'entering wedge' and a threat to the whole national school structure.[23] Thus Hincks readily joined his French-Canadian colleagues in the cabinet to support bills establishing Roman Catholic and Anglican ecclesiastical corporations with the power of holding property in perpetuity. Yet to the Clear Grits all this was plain evidence of the manner in which Reform voluntarist positions were being steadily diluted by French-Canadian influence, an opinion that George Brown was starting to share. When in December Brown took up the 'papal aggression' issue in England and endeavoured to show that 'papal aggression' also threatened Upper Canada, he became, in the eyes of many, the symbol of extreme voluntarism and unyielding anti-catholicism. Hincks, in contrast, became more and more identified with compromise and the maintenance of the Reform alliance.

Everyone, including Francis Hincks, was taken by surprise in the early summer of 1851 when Robert Baldwin abruptly decided to resign as co-premier after a majority of the Upper Canadian members declined to support his reformed Court of Chancery. Hincks immediately offered to resign with Baldwin, but this was a perfunctory gesture. He had been critical of Baldwin and LaFontaine's leadership and was certain he would make a more decisive and dynamic leader. Still, it was not the ideal moment for a change in leadership and Hincks probably would have preferred to delay it. The Clear Grits in the western section of the province and the Rouges in the eastern were threatening both the unity of the Reform party and the existence of the Canadian Union. At the same time, George Brown's *Globe* was becoming increasingly critical of concessions and compromises made to maintain the Reform alliance. Moreover, Hincks was fully occupied at the moment discussing, with Joseph Howe and E.B. Chandler, co-operative arrangements to link Nova Scotia, New Brunswick, and the Canadas by rail.

In any event, Baldwin's resignation at the end of June 1851 cleared the way for the accession of Hincks as leader of the Reform forces in Canada West. It was accompanied by LaFontaine's announcement of his own intention to retire at the end of the session. In the interval, Hincks faced the difficult task of consolidating his position and of preparing for the eventual reconstruction of the ministry.

In his initial speech as *de facto* leader of the western section of the party, Hincks was anxious to convey the impression that a firmer hand now held the reins and that he had clearly defined objectives and policies. Emphasizing his determination to preserve the Union as the essential basis for Canadian progress and development, he condemned the *Globe* for its doctrinaire voluntarism which made it critical of government support for ecclesiastical corporation bills. He warned the Reformers that division within their ranks was threatening the Reform alliance and the existence of the Union itself.[24]

Hincks obviously intended to insist that the *Globe*'s editorial policy remain in harmony with the policy adopted by the leaders of the party, but for Brown Hincks' speech was the final straw. For more than a year he had been growing less and less satisfied with the party, yet his respect for Robert Baldwin had prevented him from making the final break. Now, however, Baldwin had resigned and the prospect of Hincks placing political power ahead of principles was more than Brown was willing to accept. All his latent antipathy to Hincks welled up in him as he responded in the *Globe* to the new leader's speech. Striking out at the government's delay in secularizing the clergy reserves and the increase in sectarian grants and ecclesiastical corporations, he declared: 'When we find our friendly cautions on these exciting subjects treated with resentment and threats – we can no longer be silent.'[25] To Hincks' claim that the adoption of a thorough voluntarist policy would destroy the Reform alliance and lead to the defeat of the party, Brown retorted that true Reformers must take a firm stand against Roman Catholic aggression and 'state churchism.' Whatever the consequences, principles must take priority over power, or any other consideration.

The open break had finally occurred. George Brown and the *Globe* were wholly lost to Hincks in his efforts to reorganize and strengthen the party. Had the two men been able to work together, Brown could have provided solid strength in the cabinet; instead he became Hincks' most dangerous political opponent. Yet almost certainly, it could not have been otherwise, for they represented different and nearly irreconcilable strains within the Upper Canadian reform tradition. Moreover, on personal grounds Hincks would have found it very difficult to offer Brown a cabinet post; if he had, Brown surely would not have accepted it.

George Brown was not the only one to react to Hincks' inaugural speech as leader. The next mail brought a letter from Thomas Shenston, Hincks' campaign manager in Oxford, describing the consternation the speech had caused among his neighbours in Woodstock. In reply Hincks regretted that he should have displeased his friends, but insisted he could not abandon views which he had expressed 'after mature deliberation.' 'It is *not* true that I stated I *would join any party*,' he continued:

What I did state ... was that however I personally disliked these acts of incorporation, it was necessary for a statesman to look at the state of public opinion and the fact that one half of the entire population was Roman Catholic – that the policy of the Church was to manage its charities and its education by means of such corporations and that there must be mutual concessions of opinion on minor points if the union was to be preserved, and the present combination of parties maintained. I warned the liberal members from U.C. that if they adopted a policy so entirely at variance with the views of L. Canadians the inevitable consequence would be a new combination of parties, as in no other way could the Government be carried on ... How can we ask Lower Canadians to adopt our views on the Clergy Reserves if we refuse to make even the slightest concession of our prejudices to them.[26]

Despite the opposition of his constituents and the hostility of the *Globe*, Hincks pressed ahead in his endeavour to restore a measure of harmony in the Reform ranks. The editor of the leading Clear Grit paper, William McDougall, was willing to support a reorganized government with his *North American*, but the price he demanded was Grit representation in the cabinet. McDougall, of course, believed that Hincks could be dominated by the Grit influence in the government. Hincks, however, was confident that the responsibility of office would soon exert a moderating influence on the Grits. He readily agreed to McDougall's demand that two veteran radicals, John Rolph and Malcolm Cameron, be given office,[27] but, for his part, he insisted that the radical aspects of the Grit platform be set aside and that the new ministry should seek to carry reasonable, progressive measures. An agreement for a Clear Grit-Hincksite coalition was soon worked out, but both parties to it had deluded themselves. The Grits would gain office, but they would not dominate the ministry, and before long they would find it necessary to betray their voluntarist principles to keep the government in power. At the same time, Hincks had not reunited Upper Canadian liberals as he had hoped; he had not eliminated Clear Grittism in Canada West, though he did, perhaps, contribute to the moderation of its political radicalism.

Having done all he could to prepare for reconstruction of the cabinet, Hincks turned his attention to carrying legislation authorizing Canadian participation with Nova Scotia and New Brunswick in building a through railway line from Halifax to Canada's western boundary. Declaring that private capital was incapable of providing the extensive rail links the province needed, he insisted that the major railways in Canada would have to be publicly owned and operated. He admitted that Canadians generally were less interested in the Intercolonial Railway from Halifax to Quebec than they were in the Canadian trunk line, but he stressed the necessity of participating in the Intercolonial in order to obtain the benefits of an imperial guaranteed loan and thus cheaper financing for a portion of the Canadian line. In any case, both lines would soon be needed and it was an opportune time to build them. The idea of a Canadian trunk line was generally approved by the legislature, and Hincks' 'Main Trunk Line' bill passed without difficulty.

The passage of the railway legislation was the prelude to the resignation of LaFontaine's government in September 1851. Lord Elgin then called upon Hincks as the senior member of the retiring government, and the man whom he had described as having 'more energy than all the Canadian Statesmen I have yet had to do with put together,'[28] to form a new administration. At last the ambiguity of Hincks' position was at an end; he was now effectively joint premier, with, in fact, the formal headship of the government.

After a brief consultation he agreed with A.N. Morin, formerly Speaker of the Legislative Assembly, on an extensive programme that included secularization of the clergy reserves in Upper Canada, the reform of seigneurial tenure in Lower, and an elective Legislative Council for the province as a whole – not to mention increased representation in the assembly for a larger Canadian population, the extension of the franchise, and the encouragement of railway building. They looked forward enthusiastically both to completing reforms of this sort that had been widely expected of LaFontaine and Baldwin, and also to presiding over the advent of a new railway age.

When he began reconstructing the cabinet, Hincks offered the prominent eastern Upper Canadian Reformer, Sandfield Macdonald, the office of commissioner of crown lands. The offer was declined because Macdonald felt that having been solicitor-general since 1849 he was entitled to the senior legal appointment of attorney-general west. Instead of replying tactfully, Hincks took perverse satisfaction in informing Macdonald that if the offer had not been 'peremptorily' refused, it would have had to be withdrawn so that both Rolph and Cameron could be appointed. Rubbing salt in the wound he continued: 'You yourself appear most rashly to have committed yourself by speaking of the probability of Mr. Cameron being included in the arrangements and this you must now perceive was fatal to the success of your views.'[29] The letter came as a shock to Macdonald who had expected Hincks to yield and give him the attorney-generalship. 'I have no fixed notion of the course I will pursue tho' I am clear that I will make Hincks pay for it if I can ...'

he wrote to a friend.[30] Within less than six months of assuming command, the new government leader had broken with two very influential Reform figures, Brown and Sandfield Macdonald. Still, given the numerous factions within Upper Canadian liberalism, such losses were virtually inevitable.

Coalition with the Clear Grits created misgivings in the minds of some of the right wing of Morin's French-Canadian bloc. Joseph Cauchon refused to accept an appointment as assistant provincial secretary because he would not associate with those intent on 'pulling down everything even to earth' and beginning society anew 'precisely after the manner of European socialists.'[31] He also claimed that French-Canadian influence had been diminished by the appointment of Lewis Drummond and John Young to the Lower Canadian section of the cabinet. Hincks recognized instantly that such sentiments posed a threat to the Reform alliance from a different direction and hastened to reply to Cauchon in a letter intended for publication. He denied that Rolph or Cameron were socialists or that socialist influence had been admitted to the government. Responding to Cauchon's complaint that French-Canadian influence had been diminished, he declared: 'It was never imagined that justice to the French Canadians consisted in there being any particular number of that race in the Cabinet, or that any particular offices should be filled by gentlemen of that origin.'[32]

The appointment of John Young to the cabinet, he continued, had been made to convince the merchants of Montreal and Quebec that 'there was every desire on the part of the Government to afford them the means of representing their wishes in the most satisfactory manner, and that there was every desire to meet their reasonable demands.' Speaking on behalf of the commercial interests, however, the Conservative Montreal *Gazette* was not favourably impressed. It professed to be scandalized that Hincks and the Clear Grit Cameron could associate with each other politically. 'In the name of morality, public and private,' it proclaimed, 'the people of Canada are called upon to repudiate the base connection.'[33]

George Brown, of course, had long since made up his mind about the new ministry. During September and October he had published a series of open letters to Hincks in the *Globe* denouncing him for his betrayal of Reform principles and justifying the termination of his own connection with the party. When challenged by Thomas Shenston for his earlier failure to support the Clear Grits in their determination to secularize the clergy reserves, Brown replied that had 'Rolph and Cameron made satisfactory terms and openly declared the principles on which they joined Mr. Hincks and the French Canadians, I would have supported them. But this is so far from being the case that I know they have agreed to set aside the Reserve question until the Imperial Parliament acts ... & what they have agreed on other questions nobody knows.'[34]

Despite the opposition of Brown, Macdonald, and others, the new government advised Lord Elgin to dissolve parliament and call an election. In Hincks' own constituency as well as in Canada West generally, George Brown's attack on Hincks' leadership and on the Grits' betrayal of their principles had an immediate impact on events. Dr Rolph's influence was utilized to marshal the Clear Grits in Oxford behind Hincks but, nonetheless, with George Brown's encouragement an independent candidate, Scatchard, was nominated. By early November John Ross, Hincks' newly appointed solicitor-general west, began to fear that a split Reform vote in Oxford would result in the election of the Tory candidate. 'If Scatchard cannot be persuaded to back out & *support* Mr. Hincks,' he wrote to Thomas Shenston, 'he must be denounced as a renegade like George Brown & attacked in every possible way as George Brown's tool.'[35] As an added precaution it was decided that Hincks should run in Niagara as well as Oxford.

In the end there was no need to worry. Hincks was returned by safe margins in both Oxford and Niagara. With eighteen seats in Canada West and thirty in Canada East the Hincks-Morin government had the same strength as its predecessor. Even so, the election returns for Upper Canada must have given Hincks cause for reflection. George Brown had been elected as an independent Reformer committed to work for the defeat of Hincks and his government. Though Hincks probably still underrated Brown as a political opponent, the *Globe* was a powerful force in Upper Canadian politics and it was certain to continue deriding the Grits for joining the government. Since the Grits now constituted half of the Upper Canadian Reformers in the assembly, Brown's continued pressure on them was a constant threat.

From the outset, the new government was beset with problems which made it vulnerable to the divisions of opinion in parliament and the province. First, it soon became apparent that Joseph Howe and Lord Grey, the colonial secretary, had misunderstood each other on the issue of railway financing; an imperial guarantee was only available for a loan to build a railway from Halifax to Quebec following a route through northern New Brunswick along the south shore of the Gulf of St Lawrence. Aware that New Brunswick had insisted upon railway service for the St John Valley, Hincks feared the collapse of the arrangements for interprovincial co-operation and the loss of the opportunity to borrow railway funds at 3¾ per cent under the imperial guarantee. He had shared in the enthusiasm for railways and had benefited from it politically. His imagination was fired by a vision of railways bringing in their wake industrial and commercial expansion in the Canadas. It was important that there should be no setback at this stage. Already Hincks was thinking in terms of a compromise route that he believed would be satisfactory to New Brunswick – one that would follow the St John Valley instead of the north shore of New Brunswick. Hastily he sent off telegrams to

167 Sir Francis Hincks

Nova Scotia and New Brunswick expressing the hope that some basis for common action could still be found and suggesting a meeting in Fredericton to discuss the matter. From Joseph Howe the encouraging reply came back: 'Let Canada and New Brunswick agree to some proposition in the new state of things and Nova Scotia will not be unreasonable.'[36]

Hincks set out for Fredericton on 15 January 1852 with two of his cabinet colleagues, E.P. Taché and John Young. On the way they were surprised to learn that Howe was opposed to substituting the St John Valley for the northern route and, consequently, Nova Scotia would not be represented at Fredericton. When they found the New Brunswick government favourable to Hincks' compromise plan, the Canadians decided to attempt to overcome Howe's objections and persuaded E.B. Chandler to accompany them to Halifax.

Upon their arrival in Halifax they found rumours circulating that Canada and New Brunswick were conspiring to substitute the St John Valley route for the original one. This would give Saint John a direct rail connection with Canada and enable it to compete with Halifax. It was also rumoured that Canada and New Brunswick had intrigued with English capitalists to thwart the original plan for public ownership of the railway to prepare the way for it to be built by private interests with government assistance and guarantees.

After considerable discussion a proposal was made to the Nova Scotian cabinet that the St John Valley route be adopted together with a new cost-sharing arrangement under which Nova Scotia would pay one-quarter, New Brunswick, five-twelfths, and Canada, one-third of the cost of the line from Halifax to Quebec. In addition, Canada would pay the whole cost of the line from Quebec to Montreal, but it was assumed that the imperial guarantee would also be available for this section.[37] The Nova Scotia government made no response to this suggestion, apparently because Howe was still opposed to it. Hincks again felt thoroughly frustrated – all his efforts were apparently to end in failure. But at this point Benjamin Weir, a Halifax merchant and member of the assembly, persuaded the mayor of Halifax to call a public meeting to enable the citizens of Halifax to meet the visitors and to hear what they had to say on behalf of the railway they proposed. Hincks welcomed the chance to appeal directly to the people over the heads of Howe and his colleagues.

In a masterful speech he stressed the economic advantages of the St John Valley route not only for New Brunswick and Canada but for Nova Scotia as well, and pointed to the favourable terms that were offered to Nova Scotia. Spurred on by the evident interest of his audience, Hincks deftly sought to neutralize and isolate Howe while appealing to the Nova Scotians to express their own opinions: 'I would think it unfair to ask the Hon. Provincial Secretary to assume any more responsibility on this matter than he has – having set his heart upon it and enduring so much more than any other man; but I wish you gentlemen, in this free conference, to state your objections to our proposal. We ask you to co-operate with us in our intercolonial railway. We wish to traffic with you – our lines are open with the United States; if you co-operate with us we shall be glad; if not, in God's name, say so, and we shall reluctantly leave you with disappointment. We do not wish to press you.'[38] As he sat down amid loud and prolonged cheering and applause Hincks knew he had won the audience for his proposal and he waited with interest to see what Howe's reaction would be.

After Taché and Young had spoken briefly, Howe arose and began by expressing his pleasure at the turn of events that 'had brought the "stars" of Canada to shine upon us.' He passed lightly over the failure of the Nova Scotian cabinet to respond to the proposal put before them, declaring: 'I am not quite sure that the spirit of mischief which shows itself occasionally in my composition, did not prompt me to give them 24 or 48 hours of the anxiety and suspense that I endured for 18 months.'[39] He could not take upon himself the sole responsibility of negotiating to carry out any particular scheme; the question was before the legislature and it would make the final decision, but he intended to vote in favour of the new proposition.

Hincks returned to Canada with a full sense of accomplishment. With Howe's opposition removed, he was confident the new proposal would be approved by the Nova Scotia legislature. It was necessary now to concentrate on winning the approval of the British government for the St John Valley route. The day after the public meeting in Halifax Hincks wrote to Lord Grey, the colonial secretary, expressing 'strong hopes' that 'mere military considerations' would not cause the new proposal to be refused the imperial guarantee. If this were to happen, he warned, 'it will be vain to expect the concurrence of the three Legislatures to any new proposition.'[40] Grey was ready to accept the St John Valley route 'in the absence of a better,' but he was uncertain how his cabinet colleagues would react to the prospect of a railroad that could be easily taken in the event of war.[41] He encouraged Hincks' suggestion that the three provinces send representatives to London to explain their proposal and rally support for it.

Hincks had returned from Halifax late in February 1852 and by the twenty-sixth he was on his way to England. Howe and Chandler were to sail shortly thereafter and meet him in London. The railway guarantee was his primary objective, but he hoped to obtain the repeal of the imperial Clergy Reserve Act, which prevented the Canadian government from settling the clergy reserves question, and to accelerate the negotiations for a reciprocity agreement with the United States. He arrived in England to find that the Whigs had been defeated. Instead of Lord Grey, whom he knew was willing to consider the St John route for the guarantee, he would have to deal with his Tory successor, Sir John Pakington, an unknown quantity.

His initial impression of Pakington was unfavourable. Upon requesting an interview, he was informed he must await the arrival of Howe and Chandler, but in the interim, if he wished to prepare a memorandum on the background of his mission, the colonial secretary would be pleased to receive it. Chandler arrived in April, but Howe was delayed, having been forced by a technicality to seek re-election in a by-election. Hincks was becoming uneasy, for he would have to leave in May to prepare for the session of his own legislature.

It was 30 April before Hincks and Chandler alone were able to obtain an interview with the prime minister, Lord Derby. Sir John Pakington, who was present at the meeting, repeatedly emphasized that, regardless of any encouragement Grey might have given, the imperial government was committed only to the northern route. Hincks sensed that Pakington was laying the groundwork for a refusal of support with his emphasis on a line he knew was unacceptable to New Brunswick.

Conscious that his time was running short and annoyed at Pakington's imperious attitude and lack of courtesy, Hincks determined to force a decision from the Derby government. He still preferred to have the imperial guarantee, but he no longer considered it vital. He had done his best to preserve the arrangement for interprovincial co-operation, but if it was about to collapse for want of the imperial guarantee, he did not intend to go home empty handed. Aware that the firm of Peto, Brassey, Jackson, and Betts was ready to build Canadian railways as private enterprises, he would make his own arrangements with them.

On 1 May 1852 Hincks wrote to Pakington, stating that Canada could not submit to further delay. 'I am most anxious,' he declared, 'that Her Majesty's Government should understand most distinctly that I have not been sent to England as a humble suitor on the part of Canada for Imperial aid. Canada was invited by the Imperial Government to aid in the great national work under consideration ...' and she had responded 'generously and patriotically.'[42] But it now appeared 'far from improbable' that the negotiations would not be successful, and if this were so it was important for Canada to be informed as soon as possible. Arrangements could be made with 'eminent capitalists' to construct all the railroads Canada needed on her own unaided credit. He was certain that if the guarantee could not be made available, the British government would not wish to see Canada 'lose the opportunity of effecting other desirable arrangements.' He respectfully requested that he be given a firm answer by 15 May, adding that 'if Her Majesty's Government is unable either from want of time, or from the necessity of consulting Parliament, to come to a decision by that period, I must beg it to be understood that Canada withdraws from the present negotiations.'

Hincks had given the imperial government a virtual ultimatum, which Pakington regarded as a regrettable sign of increasing Canadian independence. For his part Hincks was beginning to think that the colonial secretary had little knowledge of the implications of responsible government. Pakington knew that the Canadian cabinet had asked Hincks to press for the repeal of the imperial Clergy Reserves Act while he was in England, but, in spite of this, he had ignored Hincks and written to Lord Elgin informing him that the government did not intend to repeal the act during the current session. In justification of this course he asserted that the views of the recently elected Canadian Assembly on the reserves issue were not known. In any case, the Derby government had 'serious doubts how far they would be able to give their consent and support to an arrangement, the result of which would probably be the diversion to other purposes of the only public fund ... for the support of Divine worship and religious instruction in the colony.'[43]

Hincks was angry. Two days after his blunt letter on railway negotiations he wrote to Pakington again, regretting to have learned through the newspapers that the government had decided to take no action on the reserves during the session. He reluctantly accepted the decision as 'irrevocable,' but he felt bound to warn Pakington 'that there will be no end to agitation in Canada if the attempt be made to settle the question permanently according to public opinion in England instead of that of the province itself.'[44] When he received a copy of Pakington's actual despatch to Elgin, he was astonished to find that the colonial secretary still contemplated resisting Canada's desire to secularize the reserves. He felt obliged to write Pakington on the subject once more:

I cannot view without grave apprehension the prospect of collision between Her Majesty's Government and the Parliament of Canada, on a question regarding which such strong feelings prevail among the great mass of the population ... It happens most unfortunately, that public opinion in England differs very widely from that in Canada on questions at all partaking of a religious character; and as the people of Canada are convinced that they are better judges than any parties in England can be of what measures will best conduce to the peace and welfare of the Province, Her Majesty's Government will, I trust, perceive that the danger which I apprehend is at least deserving of the most grave consideration.[45]

Hincks' initial unfavourable impression of Pakington had been confirmed by subsequent events; he now believed the colonial secretary to be the principal source of the frustration he had experienced – the time and effort wasted trying to save the imperial guarantee and interprovincial co-operation in railway building, and his failure to accomplish anything positive in connection with the clergy reserves. His brief discussion with Pakington concerning efforts to gain reciprocity with the United States had been equally unsatisfactory. The Canadian premier had been considering granting American vessels free navigation of the St Lawrence River as an inducement for the United States to enter into a reciprocal trade arrangement, but the secretary declared the imperial government would be opposed unless the Americans made an equivalent concession. This was disappointing, for Hincks had expected to increase the revenue from Canadian canal tolls as well as promote reciprocity by granting American vessels the right to use the St Lawrence River. Pakington was apparently unable to appreciate Canadian interests and was not impressed by Canadian arguments when they differed from his own. Hincks' mission was not a total failure, but what had been achieved was accomplished in spite of Pakington and the Derby government.

Hincks had been convinced from the outset that, whether the guarantee was available or not, most of the capital to build a Canadian trunk railway would have to come from British investors, and consequently it was important to secure the services of railway contractors in whom they would have confidence. He had left for England with the intention of examining the possibilities of entering into a contract with Peto, Brassey, Jackson, and Betts to construct the line.[46] Undoubtedly he had entered into discussions with the firm before he wrote to Pakington insisting upon an answer by 15 May. Very likely as the prospect of an imperial guarantee diminished, the enterprising William Jackson encouraged Hincks to think of alternative means of financing and constructing the railway. In any event, shortly after writing to the colonial secretary Hincks had entered into a contract subject to confirmation by the Canadian legislature.

Under the terms of the contract a railway was to be constructed from Montreal to Hamilton and from Quebec to Richmond, south-east of Montreal. It was intended that the link from Richmond to Montreal should be supplied by the St Lawrence and Atlantic Railway and that from Hamilton to Windsor at the south-western tip of Canada by the Great Western, both under construction already. One-tenth of the necessary capital was to be provided by Peto, Brassey, Jackson, and Betts; one-tenth was to come from the sale of stock to municipalities and private investors; and the sale of bonds was to provide three-tenths. The remaining 50 per cent was to be raised under Hincks' Guarantee Act of 1849. Jackson assured Hincks that with the company's connections, there would be no problem in raising the necessary funds.

There was other business to be attended to before he sailed. Knowing of Hincks' connection with Barings and other financial houses in London, the mayor of Montreal had asked him to arrange for the sale of an issue of his city's bonds. Hincks had previously recommended Canadian municipal debentures to Barings as a vast field for profitable investment and had suggested that he act as the firm's agent in this connection. Now, he wrote to Thomas Baring saying that he would like to take an offer to the city when he sailed. He asked whether Barings would be interested in handling the bonds on terms that would also allow him a 1 per cent commission as Montreal's agent. Subsequently, the negotiations collapsed and Hincks received no commission, but the incident would be used against him in the future. He saw nothing irregular, or improper, about a provincial premier acting as the financial agent for cities in his province, but it must be remembered that he lived in an age that was only starting to clarify its ideas on conflict of interest. Only a few years previously the province's receiver-general had been permitted to invest the public funds in his custody for his own private profit.

When Hincks arrived back in Canada in the late spring of 1852, he found that the strong stand he had taken with Pakington and the tentative railway contract had both created considerable excitement in the press. While government newspapers presented the contract as a positive achievement, Tory organs and George Brown's *Globe* found much to criticize. The Montreal *Gazette* charged the premier with impertinence and insincerity in his dealings with the British government and insinuated that he had been eager to kill the possibility of a guaranteed loan so that he could turn to private contractors. The *Gazette* also suggested that he had deliberately sought to manufacture a grievance against the Tory Pakington.[47]

Though he knew that he would eventually have to respond to such criticism, Hincks paid little attention to it as he prepared for the session of the legislature which began in Quebec on 19 August 1852. Once again, church-state relations and railways policy would be primary sources of concern and controversy. Hincks took an early opportunity in the debate on the reply to the speech from the throne to inform the house of Sir John Pakington's obstruction with regard to the clergy reserves. An opportunity would be given shortly, he promised, for the members to record their wishes with regard to the reserves. George Brown made his maiden speech in the debate, and queried the presence of the Clear Grits in a ministry with those they had consistently condemned. How could such opposing forces combine? Surely principles must have been ignored by one side or the other. Had Hincks been converted to the Grit faith in elective institutions? What had become of the Grits' denunciation of French-Canadian state-churchism? The plain fact of the matter was that the coalition was not based upon any principles and was thus a betrayal of the movement which had won responsible government.[48]

Nonetheless, in September, as he had promised, Hincks introduced a series of resolutions on the clergy reserves which he intended as a direct answer to Pakington. The resolutions began by asserting that the reserves were an internal problem and thus entirely within the jurisdiction of the provincial legislature. Though the Canadian people were loyal to the crown and anxious to maintain the connection with Great Britain, the second resolution declared: 'the refusal on the part of the Imperial Parliament to comply with the just demand of the representatives of the Canadian people on a matter exclusively affecting their own interests, will be viewed as a violation of their constitutional rights, and will lead to deep and widespread dissatisfaction among Her Majesty's Canadian subjects.[49]

Hincks' resolutions came under attack from both George Brown and Henry John Boulton, the latter an odd mixture of radical and Tory. Boulton proposed an amendment that condemned the threatening language of Hincks' resolutions. Brown, suspecting that the resolutions were a mask for conflicting views on the secularization of the reserves within the cabinet, called for the introduction of a secularization measure which could be suspended after it was passed until the imperial parliament had repealed the existing compromise act of 1840. After considerable debate, Boulton's and Brown's amendments were defeated and Hincks' resolutions approved; but once again it had been demonstrated that the clergy reserves were an active problem in urgent need of a solution.

When Pakington received the resolutions, he drafted a despatch regretting that the imperial government could not comply with the request that the Clergy Reserves Act be repealed because the reserves involved peculiar interests which made them a matter of imperial concern.[50] The Derby government went out of office before the despatch was sent, however, and Pakington's Whig-Liberal successor, the Duke of Newcastle, indicated he would honour Grey's promise to seek repeal of the act.

Simultaneously, the government sought to further its railways policy. Convinced that the municipalities were potentially an excellent source of investment in railways and other essential communications, Hincks was determined first to find some means of making credit more readily available to them. On 7 September he introduced a Municipal Loan Fund bill authorizing the provincial government to borrow money through the sale of Municipal Loan Fund debentures and to lend it to municipalities for investment in railway, canal, and road companies. At the time, the measure attracted very little attention in either the legislature or the newspapers. Apparently no one then foresaw the danger that it would help to over-stimulate enthusiasm for railways by making more funds locally available, and lead many cities and towns to increase their indebtedness unwisely in the belief that a railway connection would transform them into centres of industry and commerce. But regrettably, it did have that result.

The Municipal Loan Fund bill was followed on 24 September by a bill for the incorporation of the Grand Trunk Railway Company introduced by the company solicitor and rising French-Canadian politician, George Etienne Cartier. This met with immediate opposition from A.T. Galt, Luther Holton, and D.L. Macpherson, three leading businessmen who, having gained control of the charter for the Montreal-Kingston Railway, protested against granting the Grand Trunk a charter to build a line from Montreal to Toronto. Their contention that Canadian contractors ought not to be pushed aside for the benefit of an English firm was vigorously supported by the *Globe* and the Montreal *Gazette*. After a searching inquiry, the railway committee ruled in favour of the Grand Trunk, but Galt did not yield. He used his influence as president of the St Lawrence and Atlantic Railway to obtain the amalgamation of that line with the Montreal-Kingston Railway. Finally, Hincks won his agreement by proposing to include the St Lawrence and Atlantic as part of the Grand Trunk and to construct a bridge across the St Lawrence, thus giving the St Lawrence and Atlantic Railway direct access to Montreal.[51]

When the Grand Trunk bill came up for debate in the assembly, the Reform-independent, George Brown, and the rising Conservative, John A. Macdonald, led the opposition to it, continuing the attack on the use of English contractors. To such criticism Hincks steadfastly replied that Canadians could not raise the large amounts of capital necessary to build the road. British investors were the only source of sufficient funds, and if they were to have confidence in the railway it was essential that the contractors should be well known and highly respected in Britain. When the vote was taken, Hincks obtained, as he had confidently expected, a solid majority in favour of the Grand Trunk bill.

Early in November 1852 the church-state issue was revived by debate on a bill to incorporate Catholic St Mary's College in Canada East, in which it became clear how easily this question could threaten the Reform alliance. Joseph Cauchon accused Hincks of leaving the house to avoid voting on the bill, and, pointing out that all the Upper Canadian ministers had voted against the measure while their Lower Canadian colleagues supported it, he declared that 'the alliance ... of the two parties which formed the ministry was unnatural, monstrous and impossible of endurance.'[52] Hincks replied that he was not opposed to the incorporation of the college, but he preferred to see it incorporated under a general bill that would be introduced later in the session. He denied that he had ever shirked a vote and challenged Cauchon to prove otherwise. George Brown expressed his own outright opposition to all religious corporations because of their power to accumulate land that was thus forever removed from general commerce – monastic institutions had been 'the curse of all countries where they had been established.' With the exception of Hincks, Brown insisted, the Upper Canadian ministers had declared themselves opposed to ecclesiastical corporations on numerous occasions.

When parliament reconvened in February, Hincks informed the members that a despatch had been received from the colonial secretary, the Duke of Newcastle, promising that the Clergy Reserves Act would be repealed, but he gave no indication of how the government intended to settle the problem when the impediment to provincial legislation was removed. Indeed, as the session progressed, doctrinaire voluntarists found still more to criticize in the government's policy.

The Upper Canadian 'University question' now reappeared, since supporters of denominational colleges were attacking the secular, state-supported University of Toronto set up in 1849, seeking a share of public funds for their own institutions. George Brown was astonished by Hincks' answer: a proposal to make the provincial university an examining and degree-granting body, and to give its teaching functions to a non-sectarian University College, to be established in Toronto in connection with the university. Asserting that the idea of one single provincial university had not given general satisfaction, Hincks proposed that the several church colleges be given the opportunity to affiliate with the university and share in any surplus revenue. To Brown, Hincks' proposal was a shameful attack upon the 'great and noble' institution established by Robert Baldwin. 'It would be a national calamity,' he protested, 'to split up and destroy Toronto University for a set of little paltry colleges' each of which would offer an inferior education and its own sectarian bias.[53]

Brown was even more vehement in his opposition to the Ecclesiastical Corporations bill, declaring that it would be injurious to the best interests of the country. It was much worse than individual incorporation bills brought forward one at a time, for then, as each one was debated, its 'pernicious influence' could be impressed upon the public mind. If the bill passed, however, separate acts would no longer be required to incorporate religious societies. 'The province will swarm with corporations,' he warned, as he moved in amendment that the bill be given a three-month hoist.[54]

Brown's amendment was defeated, 33-39, with the Conservatives, as the Tories were now generally calling themselves, voting with Brown. Pleased that the combined efforts of Brown and the Conservatives had been ineffective, Hincks seized the opportunity to deride Sir Allan MacNab and his followers. The 'great Conservative party,' he jeered, had voted to a man with Brown, but it had been strangely silent in the debate which preceded the vote. 'Yes, they had heard the principle of the bill discussed for three nights without saying a word – without daring to say a word – without venturing to commit themselves; and they watched their chance to profit by a division created among the supporters of the government by the member for Kent.'[55]

Vigorous as Brown's opposition was on church-state issues, Hincks knew that he would be just as aggressive on the question of representation. Ever since the census returns of 1851 had revealed that the population of Canada West now exceeded that of Canada East, the demand for representation by population had been growing in the western half of the United Province. Though he rejected the Clear Grits' political radicalism, Brown had come to share their opinion that the Reform alliance was dominated by Morin and his French-Canadian followers. Because of their political power, Upper Canada was threatened with French-Canadian domination and the expansion of Roman Catholic influence and institutions in the province. For Brown and many Upper Canadians there was a simple solution – 'Rep by Pop.' If representation were based on population, Upper Canada would have the members, and thus the political power, to counteract the French threat. But no French Canadian could consider replacing equal representation with representation by population and the threat of a voluntarist majority which that implied. Firmly convinced, however, that the Union was vital for Canadian economic development, Hincks rejected 'Rep by Pop,' and clung instead to the alliance with French Canada and the maintenance of the Union.

Although they were firmly committed to equal representation, Hincks and Morin were anxious to enlarge the number of seats in the legislature and improve upon their distribution in each section of the province. To this end Morin introduced a bill increasing the number of seats in each section of the province from 42 to 65. In March the debate on Morin's bill gave Brown an opportunity to propose that representation be based upon population 'without regard to any separating line between Upper and Lower Canada.'[56] His proposal was defeated, 57-15, but he continued to oppose Morin's bill, expressing his amazement that the government proposed to perpetuate a system which gave 'one portion of our population a larger representation than another just because they live in a different part of the country.'[57]

The representation question came up again early in May, when Brown sought the repeal of the requirement for a two-thirds majority to change representation in the assembly. In support of his proposal he declared that as it had a larger population and contributed more to the consolidated revenue, Upper Canada would not consent to remain under-represented.[58] Hincks declared that Brown's argument was 'most illiberal' and that he had taken the 'narrowest of views of the union.' With the French-Canadian members crying 'hear, hear,' he continued: 'The truth was that people occupying Upper and Lower Canada were not homogeneous: but they differed in feelings, language, laws, religion and institutions: therefore the Union must be considered as between two distinct peoples each returning an equal number of representatives.'[59]

Hincks and Brown clashed again early in June 1853 over the government's supplementary Common School bill. As a result of pressure from Armand de Charbonnel, the Roman Catholic bishop of Toronto, the fourth clause of the bill authorized Roman Catholic ratepayers in Canada West to establish Boards of Trustees for separate schools with power to collect and expend money. Acting in concert with the old radical William Lyon Mackenzie, Brown endeavoured first to carry an amendment abolishing separate schools, and, when this failed, to give the bill a six-month hoist. His ire aroused, Hincks charged Brown with having mounted a crusade against separate schools in the *Globe* and arousing religious animosities and public excitement.[60] But when the charges and counter-charges had all been made, the bill was carried by Morin and the French-Canadian bloc; only ten Upper Canadian members supported the ministry while seventeen were opposed. Brown considered this a flagrant example of French-Canadian domination of Upper Canada, but Hincks understood and sympathized with the French-Canadian desire to obtain for their co-religionists in Upper Canada the same privileges enjoyed by Protestants in Canada East.

The long session finally ended on 10 June 1853, amid the vehemence and animosity generated by the Gavazzi religious riots in Quebec and Montreal. It was an atmosphere which only exalted George Brown's aggressive voluntarism in Upper Canada, and generated more criticism there of the government's continuing dependence on French-Canadian support.

As Hincks looked back over the heated session, he still could take satisfaction in having carried his railway legislation and most of his important measures. The clergy reserves remained to be secularized, but shortly before the session ended word had been received that the imperial parliament had finally cleared the way for the Canadian legislature to enact its own solution. It was true that Morin's efforts to reform seigneurial tenure and to make the Legislative Council elective had encountered snags, but he planned to bring forward new legislation when the house met again. In many ways, indeed, it had been a most successful session; but there were worrisome thoughts that cast long shadows on the future. Despite the presence of John Rolph and Malcolm Cameron in the cabinet, an open split remained within the Reform ranks. George Brown was playing upon that split with his resolutions in favour of representation by population and his attempts to make voluntarist principles prevail.

Hincks was worried too about the possibility of his speculation in Toronto debentures being discovered. Shortly after he returned from England in the spring of 1852 he had joined with John Bowes, mayor of Toronto, in purchasing, at 20 per cent discount, £50,000 in Toronto debentures which the city had originally invested in the Ontario, Simcoe and Huron Railway to encourage construction of that line. The plan was that Hincks, through his connections with the leading financial houses in England, should arrange the resale of the securities at a profit. To make the debentures more attractive to British investors – but without disclosing that he and Hincks had acquired them – Bowes persuaded the city council to include the £50,000 in a consolidation of the city's debt. Under his guidance the council petitioned the legislature for an act authorizing the issue of £100,000 in new debentures, £50,000 of which were to be exchanged for the depreciated ones. As an added inducement to British investors the new debentures were to be issued in sterling and made payable in London or elsewhere.

The Toronto Debt Consolidation Act was introduced by a Toronto member of the opposition, William Boulton, but Hincks and the president of the Ontario, Simcoe and Huron Railway, J.C. Morrison, lent their support in the legislature to push it through as quickly as possible. By combining debt consolidation and the redemption of depreciated debentures in one measure, and putting the emphasis on the former, Hincks and Bowes got their act through the legislature without opposition – and without their ownership of the debentures being discovered. Before the end of 1852 they had sold their new securities at a profit of slightly more than £8000 after expenses were deducted.

During the parliamentary recess from 11 November 1852 to February 1853, Hincks began to hear disquieting rumours of charges against Mayor Bowes regarding speculation in Toronto's debentures. Anxiously he asked George Brown about the reports when Brown returned from Toronto, but upon being informed that the rumours suggested he had been associated with Bowes, he denied any connection.[61] Before the long session ended on 10 June 1853, William Lyon Mackenzie tried to launch a parliamentary inquiry into the matter. Mackenzie was unsuccessful, but as Hincks reflected on the transaction during the summer of 1853 he knew that the city would likely sue John Bowes. If it did, his own involvment would soon be public knowledge. He did not consider that he had acted dishonestly in any way, but he knew full well how both the *Globe* and the Tory press would seize upon the matter and make political capital out of it.

By September his fears were realized as the suit uncovered the details of what the opposition soon termed 'the £10,000 job.' Upon this base, innuendo and rumour continued to build during the autumn and winter; in effect Hincks became suspected of having used his position and inside knowledge for private gain in a whole series of unscrupulous deals. Convinced of Hincks' dishonesty, George Brown determined to drive him from public life and rebuild a truly liberal party.

The attack on Hincks' character had an effect as well on the Clear Grits. William McDougall, who had promoted the entry of Rolph and Cameron into the cabinet, soon decided that Hincks must be thrown over as leader.[62] In October Thomas Shenston informed Hincks of rumours circulating in Oxford County that John Rolph had joined a conspiracy to force Hincks out and planned to submit his resignation as a means to this end. Hincks found it hard to believe such a report, but still, he could not be certain. '*If by any caballing* ... Dr. Rolph shd be *induced to* resign,' he replied, 'it will not change the policy of the Government nor will it interfere with our appealing to the people by a general election as soon as possible.' If division within the party led to defeat in the election, he continued, '*To me the only result* can be mortification for the injury done to the great cause of reform, but coupled with this will be great personal relief from the cares of office which are daily becoming more & oppressive.'[63]

Hincks had expected in fact that the construction of the Grand Trunk would promote prosperity and that this would redound to the credit of the government. Instead, by the autumn of 1853 the Grand Trunk was already encountering financial difficulties; its stock was below par and Thomas Baring was complaining that the company was being mismanaged.[64] The Grand Trunk was becoming a political liability instead of an asset. In addition, a report was being circulated that Hincks had been paid off with a block of Grand Trunk stock for giving the contract to Jackson and his partners.

Early in 1854 Lord Elgin went home on leave and, as he knew he would be consulted on the question of reciprocal free trade with the United States, he asked Hincks to accompany him. Although it had been necessary to leave the actual negotiations with the American republic to British diplomats, Hincks had been actively working to obtain a reciprocity arrangement ever since he took office in 1848. In 1849 he had agreed with Elgin that reciprocity was essential as an antidote to annexation sentiment. In 1850 and 1851 he had journeyed to Washington to assist in negotiations. He had taken advantage of a 'railway jubilee' in Boston in 1851 to tell Americans of the benefits they could expect from reciprocity. Now he readily accepted Elgin's invitation. If the elusive reciprocity agreement could finally be obtained, it might help him and his government to regain the prestige they had lost.

Elgin and Hincks arrived in England at an opportune moment. After years of unsuccessful negotiations, both the United States and Great Britain were anxious to settle the long outstanding question of access to the British North American fisheries before it produced serious friction between them. And there was a good possibility the settlement might include reciprocal trade in natural products between the United States and British North America. When the suggestion was made that Great Britain send a special plenipotentiary to the United States to assist in discussions on the fishery question, the British foreign secretary, Lord Clarendon, announced that Lord Elgin and Hincks would pay a visit to Washington on their way back to Quebec.

Upon their arrival in the American capital on 26 May 1854, Elgin and Hincks were pleased to find circumstances more favourable to reciprocity than they had been at any time in the past. Southern senators seemed less defensive and more confident of the South's ability to co-exist with the North. In addition, a period of prosperity had dispersed anti-reciprocity sentiments in the North. In a round of balls, dinners, and receptions Elgin took every opportunity to talk informally with Southern senators and to impress upon them that a reciprocity treaty was the best means of avoiding the annexation of British North America to the United States, and thus the addition of a number of free states. After ten days of social lobbying, Elgin indeed informed President Pierce that he was confident a reciprocity treaty would have the necessary majority in the Senate. It now became a relatively simple matter for Elgin and the American secretary of state, William Marcy, to agree upon the details. A draft treaty was signed on 5 June. Delighted with the success of their mission, Lord Elgin and Hincks departed for Canada.

They had barely returned to Quebec before the session of the legislature, delayed to the last legal moment, began. Twice it had been necessary to postpone the session, when fires in February and May had severely damaged the old legislative buildings and destroyed a convent that was being prepared as alternative quarters. When the assembly finally met on 13 June, the opposition expected the government to bring forward measures to deal with the clergy reserves and seigneurial tenure. Their surprise and anger mounted when they learned in the Speech from the Throne that it was considered improper to proceed with important measures now, as the next election would see the assembly enlarged from 84 members to 130. The government thus proposed a brief session to be followed by dissolution and an election. Though the ministry may have been playing for time and seeking to capitalize on having at last obtained the American reciprocity agreement, Lord Elgin fully agreed with the decision to postpone secularization of the reserves until after the election, and may have urged his cabinet to adopt this policy.

Far from accepting the government's proposals, Conservatives, Clear Grits, Brownites, Rouges, and right-wing French-Canadian independents combined in a determined effort to drive Hincks and Morin from office. The ministry was accused of procrastination, corruption, and extravagance – charges that could be sustained by rumours and its own actions. Finally, on 20 June, an amendment was carried regretting that the government did not plan to introduce a measure for the abolition of seigneurial tenure or 'one for the immediate settlement of the Clergy Reserves.'[65] It was a clear vote of no confidence.

Francis Hincks was tired and exasperated. He had used all his parliamentary debating skill to no avail in an effort to avoid defeat. His government had been censured by what seemed a hypocritical combination of those who demanded immediate secularization of the reserves and those who were utterly opposed to it. There was no way in which these forces could work together to form a government, and yet they had conspired to defeat an administration with a positive constructive programme.

Faced with the assembly's censure, the ministry decided to advise an immediate dissolution and a new election. Though this was clearly an option open to them, and one that followed logically from their insistence that only the enlarged assembly should deal with the reserves and seigneurial tenure, many members of the opposition had somehow managed to convince themselves that the government was bound to resign. They were disagreeably surprised when the assembly met on 22 June to learn that the governor was already on his way to prorogue the house. The session terminated in confusion, as the angry opposition protested loudly and irrationally that such a prorogation was both arbitrary and unconstitutional, while the Speaker, Sandfield Macdonald, attempted to lecture Lord Elgin on the constitutional points involved.

Knowing he would encounter strong opposition from the Clear Grits in South Oxford, Hincks accepted the proposal of the Ottawa Valley lumber Baron, John Egan, that he should also stand for Renfrew. He readily agreed to Egan's stipulation that he should sit for Renfrew if he secured a double return. Despite determined efforts made by William Lyon Mackenzie and George Brown to defeat him, Hincks obtained the largest majority he had ever received in South Oxford and was elected in Renfrew County. In the province as a whole the government elected more members than any other party, but they were still short of a clear majority. Hincks realized that he must find additional support, or the government would be as vulnerable as it had been before the election.

He foresaw that when the legislature met, the election of the Speaker would be a crucial test of strength, and he was convinced that if the government failed to elect its candidate it would not last a week. In search of support he wrote to Alexander Galt to inquire if the Rouges with whom Galt was then associated would combine forces with the government's supporters to elect George E. Cartier, by now a notable eastern ministerial Liberal. Galt's reply suggested little prospect of Rouge support, but it did hold out the possibility that he might act independently himself and support the ministry if he approved of its programme for the session.[66]

There were three candidates for the speakership when the assembly met: Sandfield Macdonald, who was seeking re-election to that office; George E. Cartier, the government's candidate; and Louis Sicotte, whom the Rouges intended to nominate. Cartier was nominated first, only to be defeated, 59 to 61, by the combined votes of independent western Reformers, Rouges, and seventeen Conservatives.[67]

With Cartier's defeat it appeared that the combined strategy of George Brown and Sandfield Macdonald was about to succeed. Sicotte would be nominated and defeated, and then Sandfield would be triumphantly re-elected. On the basis of this victory he was to be brought forward as the leader of a reconstructed Reform party in Canada West, dedicated to the separation of church and state, representation by population, and non-sectarian schools.

But in formulating their strategy Brown and Sandfield Macdonald had underestimated Hincks. He knew his government would soon suffer defeat and that a new political alignment would be formed, but bitter at what he considered a malicious conspiracy, he resolved to deny Brown and Sandfield their anticipated triumph. Sicotte was nominated, and one by one the Rouges cast their votes on his behalf, while Hincks, Morin, and their followers looked on without any trace of emotion. When the last Rouge vote had been cast, Hincks rose and called out, 'Put me among the ayes' and then sat down to enjoy the consternation on the faces of the opposition, as his example was followed by Morin and each of the ministerialists in turn. As it became apparent that Sicotte would be elected by a large majority, Sandfield looked across the floor at Hincks and sarcastically mouthed the words 'thank you.' The premier replied with a mocking courtly bow.[68]

When the Speech from the Throne declared that a 'measure' would be introduced to settle the clergy reserves, the independent reformers suspected further subterfuge and delay and proposed amendments specifying that the reserves were to be secularized. Galt also informed Hincks that because of the Throne Speech's ambiguities he could not in good conscience support the government. Piqued at this lack of trust, Hincks replied: 'I want no vote from any man who does not believe my word as a minister that I am prepared to secularize the Reserves ...'[69]

Hincks had already made up his mind to resign after the vote was taken on the reply to the Throne Speech, but when the government was defeated on a question of privilege, and when he was taunted by the Tory John Hillyard Cameron with being unable to control the house, he decided not to cling to office any longer. After consulting with Morin he submitted the government's resignation to Lord Elgin on 8 September 1854.

He intended to resign also as leader of the Upper Canadian Reformers, but in doing so he hoped to arrange an alternative to the political alignment envisaged by George Brown and Sandfield Macdonald. Fearful that Brown's influence would shatter the Union and destroy the province's credit, Hincks sought a reconstructed Upper Canadian Liberal party that would continue the alliance with the main body of French Canadians rather than drive them into the arms of right-wing Conservatives. Initially he proposed John Wilson, a moderate Conservative from London who was pledged to support secularization, as his successor. But he soon saw the prospect of a much stronger coalition than he had imagined possible.

The day after he had announced the government's resignation in the assembly, Hincks was pleasantly surprised to learn that Sir Allan MacNab had approached Morin on behalf of the Upper Canadian Conservatives to seek an alliance. They had tentatively agreed to form a coalition dedicated to secularization of the reserves, the abolition of seigneurial tenure, and the creation of an elective Legislative Council. At first Hincks was amazed that MacNab could bring himself to sponsor secularization after having opposed it so violently, but upon reflection he recalled that during the election many Conservative candidates had pledged themselves to support it. In reversing his stand MacNab was accepting the verdict of the electorate. At Morin's request the Tory-Conservative leader had agreed to give Hincks and his followers an opportunity to join the coalition. Hincks now realized that MacNab could bring in virtually the whole Conservative party, and that such an alignment would enjoy an overwhelming majority in the assembly. It would give MacNab and John A. Macdonald the predominant influence in Upper Canada rather than George Brown and Sandfield Macdonald, but this was entirely acceptable to Hincks, for the Conservative leaders appreciated the necessity of maintaining the alliance with French Canada. These same leaders were no less favourably inclined to railway development: a significant point for Hincksite proponents of the Grand Trunk.

When MacNab invited Hincks to support the new coalition he replied, accordingly, that although he and his followers were not likely to go into opposition, if they were to be formally associated with the government they must have two seats in the cabinet. After consulting with his colleagues, MacNab agreed. Hincks did not consider taking one of the two seats himself. Under suspicion and deserted by former colleagues, he knew that, for the moment at least, he was a 'governmental impossibility.'[70] He discussed the matter with members of his party and then named John Ross and Robert Spence as the Hincksite representatives in the Liberal-Conservative coalition. The decisive shift was complete, and the day of the old Reform party had ended in the Canadian Union.

In announcing his government's resignation to the assembly, Hincks declared: 'I am anxious to submit to the judgment of the House any charges that can possibly be brought against me.'[71] It was a foregone conclusion that there would be a parliamentary inquiry into all the charges that had been circulating, for most members felt a thorough investigation was necessary to clear the air. Consequently, once the new government was installed in office, committees of inquiry were established by both the assembly and the Legislative Council. Hincks devoted most of his attention to the hearings of the assembly's committee. And it was well that he did, for, as a member of that committee, George Brown soon assumed the dual role of prosecutor and judge and pursued him vindictively throughout the hearings. Brown may have been prompted by a stern conscience that demanded Hincks' exposure and punishment as an example and warning to others, or perhaps he was motivated by a desire for revenge on the man who had helped to thwart his plans for political realignment. Whatever his motive, he was clearly intent on ruining Hincks forever as a public man.

The hearings began on 26 October 1854 and continued until December when they adjourned for the Christmas recess. They resumed again on 16 March 1855 and continued until the committee submitted its report at the end of April.[72] Numerous witnesses were heard, many of whom repeated their suspicions regarding Hincks' activities, but no solid, factual evidence of wrong-doing was presented. George Brown appeared as a witness himself and, anxious to develop a case, he requested that he be allowed to prepare full written replies to the questions he was asked. With Hincks' concurrence the request was granted. But when Brown did not confine himself to facts within his own personal knowledge, the committee ruled that his testimony could not be admitted as evidence. In spite of this ruling Antoine Dorion, Brown's ally on the committee, contrived to read his replies into the record by proposing them as amendments. But even Brown's testimony amounted only to suspicions – there was no solid evidence upon which a criminal charge could be based. Indeed, in a number of instances Brown's factual evidence was revealed to be quite inaccurate.

Hincks handled the charges investigated by the committee in two ways. On the one hand, he insisted that in taking office he had not forfeited his right to participate in legitimate investments and denied that he had ever misused the powers of his office or utilized inside information for his own personal gain. On the other hand, he showed that many of the accusations against him were based on factual inaccuracies.

He denied there was anything improper about the profit he had made, together with Mayor Bowes, speculating in Toronto debentures. It was a legitimate transaction that was open to any investor. The Court of Chancery, it was true, had declared that Mayor Bowes could only have acted as a trustee of the city and ordered him to pay his share of the profit over to the city. But it did not rule that the transaction was dishonest. There was no suggestion that the city or any individual should enter suit against Hincks. The fact that there had been no opposition in the legislature to the bill to refinance Toronto's debt refuted the claim that he had used his influence to carry the measure – such influence had not been required.

Brown had claimed that Hincks used prior knowledge of the amalgamation of the St Lawrence and Atlantic Railway with the Grand Trunk to make a profitable private investment in the depressed shares of the former company. Much to Brown's chagrin, however, Hincks revealed that he had not bought St Lawrence and Atlantic shares until some time after the amalgamation had been announced and the shares had risen considerably. To the further charge that he had helped to arrange a loan for the city of Montreal and had received a commission for doing so, Hincks replied that the negotiations he was conducting had collapsed and, consequently, no commission had been paid. But he admitted that he would have accepted the commission if it had been possible to earn it and insisted that he had had a perfect right to do so.

The claim was also made that Hincks had been given 1008 shares of Grand Trunk stock as a reward for giving Peto, Brassey, Jackson, and Betts the contract to build the railway. It was true that the stock had been allotted to Hincks in the company's books and that Sir Morton Peto had paid the initial deposit on it in Hincks' name. But two Grand Trunk directors testified that the stock was not intended for Hincks personally; rather, it had been allotted to him in trust for distribution in Canada so that Canadian investors could be given an opportunity to acquire stock at par. Whatever the original intention, it was clear that Hincks had never received the stock.

A number of other charges based upon erroneous information collapsed in the light of the evidence presented to the committee. This was true of the claim that his financial interests had led Hincks to oppose the incorporation of a company to build a canal on the Canadian side of the border at Sault Ste Marie. Similarly, accusations that he had used his political influence on behalf of a land speculation syndicate composed of Samuel Mills, James Morris, William Matthie, and himself were shown to be groundless.

At the conclusion of the hearings the committee essentially recognized that Hincks and some of his colleagues had purchased public lands and securities 'in the same manner as other individuals in the community and Members of former administrations.' The evidence presented to it, the committee declared, would not support a charge of corruption against any member of the Hincks-Morin administration. Astonishment was also expressed that 'after the circulation of so many charges of corruption ... no person appeared before this Committee either to advance any such charge, or offer evidence in support thereof; and this Committee has been compelled to depend entirely upon its own exertions in obtaining information and evidence in respect of the charges investigated.'[73] Brown and Dorion were strongly opposed to these findings and tried unsuccessfully to carry amendments declaring that Hincks was guilty of 'official misconduct of a grave character' and that his cabinet colleagues, Taché, Morris, and Ross, had committed 'acts inconsistent with their positions as Responsible Ministers of the Crown.' There was clearly some uneasiness among members of the committee regarding the suspicions aroused when members of the government made private investments, but they were not prepared to censure Hincks and his colleagues either on the basis of the evidence or on previous practice. The select committee of the Legislative Council reported on 25 April 1855 and came to virtually the same conclusion as the assembly's committee: there was no evidence of corruption on the part of the late ministry.

Though he had never doubted the outcome, Hincks was naturally pleased to be exonerated by both parliamentary committees. He did not plan, however, to remain in politics. He continued to attend the assembly during the first two weeks of May, but shortly thereafter he left for a visit with his relatives in England and Ireland. On his return he intended to accept the presidency of the Grand Trunk Railway, which had been offered to him, but while he was travelling in Ireland he received a letter from the colonial secretary, now Sir William Molesworth, proposing his appointment as governor of Barbados and the Windward Islands. The offer came as a complete surprise, but it was most gratifying. To receive such an appointment at the hands of the queen would be the ultimate answer to those who cast aspersions on him in Canada. After only a few days' consideration he readily accepted the post.

In the islands under his charge Hincks found a much more rudimentary form of representative government than he was accustomed to, but he adjusted to it quite easily. He interested himself in improving the social conditions and education facilities of the creoles who had been freed from slavery in 1834. He would have liked to redistribute the creole population and thus reduce the Windward Islands' dependence upon indentured coolie labourers from India and China, but his efforts were thwarted by the opposition of sugar planters who feared his proposals would result in higher labour costs.

During his term as governor, Hincks won the approval of both the inhabitants of the islands and his superiors in Great Britain. In September 1861, as his term was drawing to a close, the Duke of Newcastle offered him another appointment as governor of British Guiana. The new position, carrying with it an increase in salary and rank, was a definitive mark of approbation and Hincks was pleased to accept. As an additional sign of commendation he was made a Commander of the Bath at the end of his term in Barbados.

In British Guiana Hincks was called upon to administer an authoritarian form of government based upon a modification of the original Dutch system and he found himself almost immediately in conflict with a group of professional and business men whose leaders were known as the 'Bermuda Clique.' The 'Bermuda Clique' were opposed to the continuation of the planter oligarchy and demanded a more representative form of British government. Hincks' major problem, however, grew out of a personality clash between himself and Chief Justice William Beaumont. The two men disliked each other from the beginning and the asperity between them increased as Beaumont embarked on a determined effort to curtail the governor's prerogative and to interfere with his executive powers. The perpetual quarrels between the rivals and the long complaining letters each wrote to the Colonial Office were probably the main reason that neither was reappointed at the conclusion of his term.

In 1865 Hincks' youngest son, Edward, paid a visit to his family after graduating from Oxford with a distinguished record. The pleasure of his visit turned suddenly to sorrow, however, when he contracted yellow fever and died. In the spring of 1866 Hincks went on leave to England and was still there when the delegates from Nova Scotia, New Brunswick, and Canada arrived for the London Conference on Confederation. Hincks enjoyed renewing acquaintances with John A. Macdonald, Cartier, and Galt. He attended Macdonald's wedding to Agnes Bernard in London in February 1867, and at the reception afterwards he proposed the toast to the bride.[74]

Returning to British Guiana in September, Hincks found himself once again embroiled in controversy with Chief Justice Beaumont. He was probably not sorry when he was notified in December 1868 that his successor had been appointed and would relieve him early in the new year. In recognition of his services he had been recommended for a knighthood, but there was no suggestion of a further appointment.

When he arrived in England in the spring of 1869 he learned that there was no immediate prospect of a new office. The suggestion was made that he go on half pension and Hincks agreed, though, as he was only sixty-two, he continued to hope that he might receive one more appointment. Because of the high cost of living in London he decided to pay a visit to Canada. He arrived to find John A. Macdonald searching for a minister of finance to replace John Rose who wished to resign and return to England. Macdonald offered Hincks the post and, after a number of days spent sounding out old friends and supporters, he accepted.

The one-time premier's re-entry into Canadian politics was signalled by a renewal of the *Globe*'s hostility towards him. All the old charges of the 1850s were revived when he successfully sought to win a seat in a North Renfrew by-election. The opposition of George Brown and his associates, or of Sandfield Macdonald, could perhaps be taken for granted, but he was surprised to find strong criticism of his appointment within Liberal-Conservative ranks themselves. When he was named minister of finance, Mackenzie Bowell, Richard Cartwright, and A.T. Galt tried unsuccessfully to promote a revolt against John A. Macdonald as Conservative leader and prime minister. The truth was that he was of another age, and neither the Liberals nor the Conservatives really welcomed his return to Canadian politics.

In spite of this, however, Hincks proved to be an extremely able minister of finance. He readily took on the task of laying the basis for a national currency and a national banking system. His firm stand on the administration of Canadian loans raised in Great Britain did much to free Canada from the restraints of the British Treasury and to establish Canadian fiscal autonomy. As finance minister he served as one of John A. Macdonald's principal advisers when the prime minister sought an agreement for reciprocity in natural products with the United States. He participated actively in the early discussions concerning the financing and building of a Canadian transcontinental railway. It was Hincks who first discussed the railway to the Pacific with Sir Hugh Allan on behalf of the government and encouraged him to think in terms of American financing. In fact, he put Allan in contact with the group of American financiers who subsequently became involved in the notorious Pacific Scandal, when it was revealed that Allan, who had gained the CPR charter, had contributed handsomely to Conservative election funds.

In the election of 1872 Hincks was nominated for South Brant and soon found himself engaged in a strenuous fight with William Paterson, the Liberal candidate. The *Globe* singled him out for concerted attack, rehearsing once again all the old accusations of 1854 and adding some new ones; he was threatened as well with the united opposition of the large number of Roman Catholics in his constituency. When he was defeated the *Globe* declared, triumphantly, that this was one of the worst upsets suffered by the government in the election. Without consulting him, Macdonald then had him nominated and elected in the safe Conservative constituency of Vancouver Island, but Francis Hincks had lost his zest for political life. Disillusioned and suffering from poor health, he decided to resign from the cabinet before the session of 1873 began. He would finish out his term as a private member, but he was anxious now to retire from politics.

His desire to free himself from the cabinet responsibility increased when he learned that the Liberals were preparing to charge the government with corruption in connection with the chartering of the transcontinental railway and Sir Hugh Allan's financial assistance to Conservative ministers in their election campaign. He submitted his resignation from the ministry on 10 February 1873; Macdonald reluctantly accepted it. In April the Liberal L.S. Huntington made the Pacific Scandal public in parliament. Throughout the summer Hincks worked with J.J.C. Abbott, a Conservative member and Allan's legal adviser, preparing evidence for presentation to the Royal Commission which had been appointed to investigate the charges against the government. He testified before the commission himself and explained the role he had taken in the early negotiations while, at the same time, denying he had been guilty of any wrong-doing. When the Liberals defeated the Conservatives in the legislature that autumn, and then called a new election for January 1874, he retired at last from public life and settled down in Montreal.

Shortly after moving there, Hincks was bereaved by the death of his wife, and for several months he was in poor health himself. But before the end of 1874 he had recovered and married the widow of Robert Baldwin Sullivan. Not yet ready for full retirement, he contributed editorials to the Canadian

Journal of Commerce and accepted the presidency of the Confederation Life Insurance Company. He was also president of the Consolidated Bank of Canada, but advancing age and poor health led him to neglect his duties. When the bank failed it was discovered that Hincks had been in the habit of signing, without properly checking, reports falsified by the general manager to conceal the bank's financial instability. The general manager fled to the United States and Hincks was left to face the shareholders. Required to stand trial, he was acquitted of any dishonesty, but was censured for his carelessness. When he submitted his resignation as president of the bank it was readily accepted.

Though now fully retired, he still kept active. In 1878 he accepted John A. Macdonald's invitation to serve as the federal government's representative on the Ontario-Manitoba boundary commission. He took a keen interest in the work of the historian, J.C. Dent, and spent much time and effort helping him to clarify specific points in connection with Dent's well-known works, *The Canadian Portrait Gallery* and *The Last Forty Years: Canada Since the Union of 1841.*[75] Subsequently, the former premier undertook the preparation of his own reminiscences, which were published in 1884; but unfortunately he had waited too long to begin this task and the work lacked the coherence, vigour, and spirit that one would have expected from him. His second wife had died in 1880 and he was now living with his married daughter, Ellen Ready, who increasingly had to care for him as his health declined. In August 1885 Francis Hincks fell ill with smallpox, as an epidemic swept Montreal. Within a few days, on 18 August, he died at the age of 77.

In many ways the years before Hincks became premier were the most productive and the most dynamic in his long career. It was during this time that he acquired the business and banking experience upon which his reputation as a financial administrator and 'the best public accountant in the country' was based. In the period immediately following the rebellion he became, through the *Examiner*, the spokesman and the political strategist of the Upper Canadian Reform movement. His work in explaining responsible government and rekindling hope in the possibility of political and social reform was a major factor in the revival of the movement after Lord Durham's appointment was announced. It was he who recognized the great advantages Upper Canadian Reformers could derive from an alliance with French Canada and who took the initiative to make that alliance. Although he was quite ignorant of French-Canadian values and objectives when he first wrote to LaFontaine, he learned quickly and soon became an outspoken exponent of *la survivance*. It was also during these years that he revealed another aspect of his character – his essential pragmatism, which could well appear as readiness to compromise on political principles. His temporary break with Baldwin and the French-Canadian Reformers in 1841 permanently labelled him a political opportunist.

When in 1844 he moved to Montreal and founded the *Pilot*, he hoped that he and his newspaper would serve as vital links between Upper Canadian Reformers and their French-Canadian counterparts. His move did increase his influence with French Canadians, both through frequent personal contact with their leaders and indirectly through the *Pilot*, as his editorials were translated and republished in the French-Canadian papers. But the move to Montreal isolated him to a degree from the Reformers in the western half of the province. Furthermore, he had always been a voluntarist, but his liberalism prevented his voluntarism from becoming extreme and thus threatening the Reform alliance. His ideal of civil and religious liberty together with his pragmatism brought him to accept the claim of Roman Catholics that they should be permitted to devote their school taxes to the support of their own separate school system. To ultra-voluntarists in Upper Canada, however, this appeared to be a dangerous compromise of principles – another example of Hincks' political opportunism, and a possible prelude to the rationalization of French domination of Upper Canada. The antagonism between George Brown and Hincks thus had its roots in the difference in degree of their voluntarism, while a mutual antipathy developed through the rivalry of the *Globe* and the *Pilot* and through Hincks' suspicions that Brown wished to supplant him both in Oxford County and within the party as a whole.

Hincks was thoroughly committed to railway building and economic expansion well before he became premier. When he took office under Baldwin and LaFontaine in 1848, he regarded responsible government not only as a means of secularizing the clergy reserves or of solving the seigneurial tenure problem, but also as a means of encouraging railway building and fostering economic expansion under Canadian governmental leadership. It was with these objectives in mind that he had introduced his Railway Guarantee Act. His policies, in general, were closely geared to practical, material development.

He enthusiastically took office as joint premier in the autumn of 1851, confident that he and Morin could end the procrastination and delay that he had criticized in Baldwin and LaFontaine. They would inaugurate a new era of reform and economic expansion. But the next three years contained more than their share of hindrances and disappointments. When the Hincks-Morin administration resigned in 1854 it might well have been dubbed 'the ministry of unfulfilled expectations.' They had given top priority to secularizing the clergy reserves and to settling the long-lived question of seigneurial tenure, but after three years in office they had done neither and were themselves being accused of procrastination. They were, of course, unfortunate in the long delay that occurred before the imperial Clergy Reserve Act was repealed. Yet they themselves decided on further delay instead of proceeding immediately with secularization, once that impediment had been removed. Also, differences of opinion among French-Canadian members as to whether seigneurial tenure should be reformed or abolished, and as to the compensation that should be paid to seigneurs if it were abolished, had impeded decisive action on this question.

The Grand Trunk Railway Company had been established, but the railway was still being built during Hincks' premiership; and as it encountered one financial problem after another, it was threatening to become a costly burden on the government. A reciprocity agreement with the United States had finally been obtained, but it was Lord Elgin, rather than Hincks, who had played the major role in the negotiations. In any case, the clamour for reciprocity had declined as prosperous times returned. Hence these achievements also did him no great good.

Moreover, when he took office as premier, Hincks believed he could reunite the Reform party in Upper Canada, but the old political alignments were now yielding to the force of new circumstances. Despite the appearance of unity in his cabinet, he had to contend with division within the ranks of his party during most of his term in office. As it became clear to him that he could not prevent the disintegration of the Upper Canadian Reform party, he made every effort to lead his supporters into a new political alignment that would maintain the alliance with French Canada. Paradoxically, one of his major achievements as premier was the contribution he made to the formation of the Liberal-Conservative coalition, even as he was being forced out of office.

The fall of the Hincks-Morin government was due as much to charges of scandal and corruption as it was to its failure to secularize the reserves and abolish seigneurial tenure. Many of the charges were related to Hinck's activities and could be attributed to his insistence that he had not relinquished his right to participate in legitimate investments and business transactions simply by taking office. It was a naïve and unrealistic attitude for him to adopt. The premier and his ministers were privy to confidential information and had the power to influence economic factors. Hincks maintained that no wrong was done unless the power and information were used improperly for private gain. He refused to recognize that such a claim must result in perpetual suspicion that the powers of office had been misused and in perpetual rumours of scandal – an impossible position for any politician. It is surprising that Hincks should adopt such an attitude, for he was aware of the concept of a conflict of interest. 'It strikes me,' he wrote to J.C. Dent almost forty years later, 'that members of govt. in the present day have done things ten times more objectionable. I only know that I parted with both my newspapers when I joined the Govt. I would not have been President of an Ins'ce Co. or Solicitor to a Railway Co.'[76]

Yet, if Hincks generated suspicions of corruption, both George Brown and the Tory press eagerly pounced upon each rumour and inflated it to the limit. Despite the fact that two parliamentary inquiries found no evidence of dishonesty, Canadian historians continue to accept George Brown's picture of Hincks as the man who brought large-scale corruption into Canadian politics. Like two figures in a morality play, Baldwin is invariably presented as the paragon of Whig virtue while Hincks is considered to be the exact antithesis. Baldwin held resolutely to his principles, it is true, while Hincks, as a practical, adaptable politician, was willing to compromise in order to make some progress towards his goals; yet this scarcely justifies the treatment he has received at the hands of most historians.

The years that followed his premiership were for Hincks a vindication of his reputation – a restoration of his public and private respectability. But they were also an anti-climax. When he entered office as premier he had a vision of a prosperous, burgeoning railway age. After three years of cabinet headship, of frustration and discouragement, he lost that vision; and though he was subsequently a competent colonial governor and an able minister of finance, he never fully regained his former enthusiasm and zest. Nor throughout his private career did he build up the wealth that might have been expected of him, at least by his own contemporaries.

Among them, Francis Hincks indeed was reputed to be a financial genius. He had demonstrated his banking expertise by keeping the Bank of the People solvent during extremely difficult times, and he was one of the few men in Canada who really understood and appreciated the monetary theory behind Lord Sydenham's proposed bank of issue. Moreover, it was largely because of his efforts as inspector-general that Canada's financial reputation was restored in Britain and Canadian debentures began to sell at a premium on the London money market. He was personally held in high esteem by Baring Brothers and many other financial houses in Britain. But even more important in the eyes of Canadian entrepreneurs, he created a favourable financial climate for railway building and industrial expansion with his Guarantee Act and his Municipal Loan Fund. At a banquet which he gave in Hinck's honour, Samuel Zimmerman, the millionaire canal and railway contractor, declared: 'Had it not been for the financial ability of the Hon. Francis Hincks, I would not be what I am at present nor would I have been able to entertain you here this evening.'[77]

Whatever Hincks' financial skills, he seemed unable to apply them to his own private affairs. In no personal sense was he an astute, successful businessman. The wholesale business which he began upon his arrival in York was not sufficiently remunerative to encourage him to continue it. The

Examiner was apparently a modest financial success, but Hincks felt obliged to sell it when he became a member of the government in 1842. The circumstances under which the *Pilot* was founded may indicate a devotion to the Reform party, but they say little for Hincks' acumen as a businessman. Dependent from the outset on contributions from prominent Reformers, the paper failed to yield even a decent wage for its proprietor and editor and was a constant drain on his limited finances. Hincks invested his savings in mortgages and, on tips from acquaintances, he speculated in bonds, stock, and real estate, but only occasionally did he make sizable profits. At no time did he amass great wealth, and on several occasions he was in difficult financial straits for the want of relatively small sums of money. In the late 1840s he became interested in mining speculation and was one of the founders of both the Echo Lake Mining Company and the Lake Huron Silver and Copper Mining Company. Yet, when he managed to make $4500 on his mining investments, he simply planned to use the money to pay off his debts in connection with the *Pilot*.

Finally, in his will he named his grandson, John Alexander Ready, as his executor and sole legatee, but noted that there would be 'little if any surplus' after his debts were paid.[78] Such, then, can be the differences between public legends and private facts. Nevertheless, it is no legend that Hincks in public life was one of the most influential and constructive of Ontario's pre-Confederation leaders.

Although the most important part of his political career came to an end in frustration and humiliation, its great significance lay in the fact that he helped to shape the fundamental orientation of the party system in the province of Canada and ultimately in the Canadian federation. Francis Hincks, along with his contemporaries in the Reform and Conservative camps, had a well-articulated set of values, values which in his case were derived from the general tenets of mid nineteenth-century Anglo-American liberalism. Unlike some of his opponents, such as George Brown, he sensed, as Sydenham had and John A. Macdonald would, that the politics of consensus and management would be more compatible with the smooth working of parliamentary government and the use of the state to foster economic growth than would the politics of ideology. Thus, whether consciously or not, he gradually detached many English-Canadian reformers from dogged adherence to their principles and persuaded them that to talk about convictions while pursuing consensus would be an effective way of fostering political stability and material progress. Without his efforts the work of John A. Macdonald in founding a Conservative management party probably would have been much less successful. When the Liberals under Laurier belatedly recognized the logic of Hincks' and Macdonald's careers, they too were blessed with political success.

NOTES

1 G.E. Boyce, *Hutton of Hastings* (Belleville 1972), 9. Apparently this child died in infancy.
2 *Examiner*, 11 July 1838
3 Public Archives of Canada [PAC], LaFontaine Papers, Hincks to LaFontaine, 12 April 1839
4 LaFontaine's letters to Hincks have not survived. It is thus necessary to surmise their content from Hincks' replies. The main body of Hincks' papers was destroyed when he died of smallpox, but since he made no reference to his important correspondence with LaFontaine in his *Reminiscences*, it is quite possible that he did not keep the letters he received from the French-Canadian leader.
5 LaFontaine Papers, Hincks to LaFontaine, 15 Dec. 1840
6 Ibid., Hincks to LaFontaine, 14 Feb. 1841
7 Ibid., Baldwin to Hincks, 7 Nov. 1840, enclosed in Hincks to LaFontaine, 27 Nov. 1840
8 Ibid., Hincks to LaFontaine, 6 April 1841
9 Ibid., Hincks to LaFontaine, 29 June 1841
10 Boyce, *Hutton of Hastings*, 103
11 LaFontaine Papers, Baldwin to LaFontaine, 20 Jan. 1841
12 Francis Hincks, *Reminiscences of his Public Life* (Montreal 1884), 137
13 Metropolitan Toronto Central Library [MTCL] Baldwin Papers, Hincks to Baldwin, 8 May 1844
14 Ibid., George Brown to Baldwin, 10 July 1845
15 Ibid., Hincks to Baldwin, 18 Sept. 1845
16 J.M.S. Careless, *Brown of the Globe*, 2 vols. (Toronto 1959), I, 64
17 Baldwin Papers, Hincks to Baldwin, 14 July 1846
18 A.G. Doughty, ed., *The Elgin-Grey Papers*, 4 vols. (Ottawa 1937), I, 136-7, note 1
19 Baldwin Papers, Hincks to Baldwin, 26 Oct. 1849
20 Ibid.
21 Ibid., Hincks to Baldwin, 2 Nov 1849
22 MTCL, T.S. Shenston Papers, Hincks to Shenston, 7 July 1851
23 Careless, *Brown of the Globe*, I, 120
24 *Globe*, 3 July 1851
25 Ibid.
26 Shenston Papers, Hincks to Shenston, 25 July 1851
27 Ontario Archives, Charles Clarke Papers, McDougall to Clarke, 25 July 1851
28 Quoted in C. Martin, *Empire and Commonwealth* (Oxford 1929), 324
29 PAC, J.S. Macdonald Papers, Hincks to Macdonald, 11 Oct. 1851
30 Ibid., Macdonald to Dr Barker (draft), 27 Dec. 1851
31 Hincks, *Reminiscences*, 272

32 Ibid. 267-70
33 Montreal *Gazette*, 30 Oct. 1851
34 T.S. Shenston Papers, Brown to Shenston, 23 Oct. 1851
35 Ibid., John Ross to Shenston, 6 Nov. 1851
36 Hincks, *Reminiscences*, 227
37 Ibid., 213
38 Ibid., 218-22
39 Ibid., 226
40 *Imperial Government Reports relating to Canada, 1840-67* (London 1867),
    Hincks to Grey, 5 Feb. 1852, cited in R.S. Longley, *Sir Francis Hincks* (Toronto
    1943), 211
41 Doughty, ed., *The Elgin-Grey Papers*, III, 998, Grey to Elgin, 20 Feb. 1852
42 *Imperial Reports*, Hincks to Pakington, 1 May 1852, cited in Longley, 219
43 Hincks, *Reminiscences*, 286-7
44 Ibid., 287-8, Hincks to Pakington, 3 May 1852
45 Ibid., 288-91, Hincks to Pakington, 10 May 1852
46 Ibid., 245-6
47 Montreal *Gazette*, 16 June 1852. A series of anti-Hincks editorials on the same
    theme were published in succeeding issues.
48 Careless, *Brown of the Globe*, I, 157-9
49 Hincks, *Reminiscences*, 292
50 Ibid., 292-4, Pakington to Elgin (draft), [16] Dec. 1852
51 O.D. Skelton, *The Life and Times of Sir Alexander Tilloch Galt* (Toronto 1920),
    95
52 Montreal *Gazette*, 9 Nov. 1852
53 Ibid., 2 March 1853
54 Ibid., 14, 16 March 1853
55 Ibid., 16 March 1853
56 Canada, *Journals of the Legislative Assembly, 1852-53*, Part I, 539 [hereafter
    Journals]
57 *Globe*, 15 March 1853
58 Montreal *Gazette*, 7 May 1853
59 Ibid.
60 Toronto *Leader*, 7 June 1853
61 *Journals, 1854-55*, Appendix AAAA, Testimony of George Brown
62 Clarke Papers, McDougall to Clarke, 17 Sept. 1853
63 Shenston Papers, Hincks to Shenston, 11 Oct. 1853
64 PAC, Baring Papers, Hincks to Thomas Baring, 12 Nov. and 5 Dec. 1853
65 Hincks, *Reminiscences*, 297
66 Skelton, *Galt*, 190
67 *Journals, 1854-55*, Part I, 2-3
68 J.E. Collins, *The Life and Times of John A. Macdonald* (Toronto 1883), 177

69 Skelton, *Galt*, 192
70 Hincks, *Reminiscences*, 330
71 Ibid., 328
72 *Journals, 1854-55*, Appendix AAAA
73 Ibid.
74 Joseph Pope, *Memoirs of Sir John Macdonald* (Toronto 1930), 333
75 Elizabeth Nish, 'How History is Written: The Hincks to Dent Letters,' *Revue de centre d'étude du Québec*, 2, Avril 1978, 29-96
76 Ibid., 81
77 Quoted in J.J. Talman, 'The Impact of the Railway on a Pioneer Community,' Canadian Historical Association, *Report*, 1955, 1-12
78 Probate of the Holograph Last Will of the Late Sir Francis Hincks, No 1166, Archives Judiciaires, Palais de Justice, Montreal

J.K. JOHNSON

John A. Macdonald

In pre-Confederation Ontario John A. Macdonald was not a political leader like the others. He dominated the politics of much of the Union period. Unlike other contemporary leaders he continued to dominate Canadian politics long after Confederation. He was better at politics than the others. It was not just that he survived through seven general elections and through seven out of the eight parliaments of the Province of Canada (Sandfield Macdonald sat in eight out of eight) but that for much of the time he was in command. Between 1854, when he first assumed the crucial office of attorney-general west, and the coming of Confederation in 1867, he alone was the actual leader of the Ontario section of his party, and for at least ten of those years he was the actual Ontario leader of the government. No other political figure of the time had half so long a tenure of office. No other leader left so lasting an impression on the time or on the succeeding period. Ultimately it was Macdonald who set the prevailing political tone. He absorbed and refined the experience of his predecessors, but by 1867 it was his political rules by which the game was played. It was his standards, his style, which were the norm, to be emulated, elaborated upon, envied, or deplored. John A. Macdonald's career in its formative political phase provides therefore a study in the ingredients of political good fortune and political success, at a time when both were highly unusual.

There was nothing very unusual about his background and early years. Like so many other nineteenth-century Canadians he was an immigrant, the only surviving son in a Scottish family which arrived in Kingston, Upper Canada, in 1820, when he was five years old. Though he afterwards claimed to remember his native Glasgow,[1] the fact is that his childhood was essentially Canadian rather than Scottish. By emigrating as early as 1820 his family's move pre-dated the great waves of migration of the 1830s and 1840s, so that, while he and his family were not native Canadians, they were earlier, longer-established settlers than the majority of the Irish, English, and

Scottish emigrants who later made their way to British North America. John A. Macdonald was nonetheless in part the product of a Scottish background. His family were Presbyterians, they had a Scottish faith in the benefits of a sound elementary education, and they valued and maintained close family ties. His parents, however, represented differing Scots occupational strains. His father and grandfather Macdonald were merchants. His mother's people, the Shaws (and their connections, the Clarks, Grants, and Macphersons) were mainly soldiers.[2]

It is difficult to assess with any great accuracy what characteristics John A. Macdonald may have inherited from the Macdonald and Shaw sides of his family; at any rate he did not become either a merchant or a soldier. It has been suggested that in the marriage of his parents, Hugh Macdonald and Helen Shaw, it was the mother who was the stronger, more dominant partner and that it was from her that he inherited or absorbed his intelligence and his ambition.[3] While this may be true, it must be admitted that really very little is known about his father except that he died relatively young (Helen Shaw Macdonald was not only five years older than her husband but survived him for more than twenty years) and that he was involved in intermittent business failures both in Glasgow and in Upper Canada; whether the conventional picture of Hugh Macdonald as an affable but shiftless dreamer with no real head for business[4] is a fair one will probably never be known. Failure in business in the nineteenth century was by no means a rare occurrence and it is possible that Hugh Macdonald's ill luck was due as much to bad economic conditions, a basic lack of capital, or ill health as to any intrinsic lack of business skill. In fact, Hugh Macdonald was not always a failure in business. He ran a sizeable milling business in Prince Edward County for ten years before retiring a few years before his death to a salaried position in a Kingston bank. The point is of some importance because it has been alleged that John A. Macdonald developed an antipathy to 'trade' from his father's lack of enterprise,[5] but, on the contrary, he actually from an early age showed a keen interest in business matters, as had his father and his grandfather, 'the merchant Macdonald.'

Perhaps all that can safely be said about the importance of Macdonald's heredity is that he seems to have been a lucky hybrid. If the Shaws have been correctly characterized as stubborn, strong-minded, and impetuous, and the Macdonalds as popular, affable, and commercially minded, the result of this combination for the purposes of a professional and political career was an improvement on both sets of family traits.

Macdonald's formal education, as has been observed, was about the best that was available in Upper Canada at the time, at the Midland District Grammar School and at a private school supported by the Kingston Scottish community.[6] It is likely that his school years were fairly important in shaping his later career. He had, by all accounts, good teachers and he himself was undoubtedly an apt pupil, 'a bright boy,' who liked school, did well, and was led to believe that he had a promising future. He was intelligent, sensible, and blessed with a retentive memory. If nothing else, as the letters and papers of his adult years make clear, he learned to write a clear, readable hand, to spell with usual accuracy and to handle mathematical calculations without difficulty. He learned (and probably enjoyed learning) all those Latin phrases which so frequently appear in his adult correspondence. Probably also as a school boy he acquired his life long habit of reading rapidly and widely and his capacity for furious concentrated spates of productive work.

Whatever social, political, and moral precepts Macdonald may have imbibed from his teachers, members and ministers of the Churches of England and Scotland, were certainly not radical notions. A reverence for the crown and for established religion, a due subordination to authority, a sense of duty and responsibility were not only a part of Macdonald's schooling but of his whole environment in what he later liked to call the 'loyal old town' of Kingston. His family was a minor part of the military-professional-commercial élite of Kingston, a group whose collective outlook was highly conservative. There is nothing to indicate that young John A. Macdonald ever questioned the prevailing social and political assumptions of his family and community. There was indeed no reason why he should have. To a bright, ambitious boy the community promised and sometimes delivered quick and tangible rewards. On leaving school he immediately began the process of acquiring his own place among the successful lawyers, bankers, and merchants of the town.

There were not really many options open to him in the choice of a career. Business or the law were the favoured respectable pursuits of the Kingston establishment, of men like John Watkins, Thomas Kirkpatrick, John Mowat, Christopher Hagerman, or Henry Gildersleeve.[7] A young man with no capital to back him could not easily get a start in business, but if he were intelligent and industrious and had respectable connections to arrange his entry, the law was the obvious, almost the inevitable choice.

No doubt it was the right choice. His legal career from its very beginning when he was a fifteen-year-old law student was generally successful. George Mackenzie, to whom he was articled, quickly recognized his promise and trusted him to perform difficult tasks at an early stage. Once on his own he acquired a considerable reputation not only as a trustworthy businesslike professional man with a sure knowledge of the law but also as a courtroom lawyer known for the quickness of his mind, for ingenuity in defence, and for a talent for persuasiveness. His professional ability was quickly and publicly recognized. At age thirty-one he was made a QC, 'one of Her Majesty's Counsel learned in the law.' Much has been made of Macdonald's courtroom heroics in defence of lost causes such as that of Nils Von Schoultz, the captured leader of the 'Patriot' attack on Prescott during the border raids of 1838; but his practice as it developed was really of quite a different nature. Essentially he was a business lawyer, a corporation lawyer. He had as his clients leading Kingston businessmen like James Morton, brewer, distiller, industrialist and, contractor, and the two major Kingston-centred financial institutions, the Commercial Bank of the Midland District and the Trust and Loan Company of Upper Canada. He became an 'insider' in the Kingston and Upper Canadian business world. It is not surprising that he also quickly became personally involved in various kinds of business enterprises.

He was made a director of the Commercial Bank when he was twenty-four, only three years after he had been called to the bar in 1836. By the time he was forty he was a director of a dozen Kingston firms – insurance companies, gas and water companies, road, railway, and canal companies, and building societies. But he was never merely a business adviser. He was an active speculative businessman in his own right. He invested, in a minor way, in stocks and in shipping. He even bought and sold one or two lake ships. He was financially involved in at least one major railway project. His real interest, though, was in real estate. As early as 1842, if not earlier, he began regularly to buy and sell property in Kingston. He quickly became a land speculator and developer on a broad scale. On his own or in partnership he bought and organized the land for three Kingston subdivisions, following the classic pattern of the city developer, turning former farm land on the outskirts of the city into hundreds of building lots in anticipation of urban growth. He also bought and sold purely as a speculation a great many individual lots and parcels of land throughout the city over a period of years. Macdonald was, of course, by no means unique in this regard. Most of his Kingston contemporaries, other lawyers, merchants, and financiers, also speculated in land during the 1840s, 1850s, and 1860s on a greater or lesser scale. Macdonald was simply a typical Kingston businessman of his time, but he was also a leading Kingston businessman. By the time he was forty he was a solidly established member of the professional-commercial community, as company director, corporation lawyer, business adviser, and real-estate developer. If he had never gone into politics at all he would still have been known and respected by Kingstonians as an influential member of the professional, commercial, and financial élite.

He would also have been well known in many other places outside of Kingston.[8] In the 1850s and 1860s he developed a subdivision larger than any he had begun in Kingston at Guelph. He bought eighteen city lots in downtown Toronto and a half-interest in a large modern building on King Street which was rented out as office space. He bought and sold land in parcels as large as 9700 acres at a time in a dozen counties of Upper Canada.

He had farm land, 'wild' land, railway land, suburban land, and city houses at Napanee, Owen Sound, Peterborough, Sarnia, Madoc, Gananoque, and elsewhere. This kind of province-wide business activity, carried on personally or through agents, plus the widespread concerns of many of the firms which he represented as solicitor or of which he was a director, brought him into contact with a much wider circle of prominent lawyers and businessmen. He collaborated as a lawyer and as business partner with land speculators, railway builders, and financiers like C.S. Gzowski, David L. Macpherson, A.T. Galt, and Luther Holton. They were all, as Macdonald once explained, 'mutual friends' who were 'speculatively inclined.'[9] Through them he came to know and to take his holidays with American magnates like John A. Poor of Maine and Robert Pomeroy of Massachusetts. He dealt in land with J.M. Strachan, son of the bishop, and with W.B. Robinson, brother of the chief justice.[10] He developed a close and life-long business and personal relationship with John Rose, the Montreal (and later London, England) lawyer and financier. Through the Trust and Loan Company, which was essentially a British company, dependent on British capital and run by a British board of directors, he became involved both as Canadian solicitor and as a member of the British board, in frequent contact with representatives of the London financial community like William Chapman and Frederick Fearon, and intermittently with some of the genuinely powerful financiers, Thomas Baring, George Carr Glyn, Andrew Colville, Edward Ellice.[11] His handling of the loan company's affairs was impressively adroit and led to other opportunities. He began on his own to act as agent for the investment of British capital in Canadian real estate. 'I thoroughly understand that business,' he boasted to a friend, 'and can invest without risk of loss.'[12] He was appointed to the board of directors of a British insurance company.[13] Finally, he was asked to assume the presidency of another British-backed company operating in Canada, the St Lawrence Warehouse, Dock and Wharfage Company of Quebec City, a position which he continued to hold for twenty-five years.[14]

It must be admitted that Macdonald's business affairs were not uniformly successful. At times he over-extended himself, at times he was simply unlucky. The death of his legal and business partner in 1864 and the failure shortly afterwards of both the Bank of Upper Canada and the Commercial Bank, to both of which he owed money, put a substantial crimp in his activities. Still, he always managed to avoid outright failure, a fate which periodically overtook quite a few of his contemporaries, men such as his client, James Morton, or the Hamilton wholesale merchant, Isaac Buchanan, or the Toronto land and stock speculator, John Hillyard Cameron, all of whom had much greater capital resources than he. It is impossible in fact not to be impressed by the way in which Macdonald could keep so many business schemes concurrently afloat (to say nothing obviously of his other personal and political activities). His affairs sometimes got into a muddled and even perilous state but he always managed to extricate himself, usually advantageously. He never stopped pursuing business angles, never stopped pursuing the wealth which he expected would soon be his.

One of the factors which limited both his time and his capital was his responsibility to his family. His father died when John A. Macdonald was twenty-six. He, as only son, became the family's head and sole support. His first wife, his cousin Isabella Clark, became a permanent invalid within a year of their marriage. Isabella's protracted illness made great demands upon Macdonald, not only financial demands, though they were heavy enough – for constant medication and medical attention and for extensive travels in search of a healthier climate – but also emotional demands. It is scarcely too much to say that their marriage was a kind of prolonged nightmare. From the first there seems to have been no real hope that Isabella would ever recover. Again and again she was believed to be on the point of death, yet she lingered on, dependent on frequent doses of opium (another nineteenth-century condition which was common enough), survived two hideously painful confinements, survived the death of her first born and of her younger sister, survived as a constant burden to herself and her family.

The extent to which the tragedy of his first marriage left its mark upon John A. Macdonald has been a matter of some conjecture. Certainly the circumstances provide ample scope for psychological speculation. It has been suggested, for example, that his sporadic bouts of heavy drinking (a habit that he shared with many others of his time) was a means of drowning his anxiety about his wife's condition.[15] It is likely, though, that his fondness for liquor and convivial company was well established before his marriage in 1843, at age twenty-eight, and his drinking does not appear to have been 'a problem' until some years after Isabella's death in 1858.[16] It is perhaps at least as likely that he attempted to forget his family troubles by plain hard work, if he sought to forget them at all, for it is surprising how much time Macdonald, the busy professional man, found to spend with his sick wife. The truth is that there are no easily discernible outward scars left by the climate of illness and death – of his father, his son, his wife, and his mother – in which he lived for twenty-five years. In those days illness and death also were a familiar part of the lives of everyone. Experience and religion taught that it was necessary to be prepared for the worst and to be resigned to God's mysterious ways. Macdonald bore his personal losses stoically. He carried on business as usual. Nonetheless, the evidence of his personal correspondence beginning in the Isabella years does point to something not quite definable, an impression only, of a kind of central emotional dead spot, a fatalism approaching at times to callousness, an underlying cynicism, perhaps always a part of his nature, perhaps an acquired necessary alternative to depression and despair. What John A. Macdonald really thought or felt is at no time a matter on which certainty is possible. Canadians have tended to think of him as a man of straightforward, uncomplicated nature. He was not. He was a highly complex man whose motives and actions were rarely as simple as they seemed.

When he became a politician, John A. Macdonald did not become a different person with a different outlook, attitudes, and interests. For quite a long time, perhaps for the first ten years of his political career, politics was more of an extension of his ordinary pursuits than a separate activity. By his own account his original entry into politics was to have been strictly temporary,[17] and simply by getting elected he did not commit himself to a life-long political career. It is likely that up to about the year 1864 his frequently expressed desire to quit public life at the next suitable opportunity was perfectly genuine. As a politician he often felt overworked and under-rewarded, disillusioned with his colleagues, bored, frustrated and nagged by the feeling that he really ought to be making money instead. It is impossible to separate his private and political careers, especially since he himself never did. He always tried to do everything at the same time, dealing in a day's work with politics, administration, and private business, using his parliamentary office for private and his house for public business, entering copies of political and business letters side by side in the same letterbook.[18]

It could be said that in the years before Confederation Macdonald passed through a series of occupational-career stages: lawyer, lawyer-businessman, lawyer-businessman-politician, to politician-lawyer-businessman, the last stage being reached about the time of the Great Coalition of 1864 and the subsequent Confederation negotiations. Any study of Macdonald as a political leader before or after Confederation must take into account these early stages as well as his private character. What had he learned from his early experiences? How had his background affected the political position which he took? What kind of man was he?

John A. Macdonald, the young man whose style as a politician rapidly attracted widespread attention, possessed, like most other people, a combination of qualities which were sometimes paradoxical. He was a man of cheerful, easy-going, optimistic disposition, tinged with a cynical view of mankind, given to occasional moods of depression and occasional outbursts of violent anger. He was a man who resented criticism more than he seemed to and who enjoyed, even needed, praise. He was a casual, convivial man who was also capable of enormous amounts of sustained work. He was an intelligent, not just a clever man, a man of 'intellect and general versatility,'[19] but not a man given to constant reflection or to critical examination of things as they were. He was an orthodox man following without question standard career patterns, guided instinctively by standard assumptions, who could on occasion take political 'steep turns.'

In terms of the politics of the time it would have been highly unlikely, given his background and his own pragmatic nature, had he become anything other than a Conservative. His study of the law taught him that rules must be obeyed, property must be respected, forms must be observed. His practice of the law, including ultimately his administration of the office of attorney-general of Upper Canada, demonstrated that society was divided into classes, with the 'respectable' at the top and the 'criminal element' at the bottom, and he saw nothing to indicate that the criminal element was likely to reform. For Macdonald, a part of the 'respectable' class, the *status quo*, the 'system,' worked, at least for him, in tangible ways. From the beginning of his working life he was on the inside, there were always helpful friends among whom professional favours could be exchanged, friends to point out short cuts and angles to be pursued. As a young man he accepted contemporary society as he found it and accepted the prevailing business and political morality of the time as he found it, and that was a time when, at the beginning of the first great Canadian land and railway boom, morality was taking a turn for the worse. The tight little Kingston legal-commercial élite group of which he first became a part did occasionally produce a case of mild political maverickism in men whose background was not strictly orthodox, such as John Counter, a Methodist of humble origins, or the Gildersleeves of American, Congregationalist antecedents,[20] but Macdonald suffered from no such lingering disabilities. Perhaps most important of all, he did not suffer from the demands of a devout Christian conscience, the kind of conscience which could compel a young man like Oliver Mowat, whose early circumstances were practically identical to Macdonald's, to embrace Liberalism, because of a distaste for the low conventional political standards of the time.[21] John A. Macdonald adhered of course to the normal forms of church attendance and devotion, but he would never like Mowat acquire the title of 'the Christian Politician.'

Macdonald's earliest political interest was in Kingston itself. He was an alderman for three years, 1843-6. Again he was performing exactly to type, for participation in civic politics was a normal part of the function of the Kingston business élite, which tended to see the welfare of the town as a whole and the welfare of the business community as being interdependent.[22] Having achieved local prominence as a lawyer-businessman and politician, he was quickly seen as a possible contender for the Kingston seat in the Legislative Assembly. By the time he actually entered provincial politics in 1844 he was known to Kingstonians as an alderman of ability as well as a bank director and one of the founders and promoters of the Trust and Loan Company. His contributions to the advancement of Kingston's interest were sufficient to ensure his first election. He continued to represent Kingston, in the Legislative Assembly and the House of Commons, for the next thirty-four years, evidently to the general satisfaction of his constituents.

Being member for Kingston imposed certain historical demands upon the incumbent. Kingstonians had always had a view of their town as a place of special worth. It had been the first urban centre of any consequence in Upper Canada and had continued to surpass the upstart town of York in military and commercial significance until a point in the 1830s. For many years Kingston had been represented at the provincial capital by Christopher Alexander Hagerman, a powerful and pugnacious figure and a formidable voice of Kingston's aspirations within the Family Compact itself. The citizens of the town had come to expect their member to put Kingston first, and they were quite prepared to vote in a rival (Conservative) candidate if this rule was disobeyed.[23] After the union of Upper and Lower Canada, S.B. Harrison, Macdonald's predecessor as member for Kingston, though actually only a transient Kingstonian, had thought it necessary to resign from the Executive Council to protest the government decision in 1843 to move the capital of the Province of Canada from Kingston to Montreal.

As member for Kingston Macdonald inherited the burden of Kingston's mission, which was simply the restoration of the town to its rightful place as the leading metropolis of Upper Canada. He did his best. His attendance record in his early years in the assembly, when his only roles were as a member of his party and a representative of his riding, was something less than perfect. Nonetheless, he was an effective and conscientious constituency man. He helped individuals and groups when he could by presenting petitions and recommending applicants for government jobs. He tried by private pressure and by sponsoring legislation to advance the interests of worthy Kingston corporate bodies, such as Queen's and Regiopolis colleges, the Kingston Hospital, or the Orphan's Home and Widow's Friendly Society. As his political leverage increased he was able to achieve more for the good of the town. There cannot have been many Upper Canadian communities in the 1850s in which four major public buildings, a court house and jail, a post office, a customs building and an asylum, were all under construction within a period of five years. Macdonald's best and most unremitting efforts were, however, on behalf of Kingston business enterprises.[24] His conception of his role as member for Kingston was primarily that of spokesman for the commercial leadership group of which he was a part. What was good for the town's business would ultimately be good for that centre as a whole. In the 1840s, 1850s, and 1860s the goal of the Kingston business community, as it had always been, was prosperity through growth – growth not just of population but of industry, capital, port facilities, and Kingston-centred roads and railways. All of these Macdonald laboured hard to provide, with some degree of success. The fact that so many of the Kingston bills which he guided through the legislature – the incorporation of Kingston as a city, the chartering (and frequent amending of charters) of public utilities, road, rail, finance, insurance, and other companies – involved enterprises in which he had a direct financial interest[25] seems not to have worried him even slightly. Obviously the fact did not concern most of his constituents or political colleagues either, though there were occasional objections that he was taking undue advantage of his position.[26] He was cheerfully oblivious to any suggestion of conflict of interest. He was an urban businessman representing an urban riding, doing what he could. 'It is alike my duty and my interest to promote the prosperity of this city and the adjacent country.'[27]

Macdonald spent most of the first ten years of his provincial political career that began in 1844 in 'hopeless opposition,' but he was from an early date one of the acknowledged leaders of his party. For ten months in 1847-8, while still in his first term as a member of the assembly, he held cabinet posts in the administration of William Henry Draper. Expertise in the affairs of their departments was not necessarily a requirement for ministers of the day and at first glance it might seem that he had no particular qualifications to be receiver-general of the province or, for a period of about three months, commissioner of crown lands. In fact he was, rather more than most of his colleagues, qualified for both positions. As a bank director and solicitor for a bank, as a founder, director, and solicitor of a loan company, he had more than a passing knowledge of finance and the disposal of land. His first cabinet experience in turn was valuable to him both as a public and a private man. The fact that he had been, albeit briefly, in charge of the government's funds and its land and timber reserves added to his business credentials; as it did, for instance, when he went to England in 1850 as the Canadian representative of the Trust and Loan Company to deal with British financiers.[28] He also had a chance to see at first hand the workings of the Executive Council and government departments and to test his own abilities as policy-maker and administrator.

Macdonald's work as a department head has been given scant attention in studies of his career. Such opinion as has been offered on this point is divided as to whether he was or was not an efficient administrator.[29] It is apparent, however, that at all times he took these duties seriously and performed them conscientiously and well. He worked hard, though not always to a regular schedule, and he expected industry and efficiency from his staff. A week after he became receiver-general he introduced new procedures governing the issuing of departmental cheques. A few months later he revised the hours of work and forbade absence on private business.[30] As commissioner of crown lands, according to the testimony of H.J. Morgan, himself a career public servant, he disposed of difficult departmental cases with more 'promptness and sagacity' than had any of his predecessors.[31] When he was appointed attorney-general of Upper Canada in 1854 he had less time to devote entirely to the work of his department, because of the increased demands on him as a leader of his party, but he was no less attentive to his administrative functions; he simply worked longer days. Besides being attorney-general from 1854 to 1862, and from 1864 to 1867, he was also twice minister of militia affairs, in 1861-2 and from 1865 to 1867. Finally, in 1864 he persuaded the cabinet to sanction the appointment of a 'stenographic clerk' to whom he would dictate his innumerable letters and memoranda. Characteristically, he made use of the new member of his staff for administrative, party, and private purposes all at the same time.[32]

Although Macdonald complained often of overwork, an examination of the voluminous files which he compiled as a minister leaves the distinct impression that he enjoyed the office routine. It could even be said that he went out of his way to assume extra departmental (and also policy) duties. His appointment in 1861 to the newly created post of minister of militia affairs was made because 'those matters have heretofore more particularly claimed the attention of the Hon. John A. Macdonald, Atty. Genl. U.C.'[33] He had a strong sense of duty and responsibility which compelled him to get through his work. 'Pray remember,' he replied tartly to a favour seeker, 'that I have infinitely more to do in my own legitimate sphere than any one man ought to have, and if it were not that I am a quick worker I should have been hopelessly in arrear.'[34] He needed to be a quick worker. The volume of business, especially in the Office of the Attorney-General, increased continually, partly because the province as a whole was growing rapidly, requiring constant expansion of the legal machinery, partly because other departments (perhaps as has been suggested, sometimes unnecessarily)[35] referred more and more matters to Macdonald for a legal opinion before taking action on their own.

As a department head Macdonald cannot exactly be accused of empire building, since his staff was never very large, but he did at the beginning of his tenure as attorney-general in 1854 oversee the creation of his own office staff separate from that of the attorney-general of Lower Canada.[36] He liked to have a personal staff on whom he could rely and he was both fortunate and shrewd in acquiring and keeping able administrative lieutenants. Between 1854 and 1867 he had two deputies (actually called chief clerks), R.A. Harrison, who left in 1859 to begin his own distinguished legal career, and Hewitt Bernard, who remained with Macdonald after Confederation as the first deputy minister of justice – and incidentally as his brother-in-law. Macdonald developed a very close and lasting relationship with both of these men and undoubtedly relied heavily on them for the day-to-day conduct of the office and for preliminary research and comments on the many questions requiring legal decision which were referred to the attorney-general. It is clear, however, that he made up his own mind after a careful review of each case. His position as the chief law officer of the crown in Upper Canada imposed heavy responsibilities and demanded not only broad legal knowledge but uncommon wisdom, for he was responsible for both the judicial and the penal systems of Upper Canada. He was required to decide in the line of duty questions of the length of prisoners' sentences, or the possibility of pardon, or from time to time, the commutation (or non-commutation) of the death penalty.

Not all of the problems dealt with in the attorney-general's office of course were matters of life and death. They were in fact extraordinarily varied. Surely no other government department of the day, except perhaps the provincial secretary's office, habitually dealt with such a range of human affairs. Besides the department's central concern with crime and punishment, legal opinion was sought on such matters as the needs, duties, and condition of the Upper Canadian militia, the incorporation of companies and municipalities, the division of counties and the choice of county towns, the care of the mentally retarded, labour disputes, separate schools, the financial problems of railways and toll roads, pensions alleged to have been earned in 1812 or 1837, and many, many other topics, important or trivial, concerning the province as a whole or single individuals.[37]

This endless parade of human problems and human follies occupied a large part of Macdonald's working life and formed a large part of his accumulated experience of men and affairs. If he had had no other indication his departmental duties must have demonstrated that Upper Canadian society was changing and expanding, imposing new demands upon the state. He saw in patents and charters the evidence of technological advance. He supervised the creation of the temporary Judicial District of Nipissing and the Provisional District of Algoma to accommodate the beginnings of population and resource development beyond the old settlement limits. He knew that the incidence of crime was increasing, he knew that the Provincial Lunatic Asylum in Toronto was overcrowded, he took a leading part in providing, for the first time, provincial institutions for juvenile offenders and for the criminally insane.[38] Perhaps most important of all, he was exposed for long periods of time to a broad cross-section of Canadian society at its best and worst, to learned justices and hardened criminals, to Orangemen and Irish Catholics, to aliens and Indians. It was all absorbed experience which reinforced and added to the instinctive wisdom and tolerant pragmatism with which he viewed his fellow men.

By his nature and from experience John A. Macdonald developed no very exalted view of human nature, but he was not simply a pessimist or a cynic.

He was, it is true, sometimes deeply discouraged but his basic disposition was cheerful. He enjoyed the things he did. He enjoyed the intricacies of the law, he enjoyed making money, he enjoyed departmental problem-solving. Probably most of all he came to enjoy the 'game' of politics. To politics he applied the skills and knowledge gained in all his activities since boyhood. He had no real political mentors. He had admired his first leader, William Henry Draper, and was in one sense his political heir. Like Draper, his abiding political concern was the creation of a moderate, 'progressive,' broadly-based coalition party, but he was totally different in personality and methods from the aristocratic, publicly aloof Draper who could scarcely wait to escape from a public position he found distasteful.[38] Macdonald had been, in public at least, a dutiful party follower of Draper's successor, Sir Allan MacNab, so long as MacNab remained as leader and premier. With MacNab also he shared much political ground, especially their common assumption of the right and necessary connection between private business and the business of the state, but he had no great personal respect for the abilities and pretensions of 'the gallant knight.'[40] Undoubtedly Macdonald learned from Draper and MacNab and from many others about parliamentary strategy and about the manipulation of political friends and enemies, but if he had political heroes they were not North American. His occasional references to current models of political and parliamentary behaviour were invariably to former or living British statesmen, to Pitt or Chatham, Peel or Derby. The truth is that as party leader and premier, Macdonald's style and approach to politics were largely his own.

One of the essential ingredients of his leadership style was egoism. He believed in his own intelligence and ability. He believed, probably rightly, that he could do a better job of leading his party than anyone else. Without him the Conservative party would have been in the wilderness, 'where they were when I took them up in 1854.'[41] This sense of his own value together with his strong sense of duty sustained him in bad political times. His fellow Upper Canadian Conservatives had chosen him, even before the squeezing-out of Sir Allan MacNab in 1856, to be their leader. 'When a man like myself has once entered upon the track,' he once told an audience in Hamilton, 'he cannot go back. Having assumed certain duties, he cannot, in justice to himself, in justice to the position he has voluntarily taken, in justice to his constituents, in justice to his party, or in justice to his own principles, recede.'[42] So long as his party wanted him to he would lead. So long as he was leader he expected and generally got loyalty and obedience from the ranks. It is significant that in the two major parliamentary defeats which the Conservative party suffered under the joint leadership of Macdonald and George Etienne Cartier, it was Cartier's followers who in 1858 and 1862 defected.

Macdonald claimed always to be 'a strong party man' (except when there was the prospect of a coalition when it became necessary to 'rise above party'). Maintaining party discipline among the diverse and balky elements of the political group which he led was no easy matter. The Liberal-Conservative coalition of 1854 which Macdonald had helped to form contained, besides the majority of the French-Canadian members and the moderate Conservatives of Upper Canada, reactionary remnants of the old Family Compact plus several varieties of Baldwinite or Hincksite Reformers, many of whom insisted on maintaining at least nominal adherence to their original political identification. Like Macdonald himself as well, many of the supporters of the coalition were strong-minded individualists with their own private or corporate ends to pursue through their political careers. 'Never was a poor devil surrounded by greater difficulties than myself,' Macdonald confessed to a friend during the uncertain political situation in the spring of 1862, 'and again and again disgusted with the selfishness of some or the faint heartedness of others was I tempted to throw up everything. A sense of party duty alone prevented me from doing so. By great caution and perseverance added (forgive the vanity!) to a little judicious manipulation I have got the discordant elements of our party into some shape.'[43] When, shortly after, defeat in the assembly actually occurred, he could report that 'My U.C. friends stood to me as one man and I fell in a blaze of loyalty.'[44] Eventually, the loyalty which he inspired reflected a widespread belief that he really was the party's best hope and a fear that without him the party might disintegrate. 'Your generalship can carry the party through when another man – no matter how able – would fail,' James Patton told him, 'no man on our side can take your place.'[45]

That kind of undisputed position of leadership was not achieved overnight. A great deal of 'judicious manipulation' had taken place along the way. Macdonald was always busy shoring up his political strength, encouraging the wavering, courting the undecided. He had the gift of pure, potent charm. 'The old humbug' had 'any amount of small talk' which he applied to political friends and foes alike and sometimes to susceptible ladies, with devastating effect.[46] His talent for calculated flattery, for 'soft sawder,' was as great as his legendary capacity for alcohol and he used both along with stories 'of doubtful moral tendency' and other blandishments to keep 'the refractory members' in good humour and in line.[47] He was a willing and a generous host, even, when he could afford it, a lavish host. He liked to entertain and to be entertained. 'Our administration,' he remarked on the occasion of the visit of the Prince of Wales in 1860, 'is more familiar with cocktails than cocked hats.'[48]

His ability to amuse and to persuade did not, needless to say, achieve the instant conversion of all his political enemies, but he did consider almost any opponent as a possible future ally. Some he marked out for special attention and set about with 'caution and perseverance' to effect their transmigration.

He had a sharp eye for early signs of discontent among the ranks of the opposition. Having detected a potential convert he would begin, in public and private, a patient, long-range campaign. The process could take months or it could take years but sooner or later most if not all of the people on his political shopping list – such as Galt, McGee, Foley, Sandfield Macdonald – found themselves collaborating with their former enemy. He had by nature an advantage that not all politicians possess: he was perfectly capable of working with people he disliked. Some of his surviving letters to close friends contain very candid, highly unflattering comments on other politicians. 'Put this in the fire after you have read it,' one such letter concludes, 'I have written with perfect candour, but I may have to act hereafter with some of the gentlemen I have spoken of.'[49] In private he called the erstwhile moderate Reformer, Michael Foley, 'lying Mike,' but was publicly cordial because 'Mike may be made useful yet.'[50] He was. Macdonald did not hold grudges for long because he did not believe he could afford to. He could at long intervals be provoked into a violent public rage and he periodically became so disgusted with individuals that there seemed no prospect of reconciliation. 'I don't speak to Sir Allan,' [MacNab] he wrote in 1858, 'and probably never will.' But of course he did. He became convinced that Sandfield Macdonald was 'a base bad man.' 'I have done with Lord Monck,' he declared in 1863, 'he deserves no longer any consideration.'[51] But these low character estimations too were only temporary. He said over and over again much harsher things about George Brown, but had no hesitation about forming a coalition with him in 1864. A politician, he knew, could not enjoy the luxury of prolonged personal animosity. 'Politics,' he advised a colleague, Sidney Smith, 'is a game requiring ... an utter abnegation of prejudice and personal feeling.'[52] Yet if he usually found it possible to forgive his enemies he could be quite ruthless in dealing with politicians, including colleagues and sympathizers, whom he had found untrustworthy or whose usefulness had come to an end. In the election of 1861 he abandoned David Roblin who had invariably given him faithful support because he had become 'a mounting political liability.'[53] In the same election he practically destroyed the political career of Sir Henry Smith, whom he believed to have betrayed the Conservative party and its leader.[54] This too was the mark of the successful leader. He did whatever had to be done.

Part of the reason why Macdonald found it relatively easy to deal with the majority of his political contemporaries, regardless of their formal political allegiance, was because he had a good deal in common with most of them. Being a Scot, for example, could sometimes be useful, for the Scots were well represented in politics in relation to their total numbers. He was also an Orangeman, which made him a part of a sizeable brotherhood, at least among the voters in Upper Canada, and he joined many other organizations as well, such as the Masonic Lodge, the Odd Fellows, the St Andrew's Society, the Toronto Club, and the Rideau Club. His business and professional interests were undoubtedly even more important political assets. They made him a member of a large and influential fraternity who, whether Grit or Tory, spoke a common legal-entrepreneurial language and shared a common outlook. It was not just that he was a lawyer and that the majority of his political contemporaries were, as they had always been and would continue to be, lawyers, though that in itself was of undeniable significance. He was also a part of a particular generation of Canadian entrepreneurs which differed in a number of ways from its predecessors and which bound its members together in a special way. It was a generation of young men of the urban middle class, both native and immigrant, all roughly about Macdonald's age, who began to make their way in the world in a period of rapid change and expansion. It was a generation which came to assume dominant roles in Canadian life during the mid part of the nineteenth century.

The urban professional-commercial community of Upper Canada which preceded Macdonald's generation had of necessity somewhat limited economic political and social horizons. They were hampered by a lack of capital, a faulty transportation system, a cumbersome if well-meaning form of colonial government, and perhaps to a degree by a lack of educational opportunities. The great event of their time had been the War of 1812-14, which was well remembered as a source of pride and also of profit. Their major goals were the accumulation of capital through hard work and shrewd dealing, or the acquisition of a secure public office.

The professional-commercial men of the 1840s and 1850s were better educated and began from less humble origins, sometimes with inherited capital or property. They have been described as 'more enterprising,'[55] but the truth is that they had far more opportunities. Suddenly the old restrictive colonial system of governing the province had been swept away, and perhaps just as significantly, local government also was generally revamped. Politics, local and provincial, was 'democratized' just enough to permit the enterprising urban professional-commercial class to replace the old narrow entrenched office-holding élites. Other changes occurring at the same time enhanced the pattern of change. British government loans and British private capital flowed in, canals were completed, railways were begun. The population grew at an unprecedented pace through immigration. Businesses sprang up, land values soared. In this period, centring on the mid-century point, old ways and old values changed also. 'Boom' conditions, a 'boom' mentality lasting in its first heady manifestation until the sharp economic setback of 1857, created innumerable opportunities for the 'enterprising.' Among the group of businessmen operating in the fluid conditions of the time was John A. Macdonald. Many others like him, mostly young, hustling, ambitious law-

yers, businessmen, builders, land speculators and developers, railway promoters, contractors and investors, promoters, directors and investors in road
companies, building societies, and loan companies sooner or later also became involved in provincial politics.

As a politician and party leader, John A. Macdonald did not operate as
someone removed from or independent of this context of business and politics but as a central part of it. His connections with other businessmen-politicians often bore no relation to political loyalties as such, but they were nonetheless real and capable of being turned to political advantage. He understood them and they understood him. They shared a common interest in
'developmental' policies, policies which encouraged economic growth. They
share a common interest in the expansion of business of all kinds and in the
use of the state as an aid and stimulant to business. The people Macdonald is
known to have persuaded to enter politics, men such as John Rose, David L.
Macpherson, and James Morton, were businessmen-politicians of this type,
as were the people he tried to persuade to cross the floor of the assembly and
a number of the people whom he recruited from time to time to put new
blood into his cabinet – M.H. Foley, Isaac Buchanan, and J.C. Morrison, for
example. Like Macdonald, they were businessmen-politicians.

With some of these men he had direct business connections. 'If it [the Great
Southern Railway] is going to have a chance,' he wrote to Isaac Buchanan in
1861, 'it must be strong in Parliament and Foley, you, Christie, McBeth and
myself will require all our united influence to set it on its legs again.'[56] (At
least two other sometime members of the legislature, James Morton and
Arthur Rankin, were also involved in this railway.) He bought and sold land
to, from, or with W.B. Robinson, John Rose, A.T. Galt, David L. Macpherson, Luther Holton, Malcolm Cameron, and Alexander Campbell.[57] With the
many other businessmen-politicians of the time, including Francis Hincks,
John Sandfield Macdonald and his brother D.A. Macdonald, J.G. Bowes,
James Webster, John Ross, John Hillyard Cameron, John Cameron the
banker, Sir Allan MacNab, Henry Smith, Sidney Smith, David Roblin, T.C.
Street, Robert Spence, Billa Flint, John Hamilton, John Macaulay, George
Crawford, John Carling, and others, he may or may not have had actual regular business dealings, but he had nonetheless a built-in understanding, an
insider's view shared and appreciated. As a businessman, John A. Macdonald
had no special distinction; he was by no means the most financially successful
of the group, he was neither the most honest nor the most dishonest, but he
was a better politician than the others. One of the reasons why he was lay in his
ability to exploit the unspoken understanding, the assumption of common
goals, which he shared with other businessmen-politicians.

Macdonald's superiority as a politician and leader was not simply a matter
of sympathetic intuition, however. It depended to a large degree on the

extent to which he worked at politics, and he worked at politics, as at every-thing else, very hard indeed. He wanted any administration of which he was a leading member to be known as 'a working government,' a fact about which he found it necessary to remind his cabinet colleagues at intervals.[58] He made the greatest demands of all on himself. He was prepared, in order to keep other cabinet members in good humour, to overlook occasional lapses and absences, but he himself rarely strayed from his post. Besides, he had a great deal to do. In addition to his private legal and business matters which he carried on mostly at long distance by mail, he had (except when in opposition) his departmental work to keep up. He had also to attend meet-ings of the Executive Council, which met formally on an average of twice a week throughout the year to despatch official government business. Besides all of these duties, he was a full-time leader and organizer of the western section of his party. To that role also he devoted large amount of time and energy.

Before Confederation there was no consistent province-wide Conservative party organization run from a central office, nor a permanent central office for Upper Canada alone. Macdonald, who was always more concerned about party organization when in opposition than when in power, made some efforts to create a centralized Conservative association headed by a full-time paid party official in 1863,[59] but nothing seems to have come to this scheme. No doubt the Great Coalition of 1864 complicated and delayed the plans. About this time also a number of Conservative party associations at the county or riding level were formed,[60] but there is little to show that they were widespread or vigorous. Between elections, in fact, it is hard to find much evidence of formal party organization at all, aside from occasional meetings in caucus of the elected members of the party. The day-to-day central organi-zation of the party in Upper Canada consisted mainly of one man, John A. Macdonald, who, working out of his office at the provincial capital (wherever it happened to be), planned party strategy in and out of the legislature, arbi-trated disputes, provided information and direction to party newspapers, dealt generally with party problems as they arose, and, certainly not least in importance, dispensed government patronage.

Macdonald delegated very little party responsibility. He seems to have preferred things that way. He certainly tried to keep a firm grip on such largesse as the government had to bestow on the party faithful. 'The truth is,' he told Henry Smith, 'all recommendations should come from an Execu-tive Councillor as otherwise there will be no end to cross purposes. We must keep these things as attached to the legal department, if possible.'[61] Patron-age was power, and patronage created loyalty to the party and to the leader (except in the hands of a 'Rad,' by whom it would be 'unscrupulously exerted').[62] He expected that loyalty so created would yield political rewards. 'I never desert a friend,' Macdonald once claimed.[63] His use of patronage helped to ensure that his friends would not desert him when he needed them. Needless to say, he received a great many requests for government jobs and other favours. He treated them seriously, kept them filed away either in his office or in his head, and replied to them as hopefully as he could. 'Make a civil answer,' he would instruct his secretary on the margin of a letter from an office seeker, or sometimes it was 'a very civil answer.' He screened applications by means of a number of working rules of his own devising which he applied whenever appropriate to justify a negative reply. He would not, for example, recommend anyone whom he did not actually know.[64] He would not, of course, recommend anyone who was known to be a political opponent. He would not recommend anyone who did not also have the support of his local (Conservative) member and preferably the support of another member of the cabinet as well.[65] He would not recommend anyone who applied for an office while the incumbent was still in it.[66] One other important rule by which he determined matters of patronage was that any of his ordinary rules could be broken if necessary, for sufficient political reason.

He worked hard at satisfying those whose cases he considered important. If he believed that the applicant was deserving, qualified, in genuine need, or, more important, if he was someone to whom Macdonald or the party really owed something, he would go a long way to 'meet the views' of the person involved. He was also careful to dispense patronage in due proportion between Roman Catholics and Protestants. He prided himself in fact on having given Catholics their proper share of government spoils, something which he claimed no other administration before his had ever done.[67]

In or out of office he could be extraordinarily tenacious in pressing the claims of those individuals or groups to whom he felt a commitment. Sooner or later he usually got results, even if as sometimes happened the individual involved had died before he could reap his reward.[68] 'My plan thro' life is never to give up,' he once told an impatient favour seeker, 'if I don't carry a thing this year, I will next.'[69]

On many matters, patronage included, he moved only after due deliberation, but he was capable of very rapid decisive action and on several fronts at once, especially during the period of a general election. At such times it again seems clear that if the Conservative party in Upper Canada had a central election organizer it was Macdonald himself, certainly from the election of 1857-8 on. He did not normally have to worry very much about his own election in Kingston, and he remained throughout most of each election campaign at the capital, even when the capital was Quebec City, working as usual from his office, writing innumerable letters, and dealing with the host of large and small problems which arose. His first problem was getting the right people nominated. Since he always headed the 'Liberal-Conservative' party, which was officially a coalition of Conservatives and Reformers, this was not always an easy matter. In some cases he personally named the man he wanted, or he prescribed the procedure by which the candidate should be chosen.[70] His preference was for the prearranged selection of candidates by a small group of prominent party supporters in each riding, though he did reluctantly accept the increasing use of that 'immoral and democratic' device, the nominating convention, as a means of promoting local party unity, so long as conventions were carefully organized and composed of 'a really respectable and influential body of delegates.'[71]

His incessant refrain at nomination time was 'let there be no splits'; that is, no rival coalition candidates. 'Splits' were the bane of his existence. 'A split, no matter how unimportant the man may be, discourages our friends and strengthens our foes.'[72] Not only the two wings of the coalition but Conservatives themselves showed an unfortunate tendency toward factionalism. Macdonald sometimes found as many as six candidates all claiming to support his government ranged against a single Reform candidate. He coped with these kinds of stubborn rivalries between local groups or individuals in a number of ways. The inevitable letters went out applying direct or indirect pressure on influential party supporters, appealing for party loyalty and unity. 'I am told there are a dozen candidates in the field for West Middlesex and that the consequence will be a Grit triumph,' he wrote to H.C.R. Becher of London in 1857. 'Now my dear fellow, set your wits to work, and choke off as many of them as possible, so as to have a fair fight between two.' Becher got it down to three. 'For Heaven's sake,' he appealed to Becher again a week later, 'stop old Ermatinger from dividing the ministerial interest in Elgin.' Ermatinger was stopped.[73] 'Don't let there by any splits in Peterborough,' he warned Sidney Smith and there weren't any. 'The only question should be,' Macdonald once declared, 'who will get the most votes?'[74]

Sometimes 'desperate cases require desperate remedies,'[75] fair or foul. When all else failed a 'split' might be avoided by buying one of the candidates off. There is a scarcity of hard evidence relating to such 'desperate' action but there is enough to indicate that it was an accepted practice when necessary. 'Buying off' could be done by direct cash payment but the more common method was by the promise of government office. An 1861 by-election in the riding of Grey in which the official government candidate, J.C. Morrison, was opposed by an Independent Conservative, Nassau Gowan, provides an illustration of this procedure. Macdonald's proposal was that if Gowan withdrew and worked for Morrison he would get 'some appointment as Clerk County Court or something of that kind within 6 months after the election.'[76] Gowan, as it happened, stubbornly refused to withdraw even though Macdonald eventually took 'the desperate course of using the telegraph today to buy off Nassau at any price.'[77] His use of 'buying off' as a method of improving electoral chances could be highly devious. During the general election of 1861 he proposed to Sidney Smith a means of paying off the party's obligations to Smith's brothers, James and John Shuter Smith. 'My plan as to Victoria and E. Durham,' he wrote, 'is that John Shuter should keep in the field till too late to hurt Burton, that James should not run against Cameron, that as soon as Cameron and Burton are returned John S. and James should settle who should be appointed Junior Judge for Peterborough and Vic.' Though this plan was not followed to the letter by all concerned, lucky James Smith did become judge of Victoria County in 1864.[78]

The nominating process was the first electoral hurdle which had to be got over. Then, and usually only then in most ridings, a semblance of party organization took place with the formation of 'central and other committees' to work for the election of each candidate.[79] Macdonald at this point assumed three main election functions. He intervened personally or by mail on behalf of his candidates, he gave policy guidance for candidates uncertain about the current party line, and he provided financial help. His personal involvement in specific ridings was normally late in the campaign and pretty limited. He could not 'leave the helm here for a moment, or everything will go to the devil.'[80] Under the flexible electoral system of the time, in which all elections did not necessarily take place on the same day, it was possible for him to arrange to be elected in Kingston and then to take a hand in one or two neighbouring ridings; but most of his extensive efforts in aid of candidates were achieved by writing his persuasive letters to influential people in the constituencies. This was particularly important when a 'split' had not been prevented, for it had to be made clear who Macdonald really wanted elected and why. At the riding level his correspondents were chosen, depending on how well he knew the area, from his own knowledge of who was likely to be able to sway other votes (there was of course no secret ballot at the time) or from a list of names submitted by the candidate, or a combination of both.[81]

At the provincial level he applied the same principle on a broader scale. His theory of electoral behaviour included a firm belief that sizeable numbers of voters reacted in a mass way and voted in blocs. The French in Lower Canada were naturally the shining example of this phenomenon so far as the party as a whole was concerned. They were the 'sheet anchor,'[82] as Macdonald called them. But in Upper Canada, also, he saw and attempted to manipulate at least three distinct 'blocs' – the Orange Order, the Roman Catholics, and the Wesleyan Methodists. His approach was always to work on the leaders of these groups on the assumption that they could influence the rank and file of their followers. Evidence of his wooing of his brother

Orangemen is disappointingly thin but his numerous extant letters to Upper Canadian Roman Catholic bishops and to the Reverend Egerton Ryerson[83] illustrate his technique. They were not allowed to forget which party had done or was going to do the most for their churches and their adherents. His relationship with the Orange Order was severely strained when the order was snubbed by the Prince of Wales in 1860, and he found it necessary to 'soothe the Orangemen by degrees,' but within a year he could candidly tell Ryerson that the Orangemen and Roman Catholics were 'all right' and 'we only want the Wesleyans to carry Upper Canada.'[84]

Macdonald's role as policy adviser to his candidates covered a great deal of ground and provides some indication of why he felt he could not 'leave the helm.' He did everything himself. The party leader and joint premier of the province could be found mailing out printed pamphlets and broadsheets to individual candidates, as well as writing long detailed letters suggesting 'good bunkum arguments' for candidates to use, warning of subjects which should be avoided and setting out safe limits of commitment on others.[85] (The question of how far a candidate could go in advocating 'Rep by Pop' was one which he found it necessary to deal with more and more often between 1854 and 1864.) His letters of this kind give another indication of the assumption upon which his overall election strategy was based. His instructions were often geared to local conditions in the evident belief that voters were more concerned with local than with large provincial questions or with abstract constitutional notions. He even suggested on occasion playing off one part of Upper Canada against another. The fear of the central section being dominated by 'the peninsula' west of Toronto was, he felt, exploitable material.[86] What mattered was not that all the pro-Macdonald candidates said the same thing on the hustings but that they got elected. To achieve that end his ultimate advice to candidates was to work hard and to leave as little as possible to chance. 'Canvass steadily and vigorously, yet quietly – get your own returning officer, a true man selected, and all your deputies.'[87]

Like the organization of the party in general, the systematic collection and disbursement of election funds was, prior to Confederation, in a rudimentary state of evolution. Here too Macdonald's role was central and decisive. His stated rule applying to elections was that each man paid his own expenses. Politics was no game for paupers.[88] As always, there were exceptions to the rule which could be made. If a candidate was short of cash and was also a cabinet member (or a prospective cabinet member), or if his election was considered vital, something could usually be done. The methods used by the party to collect money are obscure but Macdonald was certainly deeply involved in the process. No permanent party war chest existed in the pre-Confederation period (though so long as the party was in power the Secret Service Fund could be discreetly dipped into in a dire emergency[89]). Ordinarily each situation was treated on an *ad hoc* basis. Money was collected, mostly by Macdonald himself, from members of the administration and other well-to-do sympathizers and paid by him to particular candidates. He spent a great deal of his own money as well, either in the form of 'gifts' or as loans to candidates. It is likely in fact that the large debts he amassed at both the Bank of Upper Canada and the Commercial Bank were often as much political as commercial in origin. $100.00 here, $400.00 there, promissory notes which he might or might not collect on.[90] It is small wonder that he was himself sometimes short of funds.

By-elections created special circumstances in which the provision of funds was particularly important for concentration on a limited objective. The by-election in South Leeds in 1864 in which A.N. Richards, Liberal, was opposed by D. Ford Jones, Conservative, is the most thoroughly documented case of this type for which there is surviving evidence. Once again it shows Macdonald expending his maximum organizational and financial efforts while in opposition. He collected 'the sinews of war' by writing confidential letters 'eastward and westward' to every likely Conservative contributor in both Upper and Lower Canada, asking them to donate money (in the suggested amount of $100.00 each) and to act as sub-collectors in their areas. Not only politicians but merchants, manufacturers, railwaymen, contractors, and no doubt many others were approached by Macdonald in his temporary guise as Conservative bag man.[91] In South Leeds his efforts were rewarded – Ford Jones was elected. Money, however, could not always buy happiness. A few months later, when he was back in office, he again 'succeeded in getting liberal subscriptions'[92] in support of his own new minister, M.H. Foley, in a by-election in Waterloo North; but Foley went down to defeat.

The fact is that as an election organizer – or as what could now be called Ontario campaign chairman – Macdonald was at best only an indifferent success. In the four general elections between 1854 and 1867, the Liberal-Conservatives under his leadership managed to win a (small) majority of the seats in Upper Canada only once, in 1861. It can be argued that he was not entirely to blame for this. The party's overall election strategy did not necessarily hinge on winning a majority of seats in Upper Canada. They could usually obtain power on the strength of their 'sheet anchor,' the French Canadian Bleu bloc. Still, the usual failure of the Conservatives to get out the Upper Canadian vote must raise some questions about Macdonald's possible shortcomings as an election strategist and organizer and as an appealing public figure. As has been seen, he at one time toyed with the idea of a full-time headquarters staff which could have handled at least the mechanics of organization, party propaganda, and fund raising, but this plan was never put into effect. He may have been reluctant to lose the control which he exercised over the party and its sources of support. He may have believed that no one else could perform his many functions as well as he could. He may have been simply too busy to devote enough time to formal party organizations. Whatever his motives, it is still possible to speculate that by not delegating some of his responsibilities, by not adopting some of the 'modern' party techniques which he himself advocated and which his opponents were, after a fashion, already using,[93] he may have damaged his own side's chances to some degree. Perhaps if he had worked in different political circumstances, without Cartier's Bleus to fall back on, or if he had been oftener in opposition and been spurred on by the greater sense of urgency which being out of office roused in him, his undoubted organizing abilities might have been put to better and less single-handed use.

In view of his party's dismal record in Upper Canadian elections, it is reasonable to ask whether John A. Macdonald's personal public image was or was not a strong political asset. There is no doubt that he was an able, colourful, and entertaining speaker, both in the assembly and in public. Even his early speeches, read after a lapse of more than a century, are still impressive, not for their oratory but for their clarity, the logic of the arguments, and especially as high quality political invective. His speeches were not particularly graceful and were rarely emotional. They were highly partisan, sometimes boastful versions of recent political events. They were also, and still are, often very funny. He may have been the first Canadian politician consciously to use humour as a political weapon. His public image was easy going and familiar; he was 'John A.' the 'welcome friend' of the 'industrious farmer,' the 'enterprising merchant,' and the 'honest hardfisted mechanic'[94] who came to hear him; but his humour was anything but gentle and his jokes were never at his own expense. They were skilful exercises in political ridicule which seized upon and magnified every opposition inconsistency, every real or alleged blunder, every evidence of fallibility and ineptitude. He made the kind of speeches which delighted partisan audiences and infuriated his opponents.

On the whole the image which he sought to project – an image of informality coupled with shrewdness and native common sense – no doubt succeeded in winning some additional support for Macdonald and his party. The surprising fact about Macdonald as a public speaker in the pre-Confederation period is that he actually did so little of it. Prior to the general election of 1861 he undertook his first and only extended speaking tour of Upper Canada. This was a novel and a rather undignified, un-British, thing for a minister of the crown to do at the time, even though he spoke only to 'private' party dinners and not to open meetings; but the subsequent election results (whether as a direct consequence of the tour or not is of course open to doubt) do appear significant. The Conservatives then won a majority of the seats in Upper Canada. In the South Leeds by-election in 1864, already referred to, Macdonald, then in opposition, spoke at a number of open political meetings.[95] The Conservative candidate won. In the Waterloo North by-election a few months later Macdonald, once more a minister, stayed away. His candidate lost by 163 votes.[96]

Obviously the evidence on this point is inconclusive but it does suggest that he might have made more use of his own talents as a public speaker at election time, especially after the apparently successful experiment with the 'modern' device of the speaking tour in 1860-1. Why he didn't is not entirely clear. He often justified his refusal to make public appearances in support of particular candidates on the grounds that British parliamentary practice forbade a minister of the crown who was 'responsible for every word he utters' from going 'about the county haranguing crowds'[97] ('especially at public meetings where they may be subject to an adverse vote').[98] Macdonald, however, was not one to avoid a successful course of action merely because it wasn't 'done.' It may be that before Confederation he did not again find enough time to undertake such a tour, or it may simply have been that his first speaking tour was not a very enjoyable experience. He certainly got tired of giving the same speech over and over. 'It was good fun for a time but at last became wearisome beyond expression,' he confided to J.R. Gowan.[99] He promised at the time 'to begin again in the Spring,'[100] but before Confederation he never 'took to the stump' again, nor did he win a general election in Upper Canada again. Still the lesson of 1860-1 was not forgotten. The 1860 speaking tour was undoubtedly a forerunner of his successful public performances in the 1870s and 1880s on 'the picnic grounds of Ontario.'[101]

Elections are not won by speeches alone, by organization alone, or by money alone. It is a matter of debate whether in the circumstances of the later Union period it was really possible for the Conservatives consistently to win elections in Upper Canada against sectional Grit-Liberal strength, despite anything that Macdonald and his party might have done. Macdonald's success or failure as a party leader, however, cannot be measured only in terms of elections won or lost in Upper Canada. The essential fact is that most of the time he succeeded in staying in power. In provincial terms, his success rested on his original and continuing alliance with the majority political bloc in Lower Canada and on *their* ability to win elections. In Upper Canadian terms, his success was in making the Liberal-Conservative coalition a viable if usually a minority political force there. His success lay also in his skill in political manoeuvre after and between elections.

The Conservatives of Upper Canada, for example, were badly defeated in the election of 1854, but out of that election emerged the first Liberal-Conservative coalition under MacNab and Morin. This was the fundamental shift by which the Upper Canadian Conservatives attached themselves to their 'sheet anchor,' the French Canadian majority (as well as to the moderate Hincksite Reformers of Upper Canada), a shift that enabled them for the first time in seven years to achieve and hold power. There is good reason to believe that Macdonald's role in the formation of that coalition was critical. In advance he had established 'friendly relations with the French' and had laid his plans 'to enlarge the bounds of our party so as to embrace every person desirous of being counted as a progressive Conservative.'[102] The coalition accomplished, his self-appointed task was to keep it together and if possible to enlarge upon it. He had no patience with those who were 'fools enough to think that a purely Conservative government can be formed.'[103] The façade, at least, of a government organized 'on a popular basis' was always preserved by Macdonald, by shuffling and replacing the representatives of moderate Reform in the cabinet or by co-opting here and there a disgruntled Grit Reformer. John Ross, Robert Spence, Sidney Smith, J.C. Morrison went in and out; McGee and Foley were persuaded to cross the floor. By such shifts and ploys Macdonald kept the patchwork Upper Canadian coalition intact and usually in power from 1854 to 1862. The election of 1863, however, showed that the game was up. In previous elections the 'thesis and antithesis'[104] of Canadian politics had operated correctly. If the Conservatives lost in Upper Canada, the Bleus gained in Lower Canada, and *vice versa*. In 1863 not only were the Conservatives decimated in Upper Canada, but Cartier's Bleus actually lost a few seats as well. It was time for a new coalition.

Macdonald was not the initiator of the Great Coalition of 1864 with Brown and the Upper Canadian Grits or of the movement for Confederation which was the reason for its existence; but he gladly took the opportunity when it was handed to him. He was soon happily at work making the new political structure function, urging his followers to set mere party considerations aside, to work hand in hand with their new political allies 'in order to prevent anarchy,' 'to settle the great constitutional question of Parliamentary Reform,' and to 'restore the credit of the Province abroad.'[105] For these worthy motives, the coalition was achieved and pressed forward, with Macdonald, in fact if not in name, at its head. In the Confederation negotiations which followed he can quite genuinely be said to have risen above 'mere party' and to have shown real statesmanship, but he did not stop being a politician. The new coalition had been formed in the nick of time, to avoid 'handing over the administration of affairs to the Grit Party for the next ten years.'[106] The coalition now had to be made secure and lasting. It was especially necessary to put down the pernicious doctrine that 'this was not an ordinary coalition but a temporary junction for a temporary purpose.'[107] To make it permanent required much patient soothing of ruffled feelings and regrouping of forces. Among other things the critical area of government patronage had to be completely revamped. Jobs had to be found for new applicants, newspapers formerly in opposition now had to receive their share of government business.

Whether by appealing to high principles or to more basic human feelings which could be reached by the salve of government favours, Macdonald succeeded once again in realizing his long-term political goal, 'a union of moderate men,' a strong political base from which to meet new political circumstances. This new base carried him triumphantly through and beyond Confederation, yet almost from the very beginning the coalition began to come unstuck and to require constant patching up. In immediate post-Confederation Ontario terms its success was decidedly short-lived, not entirely to Macdonald's surprise. He had feared all along that under the federal arrangement the new Province of Ontario would 'be left to the tender mercies of the Western Grits.'[108] At the provincial level the Conservative party was no more successful after Confederation than before in winning elections in 'Upper Canada.'

The fortunes of Conservatism in Ontario after Confederation lie beyond the scope of the present study – and, as well, were no longer Macdonald's entire responsibility. Nonetheless, from an Ontario point of view, his general failure to attract support in the period before Confederation from what was after all his own region had some obvious bearing on the politics of the post-1867 period, and can therefore stand some further exploration. In particular, some examination is necessary of the basic political premises upon which he operated.

Deciding what John A. Macdonald really thought about almost anything is not easy. He made many public speeches and wrote an enormous number of private letters in many of which he was assuming a political position and attempting to persuade others to follow his lead, but it has been correctly observed that he was quite capable of taking a position to which he was not necessarily wholeheartedly committed.[109] When he described himself as 'a hot free-trader'[110] or 'an ardent Protestant,'[111] the modern reader is justified in a certain skepticism about his sincerity. Fortunately, the very volume of his writings which has survived provides a broad basis of evidence from which some notion of his basic beliefs can be extracted. In this regard not only his speeches and private correspondence are important but also the many administrative papers which he compiled, especially as attorney-general. These documents, while primarily concerned with practical legal problems, provide as well some helpful insights into the workings of his mind in politically neutral situations.

John A. Macdonald's political 'ideas' or 'beliefs' have been subjected to more learned scrutiny than those of almost any other Canadian leader,[112] a fact which is more than a little surprising, considering that the scholarly consensus has been that he was not a man of ideas at all. It has generally been agreed that though a number of broad assumptions about politics and society underlay his actions, he was not reflective by nature and did not work within any consistent theoretical or philosophical framework.[113] Like almost anything else that can be said about him, this image of Macdonald is capable of some qualification. It is true that he was essentially pragmatic, even opportunistic by nature. He did not disguise his pragmatism with political rhetoric; on the contrary, he positively boasted of it. 'I am satisfied,' he said during the Confederation debates, 'to confine myself to practical things ... I am satisfied not to have a reputation for indulging in imaginary schemes and harboring visionary ideas.'[114] This was the 'John A.' image, the plain, nononsense practical man of good sense. It was also a deliberate pose.

In fact, Macdonald had a far sounder theoretical grounding in comparative government and constitutional law than most of his contemporaries. Though he had not had a lengthy formal education, he had put himself through an extraordinary course of post-graduate reading in history, law, literature, political economy, and any number of other miscellaneous subjects. He believed that 'political reading' was necessary in order to succeed 'as a statesman.'[115] He himself had done a great deal of political reading both before and during the creation of the Canadian federal constitution and he had also done a great deal of abstract thinking on constitutional matters. It was his ability in both theory and practice that made him, largely by default, the dominant figure of the Confederation era and the principal author of the British North America Act. He complained privately in 1864, during 'the preparation of our Constitution,' that 'I must do it all alone as there is not one person connected with the Government who has the slightest idea of the nature of the work.'[116] The results of his constitution-making emerged in practical political form. He produced a pragmatic workable division of powers between an overriding senior government and subsidiary provincial governments, but this arrangement was grounded in theory. 'When there are local governments and a Central Government,' he once explained, '... in time either the General Government or Parliament absorbs the local ones, or the General body from weakness loses all its power.'[117] He believed that by stacking the deck sufficiently in favour of the 'General Government' he had created a situation in which in as little as a generation he would 'see both local Parliaments and Governments absorbed in the Central power.'[118] He had 'theorized' a federal system evolving into a unitary state. And perhaps there is some explanation here of his public avoidance of 'visionary ideas.' They seldom worked out as planned.

His stress on the desirability of a centralized, unitary form of federal government, a government approaching as near to a legislative union as possible, did not spring as a wholly new notion into his mind in 1864. An instinctive leaning toward unity, union, centrality had always been a basic part of the 'theoretical' underpinnings of his practical political actions. It had been a source of his political strength, but also, especially in Upper Canada, a source of political weakness. 'I am a sincere unionist,' he said, 'I nail my colors to the mast on that great principle.' 'Union with Great Britain' and 'the union of the two Canadas' were his watchwords.[119] It might be suggested that at the time these were altogether unexceptionable sentiments, even mere political platitudes. It is true that few people in Upper Canada questioned the value of a permanent connection with the mother country and that there was no consistent demand for outright repeal of the Union of 1841, but Macdonald had in fact very firmly taken one side of a fundamental difference in point of view. To him the Union had almost a sacred character. 'God and nature,' he declared, 'have made the two Canadas one' (presumably after an earlier period of trial and error); 'let no factious men be allowed to put them asunder.'[120]

Not everyone in Upper Canada agreed with him about the God-given status of the Union. It was not that most Upper Canadians disagreed with the idea of union in principle but that they did not consider it unalterable and did not always like some of its implications. Many Upper Canadians believed, rightly or wrongly, with the Brownite Clear Grits, that their economic interests were subservient to those of the Montreal business community or that Roman Catholic separate schools had been foisted upon them against their wishes. They did not, rightly or wrongly, like being forced into political partnership with a French-speaking, Catholic population, a partnership which they suspected prevented by 'French domination' the natural western extension of the province into the prairie regions and also denied them the political ascendancy to which, by 1860, their superiority of numbers entitled them. John A. Macdonald was well aware of such critical views of the working of the Union. He tried to head them off or explain them away where he could, but basically he accepted and defended the situation as it was in the name of the preservation of the Union and of the greater good which it embodied – co-operation between the races in the building of a great 'nation' and an integrated economic system. So, because it was the price of Union, he argued forcefully the case for separate schools in Upper Canada, he back-pedalled gracefully on the issue of representation by population, dragged his feet on Northwest annexation, and denied entirely that 'French domination' existed.

It can be said that his insistence on the value of the union of Upper Canada with Lower Canada reflects a breadth of view which much exceeded that of most of his Upper Canadian contemporaries. It can be argued that, on principle, he was prepared to sacrifice votes in Upper Canada rather than risk stirring up regional, racial, or religious animosities and thereby risking the Union as a whole. Certainly he was a tolerant man, by the standards of his time probably unusually so. He would make friends with anyone and work with anyone. 'If we get the right man in the right place, it does not matter what his race or religion may be.'[121] Tolerance was a natural attribute and a political asset. Tolerance, however, does not exclude the possibility of prejudice. In a political setting Macdonald did not ask anyone what his race or religion was, but he did not want his son to marry a Roman Catholic.[122] He did not dislike French Canadians as a 'race' but it is doubtful that he regarded them in quite the same light as Anglo-Saxons. In the words of one of his biographers, he was not 'blind to the defects of the French character,' which, among other things, was too logical and excitable.[123] The French were also ultimately doomed. In company with many other English-speaking Canadians before and since his time, Macdonald assumed the eventual assimilation of French-Canadian society. He did not think it would happen quickly, but, in his often quoted phrase, 'immigration and copulation ... will work wonders.'[124]

He thought that the period of the Union had seen a decided beginning on the process of amalgamation and absorption. 'At the Councils of the Province, British blood and Protestantism really do prevail,' he told an Upper Canadian audience in 1860.[125] What the old Union had begun, the new Union of all of British North America might well complete. His own plan for the central government, as has been seen, was for a powerful evolving organism which would absorb the lesser legislative bodies and in so doing was not likely to waste much sympathy on the 'peculiar position' of minorities. 'But of course,' as he candidly admitted to M.C. Cameron, 'it doesn't do to adopt that point of view in discussing the subject in Lower Canada.'[126] He was wrong about the inevitable assimilation of French Canada, just as he was wrong about the chances of local governments being 'absorbed' by the central power, but the point is that his instinctive attitude toward people of non-Anglo-Saxon origin did not differ very much from that of most of his British-Canadian contemporaries,[127] although both his natural tolerance and his sound political judgment kept his 'assimilationism' from surfacing in overt political form.

It is always difficult, and probably unwise, to attempt to separate principle and practice in analysing Macdonald's political acts. His 'friendly relations with the French' which he had been at such pains to establish were certainly genuine but were politically advantageous as well. They also fitted well within the larger framework of his desire for unity, of the empire, of his party, of French and English and of Upper and Lower Canada. His commitment to the Union of 1841 and its corollary, co-operation with French Canada, became a virtual political principle, almost at times, a political obsession. In its way it was also a political strait jacket, from which it was not easy to escape. Having cast in his lot with the French-Canadian majority bloc, he was dependent upon their support in order to retain power. Having committed himself to the Union through thick and thin, he almost failed to grasp the significance of the events of 1864 and the opportunities for a greater union which then awaited him. He wanted things to stay as they were. Almost alone among the members of the high-powered constitutional reform committee of the legislature chaired by George Brown in the spring of that year he held out for the old system, and rejected the idea of the Confederation of British North America because it was to be a federal and not a legislative union, and because it violated the unity of the Province of Canada.

Macdonald's belief in the value of the Union was of mixed origin – personal, traditional, geographical, and economic. He was an Upper Canadian but also as a Kingstonian, a Central Canadian. He had grown up and earned his living within the economic system which has been called 'the Commercial Empire of the St Lawrence.' 'Central Canada,' which in Macdonald's mind extended westward to about the Trent river,[128] depended, he believed, on Montreal as its vital *entrepôt*. Any disruption of the connection with Montreal could bring economic disaster. Perhaps even deeper in Macdonald's consciousness than an awareness of practical economic considerations such as these was an instinctive feeling that things as they were should be left alone. The commercial unity of the St Lawrence was a fact of Canadian history. The political Union of 1841 was a recognition of that fact. The Union had become a fact when he first began to take an interest in public questions, it had been a fact when he had first been elected to the assembly. He did not like changes, especially large, sudden changes. He was, after all, a Conservative.

He was not, of course, a reactionary conservative. He was a 'moderate' or 'progressive' conservative. In a rare public statement of political position he once described himself as 'a Conservative Liberal.'[129] Instinct and political shrewdness never found him too far from a consensus position on most issues, never far from the political 'centre' of the time. His personal philosophical position, nevertheless, was always at least a few degrees to the right of centre. On what might be termed the 'litmus paper' issues in Canadian politics he invariably turned an unmistakeable shade of blue. His first major speech as a member of the assembly, for example, was in opposition to the abolition of primogeniture in Upper Canada. This issue – whether the property of an individual dying without a will should be divided up or should pass intact to his oldest male heir – could be expressed in the form of a basic question about Upper Canadian society. Should wealth, property, and privilege be maintained by law or should they be shared out more equitably among the population? On this matter 'moderate' Conservatives like Macdonald parted company with 'moderate' Reformers like Robert Baldwin, W.H. Merritt, and J.H. Price.[130] On other similar issues Macdonald could be found on the genuinely conservative side. He did not, to cite another example, accept the prevailing Upper Canadian belief in the separation of church and state, especially in matters of education. In opposition to Baldwin's 'Godless University,' he favoured state support for a variety of denominational institutions and also the recognition of the claims of the Church of England to pre-eminence in educational matters,[131] just as he had upheld that pre-eminence in the settlement of the clergy reserves. If he lost (or partially lost) the political battles on these issues, it was because he was a little behind rather than a little ahead of the dominant mood of his time.

His conservatism did not require him to linger over lost causes. He could accept and even support measures to which he was personally opposed, such as the secularization of the clergy reserves in 1854, because he had become convinced that further resistance was useless. He was too wise a politician to worry unduly about total consistency; he did not want to be out of touch with public opinion and sought, so far as it was in his power to do so, to improve the social and economic conditions of his countrymen, but he was not by instinct an innovator. He preferred whenever possible to build slowly upon established foundations.

One piece of bedrock upon which he consistently sought to build a better Canada was the law, and his knowledge and experience of the law. It has been said that his political pragmatism stemmed from his legal training, which taught him to treat each situation as a separate case rather than as a part of a unified system of ideas.[132] While this observation is no doubt true in its way, his private view of the law went well beyond mere *ad hoc* practicality. The law was not just a tool to be manipulated as the occasion required but a basic force for the preservation of civilized society. Respect for the law, obedience to the law, was essential not only to preserve order and to deter criminal acts, but also to maintain the society as it was and as it should be. The law reflected and assumed an ordered, stratified society in which 'the persons and the property of the inhabitants' were properly protected.[133] John A. Macdonald believed in the rule of law and that no man should set himself above the law. He believed also that the existing legal and penal systems were wise, humane, and necessary and that constant vigilance was required to see that they were not weakened or tampered with. As attorney-general he deplored 'unwise laxity' in the application of the law, especially in the granting of bail or the remission of sentences. Behind his fear of 'unwise laxity' lay a concern that 'we might drift by degrees into the American system,' in which he saw justice subject to 'political influence.'[134] The law therefore had to command respect; the courts, the judges, the magistrates, the legal profession, and all officers of the law must be supported because they were the guardians of order, of the *status quo*, especially of the respectable, propertied class, which included Macdonald. When he spoke of the 'superiority of our institutions' (to those of the United States) he included, along with the monarchy and British parliamentary practice, the British-Canadian legal system. These superior institutions had produced a society which had avoided the excesses of democracy based on universal suffrage. 'Unless property was protected and made one of the principles on which representation was based,' Macdonald said in a debate on representation by population, 'they might perhaps have a people altogether equal, but they would soon cease to have a people altogether free.'[135] He maintained 'as a Conservative' that legally some Canadians were more equal than others, and that in this he was upheld by the wise provisions of the law, which held 'that one man had a right to the franchise because he was assessed for £50 of real estate, while we deprived of the right a man who was assessed for £49, a man whose natural capacity might be greater in every way.'[136]

On this question of representation Macdonald's faith in the law coincided with his belief in the need for balance and harmony in society and in the constitution. These were principles which he was bound to uphold 'as a Conservative,' for he was not only an instinctive but an intellectual Conservative, who understood in a theoretical way what Conservatism was. He believed 'as a Conservative' that it was necessary that there be a propertied 'middle power' to resist 'the tyrannical power of mere numbers.'[137] This, as he was fond of reminding his colleagues, was the British way. 'It is of the very greatest importance,' he argued, 'that the English system should be kept up in this country.'[138]

The precise degree of Macdonald's 'imperialism' has been a matter of some debate. Certainly he was not (as most writers have concluded) an imperialist in the broadest sense. He was never attracted to the notion of a highly-organized, politically-centralized empire, especially if it were to impose general military obligations. Though he wanted the connection between the colonies and the mother country to continue indefinitely, he believed that the nature of the connection would change and was changing. Canada, and eventually all the other possessions, would cease to be dependencies and would become allies of Great Britain. In the process they would form 'the greatest confederacy of civilized and intelligent men that ever had an existence on the face of the Globe.'[139] In the period prior to Confederation this was still a very long-range vision. Dependency – economic, military, constitutional, and psychological – was very much a part of the colonial condition. Macdonald accepted and defended this state of dependency.

Before the institution of responsible government he upheld on principle the use of the royal prerogative by the colonial governors and the right of the British government to intervene in local affairs when imperial interests were seen to be affected.[140] In later years and in office his feelings about British intervention were somewhat more mixed, but the British connection and the British example continued to be important guide-posts for his career – because Canada was a British colony, because all 'loyal Britons' owed allegiance to the queen, because Great Britain was his hereditary 'home,' and because he genuinely believed that the British way was the best way. British genius, refusing to be misled into 'anarchy and despotism' by revolutionary doctrines based on false notions of liberty and equality, had evolved a constitutional and social system that worked, a system in which *true* liberty and justice prevailed and in which all 'interests' were fairly represented.[141] 'The superiority of our institutions' derived from their Britishness and colonial institutions and customs suffered to a degree when they departed from British models. Macdonald frequently contrasted the low level of political conduct in Canada, where members of the government were 'open to the greatest obloquy and the most violent assault, not only on their political course but their private character,' with the situation as he saw it in England, where there was mutual respect among public men and where 'a man devoting himself to the public service' received 'a generous appreciation.'[142]

So if he was not an imperialist, he was certainly an anglophile. He had absorbed great quantities of British history and literature, old and new. He kept up with the latest magazines. He often quoted from the great British authors in speeches and letters – Shakespeare, Milton, Dr Johnson, Charles Dickens. He got his medical advice and his heartburn remedies from British sources. Despite chronic sea sickness he made many trips 'home' to England, trips which became more and more frequent throughout his life.

His attitude to England and the English was never simply one of slavish imitation or uncritical adulation. He never tried to turn himself into an Englishman and he knew from experience that not all Englishmen, even in high places, were uniformly wise, especially when colonial interests were involved. He understood both the advantages and the disadvantages of the existing relationship between the colonies and the parent state. On the whole, he had no doubt that the advantages, especially the advantages of British investment in the Canadian economy and British military protection, outweighed the disadvantages. He did not resent the colonial state of dependency and was therefore in no hurry to create an independent British North American nation. Nor was he ever led to indulge in the grandiose dream of a great imperial parliament espoused from time to time by fretful colonial politicians, William Lyon Mackenzie and Joseph Howe among them, who chafed under a 'second-rate' colonial status. Macdonald did not show such discontent, perhaps because, unlike so many prominent British Americans before him, from Benjamin Franklin to William Henry Draper, he never suffered from what might be termed 'the imperial put-down,' the sense of disillusionment at being treated at the seat of empire as something less than the equal of real British subjects. Macdonald's reception in London, on the contrary, was always cordial and even respectful. From the time of his first business trip to London in 1850 he had been granted access to the right people, both businessmen and politicians, had succeeded in most of his commercial and political objects and had been entertained in a variety of stately homes. In 1865 he and he alone among the British North American delegates then in England to discuss Confederation was asked to accept an Oxford honorary degree. In 1867 he and he alone among British North American political leaders was granted a knighthood in recognition of his services. He was not only treated as an equal by British leaders but was accepted for what he was, an unusually gifted commercial representative, politician, constitutional lawyer, and statesman in his own right. It is small wonder that he continued to see British commerce, politics, society, and leadership in a highly favourable light.

One other aspect of the colonial relationship which was more than ordinarily significant for Macdonald was the need for British military protection. He was no pacifist and there is nothing to indicate that he ever found British militarism offensive, but he was not personally sympathetic to the military profession or the military mind. It may be that the example of his mother's soldiering family, many of whom had died young in foreign lands, had something to do with his aversion; perhaps the only personal experience which he ever had of military service as a militia private during the Rebellion of 1837 left a strongly unfavourable impression on him.[143] Unlike the majority of locally prominent men of his time in Upper Canada, he did not at any time (and by deliberate choice) hold a militia commission.[144] As attorney-general his correspondence with the military, through the adjutant general of militia, can only be read as a persistent exercise in the denial of military pretensions, a steady assertion of the pre-eminence of civilian authority.[145]

When the post of minister of militia affairs was created in 1861, Macdonald appointed himself to it; not, obviously, because he was the cabinet minister most qualified on the basis of military experience, but more likely because he preferred to keep a strong non-military grip on a dangerous situation. He knew that Canada was practically indefensible, yet that Canadians had to show a willingness to defend themselves against attack. He was willing to do a good deal toward improving the efficiency of Canada's defences and the Canadian militia but he was firm in insisting that Great Britain must continue to be the prime defender of her Canadian subjects. Canadians were not an aggressive, warlike people. He did not intend to be pushed into purely Canadian defence measures which he felt the province (or the union-to-be) ought not to be expected to undertake. If war came 'it could only be an Imperial war on Imperial grounds,' and the British government should therefore 'acknowledge the obligation of defending every portion of Canada with all the resources at its command.'[146] He was personally determined that Canada was not soon to become a military power. 'There is no chance,' he told an inquirer in 1865, 'of there being any such thing in this country for a long time as a Profession of arms.'[147]

The reason why Canada had to be defended, the reason why continued imperial protection was essential, was the threat of war with the United States. The only war that had ever been fought in British North America had been with the United States. The only war that was ever likely to be fought in the future would be with the United States. Several times during Macdonald's early career – during the border disturbances after the Rebellion of 1837, at the time of the Oregon Crisis of 1846, during the Civil War and the subsequent Fenian raids – war was a real possibility. Upper Canada, and Macdonald's own town of Kingston, had been founded by United Empire Loyalists, refugees from and victims of the American War of Independence. Upper Canada had borne the brunt of the fighting in 1812-14. Upper Canadians had rejected the American political experiment with republicanism and democracy and had fought to retain the British system. If Upper Canada had an enemy it was an enemy at the very gate, a permanent, flourishing, confident, aggressive American presence.

John A. Macdonald has been called 'a pan-Americanophobe' and 'a thorough-going anti-American.'[148] Such labels too are unduly simplistic. His feelings about the United States were, in fact, about as ambivalent as were those of most Upper Canadians of the time. In one way it would have been surprising if he had been uniformly hostile to all things American, for he had close family connections in the United States. His uncle, James Shaw, had settled in Georgia and had married the daughter of a famous American general. One of his closest family friends was his wife's older sister, Margaret Greene, who had also married into the same Georgia family. Until her death in 1863 there was a good deal of mutual visiting across the border and Macdonald also visited other members of the Shaw-Greene connection in Rhode Island and New York as well as in Georgia. Until 1868 at least, Macdonald regularly took holidays in the United States, in Georgia, Rhode Island, Massachusetts, and Maine. Through his family, and through other vacationing Upper Canadians like David Macpherson, the banker C.S. Ross, and Judge James Gowan, he met a good many Americans, some of them prominent in politics and business. His personal image of the United States included, along with such American amenities as warm winters, lobsters, and peach brandy, 'a very grateful recollection' of American 'kindness and attention,' especially during his first wife's periods of convalescence in a number of American cities.[149]

None of his personal American experiences, of course, could affect his view of the American system of government, which was one of fundamental opposition. The government of the United States suffered in his opinion from some fatal flaws, chief of which were a weak central government and universal suffrage. In this restricted sense he really was 'a thorough going anti-American.' Yet he maintained even during the Civil War that there was hope for America still, because 'they were of the same blood as ourselves ... there was a vigor, a vitality, in the Anglo-Saxon character and the Anglo-Saxon institutions of the United States that would carry them through this great convulsion, as they had carried through our mother country in days of old.'[150] While condemning the levelling tendency of American political life which could bring a 'beast' like Abraham Lincoln to the presidency,[151] he himself adopted such American political techniques as nominating conventions and 'stump' speaking when they came in handy. He knew also that there were important economic considerations which made thorough-going anti-Americanism impractical. In the 1840s and 1850s he, along with the other leading Kingston businessmen, had vigorously promoted the Wolfe Island, Kingston, and Toronto Railroad and its successor, the Wolfe Island Railway and Canal Company, whose purpose had been to plug Kingston directly into the American railway network via Cape Vincent, NY. As a businessman Macdonald understood the importance of two-way access to American markets.[152] During the Civil War he may, as has been stated, have sympathized with the 'gallant defence' of the South, but he was under no illusion that Canada should or could adopt a pro-Southern policy, because, as he said, 'all our interests are Northern.'[153] It is true that there was much about the United States which he did not like. He thought that many American politicians were crude in their methods and manner and not to be trusted, but then he had learned that British politicians were not always to be trusted either.

John A. Macdonald was not 'a thorough-going anti-American' or a thorough-going Imperialist or a thorough-going anything else, except perhaps a thorough-going Canadian. In the context of pre-Confederation Ontario his Canadianism too was, of necessity, limited. It was and largely remained Central-Canadianism, but it was nonetheless very real. He had a genuine affection for the region where he had grown up and achieved so much in business and public life, and he had a genuine faith in its future. His Canadianism cannot be equated with what is now generally understood by the term 'Canadian nationalism.' It involved, except in the very long view, no concept of independent nationhood, though he often used the term 'nation' rather loosely. It was rather a vision of 'a great people' with a great potential, 'stretched the full length along the Northern Shore of the great lakes and commanding the mighty St. Lawrence,'[154] a people who were bound together by common interests, growing ever closer together in the pursuit of common goals. In public speeches Macdonald's Canadianism, his pride and his hopes for Canada, brought him about as close as he ever came to eloquence: 'I am like those who hear me, a Canadian, heart and soul. I heard the gallant officer who returned thanks for the army and navy say he was. That, I believe, is the feeling that exists in every breast here; and though I have the misfortune, like my friend the deputy adjutant general, to be a Scotchman; still I was caught young, and was brought to this country before I had been very much corrupted. Since I was five years old I have been in Canada. All my hopes and my remembrances are Canadian; and not only are my principles and prejudices Canadian, but (what as a Scotchman, I feel as much as anybody else) my interests are Canadian.'[155]

The practical application of this Canadianism required that in all internal matters Canadian interests came first and that, if need be, adverse external pressures, whether from the United States or Great Britain, had to be resisted. So it was not only sometimes necessary to call out the Canadian militia to patrol the frontier but it was also necessary to uphold the right of 'ministers of Canada, dependent on her people ... to raise our revenue in our own fashion' despite the protests of British manufacturers,[156] and it was necessary to maintain the independence of Canadian courts – to establish the principle that 'the English courts of Justice shall have no jurisdiction in Canada, and that no writ or process from them shall run into it.'[157]

Given sympathetic help from Great Britain, a free hand to manage its own legitimate concerns, and peace with the United States, Macdonald believed that his faith in Canada and its future would be justified. His faith was not based on mere optimism or on any abstract 'idea of progress.' He was not impressed by the puffing prize essays on Canada's glowing prospects turned out in such profusion in the 1850s (especially prior to the depression of 1857). He did believe that with competent leadership, Canada's population and resources could, barring accidents, eventually fit her to 'occupy no unimportant position among the nations of the world.'[158] When 'Canada' came to mean a federation of all the British North American colonies in a political union largely designed by Macdonald himself, his expectations naturally became even greater. Canada's people would grow to a population of eight or nine million, 'a subordinate nation' in alliance with the mother country.[159]

Clearly Upper Canada, soon to be Ontario, would have 'no unimportant position' within the new dominion. Ontario had the largest population of all the provinces and would have by far the largest number of members in the new federal House of Commons. Ontario was the region of British North

America which had shown the most unanimity in supporting political union. Ontarians were obviously looking forward to the political and economic advantages which they rightly believed would accrue to them after 1867. John A. Macdonald was an Upper Canadian. He was soon to be, and was to remain, an Ontarian. After Confederation, though he spent much of his time at the federal capital in Ottawa, he continued to be a partner in his law firm in Kingston and to pursue other business interests, including Toronto real estate. In 1874 he moved his law practice permanently to Toronto, Ontario's capital and metropolitan centre, and lived there during his brief period in opposition, 1874-8. He kept his Toronto business ties intact. In 1887 he became the first president of the newly-formed Manufacturer's Life Insurance Company, head office, Toronto. After Confederation his political responsibilities as prime minister and political leader became of necessity broader in scope than before but as the leader and foremost strategist of his party he continued to be most concerned with Ontario politics, both on the federal and the provincial level.[160] Ontario remained his personal, professional, and political base until his death – still Canada's prime minister – in 1891.

The community which in 1867 became the Province of Ontario had developed economically, politically, socially, and culturally from very small beginnings over a period of more than eighty years. It is reasonable to ask of John A. Macdonald (or of any other Upper Canadian leadership figure) to what extent he contributed to that development. It is reasonable to ask how closely he, as a political leader, was attuned to the needs and aspirations of his fellow Upper Canadians and how successful he was in achieving Upper Canadian goals. It is reasonable to ask how he conceived of the place of Upper Canada in the colonial scheme of things both prior to and in anticipation of the union of 1867. What, in other words, did he as a pre-Confederation leader want for Upper Canada? What did he do for Upper Canada?

In one sense the answer to both questions is nothing at all, for he had never thought of Upper Canada as a distinct region with its own destiny, but only as a part of a larger political and economic unit. He had always stood for the Union of Upper and Lower Canada, had always opposed any geographical division which would restore Upper Canada's separate existence. Though he had been forced to agree to the creation of the separate provinces of Ontario and Quebec as a part of the Confederation compromise, it was his intention that these new provinces (and the other provinces) would be subordinated as much as possible, and if possible entirely, to the general government. He was an Upper Canadian but at the same time a Central Canadian. For him, before or after Confederation, Upper Canada on its own was inconceivable – 'a miserable little back state,' cut off from the sea and cut off from Montreal, the commercial and industrial heart of the St Lawrence-

Great Lakes transportation system. Insofar as he ever saw Upper and Lower Canada as distinctive parts of a whole, it was in terms of one area which was predominantly agricultural and one which was predominantly manufacturing. This generalization occurred over and over again in his pre-Confederation speeches, including the Confederation debates.[161] Upper Canada was 'an agricultural country,' 'the more favored section of the Province' in soil and climate. Lower Canada with 'an incalculable amount of water power' and an 'industrious and frugal population ... must become a great manufacturing country.' Upper and Lower Canada therefore complemented one another perfectly. Even economic self-sufficiency was an ultimate possibility. The agricultural products of Upper Canada would be exchanged for manufactured goods from Lower Canada, where 'men women and children can work in the factories.'[162]

Macdonald does seem to have thought that Upper Canadian cities such as Toronto and Hamilton would steadily increase in size, perhaps to half the size of Montreal, mainly as a result of increased Canadian railway traffic into and out of the American mid-west.[163] He was also aware that manufacturing was on the increase in Upper as well as in Lower Canada, but basically his conception of an interdependent industrial east and an agricultural west remained largely intact throughout the pre-Confederation period. For him Upper Canada without Lower Canada did not make sense. It can even be argued that as a Central Canadian and as a politician he actually disliked and distrusted a large part of the population of Upper Canada. He was afraid that 'the peninsula' – that is, Upper Canada west of Toronto – with its rapidly growing population would come to dominate the region between Toronto and Montreal. He was also concerned about the frequency with which the people of 'the peninsula,' 'Yankees and covenanters ... the most yeasty and unsafe of populations,' voted for Reform candidates. Fear of the loss of economic interdependence and fear of political domination – 'the peninsula must not get command of the ship' – made Macdonald consistently hostile to any suggestion of a majority of Upper Canadians being free to run their own regional affairs.[164]

In purely political terms his 'Central Canada views' proved to be an Ontario failure, a failure to build and maintain a strong, consistent Conservative voting tradition in Upper Canada upon which an Ontario provincial voting pattern could readily be built. He also failed to build a strong, efficient, centralized political organization with which Ontario Conservatives could fight the political battles of the future. He did have a hand in hastily putting together a provincial coalition administration in 1867, under the leadership of John Sandfield Macdonald as first premier of Ontario, yet this 'combination,' unlike earlier coalitions with which he had been associated, had no knack for political survival. Nor can it be said that the standard of political ethics which he bequeathed to Ontario was notably high. His standards no doubt were those of the time, within which bribery, conflict of interest, graft, and an assortment of other dubious practices were tolerated within wide limits; but if his personal conduct as a politician was no worse than that of anyone else, it must still be said that he did very little to improve the situation as he found it.

With the major exception of the British North America Act itself, which literally created the Province of Ontario, John A. Macdonald as a political leader was not associated with much Ontario legislation which can be called dramatic or sweeping in its implications for the future of the province. The general nature of the legislation passed during his administrations did not differ materially from that of other governments of the day. Under his leadership there was no sudden speeding-up of the process of government, no striking increase in the length of parliamentary sessions, and only modest and probably necessary increases in the size and expense of the public service. 'As a Conservative' he rarely departed far from established paths. He preferred to have things 'running in grooves.' Nonetheless, he was never merely the head of 'caretaker' administrations. While he was joint premier and attorney-general of Upper Canada, a great many solid, constructive measures were taken – measures which kept pace with the needs of a rapidly developing, changing Upper Canadian community and which provided a basis for successful economic and political continuity into the era of the Province of Ontario.

Macdonald himself, of course, unlike all of the other Upper Canadian leaders except, briefly, John Sandfield Macdonald, extended his own political continuity into the post-Confederation period in Ontario. He continued, not as an Ontario provincial political leader, it is true, but as an Ontario politician – an Ontario politician who still exercised a great deal of control over the policy and personnel of the party in the province. He was instrumental in establishing another important kind of continuity as well. The Ontario political tradition of a close working relationship between government and private business (which in the opinion of one Canadian historian ultimately reduced the provincial government to the status of 'a client of the business community')[165] had its main roots in the period in which John A. Macdonald was the dominant political figure. He was not the first businessman-politician; his administration was not the first to come to the aid of private companies in the name of the 'national' interest, or to smooth the legislative path in a way highly favourable to the business community; but he and his colleagues who were in charge of Upper Canadian affairs throughout most of this period of rapid economic development built upon and solidified existing practices and left a pattern for others to follow. In an 'emerging' country, in a hurry to establish its credit rating and its very presence in North

America, short of capital and capitalists, the developmental policies put into effect by Upper Canadian politicians in the 1850s and 1860s were probably the most appropriate, perhaps the only possible policies suitable to the situation. A policy of economic development aided by the alliance of business and government was a practical, dynamic expression of the value of a propertied 'middle power' in society which Macdonald accepted as right and natural. So he and his colleagues initiated the policy of 'incidental' protection to home manufacturers, continued to put large sums of public money into the Grand Trunk Railway, and facilitated the passage of vast quantities of legislation to incorporate and encourage many kinds of business ventures – banks, railways, insurance companies, building societies, public utilities, mining companies, oil companies, lumber companies, turnpike companies, to name only a very few.[166] There were even some modest and not very effective attempts to encourage agriculture through grants to agricultural societies and by the building of colonization roads in 'agricultural' Upper Canada.[167]

It is not difficult to find evidence of many other ways in which the administrations which Macdonald led contributed to the process of development from pioneer Upper Canada to burgeoning Ontario. In one of the political 'steep turns' which now and then punctuated his career, Macdonald as attorney-general disposed of two perennially divisive bugbears from an earlier Upper Canadian era by secularizing the clergy reserves (though, as has been shown, more to the advantage of the Church of England than to anyone else)[168] and by instituting an ill-fated experiment with an elective upper house. As attorney-general, he was responsible for a number of necessary legal reforms (most of which were drafted in collaboration with his close friend Judge James R. Gowan) relating to the Upper Canadian courts themselves as well as to the laws concerning imprisonment for debt, usury, and jury procedures.[169] He was involved in the reorganization of an active militia force in Upper Canada, he created the civilian position of minister of militia affairs, and was the first to hold the office. He oversaw a similar upgrading of government functions in 1859, when the office of the inspector-general became the Department of Finance, and a general expansion of government took place during his periods in power (despite some cutting back under John Sandfield Macdonald in 1862-4).[170] New branches of government and agencies such as the Board of Audit (1855) were added in the interests of administrative efficiency and to keep pace with the growth of the province. Expanded postal and customs facilities were provided. New institutions for juvenile offenders and for the insane were built in an attempt to deal with increasing social problems. New responsibilities for home defence and for the administration of Indian affairs, transferred to the colonial government by the British, were assumed during the 1860s. New districts and new counties were brought into being to meet the needs of an expanding and shifting population. Towns and cities under legislation of 1857 and 1858 were encouraged to increase their boundaries and were incorporated for the same reasons. In addition, the growth and improvement of the Upper Canadian school system went steadily on, planned by the energetic superintendent, Egerton Ryerson, and put mainly into effect by his political ally, John A. Macdonald.

No mere list of acts passed or activities undertaken by departments of government can do entire justice to the contribution made by John A. Macdonald to the development of the Province of Ontario. No doubt if there had been no John A. Macdonald other politicians would have followed policies which were not greatly different. But it is doubtful if any other leader could have been so successful in reconciling opposing views, in finding moderate solutions and acceptable compromises. Macdonald's government was good government, practical government, and, for its time, stable government. If his own example is a reliable guide, it was also, for its time, efficient and hardworking government. By good sense, good luck, and good humour, he managed most of the time to sustain a political climate in which the problems of growth and development could be worked out free from the extremes of distracting and divisive debate on racial, religious, and constitutional questions. On the occasion of his first election in 1844 he told the electors of Kingston that 'in a young Country like Canada, I am of opinion that it is of more consequence to endeavour to develop its resources and improve its physical advantages than to waste the time of the Legislature, and the money of the people, in fruitless discussions of abstract and theoretical questions of government.'[171] That practical approach to political life he never abandoned, because, most of the time, it worked. It was an approach which, over the succeeding twenty-three years, contributed a great deal to the realization of his own overriding 'theoretical' goal: 'one people – great in territory, great in resources, great in enterprize, great in credit, great in capital.'[172] And in the process it contributed a great deal also to the creation of nineteenth- and twentieth-century Ontario.

There are five public statues of John A. Macdonald in Canada, four of them in Ontario. Of course, these posthumous tributes from a grateful people reflect primarily his significance as a national figure, yet they are not inaccurate indicators of his importance to the history of Ontario, especially in its formative years. His place in that history, beyond his many achievements as a leader and legislator, is a highly personal one. During the critical years of the old Canadian Union that were a prologue to modern Ontario, his life and his activities touched almost every aspect of the life of Upper Canada as a whole. Before there was a Province of Ontario, John A. Macdonald was an Ontario institution. 'John A.' is an Ontario institution still.

240 J.K. Johnson

1 Sir Joseph Pope, *Memoirs of the Right Honourable Sir John Alexander Macdonald G.C.B.* (Toronto 1930), 5
2 John A. Macdonald's family background is examined at length in J.K. Johnson, ed., *Affectionately Yours: The Letters of Sir John A. Macdonald and his Family 1842-1891* (Toronto 1969), 1-23.
3 D.G. Creighton, *John A. Macdonald: The Young Politician* (Toronto 1956), 13
4 Ibid., 11-13. Pope, *Macdonald*, 6
5 Creighton, *Macdonald: The Young Politician*, 19. It is worth noting that Hugh Macdonald was sufficiently respected as a member of his community to be appointed a magistrate of the Midland District in 1829 and a magistrate and commissioner of the Court of Requests in the Prince Edward District in 1834. Public Archives of Canada [PAC], RG 68, General Index to Commissions, Upper and Lower Canada 1651-1841
6 Creighton, *Macdonald*, 18. The printed reports of the Midland District School for the years 1827 and 1828 list Macdonald as a pupil in those years. In 1827 he studied geography, arithmetic, testament, Virgil, rhetoric and reading, and in 1828, Homer, Virgil, English grammar, Euclid, and arithmetic. Upper Canada, Legislative Assembly, *Journals*, 1828, 1829, Appendices
7 J.K. Johnson, 'John A. Macdonald and the Kingston Business Community, 1842-1867,' in G. Tulchinsky, ed., *To Preserve and Defend: Essays on Kingston in the Nineteenth Century* (Montreal 1975), 147-50
8 Macdonald's business activities in Kingston are traced in detail in ibid., 141-55, and outside of Kingston in J.K. Johnson, 'John A. Macdonald, the Young non-Politician,' Canadian Historical Association, *Historical Papers*, 1971, 139-47.
9 John A. Macdonald, *Address of the Hon. John A. Macdonald to the Electors of the City of Kingston* (1861), 116
10 PAC, Macdonald Papers, MG 26 A, vol. 221, 94285-8; vol. 386, 181996-2000; Johnson, 'Young non-Politician,' 142; J.K. Johnson, ed., *The Letters of Sir John A. Macdonald*, II: *1858-1861* (Ottawa 1969), 302, 304
11 Macdonald Papers, vols. 539-40
12 PAC, Buchanan Papers, MG 24, D16, vol. 41, 33225
13 Kingston *Daily News*, 10 Dec. 1857
14 Johnson, 'Macdonald, the Young non-Politician,' 147
15 Creighton, *Macdonald*, 260-1
16 He was prone to periodic 'illnesses' throughout his political career, but the first time that he seriously neglected his responsibilities because of heavy drinking seems to have occurred in the spring of 1862. Ibid., 331-2
17 Pope, *Macdonald*, 786
18 See, for example, letters to Rev. P. Watson, Bischoff, Coxe and Bompas, and M.C. Cameron, Dec. 1864, in Macdonald Papers, Letterbook 6.

19 Buchanan Papers, vol. 18, 15164
20 Johnson, 'Macdonald and the Business Community,' 148, 150
21 A.M. Evans, 'Oliver Mowat: the Pre-Premier and Post-Premier Years,' *Ontario History*, LXII, Sept. 1970, 143
22 Johnson, ed., *Letters*, I, 11, 30; Johnson, 'Macdonald and the Business Community,' 151
23 Kingston's political background is ably discussed in S.F. Wise, 'Tory Factionalism: Kingston Elections and Upper Canadian Politics, 1820-1836,' *Ontario History*, LVII, Dec. 1965, 205-25
24 Johnson, 'Macdonald and the Business Community,' 153; Johnson, ed., *Letters*, I: *1836-1857* (Ottawa 1968), 224, 371
25 Johnson, 'Macdonald and the Business Community,' 153
26 Elizabeth Gibbs, ed., *Debates of the Legislative Assembly of United Canada* (Montreal 1970-) IV, Pt II, 2499-500 [hereafter *Debates*]
27 Kingston *Chronicle and Gazette*, 5 Oct. 1844
28 Macdonald Papers, vol. 539, 255082-251
29 J.E. Hodgetts, *Pioneer Public Service: An Administrative History of the United Canadas, 1841-1867* (Toronto 1955), 65-6
30 Johnson, ed., *Letters*, I, 57, 79
31 H.J. Morgan, *Sketches of Celebrated Canadians and Persons Connected with Canada* (Quebec 1962), 584
32 See, for example, Macdonald Papers, Letterbook 7, letters for Dec. 1864-Jan. 1865.
33 Johnson, ed., *Letters*, II, 425
34 Macdonald Papers, Letterbook 7, Macdonald to James McCarrol, 27 March 1865
35 Hodgetts, *Pioneer Public Service*, 83
36 PAC, RG 1, E 13, vols. 30, 31, 'Blue Books,' 1853, 1854
37 See, for example, Johnson, ed., *Letters*, I, 293-300, 310-12; II, 136-43, 236-42.
38 Ibid., II, x-xi
39 G. Metcalf, 'Draper Conservatism and Responsible Government in the Canadas, 1836-1847,' *Canadian Historical Review*, XLII, Dec. 1961, 300
40 Johnson, ed., *Letters*, I, 398-9
41 Buchanan Papers, MG 24, D 16, vol. 41, 33089
42 Macdonald, *Address*, 8
43 PAC, J.R. Gowan Papers, MG 27, I, E 17, Macdonald to Gowan, 21 April 1862
44 Ibid., Macdonald to Gowan, 3 June 1862
45 Macdonald Papers, vol. 338, Patton to Macdonald, 19 Nov. 1863
46 See 'The Diary of Mercy Ann Coles,' PAC, MG 24, B 66, and Macdonald Papers, vol. 545, 257930, Elizabeth Hall to Macdonald, 21 Dec. 1860.
47 Macdonald Papers, vol. 194, Campbell to Macdonald, 8 March 1855
48 Johnson, ed., *Letters*, II, 258

242 J.K. Johnson

49 Ibid., I, 203
50 Ibid., II, 84
51 Ibid., 98; PAC, Amsden Papers, MG 24, B 65, Macdonald to Amsden, 25 Dec. 1863; PAC, Watkin Papers, MG 24, E 17, Macdonald to Watkin, 23 Oct. 1863
52 Johnson, ed., *Letters*, II, 268
53 J. Eadie, 'Politics in Lennox and Addington County in the pre-Confederation Period, 1854-1867,' (unpublished MA thesis, Queen's University, 1967), 92
54 D. Swainson, 'Sir Henry Smith and the Politics of the Union,' *Ontario History*, LXVII, Sept. 1974, 175
55 C.W. Cooper, *Frontenac, Lennox and Addington* (Kingston 1856), 18
56 Johnson, ed., *Letters*, II, 338
57 Johnson, 'Macdonald, the Young non-Politician,' 140-4
58 Johnson, ed., *Letters*, I, 301-2
59 Amsden Papers, Macdonald to Amsden, 29 Dec. 1863; Toronto *Leader*, 21 Dec. 1863
60 Macdonald Papers, Letterbook 6, Macdonald to J.P. Martyn, 31 March 1864
61 Johnson, ed., *Letters*, I, 227
62 Ibid., 202
63 Ibid., II, 182
64 Macdonald Papers, Letterbook 6, Macdonald to T.H. Hodge, 12 Nov. 1864
65 Letterbook 7, Macdonald to A. Armstrong, 13 Dec. 1864; Johnson, ed., *Letters*, I, 227
66 Macdonald Papers, Letterbook 7, Macdonald to P. Watson, 13 Dec. 1864
67 Ibid., Macdonald to John Farrell, 2 Jan. 1865
68 David Roblin, for example, whom Macdonald had promised a job, died while the Conservatives were in opposition in 1863.
69 PAC, Moylan Papers, MG 29, C 29, Macdonald to Moylan, 14 Dec. 1864
70 Johnson, ed., *Letters*, II, 75
71 PAC, Becher Papers, MG 24, C 29, Macdonald to Becher, 15 March 1862
72 Ibid., Macdonald to Becher, 13 Dec. 1857
73 Johnson, ed., *Letters*, I, 466-7
74 PAC, Sidney Smith Papers, MG 24, B 63, Macdonald to Smith, 18 May 1863; Johnson, ed., *Letters*, II, 75
75 Ibid., 301
76 Ibid.
77 Ibid., 303
78 Ibid., 339
79 Ibid., 333; Macdonald Papers, vol. 338, Pt II, 154001, George Benjamin to Macdonald, 8 June 1863
80 Johnson, ed., *Letters*, I, 467
81 See, for example, Macdonald Papers, vol. 229, Macdonald to W. McDougall, 8 and 12 July 1864; Letterbook 6, Macdonald to James Vrooman, 7 July 1864; vol. 229, Macdonald to Thomas Pyne, 16 July 1864.

82 Johnson, ed., *Letters*, II, 342
83 Ibid., I, 227; II, 332, 340, 360; PAC, Ferguson Collection, MG 27, IE 30, vol. 1, Macdonald to O.R. Gowan, 22 Nov. 1847
84 Johnson, ed., *Letters*, II, 332
85 Ibid., I, 469; II, 342, 352
86 Ibid., 468-9
87 Ferguson Collection, MG 27, IE 30, vol. 1, Macdonald to O.R. Gowan, 22 March 1847
88 Macdonald Papers, vol. 229, Macdonald to McDougall, 8 July 1864
89 Ibid.
90 Johnson, ed., *Letters*, I, 467-8; II, 301; Macdonald Papers, vol. 338, Pt I, 154001, Benjamin to Macdonald, 8 June 1863
91 Buchanan Papers, MG 24, D 16, Macdonald to Buchanan, 20 Nov. 1863, 11 Jan. 1864; PAC, Brown Chamberlin Papers, MG 24, B 19, Macdonald to Chamberlin, 20 Nov. 1863
92 Macdonald Papers, vol. 229, Macdonald to McDougall, 8 July 1864
93 E. Jackson, 'The Organization of Upper Canadian Reformers, 1818-1867,' *Ontario History*, LIII, June 1961, 109-15
94 Macdonald, *Address*, 4
95 Creighton, *Macdonald: The Young Politician*, 346
96 Macdonald Papers, vol. 215, 91660, Foley to Macdonald, 25 April 1864
97 Macdonald, *Address*, 3
98 Johnson, ed., *Letters*, II, 276
99 Ibid., 312
100 Ibid.
101 D.G. Creighton, *John A. Macdonald: The Old Chieftain* (Toronto 1955), 219-25
102 Johnson, ed., *Letters*, I, 202
103 Ibid., II, 355
104 Creighton, *Macdonald: The Young Politician*, 344
105 Macdonald Papers, Letterbook 6, Macdonald to James Vrooman, 7 July 1864
106 Ibid., Letterbook 9, Macdonald to S.G. Lynn, 10 April 1866
107 Ibid., vol. 229, Macdonald to McDougall, 8 July 1864
108 Ibid., Letterbook 8, Macdonald to J.S. Smith, 22 Sept. 1865
109 P.B. Waite, 'The Political Ideas of John A. Macdonald,' in M. Hamelin, ed., *The Political Ideas of the Prime Ministers of Canada* (Ottawa 1969), 55
110 Macdonald Papers, Letterbook 17, Macdonald to D.L. Macpherson, 20 Feb. 1872
111 Macdonald, *Address*, 26
112 See, for example, Waite, 'Political Ideas,' 51-67; T.W.L. MacDermot, 'The Political Ideas of John A. Macdonald,' *Canadian Historical Review*, XIV, Sept. 1933, 247-64; A.D. Lockhart, 'The Contribution of Macdonald Conservatism to National Unity,' Canadian Historical Association, *Report*, 1939, 124-32.

113 Waite, 'Political Ideas,' 61-2; MacDermot, 'Political Ideas,' 264

114 *Parliamentary Debates on the Subject of the Confederation of the British North American Provinces* (Quebec 1865), 1002

115 Johnson, ed., *Letters*, I, 201

116 Gowan Papers, MG 27, IE 17, Macdonald to Gowan, 27 Nov. 1864

117 Macdonald Papers, Letterbook 7, Macdonald to M.C. Cameron, 19 Dec. 1864

118 Ibid.

119 Macdonald, *Address*, 90

120 Ibid., 93

121 Ibid., 25

122 Johnson, ed., *Affectionately Yours*, 17-18, 117-18

123 Pope, *Macdonald*, 620

124 Johnson, ed., *Letters*, I, 338

125 Macdonald, *Address*, 25

126 Macdonald Papers, Letterbook 7, Macdonald to M.C. Cameron, 19 Dec. 1864

127 Any doubt on this point is dispelled by reading accounts of a speech which Macdonald made in Hamilton in 1882, in which he touched on Chinese immigration. 'I do not want the yellow or the brown man,' he said. 'Seriously speaking, I believe it a misfortune to introduce a different race, of a different cast of mind, of inferior civilization and lower morals.' *Toronto Daily Mail*, 9 June 1882

128 Macdonald, *Address*, 88

129 Ibid., 9

130 Gibbs, ed., *Debates*, V, Pt I, 1236-7

131 Creighton, *Macdonald: The Young Politician*, 122-3

132 Waite, 'Political Ideas,' 52

133 Johnson, ed., *Letters*, II, 306

134 Ibid., 285-6

135 Macdonald, *Address*, 99

136 Ibid., 100

137 Ibid.

138 Ibid.

139 Ibid., 114

140 Gibbs, ed., *Debates*, V, Pt I, 1010

141 Macdonald, *Address*, 100-1

142 Ibid., 6-8

143 Pope, *Macdonald*, 9

144 Johnson, ed., *Letters*, II, 589

145 Ibid., I, 363, 378, 381, 394, 403, 419-20, 429-30

146 Canada, *Journals of the Legislative Assembly, 1865*, XXV, 9-13, Macdonald, Cartier, Morin, and Galt to Viscount Monck, 12 July 1865

147 Macdonald Papers, Letterbook 8, Macdonald to F.G. Johnson, 22 Aug. 1865

148 McDermot, 'Political Ideas,' 254-5

149 Johnson, ed., *Affectionately Yours*, 4-10, 69, 109; Gowan Papers, MG 27, I, E 17, Macdonald to Gowan, 27 Nov. 1864

150 Macdonald, *Address*, 109

151 Gowan Papers, MG 27, I, E 17, Macdonald to Gowan, 27 Nov. 1864

152 Johnson, 'Macdonald and the Business Community,' 155

153 Hamilton Public Library, Buchanan Papers, Macdonald to Buchanan, 16 Oct. 1864

154 Macdonald, *Address*, 113

155 Ibid., 6

156 Ibid., 64

157 Johnson, ed., *Letters*, II, 307

158 Macdonald, *Address*, 114

159 *Parliamentary Debates on the Subject of Confederation*, 43-4

160 For one illustration (among many) of this point, see Macdonald's correspondence with C.A. Munson, A. Boultbee, A. Holmes, and others regarding a provincial by-election in Lennox in 1884, Macdonald Papers, vols. 406, 407.

161 *Parliamentary Debates on the Subject of Confederation*, 35

162 Macdonald, *Address*, 91, 94

163 Johnson, ed., *Letters*, I, 468

164 Ibid., 340

165 H.V. Nelles, *The Politics of Development: Forests, Mines & Hydro-Electric Power in Ontario, 1849-1941* (Toronto 1974), 495

166 See *General Index to the Journals of the Legislative Assembly of Canada in the 4th, 5th, 6th, 7th and 8th Parliaments, 1852-1867* (Ottawa 1867) under such headings as banks, building societies, harbours and wharves, mining companies, mortgages, navigation, railways, roads, timber.

167 Ibid. See entries for agriculture and colonization.

168 Alan Wilson, *The Clergy Reserves of Upper Canada* (Toronto 1968), 216

169 Johnson, ed., *Letters*, II, 37, 39, 228, 324; H.J. Morgan, *Sketches of Celebrated Canadians and Persons Connected with Canada* (Quebec 1862), 598

170 PAC, RG 13, vols. 38-40, 'Blue Books,' 1862, 1863. The Militia Department, for example (which Sandfield Macdonald took over from John A. Macdonald), was cut back sharply. A number of new appointees were also brought in to replace former employees.

171 Johnson, ed., *Letters* I, 12

172 Macdonald, *Address*, 92

John Sandfield Macdonald

In Quebec City, the formal opening of parliament on 12 February 1863 was considerably more martial than usual. Canadian volunteers and British regulars were both out in great strength lining the route of Governor General Monck and his vice-regal party. Fifteen volunteer companies from the city were under arms, while from far to the west the Wellington Rifles and the Victoria Rifles formed the guard of honour in the interior of the great hall. The governor general was transported in a covered carriage drawn by four magnificent horses. Arms were presented with 'the volunteers equalling the "regulars" in precision.' Cannons boomed from both 'Terrace and Citadel.' Inside the chambers, a large crowd filled the galleries, including 'an unusual number of the fair sex,' brilliantly attired.[1] The next day in the Speech from the Throne, Monck thanked Canadians for their generous donations toward alleviating distress in the Lancashire textile towns of England, towns hard-hit by the absence of cotton from war-torn America. The speech emphasized progress in expanding the militia and announced plans to improve contacts with the Northwest. Premier John Sandfield Macdonald, in office now for almost nine months, then delivered a short, careful speech of his own further outlining the projected course of his government.[2]

Back in May 1862, when George Etienne Cartier's Militia bill had been defeated and the Conservative Cartier-John A. Macdonald government had resigned, many people had been puzzled by Monck's selection of Sandfield Macdonald from the Reform opposition to form a new ministry. The ailing forty-nine-year-old member from Cornwall had never had a large personal following, nor was it clear that he would be able to command the largest section of a decidedly disunited Reform party. Yet he more than most other Reformers, seemed prepared to operate with a minimum of sectional, sectarian, and regional motivation. These centrifugal forces, together with the clash of personalities, had been the curse bedevilling a Reform party which paid insufficient heed to Robert Baldwin's old admonitions in favour of toleration and patience. The Liberal party found it hard to be liberal. At least as a liberal Baldwinite, Sandfield's credentials to lead were impeccable.

No newcomer to politics, Sandfield had, back in 1841, first been elected to the legislature as a Conservative for the tradition-bound riding of Glengarry. He had never been a part, however, of that oligarchy which had once dominated unreformed Upper Canada. Few Glengarry Catholics could have expected to be significant in a Family Compact centred in distant Toronto. Furthermore, Sandfield once referred to himself as a 'political Ishmaelite'; he was not easily controlled.

His father, Alexander Sandfield Macdonald of Clan Ranald, had been born in Scotland, in the poverty-stricken Roman Catholic, Highland parish of Knoydart.[3] All five hundred of its people had immigrated as a group with their priest to the New World in 1786. They had settled in Charlottenburgh, a back or rear township of Glengarry, in what was to become Upper Canada's easternmost county. The 'front' of Glengarry, had already been settled by Loyalist Scots. In Charlottenburgh, St Raphael's West became the centre of the new community.

At the time of the Knoydart migration, Alexander had been only a young boy in the company of his father, Allan Macdonald. In Glengarry Alexander grew to maturity and married Nancy, a distant cousin who was the daughter of a John Macdonald. In little St Raphael's West, on 12 December 1812, John Sandfield became their firstborn child. Two months previously a famous Glengarrian, Colonel John Macdonell (Greenfield), acting attorney-general and aide-de-camp to General Brock, had died in the battle of Queenston Heights. Local lore has it that Sandfield's first name ('Sandfield' was the common sub-surname for the whole family), was given him in the Loyalist Greenfield's honour. Otherwise, the future premier's beginnings were unpretentious. Lot seven, north across the King's Road and slightly to the west of the church, was the Sandfield homestead. There, four other children were born of the marriage: the unpredictable Ranald Sandfield, the temperamental and brilliant Donald Alexander, the stable and quiet Alexander Francis, and a girl who died an infant.

About two years after the birth of her fourth son, the fragile Nancy Macdonald died, after catching cold following a sleigh ride in the country on a bitter winter's night. Father Alexander Macdonell, the village priest who was later to become the first bishop of Upper Canada (and who was then finishing the impressive and massive Georgian church which would ever remain St Raphael's great pride), declared at her funeral that, 'any good that will come of her boys will be on account of their sainted mother.'

Saintliness was hardly a characteristic of the young John Sandfield. Motherless at eight, he, not unnaturally, grew up as a lad noted for his independent spirit. At only eleven, he attempted to run away from home and had to be carried back forcibly. Soon afterwards, he was apprehended while negotiating with an Indian at Cornwall; the precocious boy had tried to persuade the Indian to paddle him over to the American side for a small fee. Young John was restless at the parish school, which he only attended for a few years. At age sixteen he obtained a junior position as a clerk in a general store in Lancaster. Later, moving to Cornwall, he took up a similar post. Humiliated by the jibes of children who taunted him with the label 'counter-hopper,' and encouraged by a lawyer who frequented the store, he decided to take up the study of law. The month of November 1832 marked a decisive change in his life. Admitted as a special student, Sandfield entered the Eastern District Grammar School at Cornwall. This noteworthy school had been founded in 1803 by the Rev. John Strachan, who had become the inspirational leader of the Family Compact. It was under the principalship of the Presbyterian clergyman, the Rev. Hugh Urquhart, when Sandfield entered it. By allowing him to defer payment of his tuition fees, Dr Urquhart performed a vital service to the aspiring young Scots Canadian. Two years later he graduated from the institution a the top of his class; and early in 1835 John Sandfield Macdonald was accepted as a student-at-law by the Law Society of Upper Canada.

In the fall of 1835 Dr Urquhart's prize pupil was articled to another famous graduate of the Grammar School, Archibald McLean. McLean was then the leading lawyer in Cornwall and the Tory member for Stormont; he had intimate connections with those who governed and dominated the province. In April 1837 McLean was appointed to the Court of King's Bench, thus beginning a distinguished judicial career which was to last until his death in 1865. This disrupted the law student's ordered progress, but McLean saw to it that the interruption was put to good use. His former apprentice became a queen's messenger charged with carrying dispatches between the British embassy in Washington and the lieutenant-governor in Toronto. On one of these missions he met at Saratoga Springs with his future wife, Marie Christine, the daughter of George A. Waggaman, who was a former senator from Louisiana and a prominent American Whig.

Meanwhile, McLean had arranged for Sandfield to accompany him on the western circuit. It was a rewarding and lucrative experience. He was introduced to many prominent men of the day including Allan MacNab, Isaac Buchanan, and William Henry Draper. This meeting with Draper would prove auspicious. The brilliant Toronto lawyer, who moved in the charmed circle, was a rising force in provincial politics; in 1836 he had been appointed to the Executive Council and was now solicitor-general. Soon afterwards, probably early in 1838, John Sandfield entered Draper's law firm in Toronto to continue his articling.

His duties as occasional queen's messenger to Washington continued. Waggaman apparently forbade Christine to see Sandfield. To insulate her from the unpropitious Canadian adventurer, George Waggaman sent his daughter to a French finishing school in Baltimore. Christine's mother, the former Camille Armault, was a descendant of the French and Spanish gentry of Louisiana, and Christine's first language was French. George Waggaman had come from Maryland, of old, established stock. The school at Baltimore was a logical place to isolate Christine. Undaunted, Sandfield, posing as a distant relative, managed to obtain some time with her in Baltimore. In the fall of 1840, at the risk of permanent familial alienation, Christine eloped with the determined Glengarrian.[4] With his articling completed, Sandfield moved to Cornwall to establish a home with his young bride and to open his own law practice.

Cornwall, in which the Macdonalds' social position continued to rise, was now distinctly the centre of the Eastern District, the administrative area made up of the three counties of Dundas, Stormont, and Glengarry. Politics there evidenced the strong power of tradition, a tradition stemming both from the Highland past and the organized, even hierarchical nature of pre-Victorian Upper Canadian society. Particularly in Glengarry, a few great landed squires, most of them upstate New York Loyalists of Scottish descent, assumed social positions approaching that of the Scottish chieftains; generally they combined their social leadership with a senior rank in the militia and an abiding influence in political life. Sandfield was to benefit greatly by this rather convenient arrangement. Col. Alexander Fraser and John McGillivray, respectively the Roman Catholic and Church of Scotland political lairds of the district, chose him to be the Conservative standard-bearer for Glengarry in the elections of March 1841. The tall, slender barrister easily won his election, and became the assemblyman for Glengarry in the first parliament of the newly-united Province of Canada.

Sandfield thereupon received a letter from Draper, his former master, who was now attorney-general west, the most powerful member of the Executive Council, and the leader of the moderate Conservatives. It was with him that Sandfield became initially identified, although Col. Fraser, reappointed as a legislative councillor, was regarded as an old-line Tory. Draper advised Sandfield to beware of the 'ultra party' represented by High Tories such as Allan MacNab, who were not yet reconciled to the Union. He cautioned too against Reformers of Francis Hincks' ilk, who, so he thought, would endanger the imperial connection: 'Ponder this well and make as I do the first question on every political dogma advanced no matter by whom, what will its effect be on the British connection.'[5] Young Sandfield was thus clearly in the fold of respectability and not unknown to those in power.

The member for Glengarry, however, betrayed, at parliament in Kingston, all those who attempted to place him irrevocably in any political camp. For, while he generally supported Draper in opposition to the old-line Tories, on a bill concerning the naturalization of aliens he was to be found set solidly against the centre-line government. The intent of the bill was to expedite the naturalization of post-Loyalist Americans. Apparently overlooking the fact that he was married to an American, the son-in-law of the former senator from Louisiana argued that it would be just as likely for the River St Lawrence to 'turn its current toward Niagara' as for Americans in general to become 'good subjects of this province.'[6] It was an attitude not shared by the house, and the bill passed, Sandfield voting with the Tory minority of five.[7]

He followed a similar course in connection with the Upper Canadian District Councils bill, the first major piece of Governor General Sydenham's proposed legislative programme. All four members from the Eastern District voted with the right and left against the centre – that is, with Compact Tories and the Baldwin Reform core against the government. The measure provided for the establishment of elected district councils, presided over by centrally-appointed wardens, which would replace the administrative functions of the old courts of quarter sessions. The old-line Tories opposed the bill because it struck at the very roots of their local oligarchical power; the Baldwinites opposed it because the office of centrally-appointed warden violated the principle of municipal self-government. The bill passed forty-two to thirty, with Sandfield again in the minority.[8] He was there once more, three days before the end of the session, when he seconded an unsuccessful amendment by the Reform veteran, Malcolm Cameron, that would have cut a member's personal indemnity to fifty pounds from the sixty-five proposed by the government.[9] Throughout his career, indeed, this Scottish Canadian was to remain a champion of retrenchment.[10]

When Sandfield returned to Cornwall after the close of the session it was not the first time that he had been home since parliament had opened. Personal matters were not going well. Christine, his bride of one year, had given birth on 11 August to a frail son who had but a precarious hold on life. He died about the time that the session ended. It could hardly have been a very cheery homecoming for the young freshman member.

At the opening of the next session, in September 1842, it fell rather strangely to him to second the Address in Reply. In the meantime, the authorities had placated local interests by appointing Col. Fraser first warden of the Eastern District. Admitting that the operation of the Elective Councils Act was not as deleterious as he had at first expected, Sandfield added words of praise for the imperial authorities for the solicitude shown to British North America, a reference undoubtedly to the recent Webster-Ashburton Treaty.[11]

But now came the government crisis of September 1842, when Sydenham's successor, Bagot, was impelled to reorganize the ministry and bring LaFontaine and Baldwin and their friends into office. And in the process Sandfield's own political position further clarified itself. When the controversy over the composition of the Executive Council was reaching its peak, he expressed to McGillivray his conviction that many in the Conservative ranks, those with whom he had previously voted, were, by their obstinacy toward the mixed council, ensuring the complete triumph of the Reformers and threatening the position of the moderate 'liberals.'[12] On 16 September, the same day that the government's reconstruction was announced, Sandfield secured permission to be absent, for personal reasons, until 26 September; his delicate wife was again about to give birth. On 30 September he was back in the house – but now voting with the new administration and against his old colleagues.[13]

Macdonald's decision to stick by Governor Bagot when he redesigned his council in favour of Baldwin and LaFontaine provoked consternation among most Conservatives. That Sandfield believed he could accomplish this feat without serious repercussions in Glengarry is testimony to his own increasing sense of security, attributable, no doubt, to the fact that his hold over the Eastern District, through patronage, was becoming more personal. In any event, Baldwin, although warned about Sandfield's questionable fidelity, rewarded the Cornwall lawyer with a promotion to the rank of lieutenant-colonel in the local militia[14] and extended a generous education grant to his constituents. These developments, coincident with the rapid expansion of his own business connections in the area, were quickly transforming Sandfield's role from one of dependency on the goodwill of his patrons to that of political patron in his own right. Meanwhile, at home, things were going well. On 3 October Christine had given birth to a healthy daughter, whom they christened Lilla.

Provincially, the situation which had looked so encouraging to the advocates of responsible government and Reform ascendancy deteriorated the next year after Metcalfe had replaced Bagot as governor general. When the Reform ministers resigned in the dispute over patronage, late in 1843, Sandfield, now firmly committed to the principles of the Baldwinite school, supported the ministers and voted for the resolutions in the house that censured the governor and expressed confidence in His Excellency's late advisers. The ensuing election of 1844, won by the supporters of the conscientious Metcalfe, who took great pains to emphasize patriotism and the British connection, saw the Reformers make net gains in the Eastern District although they lost ground severely throughout most of Upper Canada. Sandfield clearly had his part in this local Reform success. With the journals of the district now against him, he countered by temporarily establishing a rival weekly newspaper at Cornwall, the *Freeholder*, which, while dedicated to the preservation of the British connection, insisted on 'liberal principles' and responsible government.[15] He was easily re-elected.

Over the next few years the Conservative government, led by Draper, rent with dissension, and weak in French Canada, gradually floundered. Sandfield pressed the attack with several speeches.[16] His prestige was rising. He was quickly becoming Baldwin's principal adviser for the Eastern District and an important man in party circles. Similarly, in Cornwall, fortune shone on the Macdonalds. Sandfield's legal business was booming, and he had acquired more property.[17] Life was going well. A second daughter, Mary Josephine, was born on 5 November 1844, and a third, Louisa Christine, on 16 August 1846. The worst personal blow during these years was probably the violent death in March 1843 of Christine's father, in a New Orleans duel.

Sandfield and the Reformers were optimistic when, on 6 December 1847, the Earl of Elgin, who had arrived as governor general the previous January, dissolved the second parliament of the Union. During the first half of 1847 dispatches between Earl Grey at the Colonial Office and Governor Elgin had confirmed the fact that the new Whig ministry in Britain was no longer opposed to responsible government for British North America. Moreover, the weak Canadian Executive Council had failed either to win over or to break up the LaFontaine Reform bloc or to stop the growing dissension between its moderate and Tory old-guard supporters. And it seemed obvious that Draper's successor, Tory Henry Sherwood, would prove unable to command the confidence of the legislature.

The election at hand, Sandfield re-established his *Freeholder*, this time permanently, and he and Baldwin set about persuading good men to run for the Reform cause in the Eastern District and other parts of eastern Upper Canada. The *Freeholder* alleged that the government had called elections in three of the district's ridings for the same day in order to tie the influential Sandfield to his own constituency.[18] If that was indeed the plan, it was successful for, while the member for Glengarry was returned, his Reform candidates, Dr Roderick McDonald and D.A. Macdonell in Cornwall and Stormont, respectively, were unsuccessful. Although the government candidate won in Dundas too, the Reformers had scored gains in other St Lawrence and Ottawa ridings and indeed had won a tremendous success provincially. Baldwin had secured easy victory in Upper Canada, and LaFontaine had swept Lower Canada. The result was confirmed in the new parliament of 1848, when the LaFontaine-Baldwin régime took office – and responsible government became an acknowledged reality.

During 1848 and 1849 Sandfield's political role increased, especially outside the house. Inside, he supported Baldwin's Municipal Corporations bill, but managed to preserve the territorial and administrative integrity of the Eastern District. It still survives as the 'United Counties of Stormont, Dundas, and Glengarry.' In December 1849 Elgin, on advice from Baldwin, appointed Sandfield to the post of solicitor-general west and made him a 'queen's counsel.' His re-election in Glengarry was by acclamation; thereafter, he was escorted into Cornwall in a triumphant procession.[19] John Sandfield Macdonald was now a very prominent man in Eastern Upper Canada.

Not only were his political affairs going well, but also his family and his business were in splendid shape. Christine had, on 11 September 1848, given birth to a hearty son, Henry Sandfield. Ivy Hall, a stately brick residence in Cornwall, soon became the family home and the centre for many entertaining evenings. Having once housed imperial troops, the spacious Ivy Hall stood at the corner of York and Water Streets, less than a hundred yards from the Cornwall Canal, which ran along the other side of Water Street and was now bustling in summer with steamers plying back and forth between the interior and Montreal. Sandfield's legal practice was rapidly expanding and becoming increasingly lucrative. Montreal merchants retained him to collect their debts locally. Often he was involved in every case before the eastern assizes. Two other lawyers. John Walker and A.M. MacKenzie, now worked under him, assisting him with the legal practice and the vast quantity of land management that accompanied that practice. They also, incidentally, kept their master informed on local political trends while he was necessarily away for long periods of time. Walker lived in with the family at Ivy Hall and acted rather like a family steward (unfortunately, he also drank too much). 'No barrister in Upper Canada,' commented George Brown's *Globe* of Sandfield, 'stands higher in the estimation of mercantile men.'[20]

These halcyon days were not to last. If the patronage available to Reformers was able to cure some ills, the growing rift between Baldwin's moderate followers and more radical Reformers began to widen. Enamoured of more democratic, even republican, institutions, the radicals at their gatherings began passing resolutions in favour of the strict separation of church and state and the establishment of manhood suffrage. Expanding the possibilities for opening separate schools and temporizing on the clergy reserves, the administration only exacerbated its relations with these emerging Clear Grits. Even the *Globe*'s support cooled in 1850.[21] To these developments the Conservatives reacted with gleeful applause.

Religious passions were also inflaming the political situation in the Cornwall area. Argument over the clergy reserves embittered relations between Church of Scotland and Free Church Presbyterian groups, while the Tractarian movement, growing among Anglicans, aroused Protestants generally against its adherents, 'the Puseyites' or High Churchmen. Sheriff D.E. McIntyre, John Sandfield's friend and confidant, reported that some over-zealous people were trying to start trouble with the Roman Catholics in Alexandria (in northern Glengarry) over assertive Catholic claims in Britain, the so-called 'papal aggression' question. McIntyre affirmed that the increasingly anti-Catholic tone of George Brown's *Globe* was doing great harm both to the party and to the country. It was a view that his friend could not help but share. Sandfield, McIntyre warned, would have 'work to do' before the next election.[22]

Meanwhile, in parliament, the 'Great Ministry' was breaking up. In the session of 1851 William Lyon Mackenzie, back in the assembly, moved with Clear Grit support for the abolition of Baldwin's reformed but still cumbersome and costly Court of Chancery, and won a majority of Upper Canadian votes. The hero of responsible government announced his resignation on 30 June, and withdrew immediately from the leadership of the Upper Canadian party in favour of Francis Hincks. LaFontaine, dedicated as he was both to his friend and to the principle of double majority, would also leave. Accordingly, the solicitor-general west became the object of much speculation.[23]

Would Sandfield, a ten-year political veteran at the age of thirty-nine, be appointed to fill Baldwin's old job as attorney-general west? That decision was left to Francis Hincks. LaFontaine tarried into the autumn before he actually submitted his resignation to Lord Elgin, but Hincks, the inspector-general, was clearly to be the new premier with A.N. Morin as his chief Lower Canadian colleague. LaFontaine thought that George Brown should be brought in; Hincks disagreed. There had long been distrust between the two men, and Brown's dogmatism annoyed Hincks, the opportunist.[24] On 3 July the *Globe* came out against the government. Since Hincks was determined to increase the size of the Executive Council only from eight to ten, he merely had three more positions to use to political advantage. Thinking it essential to placate the Grit radical element, he decided that one post must go to them, and used Sandfield, unwittingly, to make the approach to the Grits. Then, Hincks announced that the attorney-generalship would be given to a trusted friend, the unwavering W.B. Richards, who was a Brockville lawyer sure to cause the inspector-general no trouble. So Sandfield Macdonald was left the lesser office of commissioner of crown lands. Hincks later withdrew even that offer, claiming that Sandfield had promised yet another Clear Grit a post and that the Grits were now insisting upon its being given. Sandfield was asked to be content with his current position of solicitor-general west, which was actually now outside the cabinet.[25]

The member from Glengarry was furious with Hincks. He declined the 'generous' offer and claimed that he had been 'let go to pasture like an old horse.'[26] He suggested that the ungrateful Hincks had feared that the Clear Grits would look to Sandfield for leadership rather than to the premier. Hincks probably knew too, he thought, that Sandfield was not a man to be led about blindly. Now the indignant Scot was determined to 'pay him off.'[27]

On Hincks' advice Elgin dissolved parliament. In the elections which followed late in 1851, Sandfield, who had suffered humiliation on the provincial scene, secured his greatest regional triumph. Throughout the year he had kept a close eye on the local scene in the Eastern District, travelling 'to and fro' nurturing and expanding his influence. In the county municipal contests there only two of the twenty councillors elected had been Conservative, and these Sandfield himself had nominated at the township meetings.[28] In the provincial contest, Glengarry returned him by acclamation. He would have a considerable 'tail' of followers. Provincially, Hincks and Morin gained only tenuous majorities, yet their strength would lie in their ability to keep moderates and radicals co-operating. That was a task which might confound even more capable men.

The subsequent years, 1852 to 1858, in any case were ones of political frustration for Sandfield. Yet the Canadian economy, in the midst of its first railway boom, was expanding rapidly and he and his family benefitted from that expansion. His growing law office was intimately concerned with the buying, selling, and leasing of land, and Sandfield obtained considerable holdings himself.[29] In 1852, for example, he secured possession of a grist mill with a dam, house, and surrounding fields; he quickly had the mill repaired and brought into productive service.[30]

The wider family also prospered. Around 1840 Donald Alexander Macdonald, his ambitious brother, had gone to Chicago in search of adventure and fortune. He found both. He obtained a contract to construct a part of the Illinois Canal. Returning home to Glengarry in the possession of considerable money, Donald purchased the largest house in Alexandria. There he established a store and grist mill. He also obtained a lucrative contract to build a portion of the Beauharnois Canal. His first wife had died shortly after their marriage and, in the mid-forties, he had remarried; this time his bride was Catherine Fraser, daughter of Sandfield's old patron.[31] With his wealth and power increasing, and with a character more aggressive and dynamic than John Sandfield's, Donald became a great political assistant to his brother and the champion of the rear townships. Currently he was the reeve of the township of Kenyon and, therefore, on the United Counties Council.[32] Meanwhile, Ranald, the second son of the old family, with financial help from his brothers,[33] had been establishing himself on a land-holding along the front at Lancaster. Ranald had, for a time, been the black sheep of the family. He apparently kept company with 'the lowest sort,' and in 1851 had scandalized the family by marrying, outside the church, a grasping girl considered disreputable by Donald – a girl who was 'keeping company with all the Riff-Raff of a dirty village.'[34]

To return to politics, the first session of the new parliament elected at the start of 1852 began on the following 19 August. For the first time since Union it met in the city of Quebec. This greatest of French centres in North America carried off the opening ceremonies with finest British pomp and ceremony.[35] Long before opening day arrived, however, a rumour circulated that the assembly would elect J.S. Macdonald as its Speaker. Correspondents inquired about the state of his French. Although he admitted speaking it tolerably well (his wife's first language had, after all, been French), he was initially 'loathe to forego the floor for the chair,' and he kept the Hincks-Morin ministry in some suspense.[36] Eventually, he hesitatingly accepted the premier's offer, wary still of Hincks' motives. In time he was to regret this decision. The speakership tended to mute the voice of the Eastern District; increasingly that independent voice was needed in the house, as sectional and sectarian squabbles continued to fracture the Upper Canadian social fabric. These matters aside, the tall and rather dignified, high-collared Sandfield nevertheless cut a fine figure, adorned in a long black gown, tri-cornered hat, white kid gloves, and a huge ring over a gloved finger.[37] Throughout the session Sandfield performed his duties as Speaker with ease. He even took time to improve his French.[38] Late in May he played host at a gala *Bal de l'Orateur* which lasted all night and which 'fait honneur à la libéralité et à la splendide hospitalité du président de nos communes canadiennes'; while at the dance Lord Elgin made a particular point of praising Sandfield for his handling of the speakership.[39] Actually, dispensing laird-like hospitality was a role for which he and his wife were well suited; frequently Ivy Hall had been the scene of similar festive occasions.

During 1853 in parliament, however, things did not go well. If to many Upper Canadian Reformers the government's continued paralysis on the matter of the clergy reserves, its emasculation of Baldwin's University Act of 1849, and its continued concessions to the advocates of separate schools were not enough, to this was added the premier's preoccupation with lavishly expensive railways. The long-awaited Grand Trunk legislation revealed that, despite massive Canadian public financing, the rail line was to be built by private British contractors. This was sufficient to upset the most loyal Hinckksite, and Donald Alexander Macdonald was furious.[40] Much to their dismay Upper Canadians learned, too, that six of the twelve directors of the new venture were ministers of the crown, including Hincks himself. Scandals soon proliferated, reaching right to the premier. It was not only his brother Donald, accordingly, who was annoyed and worried about Sandfield's identification with the increasingly unpopular government. His relatively apolitical brother Ranald,[41] Sheriff McIntyre,[42] and the two lawyers in Sandfield's own office, MacKenzie[43] and Walker,[44] all warned Sandfield of serious trouble in store unless he could be seen to be striking out on his own.

'Shame, Shame,' wrote Donald: under the 'unprincipled Hincks,' Reform was 'nowadays but a sham.'[45]

Sandfield had other problems, deeply personal ones. For some time now his lungs had been giving him trouble. He needed to rest. Returning to Cornwall, he tried to do so, amid heavy political consultations with his friends and associates. He was there when Christine gave birth on 28 June to a fourth daughter, Adele. The next month he left the country on a six months' tour of Britain and the continent. With relaxation and excellent medical help, he partly recovered but would, for the remainder of his days continue in weak uncertain health. The trip had other rewards. He visited Windsor Castle, had dinner with the Duke of Newcastle, attended divine services at Westminster Abbey, and met some of London's leading businessmen. In France he saw the coronation of Napoleon III. In Scotland he visited ancestral haunts, astounding some of the locals by addressing them in the Gaelic.[46] Back in London he secured for Donald, Ranald, and himself the sub-contract to build most of the Grand Trunk from Montreal Island to Farran's Point in western Stormont. But brother Donald and his friends had earnestly wanted Hincks to facilitate construction of a line running from Montreal to Bytown via Alexandria, throught the back country of Glengarry that Donald wanted to develop. In reality, the future Canada Atlantic Railway was a long way off. If now this subcontract for the Grand Trunk had been facilitated by Premier Hincks (as it probably had), and even made £60,000 for the three Sandfield brothers, as some alleged, it could not hold the Speaker and his extended family loyal to the unpopular premier.[47]

On 13 June the long delayed parliamentary session of 1854 finally began. The Speaker, with difficulty but skill, umpired the attacks on Hincks from both the Conservatives led by John A. Macdonald and the wide array of disaffected Reformers, now led by George Brown and Louis Victor Sicotte. The debate on the Throne Speech ended in the overwhelming defeat of the government, with Sandfield's tail of followers voting with the majority. Hincks seemed finished – or so most observers believed. Instead, two days after the adverse vote, the members of the assembly were amazed to hear the sounds of the arrival of the governor general at the Legislative Council, where Elgin, at Hincks' behest, came to dissolve parliament before it had finished even a single item of business. The opposition members roared their protests. Speaker Macdonald, with studied deliberation, rose and left for the upper house.[48] There, before the governor general could read his address, he delivered in French and English a scathing speech on the unconstitutional nature of the action then in progress.[49] Suddenly Sandfield became a popular hero, champion of the people and protector of their sacred rights. Opposition Reformers caucussed shortly afterwards, and even George Brown admitted his readiness to serve under Sandfield.[50] Although prorogation and dissolution followed forthwith, it had been one of Sandfield's greatest moments. In tribute, 'a large body' of his admirers raised money and commissioned Théophile Hamel to prepare his portrait.[51] The rather gentle and placid countenance portrayed by Hamel reveals but a trace of the stern Sandfield who could be expected to be the staunch adversary of any attempts to erode the rights of parliament.

The elections which followed were hardly helpful. Reform remained in disarray, and when parliament met on 5 September 1854 this was obvious to all. Hincks further split opposition Reformers by backing Sicotte for the speakership at the last moment, thus preventing Sandfield's own re-election. Defeated on a routine vote after an innocuous Speech from the Throne, the Hincks-Morin ministry thereupon resigned. Perhaps now Sandfield, backed by Brown and the moderates of the party, would be called upon by Lord Elgin to form a ministry?

What happened was quite different. Elgin summoned Sir Allan MacNab, his old Tory critic. The French-Canadian bloc made its fateful decision to shift from the nominally Reform ranks to – more logically – the Conservative fold. Its members would soon be called the 'Bleus.' With the able assistance of John A. Macdonald, and Hincks, the erstwhile Reform leader, the MacNab-Morin ministry and the Liberal-Conservative 'coalition' behind it thus were formed. Soon the new government was receiving the support of convincing double majorities.[52]

Leading only a group of dissident and disunited Upper Canadian Reformers, Sandfield's prospects looked dim indeed. In Lower Canada, moreover, the only prospective allies appeared to be the radical, anti-clerical Rouges, led by A.A. Dorion. Furthermore, the Glengarrian suffered the extreme disadvantage of not having a large personal following in the assembly, although a few Reformers outside of his area, men such as Michael Foley, seemed to look to him for leadership. Still further, his early accommodation with George Brown gradually deteriorated.[53] Brown was now in the process of absorbing and moderating the original Clear Grits. By 1856 the opposition would no longer recognize any official leader. Sandfield's political fortunes were in decline.

Back in Glengarry, in late 1854, more trouble, religious trouble, had presented itself. Especially his brother Donald, but also John Sandfield, were under severe attack from the now Irish-dominated Roman Catholic clergy because of their personal opposition to the establishment of local separate schools in particular, and their religious liberalism in general. In Alexandria, Donald, its leading citizen, was denounced from the pulpit; the audacious 'miller' (and future lieutenant-governor of Ontario) in turn harangued the village folk from outside the church doorway and unsuccessfully took his priest to court. The Montreal *True Witness* picked up the attack and denounced all three Macdonald brothers, John Sandfield, Donald, and Ranald. The Alexandria priest declared that the three were not really Catholics at all. Donald lashed back at both, 'helped' by Sandfield's Free Kirk assistant, A.M. MacKenzie, and by other Protestant friends in Cornwall.[54] Before Christmas Sandfield had to come up from Quebec to quiet down Donald and the rest, while trying to smooth things over. This he largely did during the winter, but not without creating temporary tension with his more radical brother. Fortunately, the winter of 1855 lingered on into early May, allowing the miller of Alexandria to play Joseph by distributing large quantities of hay he had in store to farmers and villagers for their livestock.[55]

In Cornwall, meanwhile, the very success of Sandfield's lucrative law practice taxed his time and energy. In both 1855 and 1856 his firm was involved in over two-thirds of all cases at the fall assizes. With boom times, land was changing hands rapidly, and it all meant more business for the leading lawyer of Stormont and Glengarry. But his chief aide, Walker, had become a hopeless alcoholic and would soon have to leave, and a junior assistant was little better. A.M. MacKenzie, who did not drink, was made virtual steward of the family's whole business when Sandfield was out of town, but then hinted that he would soon leave to set up his own practice.[56] It was all too much.

It was during the session of 1856, when the government was running without an Upper Canadian majority, that Sandfield delivered his first major, elaborate, and rather fiery speech on the principle of the double majority. Seconded by Louis Laberge, a leading Rouge, Sandfield moved that as a rule cabinet ministers from each section should have the support of a majority of members from their sections. Reviewing provincial history since 1841, he claimed that the principle had been inherent in the Harrison resolutions of that year and in the basic achievement and operation of responsible government by LaFontaine and Baldwin. This was a slight exaggeration. There is no evidence that either Harrison or Baldwin believed in it, though in his own way LaFontaine certainly did. Ironically, however, it was first fully articulated by D.B. Viger in 1844 during the Metcalfe-Draper years. This was part of a bold move to undercut LaFontaine and win over *la nation canadienne* to temporary co-operation with the British authorities, as the first stage toward securing autonomy for Lower Canada through the peaceful dissolution of the Union. It was virtually an alternative to responsible government. It was also an adaptation of what John Neilson had called in 1841 the Irish Daniel 'O'Connell-tail system,' under which Lower Canadian nationalists would have kept aloof from the two parties and made temporary alliances to suit their cause. So popular did the idea of the double majority become in French Canada that LaFontaine and R.E. Caron had to accept it in a modified form, which tried to make it compatible with their commitment to the alliance with Baldwin and to responsible government. LaFontaine continued to defend double majority as a vague principle during his premiership, and Hincks alluded to it in 1854. It also seemed to be important in the formation of the MacNab régime later that year.

And in other parts of the western world around 1850, other propositions, analogous to the double majority, were being advanced as a means of preserving unions involving two (or more) nationalities or identities. For the United States, J.C. Calhoun of South Carolina advanced his plan for a 'concurrent majority' and a dual executive. Similarly, in Europe various constitutions were introduced (with much bloodshed) by Hungarians and other national leaders for the reorganization of the Hapsburg dominions. Sandfield was aware of all this, but no evidence exists of direct borrowing. In his speech Sandfield argued that the double majority had become virtually essential to the smooth and lasting operation of the Union, once the British had wisely abandoned their policy of trying to absorb the French. For Sandfield, unlike Viger, the double majority was the device to preserve the Union, not to lead to its eventual peaceful dissolution. He warned French Canada that while temporarily the government survived with only a Lower Canadian majority, without this principle an aroused Upper Canada would soon win power and then enact 'measures which the Lower Canadians would not like.' Indeed, Brown and his *Globe* did denounce the speech, and argued forcibly that shortly, with a large Upper Canadian majority but probably no Lower Canadian one, Reformers would obtain power and rule decisively with a single majority. Brown, like Sandfield, also argued in favour of preserving the Union, but he admitted that 'we have two countries, two languages, two regions, two habits of thought and action.' Despite obvious sympathy for the concept in the abstract, the government held its supporters in check, and only fifteen members of the assembly voted for the resolution.[57]

For a good deal of the session of 1856 Sandfield was sick in bed. Gradually, his tuberculosis worsened. Early in December he again left on an extended trip, this time to the South. He visited the Waggamans and took a relaxing Caribbean cruise.[58] It was no real cure. The disease cost him the use of one lung. Although he returned to Canada in late spring, he attended the session of 1857 for less than a week. Still a relatively young man, the depressed member for Glengarry entertained thoughts of retirement from political life; but he carried on.

In late 1857 Governor General Edmund Head dissolved parliament. Elections were in the offing. Sandfield's health forced him to relinquish the large riding of Glengarry in favour of the smaller, and therefore less taxing, constituency of Cornwall. His robust brother, Donald, would take over in Glengarry. When the polling ended, Sandfield had won by a vote of 428 to 246; in Glengarry, Donald had easily defeated his brother-in-law, the Tory, Archibald Fraser, by a vote of 1556 to 246.[59] Provincially, a growing polarization seemed evident in politics. Cartier had increased his hold on Lower Canada, although a few Rouges led by A.A. Dorion had retained their seats. Reformers had captured a slim majority in Upper Canada. John A. Macdonald, now the premier, was in an extremely delicate position. He attempted to strengthen his Upper Canadian support with the introduction of several non-Brownite Reformers into the cabinet. He made overtures to Sandfield.[60] The latter had had cordial relations with John A. in the past; indeed, frequently more cordial than his relationship had been with many Reformers. Nevertheless, when Sandfield demanded office for himself and two other Reformers as the price of his acceptance, negotiations broke down.[61] Sceptical of the game from the outset, the Cornwall member wired the premier a simple, 'No go.'[62]

The new parliament met in late February 1858, and from the beginning the cabinet was in serious difficulty. Progress was slow. All the various proposals for constitutional change were trotted out again and argued at great length. On the double majority, his 'hobby,' Sandfield delivered what even the *Globe* had to admit was his ablest speech ever. It was more temperate, lucid, and patient than his performance in 1856. He appealed to French Canada's sense of fair play, and warned that persistently governing without an Upper Canadian majority would lead to representation by population and a severe blacklash against the interests of the French-speaking people, thereby endangering *la survivance*. The double majority would preserve the noble Canadian experiment. This time the motion secured 33 votes, but it was still opposed by the ministry and by Brown and Dorion.[63]

It was the question of the seat of government, however, which ultimately led to the cabinet's resignation. The queen had chosen Ottawa, on advice from her Canadian ministers, as the permanent Canadian capital. It was an unpopular decision – though no other city could command a consensus. A motion simply asserting its inadvisability united the opposition and passed 64 to 50. Alleging that the members had insulted Queen Victoria, the cabinet resigned.

Governor General Head coldly offered Brown the premiership. Her Majesty's 'most ephemeral government,' led by Brown and Dorion and with Sandfield finally in the coveted office of attorney-general west, lasted but two days. With its ministers out of the house seeking re-election, the government fell on a division of seventy-one to thirty-one. Head refused dissolution. John Sandfield had filled the ministerial shoes of Robert Baldwin for about forty-eight hours. The old crowd came back, with George Cartier and John A. Macdonald in the leadership.

Although Brown had the largest following of any leader from Upper Canada, the fighting journalist was still anathema to much of French Canada. Sandfield was not. He would have had a remote but perhaps better chance of success than Brown. His friendship with French-Canadian moderates such as Louis Sicotte (who left Cartier's cabinet late in 1858), and Joseph Cauchon might have facilitated the breaking of the Bleu phalanx away from Cartier and John A. Macdonald. He might even have won over several former Hincksites, such as Isaac Buchanan, who otherwise were to drift inexorably into the Conservative fold. But the particularism, sectionalism, and sectarianism of Upper Canadians, exacerbated by the constitutional dilemma of the Union, had polarized opinion and weakened 'the middle way' which he wished to represent. This polarization, together with his own poor health, had destroyed his claims to leadership and given Upper Canadian Reform ascendancy to George Brown, a man who because of his nature and reputation would not and perhaps could not be premier of Canada for more than a few days.

During the session of 1859 the disagreement between Sandfield and Brown developed into a bitter personal feud. The issue was seigneurial compensation, a legacy of the act of 1854, which had technically abolished seigneurial tenure in Lower Canada. Cartier and his government planned to pay compensation to the seigneurs for the loss of their historic casual dues from general provincial revenue. The Upper Canadian Grit Reformers balked. Brown argued that his brief government had intended to charge the costs strictly to Lower Canadian revenues.[64] Sandfield questioned his accuracy and contended that the province had but one revenue, from which compensation would have had to come.[65] The former *censitaires* could hardly be forced, in effect, to recompense themselves. It was a legitimate constitutional position. But Brown would have none of it; to admit Sandfield's point would have been to alienate his Grit support.[66] Voting on Cartier's seigneurial bill revealed that, on that issue, all of the French-Canadian members supported the government. In Sandfield's eyes Brown had succeeded in disrupting the always-tenuous alliance with Dorion and the Rouges. With his health temporarily better, Sandfield was gradually becoming convinced that he ought to assert himself, challenge Brown, and establish temperate liberal leadership over Upper Canadian Reform.

With new-found help from Josiah Blackburn and his influential *London Free Press*, which had backed his stand on the seigneurial question, Sandfield began to work in earnest with Sicotte and other moderates to rebuild Reform and challenge the government. Sicotte in Lower Canada was operating autonomously from the official Rouge leadership.[67] Some of Cartier's own followers, fearful of their leader's intransigence with regard to Upper Canadian grievances, were becoming uneasy and restless. As talk of Bleu defections began to escalate, Sicotte and his friends were convinced that the opposition could win in the house. L.H. Holton, the brilliant Lower Canadian Liberal and financial wizard, urged Brown to let Cartier hang himself and not 'play the game of Sicotte and his little JUSTE MILIEU clique East and West.'[68] Thus, by the fall of 1859, there was already the hint of a possible Sandfield Macdonald-Sicotte combination.

Sandfield absented himself from the great Upper Canadian Reform Convention of November 1859 that was engineered by George Brown and his Toronto cohorts. While re-endorsing representation by population, it more importantly passed resolutions calling for the splitting of provincial Canada into two or more units linked by 'some joint authority.' By far the largest group at the convention had been Grits determined on simple dissolution of the Union. It was only Brown's skilful manipulation which prevented the gathering from endorsing a resolution aimed at accomplishing that goal.[69] But Sandfield, deeply convinced that Canada should remain a unitary state with a dual administration based on the historic division of 1791 and led by a broad, tolerant ministry commanding the support of a majority of members from each section, could accept neither alternative. The duality of Canada should find expression, he argued, in the cabinet, in the confidence of the assembly which held it responsible, and, for the time being, in the sectional equality of representation. Government, he believed, should reflect the plurality of Canadian life and militate against the divisive effects of sectionalism and sectarianism. Only broad, tolerant, and pragmatic liberalism, of the sort earlier advocated by Baldwin, and genuine, meaningful reform could achieve these ends.[70]

The session of 1860 saw Brown introduce in the assembly his resolutions from the Reform convention of the previous autumn, but interpreted in a more federal and less dissolutionist direction. The Lower Canadian Rouge caucus formally dissociated itself from the Brownite leadership. Foley spoke against the federal scheme. Almost every day the Upper Canadian opposition held a caucus in an attempt to iron out intra-party squabbles. Brown's leadership at length was re-endorsed; nevertheless, Foley and four others refused to declare how they would vote on the resolutions, and five eastern members, including Sandfield and his 'tail,' announced their implacable opposition. The *Free Press* wrote about the emergence of a Sandfield-Sicotte entente opposed to both the Brown-Dorion and the Cartier-Macdonald régimes, 'likely to be stronger than the former and therefore more likely to supplant the latter.'[71] Sandfield wrote to Blackburn: 'I look forward to the consummation of my long cherished hope of rescuing the real reform party from the odious trammels which has [sic] so long checked its manifest destiny.'[72] That time was approaching. But during this session, although Brown's motions failed, they received a nominal Upper Canadian majority after Foley capitulated under pressure.

Sandfield, but not Brown, was on hand when the last session of the sixth Union parliament met on 16 March 1861. While the old battles continued, attention was drawn southward, where the American Civil War burst forth in

April. In Canada the overtaxed Brown was seriously ill; he would miss the entire session. Without repudiating federation, the *Globe* had returned to its earlier emphasis on representation by population as the immediate solution to the Canadian malaise and was looking longingly for the census returns.[73] In the assembly the old 'Rep by Pop' line was picked up by the Grits. Sandfield's motion, criticizing the ministry for governing without the confidence of a majority from Upper Canada, narrowly lost.[74] It was the closest that the government had come to defeat.

Later in the session, a private member's motion favouring a modified system of representation by population was introduced. When it attracted many Western Conservatives, the cabinet was forced to declare the representational question an open matter. The most remarkable feature of the session was, however, the steady rise of Sicotte's influence and his co-operation with John Sandfield.[75] Sandfield and Sicotte, wrote the *London Free Press*, might appear 'isolated' to the 'uninitiated.' In fact, it continued, their position was very strong. Ultimately these two men would be able to combine 'the largest party from both sections of the Province,' and would conduct business on the basis of the double majority; they thus would satisfy the aspirations of the mass of Upper Canadians.[76]

In May 1861 Governor General Head dissolved parliament and had writs issued for an election. The Conservatives, despite the storms, were remarkably unified. In contrast, division epitomized the Reformers. Brown was ill, and still a 'governmental impossibility.' Foley, unable to reconcile the Baldwinites and Brownites, had no standing in Lower Canada. Oliver Mowat was competent but thus far inexperienced. In Upper Canada this left Sandfield Macdonald; but while his position was stronger than it had been in 1857, he was anathema to Brown and without a large personal following. In Lower Canada the brave Dorion was discredited because of his erstwhile friendship with Brown and because of his radicalism. Sicotte suffered few of these disabilities. He was a natural leader for disaffected Bleus. Now totally committed to opposition, he was thundering against the laxity, prodigality, illiberality, and corruption of the régime in power.[77] But he too lacked a large, personally-dedicated following.

Together with the scandals surrounding the construction of parliament buildings for the now accepted future capital of Ottawa, the census returns became a central issue in the elections of 1861 in Upper Canada. The figures indicated that Upper Canada had outstripped Lower Canada in population by a quarter of a million souls. In Stormont, where Sandfield had decided to run as well as in Cornwall, Brown and his friends ran a Grit against him. When the votes were in, Donald A. held Glengarry and Sandfield held Cornwall. Stormont went to the Grits by a margin of one hundred and fifty-five votes. In all, John A. Macdonald had secured, thanks to Reform disunity, a very tenuous majority in Upper Canada, but Sicotte had made large inroads into Cartier's Lower Canadian strength. Brown and Dorion were both personally defeated.

During the remainder of 1861 party politics took second place to concern and dispute over the American Civil War and over Canada's possible involvement in it. Yet the political pot was far from cold. The representation question continued to prevent Upper Canadian Reformers from working together. Brown continued to denounce Sandfield and deprecate Foley.[78] The *Free Press* and Sandfield continued to do the reverse.[79]

In November 1861 the British steamer *Trent* was stopped by an American federal warship while on the high seas, and two Confederate agents were forcibly removed. Anglo-American war, for a time, seemed inevitable, with Canada as a battleground. The *Trent* affair brought home to Canadians (and to the British) how vulnerable British North America was to any American invasion. Once, thanks to sober heads, the crisis itself had eased, a debate over Canada's role in its own defence rose in vigour. Early in 1862 the new governor general, Viscount Monck (whose future career was predicated on getting Canadians to increase their own defence expenditures in order to relieve British taxpayers), appointed a Militia Commission. Composed of cabinet ministers and army officers, its purpose was to review the local situation and to make recommendations with regard to possible legislation. In March the British House of Commons passed a resolution reaffirming that the main responsibility for the defence of self-governing colonies rested on those colonies themselves. These events, which led in the end to Cartier's ill-fated Militia bill, were ultimately to catapult John Sandfield Macdonald to the premiership of Canada.

The government's defence policy set forth in this bill provided for a reorganization and considerable expansion of the militia at a greatly increased cost, when already governmental expenditures were overreaching revenue. Even so, it fell short of the recommendations of the commission. The most politically dangerous aspect of the measure was the provision that the regular militia would be raised on a regional basis, and in localities where the volunteer system failed to produce the assigned quota, conscription or the draft would be employed. Sicotte led the attack for the combined opposition, including Sandfield, against the bill, while John A. Macdonald who was minister of militia affairs as well as attorney-general west, was unavailable and drunk during most of the days of debate, rallying only to give a final, brave, but futile speech. On 20 May 1862 the opposition defeated the militia bill on second reading 61 to 54.[80] Over the question of conscription and increased expenditure for defence – after the international crisis seemed to have passed – sixteen Lower Canadians moved from Cartier to Sicotte, that is from Bleu to 'Mauve.' The government resigned.

An angered Monck could now have justified calling on Sicotte, or Foley (who had secured election over Mowat as house leader for most of the Upper Canadian Reformers), or on Sandfield. He chose Sandfield. Sicotte was the architect of the Reform victory in the house, but in British eyes he was the wrecker of Canadian self-defence. Foley had no standing in Lower Canada, only a precarious hold over the Brownites, and like John A., a liquor problem. Sandfield was heartily disliked by many Western Brownites, but he had an experienced political past and close ties with Sicotte, the Mauves, and the Montreal business community. He was indeed a logical choice in an unusual parliamentary situation.

On Victoria Day, 24 May 1862, John Sandfield Macdonald, the liberal Catholic, almost-independent Reformer from Cornwall, became attorney-general west and premier of Canada. His leading colleague from Lower Canada, his LaFontaine, was the Mauve leader, L.V. Sicotte, who served as attorney-general east. Glad to be rid of the 'old gang,' even George Brown in his *Globe* gave the new ministry his qualified support: 'Mr Macdonald, the Premier, is a very crotchety individual for whose eccentricities considerable allowance has often to be made; and it is possible that one or two of the departmental offices might have been more efficiently filled; but as a whole, the standing, the ability, and the influence of the new Government are highly satisfactory.'[81] The régime pledged itself to double majority, cheap, efficient government, and pragmatic reform. These goals, it claimed, should be able to unite Reformers across the province; particularism and sectionalism, divisive forces long disrupting the Union, should be minimized. The ideals motivating the government could only be frustrated by the character of current Canadian politics.

The administration itself had severe deficiencies. Both Sandfield and Sicotte were cordially disliked by large numbers of Reformers from their respective sections. Neither came from nor represented the geographic areas of the province where political and economic power was concentrated. Sandfield, native-born, was rather a maverick in lacking many of the prejudices characteristic of Victorian British Upper Canadians. Sicotte led a group of mainly French-Canadian malcontents without the normal cohesiveness of a formal political party. Moreover, from the beginning the new régime was beset by serious difficulties. Its ministers were most unpopular with the British Colonial and War Offices and with the British press, because of their rejection of the Militia bill. And the basic Canadian issues – the constitutional dilemma and the interrelated religious questions – which had kept Reformers divided and out of office remained to vex them.

This Reform government was, like its short-lived, ill-conceived predecessor of August 1858, predominantly moderate. Although a combination of various factions, it had at its double head (unlike that predecessor) the more moderate Liberal chieftains, for A.A. Dorion, the Rouge leader who yet lacked a seat in the assembly, held only the relatively junior post of provincial secretary. The other members from Lower Canada were the flamboyant Thomas D'Arcy McGee, who became president of the council; J.J.C. Abbott, a recent political convert who became solicitor-general east; François Evanturel, a Mauve who became minister of agriculture; and J.U. Tessier, of the upper house, who became commissioner of public works. In Upper Canada, three of the positions went to prominent Grits: William McDougall assumed the office of commissioner of crown lands; William Howland, minister of finance; and Adam Wilson, solicitor-general west. The mercurial Michael Foley became postmaster-general; and the veteran moderate, James Morris, the receiver-general.[82]

The new ministry outlined its initial policy to the assembly in eight points. 'Recognizing the Federal character of the act of Union, and the danger at the present critical emergency of any change of the basis of that Union,' its first principle emphasized that ministers from each section would primarily be responsible for the local affairs of their section, leaving the cabinet as a whole to deal with matters 'necessarily common to both sections.' 'Secondly, it will be admitted, as a rule, that local legislation should not be forced on either section of the Province against the wishes of a majority of its representatives, and that the Administration of each section should possess the confidence of a majority of its representatives.' The government would propose legislation to redistribute representation within each section on a more equitable basis. It would propose reorganizing and expanding the militia, particularly by encouraging the volunteer movement. The tariff would be adjusted. Legislation dealing with debtors, creditors, and bankruptcy would be supported. Retrenchment would be rigidly applied in every branch of the government in order to balance the budget. Finally, it would uphold the decision to make Ottawa the capital but would instigate a thorough investigation into the construction, now arrested, of the public buildings and then take appropriate action. Premier Sandfield Macdonald proposed that parliament deal with routine and emergency matters and then be prorogued until the new year.[83]

The qualified support initially tendered the new régime by the *Globe* disappeared over the constitutional question. Faced with a policy which he considered to be worse than that of the previous government, Brown was livid. The paper and its publisher had no use for Sandfield's double majority. What particularly galled the Toronto Grit was the 'desertion' of his own chief lieutenant, William McDougall, who less than two months earlier had moved impatiently for 'Rep by Pop' in the assembly. Now he had joined a ministry which did not support it. A Grit caucus reluctantly agreed, however, to give the administration 'a fair and liberal trial,' even though the *Globe* declared that it was 'enough to sicken a horse.'[84] The *London Free Press*, while dedicated to 'Rep by Pop' as the ultimate solution, argued that it was 'impossible' at present to form a government organized on that principle. Chastising Brown and extolling Sandfield's virtues, it gave the new régime its total confidence.[85]

Sandfield and his ministers were now out of the house pending re-election, but he worked through friends in the assembly to tidy up affairs of the session. Parliament considered and passed a bill which temporarily dealt with the militia. The measure provided for an expansion of the volunteer force from five to ten thousand paid individuals, plus more persons in non-paid units, at a cost not exceeding $250,000. While this would be about three times[86] the amount spent in 1861, neither Governor General Monck nor Colonial Secretary Newcastle was satisfied. The defence issue would plague Sandfield throughout the remainder of the year. Moreover, for some time now the separate school issue had again been stirring. A legislative committee aided by Dr Egerton Ryerson had already severely watered down a draft bill pushed by a Catholic Ottawa Valley Conservative, R.W. Scott, which would virtually have established a full dual educational system in Upper Canada. Scott had reluctantly accepted the modifications, and said in the assembly that the bill would be a final 'settlement of the question.' Because Sandfield wanted to end the session quickly, Scott agreed to hold his measure over until the next year.[87] After prorogation on 9 June, all of the ministers were successful in their bids for election, including Dorion in Hochelaga.

Meanwhile, Monck still regarded defence as the principal problem. When the governor general had asked Sandfield to become premier, he had insisted that the new government consider the militia immediately.[88] Sandfield had done so. Now Monck officially explained the situation to Newcastle and urged the sending of British arms, ammunition, and equipment.[89]

In view of opinion in Britain, Monck was justified in his urging. Newcastle was greatly annoyed at the fall of the Cartier-Macdonald régime over the Militia bill. He ridiculed the double majority and urged Monck to set his face 'against so foolish a compromise.'[91] No effort was undertaken in Britain to try to understand Canada's political problems or the Canadian point of view. Canada had not, in fact, repudiated her own defence responsibilities; the government had tripled appropriations. Canada had not caused the *Trent* crisis, yet all agreed that Canadians had responded most favourably during the time of the crisis itself. Finally, in the last analysis, Canada was indefensible in any case without major British support. Nevertheless, the *Times* of London and Little Englanders generally continued to assault the troublesome colony.[92] Then, in August, Monck became suddenly exasperated by Sandfield's apparent intransigence and by Newcastle's continued criticism. Bitterly he wrote privately to his superior: 'I have not a very high opinion of

Mr. John Sandfield Macdonald's abilities and none at all of his firmness of purpose ... The new Ministers are a wretched lot! Not one of them is capable of rising above the level of a parish politician and they are led away by all the small jealousies and suspicions to which minds of that class are prone.'[93] Not unlike most other governors general before him, Monck simply failed to appreciate that 'great matters of state' divided Canadian politicians just as they did their British counterparts. The issues with which Sandfield was confronted were far from petty, and he was at least as prepared as any premier before him to face them. Fortunately, Sandfield never saw Monck's unfair, depreciating note. The governor general's opinion of Sandfield would change, and a lasting close friendship between them develop.

On 21 August 1862 Newcastle issued a challenge, almost an ultimatum, to the Canadian premier and his cabinet. Reiterating the theme of Canada's responsibility for its own defence, he argued that an active militia of fifty thousand men was an absolute minimum.[94] This was clearly an impractical suggestion. Any Canadian ministry which undertook the expenditure to support such a force would be immediately overthrown. Flatly rejecting Newcastle's recommendations, Sandfield's most important state paper, sent to Monck to be forwarded to Britain, stated that a force of such size would be justifiable only in 'periods of imminent danger or actual war': 'The people of Canada doing nothing to produce a rupture with the United States, and having no knowledge of any intention on the part of her Majesty's Government to pursue a policy from which so dire a calamity to proceed, are unwilling to impose upon themselves extraordinary burdens. They feel that, should war occur, it will be produced by no act of theirs, and they have no inclination to do anything that might seem to foreshadow, perhaps to provoke, a state of things which would be disastrous to every interest of the Province.'[95] The ministers had met the challenge. They would further expand the volunteer force, but they would not adopt Newcastle's unrealistic programme. Preparation of permanent militia legislation began.

With Newcastle answered and work proceeding on legislation relating to the militia, Sandfield in September turned his attention to a pressing matter concerning Indian rights on Manitoulin Island. In Upper Canada settlement had pushed hard up against the rocky line of the Canadian Shield. This was one of the chief reasons why the Grit farmers and their merchant backers and leaders were so interested in the acquisition of the Northwest. Great Manitoulin Island, along the North shore of Lake Huron, was not in the Shield; it was, therefore, an important agricultural jewel lying in the direct path of settlement north from the Bruce Peninsula. Somewhat more than 1500 Indians, mainly Ottawas and Ojibwas, held the island. The attempt to extinguish their claims and restrict them to small reservations now brought on the principal clash between expansionist Euro-Canadians and the native peoples during the life of the Province of Canada. As such, it deserves careful consideration.

Sandfield inherited a complicated problem which technically had only become a Canadian one in 1860 when Britain finally handed over control of Indian affairs. On 12 September 1862 William McDougall, who was both commissioner of crown lands and chief superintendent of Indian affairs – the dual portfolio was symptomatic of current attitudes – asked cabinet for authority to negotiate with the Indians on Manitoulin. The land, he argued, should be reclaimed and opened for settlement: 'at present its only inhabitants are Indians and half-breeds ... who obtain a precarious subsistence from the cultivation of a few patches of soil and from the fish which they take in the neighbourhood.' Its importance was undeniable, situated as it was, 'in the direct line of communication between the great cities and Marts of the Province, and the mineral regions of Lakes Huron and Superior, and the yet undeveloped but fertile territory of the North West.'[96]

Confronted, however, with Indian militance, particularly at Wikwemikong on the eastern part of the island, the government through McDougall proved willing to negotiate a new treaty which offered, among other things, a small initial financial settlement coupled with 'at least' one hundred acres per head of family and fifty acres more for each child. Although the Indians around Wiki remained opposed, most of the native population accepted these terms, and on 6 October 1862 a treaty was signed which excluded the eastern peninsula from its terms.[97] Immediately the land rush was on and a period of tense relations ensued, complicated by a dispute over fishing rights. Despite various incidents, Sandfield's government ignored the fulminations of the *Globe* against 'rebellious' and 'outrageous' Indians and followed a moderate path. Ultimately, Indian rights in the fishery were reaffirmed, the brave folk of Wikwemikong never did cede their land, and the Macdonald-Sicotte government accepted the situation. Like other Victorian Canadians, Sandfield and his ministers believed in the onward march of progress and were paternalistic and condescending toward Indians. Within that mental framework, however, their performance during the potentially explosive Manitoulin Indian incidents of 1862-3 was rather creditable.

Meanwhile, in September 1862, Sandfield had been obliged to give greater attention to railways than to Indians. He worked hard to promote the construction of the long-projected Intercolonial Railway. He had indeed strong hopes that Canadian expenditure on the Intercolonial would be considered as part of Canada's financial commitment to the defence of the British Empire. Premier Joseph Howe of Nova Scotia, an advocate of the Intercolonial link from Rivière-du-Loup to Halifax, persuaded the Canadian premier to convene a conference to discuss the project. On 10 September 1862 it opened at Quebec, with Leonard Tilley leading the New Brunswick delegation and Joseph Howe that of Nova Scotia. The delegates resolved that the proposed railway was an essential link in an unbroken highway which should be constructed through British territory from the Atlantic to the Pacific. They agreed that the colonies should again approach Britain about conditions for an imperial guarantee of the needed loan, and that costs should be split so that Canada paid five-twelfths and Nova Scotia and New Brunswick three-and-one-half-twelfths each. Sicotte and Howland were appointed to be delegates at the forthcoming meeting with the authorities in London.

The successful negotiations were politically costly. Two days after their completion Antoine Dorion ceased attending meetings of the Executive Council, and on 28 October he resigned. Opposed to big, costly projects like the Intercolonial, he had also never really been comfortable playing lieutenant to Sicotte. His departure damaged Sandfield's administration among Liberal French Canadians in the Montreal area.[98] The *Globe* also opposed the Intercolonial. And in England, the negotiations broke down over the terms of the guarantee.

Before the discussions in London had ended, Newcastle had already informed Monck privately that he 'utterly' repudiated the 'monstrous proposal' that Canada should consider money spent on the Intercolonial as money spent for defence. He also told Monck that he considered the minute of the Executive Council on defence full of 'bunkum.'[99] The defence question was far from settled, the Intercolonial far from built.

Early in January 1863 Tilley wrote to Sandfield strongly 'hoping for the best' concerning the Intercolonial.[100] No doubt Tilley was encouraged by his lieutenant-governor, Arthur Gordon, in his application of pressure on the Canadian government. At a meeting in Quebec with several members of the cabinet, Sandfield told Tilley that the Canadians had not abandoned the project, but that, in the light of its reception in England, it must be postponed. In the interim he pledged assistance for a joint survey of the route. This would prevent delay, and allow parliament in 1864, 'if existing difficulties were then removed,' to proceed with enabling legislation.

Throughout this busy period, Sandfield had also been active in securing stable journalistic support at the seat of government. He tried to operate through the *Quebec Mercury*, a rather inconsequential independent and somewhat conservative tri-weekly. Gradually, the *Mercury*'s policy and that of the government came to coincide.[101] This was particularly noticeable in the autumn after the brilliant, ubiquitous, and erratic journalist, George Sheppard, transferred his pen to that paper. Sandfield negotiated an agreement whereby he could lease the *Mercury* and hire the management. The premier then wired his friend Blackburn of the *Free Press* asking him to become publisher. Hesitating, the latter decided to travel to Quebec City to discuss the matter.[102] Having been persuaded, he took over, with Sheppard as editor, on 2 December 1862.[103] It would be an expensive but politically profitable venture for the premier.

Supervising the routine work in the office of the attorney-general west further took up much of Sandfield's time and energy. He also had the taxing responsibilities of the militia office – a post which was made a permanent addition to the office of attorney-general during his administration. In late December he had finally secured the appointment of T.B. Brown, W. Bristow, and George Sheppard as members of the important royal commission on financial and departmental reorganization.[104] Through the *Mercury* the government was suggesting many reforms in the civil service, including changes in the direction of using serious examinations and of securing promotion by merit rather than seniority.[105]

Sandfield had been so overwhelmed with work that it was 23 December 1862 before he was able to spend time with his wife and six children[106] at Ivy Hall. But the visit was not entirely carefree. The raging war south of the border had threatened the safety of his wife's family. In fact, at the battle of Malvern Hill, Federal troops had captured her brother, Colonel Eugene Waggaman, commander of the 10th Louisiana Regiment. Sandfield had been devoting some time and effort in negotiations with New York banking connections of the Waggamans and with Secretary of State W.H. Seward, whom he knew 'well,' in an attempt to have the captive released from a camp near Boston and sent to Canada for the duration. After matters were satisfactorily arranged, however, Eugene declined the offer and eventually benefitted by an exchange of prisoners. Meanwhile, with the brief visit to his family in Cornwall completed, the premier had hoped to take the train down to Washington for a hasty visit, especially to see Seward and Senator Charles Sumner, but on reaching Montreal urgent 'matters of state' called him back to the capital.[107]

Parliament would open on 12 February 1863, and, as the date approached, the political tempo quickened. For one thing, there was the problem of George Brown. The owner of the *Globe* arrived back in Toronto with his bride, Anne Nelson, the day after Christmas. Sandfield did not know what Brown's plans were with regard to a return to active politics. Even Brown himself was unsure. Since his marriage, his personality seemed to have mellowed. The *Mercury* expressed the hope that Brown would be 'less sectional.' A patriot, it argued, ought to heal the differences existing 'between two peoples,' whereas Brown had preyed upon men's 'passions and prejudices' to inflame those differences. 'It is not too late,' suggested Blackburn, 'even for Mr Brown to mend.'[108] But, on 5 January 1863 the *Globe* bitterly attacked the Roman Catholic hierarchy and warned against any new separate school legislation whatsoever. The Conservative Montreal *Gazette*, which had shown some sympathy for Sandfield, now also became more openly critical.[109] It was also rumoured that Brown was engaged in reconstruction machinations with certain Conservatives, including the prominent John Hillyard

Cameron. Brown denied this, both publicly and privately.[110] He told Holton that when he did 'go to open war with the present Ministry,' it would be as a Reformer fighting for Upper Canadian interests.[111]

The morale of Sandfield's administration was, however, rising. 'The strength of the Ministry,' the *Mercury* noted, 'no less in Lower than in Upper Canada, instead of diminishing is in daily growth.'[112] For the present, the paper asserted, the double majority was the only way to preserve the Union. Liberals had succeeded, said the *Free Press*, only when Brown's influence had lessened, when people had turned to Sandfield Macdonald, the man who stood 'between the extremes of party and was obnoxious to neither. Moderate in his political principles, he was, at the same time a constant reformer.' His integrity was beyond question. 'Throughout his long public life,' it exaggerated, 'no stain has even sullied his reputation.'[113]

Sandfield made a fatal blunder, however, when he had a faithful supporter, Dr Skeffington Connor, appointed to the bench; immediately rumours flew that Brown would seek his seat, the traditionally Reform riding of South Oxford. The *Free Press*, nervously thinking that Brown might concert with the opposition, was happy to report that he was probably not going to run.[114] Brown himself was undecided, but he wrote to Holton on the day parliament opened that he was glad to have Dorion out of a ministry which he would ultimately have to fight. He opposed the Intercolonial, on the typically Grit ground that northwestern expansion should have top priority. He also opposed any increase in the postal subsidy and the maintenance of the temporary capital at Quebec. He feared a separate school bill. Still, he hoped that the ministry would survive the session and do so without Grit support on any 'bad votes.'[115]

In contrast to the colourful, formal opening of parliament, the Speech from the Throne was undramatic. It outlined the progress made with the volunteer force and the plans to expand the militia. In reviewing the situation with regard to the Intercolonial and the Northwest, it stressed developments leading to the opening up of the western territory and to direct communications with it and with British Columbia. The two royal commissions, one on the parliamentary buildings and one on departmental reform, were proceeding with their work.[116] The speech did not mention double majority. Probably, mused the *Globe*, it would be employed only as a guide and not in the form of legislation.[117] Sandfield's careful speech was followed by Cartier's in his new, ill-fitting role as leader of the opposition.[118] John A. Macdonald was absent.

During the debate on the Address in Reply, Sandfield's ministers survived attempted amendments calling for 'Rep by Pop'; and although embarrassed, McDougall and Howland were forced to vote against these hopeless attempts. It was, however, an ominous sign that a majority of

Upper Canadian members voted in their favour.[119] Moreover, on 26 February, two days after the defeat of the second amendment, the *Globe* announced that George Brown, urged on by a petition signed by more than a thousand South Oxford Reformers, had agreed to run in the by-election. Besides the local exhortation, he had received great prodding from Luther Holton who had recently secured election to the upper house and who reminded Brown that the latter had promised to return to parliament.[120] For Sandfield, the announcement was not good news. On 5 March Brown carried South Oxford; the session would be livelier for it.[121]

Now came R.W. Scott's Upper Canadian Separate School bill, backed as promised by the government. Trouble was not anticipated by the ministers; the Scott bill was hardly a bill of substance, and it did not involve any new principle. It merely straightened out several administrative anomalies and errors in the existing Taché Act of 1855, but posed no additional threat to the common school system. It was, however, not in the form of a short amendment to existing acts, the form which Chief Superintendent Ryerson had suggested; instead, Scott had produced a lengthy bill replacing earlier efforts. Basically, both common and separate schools remained essentially public, supervised and partly financed as they were by the provincial government. At this point, however, there was one important exception in the matter of control: the separate school boards of trustees were henceforth to license their own teachers.

The political explosion came with the debate and vote on second reading, which took place on 5 March, the very day when Brown secured election in South Oxford. For John Sandfield the result should not have been unexpected. The Grit core, led by Oliver Mowat and Alexander Mackenzie, was taking its lead from the *Globe*. The newspaper had not been the least bit ambivalent:

The teacher is the great enemy of the priest, and as modern civilization has made the teacher essential, and he cannot be abolished, the priest tries to control him for the benefit of the Church. The child must go to school; there is no help for it, but let him be taught by a stupid and ignorant *frère chrétien*, who will never make learning pleasing to him, nor awake in him the love of knowledge which is, under God, the chief source of human progress ... The point of attack on the school system during the session will be an extension of the separate schools. The people will be told that the clergy are easily satisfied; that very slight concessions only are demanded; that a little pliability now will bring about the settlement of a question which has caused infinite trouble. If Reformers yield to these persuasions, they are lost. The clergy are wily. They know how and when to ask concessions. It is only a trifle, only right for Catholic trustees to do this and that, and the Catholic laity to do another thing, but the end of it all is the destruction of the common school system. Be not tempted by these devices of the enemy.[122]

As the *Mercury* was soon to say, the hatred of popery was, with some people, 'a good deal stronger than their hatred of original sin.'[123]

In the debate Scott stressed the basic principle of the advocates of separate schools, that 'religious teaching should go hand in hand with secular education.'[124] On second reading the bill passed, boasting an Upper Canadian majority of thirteen.[125] The *Globe*, enraged by the results, stepped up its campaign against the measure. Meanwhile, the *Quebec Mercury* described opponents of the bill, especially the Orangeman, T.R. Ferguson, as bigots and the disinterested supporters of the bill as liberals; the bigots, it argued, were refusing to Upper Canadian Catholics the rights enjoyed by Lower Canadian Protestants.[126] The *Globe* retorted that the *Mercury* had its bigots and its liberals reversed. The bigots were those who argued that Catholics could not sit on the same school benches as Protestants.[127] Despite his personal reservations about segregated schools, there was no doubt about Sandfield's attitude; nevertheless to be safe, he and his Grit colleague McDougall had Scott delete the offensive paragraph referring to the right of Catholic trustees to license teachers.

On 12 March Scott moved his bill's third reading, assuring the house that he and others had gone over it carefully with Ryerson, and that no one could accuse the Methodist divine of 'Popish proclivities.' He did not mention anything about the finality of the bill. Of Sandfield's ministers, McGee played the largest role. In eloquently supporting the measure as it stood, he stressed that he himself 'would be no party to further agitation. If this last politico-religious question were settled, he never again would be a party to re-opening it.'[128] As the debate progressed, bitterness increased. The opponents of the bill (and some of its Conservative supporters) taunted the ministers with inconsistency. John A. Macdonald, in one of his wittiest speeches, read from the *Journals* to show how the premier and McDougall had fought against separate schools. He then chided the Brownite Reformers as 'shabby' for deserting their premier. 'Hear, hear,' interjected Sandfield.[129] In the final division the bill carried, 74 to 30. But the Upper Canadian representatives rejected it, 30 to 23. In the 'Nays' were the Brownites and three or four Orange Conservatives. The premier's anti-clerical brother, Donald, had, conveniently, been absent on the two crucial votes. In Upper Canada only two Reformers who were not in the government voted with the administration.

John Sandfield Macdonald was trapped and was infuriated with the Grits.[130] On much less provocation his old chief, Baldwin, had resigned. Sandfield had been sustained by a simple majority, thanks to the combined votes of Lower Canada, Bleu, Mauve, and Rouge, and to the votes of John A. Macdonald and most of his Upper Canadian Conservatives. Were sectarian and sectional divisions permanently to frustrate liberalism and prevent Reform ascendancy? If he were to resign, clearly no other Reform leader

could form an administration. If he remained in office, was the double majority dead? The *London Free Press* did not minimize the crisis. It laid responsibility clearly at the door of the Brownites.[131] What Sandfield had accepted
was, argued the *Mercury*, only what the Brown-Dorion ministry had pledged
itself to achieve in 1858.[132]

The premier was not yet ready to give up the fight. On Saturday, 14
March, the day after the vote, he called together a caucus of Upper Canadian
Reformers from both houses. Apparently he held firm, threatening to resign
unless the Grits capitulated. He suggested that the upper house make some
minor changes in the bill, thereby causing it to be returned to the assembly,
where it could this time be passed with the desired double majority. On
Monday, before the caucus met again, Sandfield informed Ryerson that
unless the Grits met his terms he would 'play them a game that they little
anticipated.'[133] What happened at the Monday meeting is not entirely clear.
Although it was poorly attended – by only seventeen according to the
Globe – a decided majority apparently gave in. The *Globe*, which questioned
the rumoured surrender, said that Sandfield's main card had been his ability
to threaten that without him it was 'Cartier and Corruption.'[134] The Toronto
Leader, however, emphasized the premier's veiled threat to negotiate with
the Conservatives for a ministerial reconstruction involving coalition.[135]

As if these difficulties were not enough, Sandfield now sustained a new
blow from a most unexpected source. The *Canadian Freeman*, the leading
Irish Catholic newspaper in Toronto, denied the finality of the Scott bill: 'We
regard the slight concessions contained in Mr. Scott's bill only in the light of
an installment of our legitimate demands. Sooner or later the whole debt
must be acknowledged and paid.'[136] McGee's assurances to the contrary, the
troublesome question was not about to be so neatly settled. As the *Globe* was
quick to point out, this was exactly what it had said would happen. Here was
what it called 'the regularly authorized organ of the Bishop of Toronto, Dr
Lynch,' speaking of new concessions to Catholics even before the present
bill had become law. The *Freeman* chastised McGee severely for regarding
the measure as a final solution, to which the *Globe* replied that McGee had
about as much influence over the hierarchy 'as the Pope has over the
Tycoon of Japan.'[137] Bishop Lynch's and other Catholic protestations about
the unofficial nature of the article in the *Freeman* did little good. In Upper
Canada, public demonstrations against the bill became numerous.[138]

While the assembly debated less explosive measures such as the new
militia bill, the Conservative majority in the upper house secured passage
there of the Scott bill. On 5 May Monck gave the measure royal assent. One
of the main features of the principle of double majority was now clearly
destroyed. A law had been passed against the wishes of a majority of the
representatives from the affected section. Sandfield could offer few excuses,

although he attempted to use the fact that the bill had been that of a private member. Still, the government did continue and, because few Reformers wanted 'Cartier and Corruption,' it retained the shaky support of a majority from each section of the province.

Despite the Scott Act, many claimed that Sandfield's influence was on the rise and that Brown's was in decline. The *Free Press* and the *Mercury* asserted that the Reform press was 'almost unanimous' in support of the government and that the *Globe*'s divisive posture was 'comparatively trifling.'[139] Actually, by mid-April, the animosity between the Brownites and the ministry seemed to have passed its peak. Once in the assembly and involved in personal relationships with members of caucus, Brown became less violent in his criticisms. He gradually returned to his initial position of qualified support. 'If the Ministry has been weak in making concessions to Upper Canada,' stated the *Globe*, 'the Opposition has been still more weak.' John A. was worse than John S.[140] The premier did, however, continue to tangle on secondary issues with Alexander Mackenzie, Brown, and some of their followers. More important, with Brown's return, Sandfield's hold through Sicotte over the Mauves became more and more precarious. Brown, moreover, sat at his desk in parliament with Sicotte's rival, Dorion. McGee was reported to have said that Brown's mere presence in the house was enough to send many French-Canadian backbenchers scurrying back like baby chicks to 'mother Cartier.'[141]

The second stage of the ministry's crisis was fast approaching. The question of confidence seemed paramount. The Conservatives were applying pressure on John A. to undertake a frontal assault on the government.[142] On 1 May 1863, with galleries crowded, John A. Macdonald, seconded by Cartier, moved want of confidence. Macdonald chided McDougall for previously advocating 'Rep by Pop' and now opposing it, Sicotte for previously opposing the double majority and now accepting it, Sandfield for promoting the double majority and now accepting the Scott bill, and the ministry in general for antagonizing Britain, for allegedly wrecking the Intercolonial project, and for an inadequate militia policy. It was a scathing attack, and Sandfield's reply was rather feeble. The premier scorned the member for Kingston, suggesting that he was an anomaly as the leader of a group the vast majority of which did not agree with him on vital matters affecting Upper Canada. As for the double majority, the Scott bill was not 'exactly applicable.'[143] Some, however, thought the speech an able defence. The *Free Press* argued that John A.'s speech, although spirited as usual, lacked soundness, while Sandfield had spoken as a man 'convinced' of the righteousness of the cause he defended.[144] For a whole week the debate raged. All other business was suspended. Dorion, in a brilliant address, Mackenzie, and Mowat all spoke against the motion.[145] But Brown merely attacked the opposition and

278 Bruce W. Hodgins

boasted that he would 'kill off' the present ministers 'when he could get better.' That line hurt Sicotte.[146] Joseph Cauchon predicted that the opposition would have thirty-seven of the sixty-four votes in Lower Canada;[147] Friday, 8 May, revealed his prescience. At 1:25 AM, with only six members absent (one seat was vacant), the government was beaten, 59 to 64. Capturing a majority of three in Upper Canada, it lost badly in Lower Canada.[148] As McGee would have said, the chicks had scurried back. Cartier had obtained only one less vote than Cauchon had predicted. The Mauves scarcely existed any longer.

The defeated premier had an audience with Monck, who agreed to a dissolution and election after the passage of the various non-controversial measures before the house.[149] That weekend saw Sandfield negotiate with Brown, Dorion, Holton, and Mowat. The only detailed account of the meetings which survives is that contained in a letter from George Brown to his brother, Gordon; allowing for Brown's proclivity for over-dramatizing his own role, there is no reason to doubt its main content.[150] According to the letter, Monck had already had a friendly interview with Brown during the course of the confidence debate. During it, the governor admitted the evils of the system about which Brown complained and asked if the latter could repeat what he had achieved with Dorion in 1858. Brown indicated that circumstances had changed drastically, but that it might still be possible. Then, apparently, Monck sent for Sandfield and explained the situation. Brown surmised that His Excellency had suggested that Sandfield would have to throw himself into the hands of Dorion and the Grit leader. Until the vote of confidence was taken the premier gave no hint of all this, except to inform Brown that, if he obtained an Upper Canadian majority, he would adjust the personnel and policy of the ministry to make it more acceptable to the Grits and the Rouges. Brown claimed to have told no one about his own intended vote, not even Mowat. He wanted to 'frighten Sandfield into modifying his policy.' He further argued that he had no choice but to vote for the Reform government, because to do otherwise would have ruptured the party. Many, he admitted, would not have followed him into opposition. Besides, a 'coalition between John S. and John A. would have resulted immediately, rep by pop postponed indefinitely,' and he himself 'blamed for the whole.'

After the vote, Sandfield sent his brother Donald to talk to Brown about reconstruction. Brown, declaring his absolute determination not to enter the government himself, asserted that Dorion would have to be made leader of the Lower Canadian supporters, and Mowat and 'other reliables' would have to be included. Then he added: 'Pitch over the Intercolonial, the postal subsidy, the re-adjustment, and the Ottawa Grant, and cut down the expenditures to the lowest shilling. Then give us an acceptable policy on Rep by Pop and all will be right.' Sandfield must have been incensed when this was reported to him. In any case, after seeing Dorion and Holton, who informed him that everything depended upon what he could do in Upper Canada, the premier offered a post to Oliver Mowat. The latter would say nothing without seeing Brown. Brown urged Mowat to accept, providing all conditions were fulfilled. Then Sandfield met with all four. The editor, leading the attack, demanded full power for Dorion in Lower Canada. Agreed. Secondly, Mowat would have to enter the cabinet with such others as would convince Upper Canadians that a real change had been made. Agreed, only that, for political reasons, McDougall could not be 'unnecessarily thrown' overboard. Thirdly, the financial measures Brown had mentioned must be carried out. Agreed. Lastly, said Brown, 'Rep by Pop' must be accepted as government policy. Sandfield replied that in this matter he would be guided by the advice of Dorion and Holton. These two leading Lower Canadian Liberals indicated that making the representation question an open matter was as far as they dared go. Brown was bitterly disappointed and broke off negotiations. The premier warned that if the group refused the compromise it would be offered elsewhere. Reluctantly, Brown was forced to come around.[151]

On Tuesday, 12 May, Sicotte, Evanturel, and McGee perforce tendered their resignations. Sandfield asked Dorion to lead the Lower Canadian section as attorney-general east. The main form of the new Macdonald-Dorion ministry was announced on 16 May, with further changes following. The moderate Reformers, Tessier, Foley, Wilson, and Abbott were gone. Howland had to leave finance and be satisfied with receiver-general. Holton brought the administration great strength as minister of finance; McDougall stayed, and Mowat entered as postmaster-general. The western Reformer, Fergusson-Blair, became provincial secretary; Luc Letellier de St Just, minister of agriculture. To represent the Irish Catholics, the veteran L.T. Drummond was named commissioner of public works. Lewis Wallbridge, Reformer from Hastings and friend of the premier, assumed the duties of the solicitor-general west, with L.S. Huntington as his Lower Canadian counterpart. The *Mercury* mourned the departure of Sicotte and Foley and naïvely expressed the hope that they would loyally work for the government in the approaching elections.[152]

The *Globe* had already placed Holton and Dorion among the saints. It rejoiced, for the first time in years, over the composition of the government and over the announcement that 'Rep by Pop' would be an open question.[153] But for Sandfield, the reconstruction provoked anything but joy. While he had won the personal battle for survival as premier, he had, more fundamentally, lost. It was no longer his kind of government. Moderate Reform was disappearing. The double majority was no longer government policy. His former ministers were furious; in the elections which followed, they were to run as independent Reformers. The Grits were on the march.

Thus, the first and only Canadian government officially dedicated to the concept of the double majority as the guiding principle under which responsible parliamentary government should operate had to abandon that principle. Individual ministers, including the premier, continued to hold that it was the desirable way in which the Canadian parliament should function, but sectional diversity, which had given rise to the idea in the first place, frustrated its practice.

Was double majority just Sandfield's impractical 'hobby'? Did the concept in fact die as the phrase declined in usage? Hardly. In fact, it remained very much alive as a goal, but as a solid rule it could not be made to work. Sandfield seemed to sense the need to be more subtle when, some months later, he tried unsuccessfully to get back his double majority by means of a coalition with the old ex-Bleu chieftain, Sir E.P. Taché, while endeavouring to hold on to his links with the Rouges. In a very significant way, the great coalition of June 1864 (which included Brown but not Sandfield) functioned because it established a double majority. But it could only exist by making a major commitment to politics-out-of-the-ordinary, to altering in a major way the constitution of Canada and probably of the other provinces of British North America. Fortunately for the future of the country, the Canadian legislature, representing the people of what were soon to become Ontario and Quebec, approved by a double majority in 1865 the plan of federal union. Leading pro-unionists knew how important it was to get that double majority if Confederation was to be achieved and made lastingly legitimate. But Confederation made Ontario and Quebec into two of four units in a federation, later two of ten units. The singularity of a parliamentary majority was reconfirmed as the rule at the centre, while plurality seemed to be the norm for the units of the federation, considered as a group.

Or was it? Cartier and many French-Canadian leaders continued to see the new Canada in dualistic rather than pluralistic terms. Generally they tended to follow both LaFontaine's and Viger's old admonitions to try to operate as a 'national' bloc in the politics of the Canadian union. Usually that bloc sat to the right of Mr Speaker in the parliament at Ottawa, in close alliance with the party which – partly because of the alliance itself – tended to hold, or potentially to hold, the greatest amount of English-Canadian support. Until 1891 this was the Conservative party of John A. Macdonald, even though the 'Macdonaldian' constitution seemed to reject the politics of duality. After 1896, certainly after 1917, that dominant body tended to be the Liberals – whose great appeal has been that they have been the party of 'national unity.' In 1917, when the two majorities were deeply divided, the country was in dire straits. Later, for many Ontarians, the idea of 'national unity' came quite unconsciously to mean something not too far from Sandfield's double majority.

Yet because the double majority had spoken so clearly, if impractically, to the Canadian reality of the early 1860s, it had a second lasting application: only intellectual, no doubt, yet more direct than that subsumed in 'national unity,' an application much more acceptable in Quebec than in Ontario. This looked rather to something like the Austro-Hungarian dual monarchy; or, more recently, to two associated or reassociated Canadian states (or else to the much less extreme project of 'special status for Quebec'). Major decisions in such a dual confederacy would positively require two majorities, and perhaps the confederal assembly might require the re-establishing of equality of representation.

A third transmuted version of double majority looked to the government of Ontario, and not of Canada, as somehow the chief spokesman for the one majority, while the government of Quebec, as in the second version, was the spokesman for the other majority. This concept could hardly be fully articulated, though post-Confederation Ontario premiers often acted as if they loosely acknowledged it. Certainly Premiers Mowat and Mercier tended to operate that way in 1887, and to some degree it underlay the frequent close (if strange) Toronto-Quebec City political ententes of the mid-twentieth century. Naturally, such a version was always vehemently rejected in the West and the Maritimes.

But whenever the concept of the double majority (by whatever name) has been put forth directly or formally, it has been rejected forthrightly by most Ontarians as it was in 1863 – vehemently, then, by George Brown and his Grits, subtly by John A. and his Conservatives. Ontarians, by and large, have regarded Canada as one nation made up of individual people and individual provinces (one of which was predominantly French speaking); not as two collectivities or nations. Several Ontario leaders of various political persuasions and many Ontario intellectuals have seen and accepted various aspects of Sandfield's double majority; but they have not been able to convince most Ontarians – except, and then without consensus, at the federal level in the transformed guise of an appeal to 'national unity.' These limits of politics, much more important than mere prejudice, have even helped prevent Ontario leadership from making Ontario officially or symbolically bilingual. With imperfect vision, Sandfield sensed a reality of the Canadian experience that most of his Upper Canadian compatriots did not and have not sensed. The idea of the double majority has thus quite naturally had much more credibility in Quebec than in Ontario. And that dichotomy in perception has been a part of the great Canadian dilemma.[154]

In any event, back in May 1863, Premier Sandfield Macdonald devoted his energies to the election campaign at hand. His attention was centred mainly in eastern Upper Canada – that is, the constituencies fronting on the St Lawrence and the Ottawa.[155] Ironically, he was forced to work particularly hard against R.W. Scott, who had built up an impressive machine in Ottawa. It was important to capture that seat because Scott had been attempting to deliver the Upper Canadian Catholic vote solidly to the Conservatives. In eastern Upper Canada the business and political empires of the Scotts and Sandfield and his brothers overlapped. Probably this supplied the premier with another motive for welcoming the defeat of the author of the separate school bill. In the end, Scott, visibly unsupported by John A., who feared an Orange backlash, went down to defeat. Complaining bitterly to his Conservative chief, the vanquished candidate wrote: 'Had you come down and remained two hours in the city my election was a certainty ... Sandfield remained in town on both days of the polling enjoying his victory and working personally against me ... Bribery was openly practised, from $10 to $20 being paid for votes.'[156]

The Sandfield-Brown victory in Upper Canada was overwhelming. John A. was humiliated: the Reformers captured at least forty-one secure seats and four more possibles. But there were fewer of Sandfield's Baldwinites and more of Brown's Grits, and the government needed more support in Lower Canada. There Dorion and Holton proved unable to work miracles, though they had not been badly routed. Although Dorion had openly pledged to oppose both the Intercolonial and 'Rep by Pop,' defection by the Mauves had continued. The first votes in the new session were to reveal that only two of those Lower Canadians who had deserted Cartier in the spring of 1862 still remained with Sandfield. The new assembly, called on 13 August 1863, would give the premier an uncertain twenty-five Lower Canadian votes; that is, eight short of a majority in that section. The double majority was no longer possible for Sandfield Macdonald.

Disheartened, he fought on, still dedicated to the surviving portions of his Reform programme. In this he was now backed by all the diverse Reform press, but opposed more vehemently by papers such as the Toronto *Leader* and Montreal *Gazette*. Most enthusiastic, the *Mercury* claimed that Sandfield was governing in the moderate image of Baldwin and LaFontaine. Lower Canadians had nothing to fear. The Conservatives, it argued, having once opposed LaFontaine, but now praising his memory, accused the present Reform régime of 'democratic and revolutionary tendencies'; but they would soon after its departure be extolling its virtue and condemning a still more liberal successor.[157]

A variety of matters thrust aside by the whirlwind of political reconstruction also required Sandfield's attention. In July he was pleased to be able to appoint his old tutor, Archibald McLean, to the post of presiding judge of the Court of Error and Appeal. W.H. Draper, another of the Reform premier's Conservative tutors, succeeded McLean in chief justiceship. The first report of the royal commission on financial and departmental reorganization, made public late in May, revealed a totally unsatisfactory relationship between governmental spending and its legislative, and hence public, supervision. The comprehensive reforms which the commission advocated occasioned lively discussion and necessitated careful cabinet scrutiny.

In Lower Canada the situation slightly worsened. The veteran Drummond lost to Bleus in two attempts to secure election to the assembly. On 24 July the Rouge L. Laframboise replaced him as commissioner of public works. Henceforth, the cabinet would lack an Irish Catholic; this, in the light of McGee's now voluble opposition to the régime, was a serious deficiency.[158]

Questions concerning Canada's relations with other parts of British America and with Britain itself were again becoming pressing. The Duke of Newcastle still had little use for the Reform régime. Before he learned of the dissolution, but after it had been accomplished, he had written Monck that he was skeptical of Sandfield's abilities and that he hoped that dissolution would not take place.[159] Now he clearly informed Monck that he disapproved of the premier's actions during the May crisis. He sympathized with Cartier's efforts to secure the resignation instead of the reconstruction of the ministry. The governor general, who was becoming quite fond of his first minister, assured his British superior that his ministers were reliable and that, in fact, Cartier's action in May had been 'factious.'[160] Gone was any trace of Monck's earlier disparaging attitude. With trouble emanating from so many quarters, Sandfield was fortunate to enjoy the warm friendship of the governor.

The Maritimers were still agitated about the Intercolonial, and the premier had not given up hope that he could yet accomplish something toward that worthwhile project. He had no intention of letting the matter lie dormant as the Grit and Rouge leaders had demanded. In August, Tilley and Tupper again came to Quebec to press for action, and remained well into September. Sandfield persuaded an unenthusiastic Dorion to agree to an outlay of ten thousand dollars, by Canada, for the purpose of a joint survey of the best route for the line.[161] With the prior knowledge of the Maritime delegates but without the formal consent of New Brunswick, the Canadian government appointed the engineer, Sandford Fleming, as the surveyor for Canada.[162] 'I declare to God, Tilley,' said Sandfield. 'if I thought by resigning my office we could get the Intercolonial Railway, I would do it.'[163]

Finally, there was the question of the Northwest. Sandfield had previously favoured the termination of all the territorial jurisdiction which the Hudson's Bay Company had asserted over the Red River area. He looked to the establishment there of a separate crown colony, though the Grits still hankered after outright annexation by Canada. In Britain, there was a general reluctance both to define, in any sufficiently confining manner, the jurisdictional limits of the company and to see Canada incur financial obligations in that direction. It was clear that, without the Intercolonial, Western development would not even be considered. Newcastle blatantly informed Monck that he intended to use the Northwest as blackmail against the Canadian government. If the latter behaved in matters of defence and the Intercolonial, Britain would tend to regard with 'liberality' Canadian territorial claims against the company.[164]

Sandfield planned that the session which began on 13 August 1863 would only be a short one to deal with the militia bills and with supply, not voted on before dissolution.[165] Parliament would hold a regular session early in the new year. The special session, however, turned out to be a long one, not finishing until 15 October. The opposition was intent on toppling the premier. At one point Cartier spoke for nine hours supporting the offended Sicotte's motion condemning the reconstruction.[166] Rumours flew that Cartier was about to retire and that his mantle would fall to Sicotte. This John Sandfield could not afford. Accordingly, on 5 September, the premier secured his former colleague's appointment to the Superior Court of Lower Canada. Thus did Louis Sicotte, an important might-have-been, remove himself from Canadian politics.

The two impressive militia bills did pass. Ironically, the first measure contained an element of coercion, one of the principles on which the Cartier-Macdonald government had been defeated. Starting in 1864 the government was annually to draw up the list of a service militia from the old and ineffective universal sedentary militia that included all able-bodied men between the ages of eighteen and forty-five. From the list, the government would establish 'service battalions,' one for each of the smaller and several for each of the larger counties. Selection would be by ballot from the first class, or more able group, to be supplemented from a second class, if the quota was not filled. Each year these men would be trained for up to six days by paid instructors. Two military schools were also proposed. The second bill, dealing with the volunteer force, raised the enrolment level from twenty-five to thirty-five thousand unpaid individuals who were to be eligible for clothing and equipment. It was a more ambitious and costly scheme than the one defeated in 1862.[167] The bills passed with Cartier supporting them, but with about twenty of his 'followers' voting negatively. No Upper Canadians voted against the bills.

Sandfield's defence programme was inextricably bound up with his approach to general governmental financing. The premier was dedicated to the principle that carefully detailed parliamentary approval should precede the spending of public funds. This was one of the chief recommendations of the royal commission, and the government planned legislation to see that it was enforced. In the task of grappling with the formidable problem of the budget, the penetrating mind of Luther Holton was put to good use. On 15

September Holton presented his first budget, one involving expenditures of slightly over fifteen million dollars. He also announced that the government had decided to eschew raising the tariff to protective levels or to cover the deficits; instead, it was preparing a major tax bill for presentation to the regular session. The opposition was, however, more interested in trying to cause an upset than in dealing with substantive measures. On 19 September a highly political motion expressing regret at Sicotte's appointment to the bench failed by only two votes. A non-confidence motion on 8 October failed by only three votes. Nevertheless, although under severe attack, Holton's budget was finally approved. When the news of its contents reached England, it met with enthusiastic support. The *Times* was eulogistic,[168] and praise was heaped upon Holton and Sandfield. Canadian securities began a substantial rise in value. The crisis of confidence in Canada had passed.

Administratively and legislatively, matters looked very good for the government, but political problems still rankled. McGee was becoming more and more obstreperous and personal in his attacks. He accused Holton of dishonesty and Alexander Mackenzie and other Grits of favouring Americanism and 'democracy,' and he praised Cartier and John A. for their vision and their loyalty. He reserved his most bitter thrusts, however, for the premier, calling into question Sandfield's personal honour by accusing him of corruption.[169] The latter's Highland temper was aroused; he had always had trouble with the Irish. In a furious reply, he declared that he had taken all he could from the audacious McGee who never seemed to speak on the subject before the house, who always denounced ethnic or 'class legislation' yet claimed to speak for all the Irish in Canada, and whose only achievement as a minister had been a report on immigration. The premier admitted that he might not equal McGee in eloquence, but he claimed that he equalled him in his concern for Canada, 'the country in which he [Sandfield] was born and with which all his interests were bound up. (Cheers).'[170] George Brown liked the reply. He even seemed to be showing a slight affection for the plucky premier. He attended 'a quiet little family party of eight' given at their rented quarters by Sandfield and Christine, where various persons played the piano or took 'a turn on the fiddle.'[171]

In the assembly, Brown sensed the significance of the great dilemma of the Union. On 12 October he introduced a motion proposing the establishment of a select committee of thirteen persons to examine the constitutional question and recommend remedies acceptable to both sections. Meanwhile, he said, the government should undertake 'the strongest efforts' to secure 'a majority in Lower Canada as well as in Upper Canada.' Although no one could censure the present régime for the current state of affairs, he could not support 'continuously' a ministry which survived without a Lower Canadian majority. It would be 'deeply regretted' if the ministry 'met parliament again' without securing that majority. George Brown had shifted his ground. He could hardly have come closer to Sandfield's current concept of double majority. After finishing the speech, Brown withdrew the motion on the understanding that it would be considered early in the regular session.[172] Even the *Mercury* lauded the Torontonian's statement.[173] The *Leader* apparently sensed the changed atmosphere and, not wanting Reform wounds healed, suddenly reported that Sandfield was intriguing with the opposition, with reconstruction as the goal. The *Mercury* admitted that differences between Brown and the premier remained, but it asserted that such base tactics by the *Leader* could not destroy the present improved relationship.[174]

On 15 October Monck prorogued parliament. The opposition had subjected the government to a tremendous onslaught, yet the ministry had survived. Sectional strife had eased and Reform dissension subsided. Yet between the end of the special session and the opening of the regular one, on 19 February 1864, the position of Sandfield's administration gradually grew worse.

The question of the Intercolonial Railway returned again to tarnish his reputation, thanks to Tilley's machinations. Several months before, Sandfield had made it obvious in the pages of the *Mercury* and elsewhere that because of stringent new British conditions for an imperial guarantee the government had abandoned the old agreement with the Maritimes concerning financing.[175] In a letter to Governor Gordon, Tilley had admitted that he understood this fact.[176] Yet on 7 October, when word reached him that negotiations must begin anew, he feigned great surprise, and also refused to participate in the cost of the Sandford Fleming survey.[177] Tilley's reasons for this duplicity related to his own political troubles. Sandfield had been and was still a strong advocate of the line; he argued that Tilley and Tupper of Nova Scotia knew full well that new financial arrangements had to be made. That Nova Scotia was not then angry with the Canadians, and was in fact critical of New Brunswick's intransigence over the survey, substantiates Sandfield's testimony.[178] Without colonial agreement, however, Britain refused to assist even with the survey costs. In February 1864 Sandfield announced, as a gesture of good faith, that Canada would foot the whole bill for Fleming's field work.[179] Nevertheless, recriminations about the rail line hurt his government's prestige.

The sudden emergence of a serious disagreement over policy between the old friends Brown and Holton, moreover, began to dissipate any benefit accruing from the re-establishment of personal relations and a partial entente between the premier and Brown. Holton had decided both to float his big bond issue initially in Canada and also to transfer most treasury deposits and the government's fiscal agency from the wobbly Bank of Upper Canada, in Toronto, to the strong, expansive Bank of Montreal. The Bank of Montreal would then market the securities in England and in Canada. Enough money was to be left in the Bank of Upper Canada to prevent its collapse. Holton informed Brown of his plans, apparently not expecting any great political difficulties[180] given that the Toronto bank was controlled by interests not at all politically sympathetic to George Brown. Yet that loyal Toronto business-man reacted strongly. Montreal was not to be favoured over his city. Brown also opposed financing the bonds in Canada. Holton, convinced that he was acting in the interests of the country, reluctantly proceeded with his plans.[181]

The promising reconciliation between Brown and Sandfield was also some-what undermined when the premier, without consulting Brown, appointed as solicitor-general west A.N. Richards, the brother of W.B. Richards of Hincksite fame whom Sandfield had just appointed chief justice of the Court of Common Pleas. It was clearly a logical choice, if awkwardly handled. The post had become vacant with the election of Wallbridge as Speaker. A.N. Richards, member from South Leeds, was a moderate and loyal Baldwinite, but a little too independent for Brown to have much faith in him. The editor argued that the post should have gone to a Western Grit.[182]

Partly as a result of this difference of opinion, Brown declined Sandfield's request that he go to Washington to represent the cabinet in an effort to continue the threatened Reciprocity Treaty. The dominant Republicans there, in an angry mood over British conduct during the Civil War, were threatening not to renew the agreement. Brown dodged the request, although earlier he had chastised the government for its procrastination on this serious matter, and suggested that Holton was the man to go. This was hardly realistic with a session of parliament less than a month away, a session which was supposed to emphasize financial reforms.

The by-election fight over Richards in South Leeds proved ferocious. John A. and McGee personally took charge of the Conservative campaign. McGee successfully wooed the local Irish-Catholic authorities who gave the Conservatives their support. Conservative money poured in from the Mont-real business community.[183] C.J. Brydges, despite previous protests of poli-tical impartiality, lent the not inconsiderable weight of the Grand Trunk interests in favour of D.F. Jones, the opposition candidate. On 28 January 1864 Jones defeated Richards by seventy-five votes, although the latter had taken the seat in 1863 by a 135-vote margin. Two days later the solicitor-general resigned.[184] It was a defeat which Sandfield could ill afford.

He was trying desperately to win more political support from the mem-bership of the assembly and not lose it on the by-election hustings. He attempted, without success, to regain the support of his old friend, Isaac Buchanan, of Hamilton. Buchanan admired Sandfield but loathed George Brown, and Brown was too close to the government.[185] The Ottawa Valley also offered some hope – which had strengthened Sandfield's determination to have an eastern moderate like Richards succeed Wallbridge as solicitor-general. The position of the Brownites on the seat-of-government question had put him at a disadvantage in the Ottawa area, but the construction of the parliament buildings was moving along satisfactorily there. Accordingly, Sandfield's supporters had organized a great banquet in Ottawa on 22 December 1863, in honour of his régime. In the weeks which followed the gala affair, quiet talks took place involving various notorious 'loose-fish' from the Ottawa Valley.[186] Then, as parliament opened, George Brown, threatening to break up the Reform alliance, vetoed the entry into the cabinet of the flexible Robert Bell from Russell, just east of Ottawa. This appointment might have meant the difference of up to five seats and, in divisions, that would have meant up to ten votes. Brown's response indicated a great deal about his approach, as opposed to that of the premier's, toward political life. He had no use for Bell or 'his sort'; he thought that it must have been 'very humiliating' for ministers to treat with 'men they utterly despise.' 'For my part,' he wrote, to his wife, 'I would a thousand times rather go out of public life forever than to be at the mercy of such people.'[187] Sandfield and Holton 'kicked hard,' but Brown forced them to submit. Brown naïvely believed that, with matters 'all serene' again between himself and the ministers, they were probably all glad to be rid of the 'vile deed.'[188] In reality, it had probably been Sandfield's last chance to save his administration.

Shortly thereafter Brown gratuitously suggested to Sandfield that he try to win back some of the principal figures alienated in May 1863 – alienated largely at Brown's instigation.[189] It was surely too late; Sicotte was gone, Abbott was firmly in the Conservative fold, Evanturel lacked a seat in the assembly, and Foley and McGee were irrevocably embittered. Holton, Dorion, and Mowat also urged Sandfield to work toward a Reform reconstruction – perhaps the same one that Brown had advocated – but the premier would now have none of it.[190]

Although domestic politics were his main preoccupation, Sandfield also had cause to worry about external problems. Relations between Britain and the United States were again deteriorating, and with their victories at Gettysburg and Vicksburg behind them, the Northern armies were rolling onward. The British authorities were exercised again about the perennial problem of British North American defence. In the autumn of 1863 the War Office had sent Lieutenant-Colonel W.F.D. Jervois to the provinces to examine the military situation. He was particularly pessimistic about the defence arrangements for western Upper Canada. Furthermore, the presence there of Confederate refugees raised dangers. In November, a Confederate plot to undertake a major raid from Canada, in order to free Union-held prisoners on Johnson Island in Lake Erie, was thwarted at the last minute by Sandfield's personal intervention. He warned General Dix in Buffalo and, through the

British embassy, the American authorities in Washington.[191] A few days later McDougall had travelled to Gettysburg at Seward's invitation and Sandfield's request, to be present for what became Lincoln's famous address.[192] In late December 1863 the premier slipped away quietly to New York City for personal talks with Secretary of State Seward, but the Leeds by-election and other political problems forced him to abandon a major visit to Washington and the theatre of battle south of the Potomac.[193] In spite of these and other useful contacts, it was still probable that Congress would abrogate the Reciprocity Treaty.

The Speech from the Throne, on 19 February 1864, was a bland document; the weakened government kept its cards close to its chest. After explaining what everyone already knew about the militia, the Reciprocity Treaty, the Intercolonial, and the Northwest, it mentioned that the government would soon move the civil servants to Ottawa. Legislation was planned to improve inland navigation, to deal with bankruptcy, and to reform the electoral laws. Moreover, although revenue had happily exceeded the estimate, the government would still have to propose a measure 'to equalize the annual income with the annual expenditure.'[194]

Fiscal and departmental reforms were occupying a great deal of the time which the harassed ministers could have devoted to the task of governing. The régime expired, in fact, before it could introduce its taxation reform. Similarly, the principal recommendations of the financial and departmental commission, involving a tightening up of loose cabinet procedures, fell by the wayside. Yet the Audit Act, which received royal assent only on 30 June 1864, was the product of Sandfield's administration and, in particular, of Luther Holton. Behind both Sandfield and Holton lay the painstaking work of the devoted civil servant, John Langton, the crusading provincial auditor.[195] The bill itself, undoubtedly the ministry's greatest legislative achievement, largely established the remaining necessary principles for the creation of 'effective responsible government in public expenditures';[196] it 'marked a revolution in the methods of internal and external financial control.'[197]

The Royal Commission on Finances had stressed the inadequacy of current legislative supervision of public expenditures. The Act of 1864 expanded the Board of Audit from three members to seven. The auditor became its chairman, with full responsibility for the final audit, and with the function of ensuring that no warrants were issued for public expenditure without the direct authority of parliament. As a result of a last-minute amendment, the one exception to this rule was that the cabinet could use governor general's warrants to spend money in an emergency. The fiscal year was rearranged so as to facilitate prior consideration of spending by parliament. The minister of finance was obliged to present estimates to parliament in advance. The single deficiency in the bill, corrected in 1878, was that the auditor remained a servant of the crown rather than a servant of parliament.

All this lay ahead as the stormy debate on the Address in Reply focussed attention on the politics of the moment. Brown told Brydges of the Grand Trunk that he was quite unhappy with the ministry.[198] Given that the opposition obviously had no intention of permitting 'progress with the public business,' he thought that some 'shake-up' was imminent and even desirable.[199] Cartier, whom Brown described as 'the little wretch,' spoke for thirteen hours, castigating Sandfield's administration.[200] Yet, a few days later Cartier was sending Christine Macdonald, who was in Quebec with her husband, a very friendly letter in French, enclosing his chanson, 'O Canada, mon pays, mes amours.'[201]

On 2 March the Address finally passed. The assembly plodded on. Brown wanted to bring on another internal crisis within the Reform party to achieve some sort of reconstruction.[202] Sensing the dangers inherent in a defeat in the house, he perhaps hoped to bring McGee, with whom he was now keeping up a friendly correspondence, back into the government. Given the strained relationship between the premier and the eloquent Irishman, it was obvious that McGee would not submit to Sandfield's leadership. Any such scheme would, therefore, have involved getting rid of the latter. In any event, on 14 March, Brown, with his first major speech of the session, tried to get his constitutional committee established. Galt, John A., Cartier, and lesser figures in the opposition all opposed it. Bleus argued that sectional equality of representation should survive forever. John A. suggested that the American Civil War conclusively revealed the weakness of a federal system and that when union came to British North America it should be a legislative union, in fact and in theory. The assembly postponed for a week further debate on the resolution – though Sandfield would probably have liked to shelve it permanently.[203] Parliamentary business virtually ground to a halt.

In desperation Sandfield secretly contacted old Sir Etienne Taché of the Legislative Council, to suggest the formation of a genuine new coalition of moderate Reformers and moderate Conservatives, including John A. Macdonald and Cartier. Taché and his friends were interested. Monck thoroughly supported his now-favoured first minister with enthusiasm. A Peelite in Britain[204] and a realist in Canada, he had become a devotee of the concept of a grand coalition. The premier offered Taché the selection of two of the six cabinet positions in Upper Canada and four of the six in Lower Canada. It was not enough. Taché declined the offer.[205]

On 21 March, four days after the collapse of the talks with Taché and two days after Brown finally secured the appointment of his key committee – with the government's fate hanging precariously before the assembly, Dorion tendered Sandfield his resignation and that of his Lower Canadian colleagues.[206] That same day John Sandfield Macdonald, though still unde-feated, submitted the resignation of his administration to the governor. He then addressed the house on the nature of the crisis. His government was finished.[207] Had he waited for the first division, and if everyone had attended, the government would probably have been in a minority by one vote.[208] Futilely, the Upper Canadian Reform caucus voted total confidence in (and thanks to) the outgoing government leader.

Sandfield suggested to Monck that his provincial secretary, the Reformer Fergusson-Blair, might be able to form a coalition régime. Monck followed the advice, but Blair, who contacted Taché, again was unsuccessful. Follow-ing several other efforts, Monck finally turned to Taché himself who, after discussing the matter with Cartier and John A., agreed to try. The new Taché-John A. Macdonald ministry, sworn in on 31 March 1864, contained three wayward Reformers: Foley, McGee, and Buchanan. Still, in substance, it was really a return to office of the régime which Sandfield and Sicotte had overthrown in May 1862.[209]

Although always politically unstable, Sandfield's premiership had been a significant and important one. Racked by crises, it had probably achieved substantively more than any premiership since the overthrow of MacNab in 1856. And several other measures were on the order paper when the minis-try resigned. Many of these measures would be picked up by Sandfield at a later date, under far different circumstances. Sandfield had, with Holton's help and after a very rocky start, brought Canada back into favour with Brit-ish authorities and the British press; in the difficult months ahead this would prove very useful. Above all, however, he had given Canada two years of Reform administration; and although the political and even constitutional situation seemed to have worsened, he had played a major role in lowering the emotional temperature. There was less talk of civil strife, possible bloodshed, and disruption, and more talk of reconciliation, reorganization, and compromise. For this Sandfield was responsible. The idea of grand coali-tion was in the air, and for this, both Governor General Monck and Premier J.S. Macdonald must share the credit.

At first, in March 1863, the idea had been advanced as a threat, to try to persuade the Brownites, who would have been left out, to be more pliable on the educational question and sectional issues generally. Two months later Brown himself had recognized the threatening power of the coalition alterna-tive, during the discussion on reorganizing the ministry. He had still opposed and feared the idea of coalition, and while in theory he had wanted Sandfield to broaden out, his successful blocking of the latter's overtures to the Ottawa 'loose fish' meant that the sectional dilemma could not be solved by some pragmatic aggrandizement of either Reform or Conservatism. The Sandfield-Taché talks, followed by those involving Blair and urged on by Monck, were more significant attempts at coalition, though Taché had especially balked at the idea of working with Dorion and the Rouges, whom he considered too radical and 'socialist.' These attempts by Sandfield indicated that, despite severe personal animosities and jealousies, coalition would be easier for Upper Canada than Lower Canada. They failed largely because as yet they did not centre on major constitutional change. For that ingredient, Brown and not Sandfield was essential.

In any event, the new Taché government fared no better than the old Sandfield one. By 14 June it in turn had been defeated by two votes. In the past decade a stable working majority had increasingly eluded the best of men. Canada now seemed to be an ungovernable land of opposition majorities. While many would doubt its future efficacy, some form of constitutional change seemed unavoidable. And the process that produced it was about to begin.

The great events of June 1864 to June 1867 that resulted in Confederation were largely to bypass Sandfield Macdonald. It was ironic that he, who believed so deeply in the organic unity of the St Lawrence, in the permanent interrelationship of English- and French-speaking Canadians, and in the desirability of party coalition, should find himself one of the few Upper Canadians excluded from the achievements of these years. It was, however, inconceivable that the three main Ontario leaders, John A., Brown, and Sandfield, could work on the same team; any two would be a strain, and Brown and John A. became part of the Great Coalition. It was only when Brown left the Coalition in late 1865 that the way was open for the two Macdonalds to reach a rapprochement. Ultimately, it would be Sandfield who would bring an important strand of tolerant, pragmatic liberalism into what became the post-Confederation Conservative party. In contrast, around Brown and his successors would form the post-Confederation Liberal party. In the meantime, Sandfield was cast in the part of the leading Upper Canadian critic in the battle against the emergent scheme of Confederation.

The same day in June 1864 that the Taché régime lost the confidence of the assembly, Brown's constitutional committee had submitted its report. It declared that 'a strong feeling was found to exist among the members of the committee in favour of changes in the direction of a Federal system, applied either to Canada alone, or to the whole British North American Provinces.'[210] Twelve people signed the report. Three members of the group signed in opposition to the document's thrust; among them were John Sandfield Macdonald and John A. Macdonald. Sandfield had always been an opponent of formal constitutional change; arguing that the Union would have worked if governed by good men, he laid the responsibility for its failure on the doorstep of 'demagogues and designing persons who sought to create strife between the sections.'[211] He inevitably stood out against the new cabinet shortly formed by Cartier, Macdonald, and Brown to make a new union.

The former premier seriously distrusted the division of powers inherent in any federal system, including the one that was articulated at the Charlottetown and Quebec conferences later in 1864. The proposed union seemed too elaborate and too decentralist. Besides, to re-establish a separate Upper Canadian province was to cut off the Ottawa and upper St Lawrence valleys from their natural entrepôt at Montreal and to submit them to the political domination of the Ontario peninsula. Above all, Sandfield was troubled by what he regarded as the illiberal manner in which the government was attempting to implement the project. By March 1865 the people of New Brunswick seemed to have rejected it. Nova Scotians appeared hostile. In Canada, the 'outrageously strong' Coalition was forcing changes before the electorate had had a chance to reflect.[212]

His first important speech against the Quebec Resolutions delivered in the assembly on 6 March 1865 was provoked by John A.'s announcement of the defeat of Tilley's pro-Confederation party in New Brunswick. It was clearly implied that the New Brunswickers were to be coerced into accepting union. Some Conservative papers had suggested that Tilley's defeat was attributable to the presence in New Brunswick of many people with annexationist sympathies. Sandfield commented that if the press were correct, and he doubted it, then Canadians were fortunate to have been spared uniting with such people. Continuing the speech in a more serious vein the following day, the now-irate member from Cornwall denounced the scheme as one sure to impoverish Canadians. Here he showed himself to be less the liberal capitalist and more the lawyer who was the champion of the debt-ridden farmer and the local merchant, people who were being led to believe that the elixir of Confederation would cure their many ills.[213] Once again the 'political Ishmaelite,' Sandfield saw the assembly pass the Quebec Resolutions with a comfortable double majority.[214] In combination with several other members, he also tried formally to secure a modicum of popular involvement, by means of a general election, in the decision-making process leading to Confederation. The attempt was a dismal failure.[215] His own motion proposing that the new local legislatures be given full legislative authority over educational matters 'subject only to the approval or disapproval of the General Parliament'[216] failed by a large margin. The measure would have eliminated entrenched guarantees but would not have removed the standard central supervision of provincial legislation. No French-Canadian member was prepared to let the question rest on the 'sense of justice' of the 'local,' that is, the provincial legislatures.[217]

Shortly thereafter, Sandfield was injured in a traffic accident which, he reported, 'came near finishing me.'[218] His convalescence at Ivy Hall provided him with an opportunity to chart his future course and with time to devote to his personal affairs. The *Freeholder* needed more effective management. The three-storey stone hotel, in the process of being constructed on a portion of his extensive St Andrew's property, needed his attention. On St Andrew's Day, 30 November 1865, the as-yet-uncompleted structure housed a huge party, given by Sandfield, for the village. Six or seven hundred 'lads and lasses' danced Scottish reels while Sandfield's young son Henry and a daughter played host and hostess. With the Civil War over, Christine was on an extended visit to the Waggamans, but her husband found great pleasure in the company of many of his old friends and loyal supporters.[219] Early the next year, with brother Donald, the senior officer of the entire Glengarry militia, John Sandfield urged preparedness and vigilance in the face of the then-current Fenian threat.[220]

By August 1866 the former premier was almost reconciled to Confederation; it would have been out of character for him not to accept what was, by now, so obviously the inevitable. But he did his utmost to have offending sections of the 'treaty' amended during the subsequent debates on the provincial consitutions for Ontario and Quebec. Over Brown's loud disagreement, he suggested that the people ought to have some say in the government's plan to extend educational guarantees to Lower Canadian Protestants without a similar extension to the Catholics of Upper Canada. This government measure was withdrawn when a private bill, seeking to extend the provisions to Upper Canadian Catholics, was introduced. The *status quo* survived.[221] The debates on the nature of the provincial constitutions over, Macdonald's attention could be turned back to a more familiar focus: what to do about Reform and his place in it?

George Brown had, in December 1865, left the Coalition ministry in a huff. He had not been followed by McDougall and Howland, and at the Upper Canadian Reform Convention, in June 1867, those two were read out of the party. The process of rebuilding a unified Liberal core would nevertheless not be an easy one. Holton, for instance, was worried that Sandfield might desert if offered the sufficiently-tempting post of lieutenant-governor of Ontario.[222] The two Macdonalds had in fact met, but nothing final had materialized.

John A. Macdonald, politically weak in his own section ever since the election of 1863, wanted to continue to broaden the coalition system. It was his determined plan to have a 'nation-building' coalition at the Ontario level as well as the federal. Counselled by his confidant and adviser, D.L. Macpherson, that Sandfield was the man best able to effect that continued coalition, John A. offered the Ontario premiership to him.[223] On 8 July 1867 Sandfield himself was warning Dorion and Holton in Montreal that he anticipated such a proposal.[224] That same day, ideed, the interim lieutenant-governor, Major General Stisted, wrote out the offer. The reply indicated that the recipient would be willing to travel to Toronto to discuss the subject.[225] On 10 July an accord was reached,[226] and the *Globe* trumpeted its strong displeasure.[227]

The premiership would not be easy.[228] Ontario's first minister was unable to fill his cabinet with any Reformers of stature. He depended primarily on two Conservatives, M.C. Cameron and John Carling. Cameron became Ontario's first provincial secretary and Carling first commissioner of agriculture and public works. The Brantford Reformer, Edmund Burke Wood, was name provincial treasurer, while the commissionership of crown lands went to Stephen Richards, an eastern Reformer. For the approaching elections, wherein the Ontario and Canadian contest would take place at the same time, there were three types of candidates: Conservative, Coalition Reformer, and Grit Reformer. John A. and Sandfield worked to eliminate contests between Conservatives and Coalition Reformers. That September, the advantages of incumbency and the euphoria of Confederation frustrated the Brownites and gave victory to the coalition forces. For Sandfield, the only disappointment was that the Conservatives had fared much better than had his Liberal portion of the Ontario coalition. But now secure in office, backed by about 50 of the 84 members, he prepared for the new province's first parliamentary session.

Its opening on 27 December was a gala affair. Only the cold, disagreeable weather was inauspicious. Tickets had been carefully doled out personally by the premier for every available spot not needed by the members and the official party. The lieutenant-governor, Major General Stisted, arrived in a coach-and-four to go through the formal opening procedures. On the floor of the house were many men who played major roles with Sandfield in the life of old Upper Canada, among them Chief Justice Draper, Justices W.B. Richards and Adam Wilson, Chancellor Philip Vankoughnet and Vice-Chancellor Oliver Mowat, Dr Egerton Ryerson and Bishop Lynch. The next day Stisted returned to read the Speech from the Throne, which declared the government's intention of completing the structure of the Ontario administration and encouraging immigration and settlement through a liberal homestead law. Several days later the premier made his first major speech in the asembly, further elaborating on the ministry's programme and defending the continued existence of coalition. He had always been a party man, he contended, for party was vital to the securing of true liberty in free countries. He definitely remained a Reformer but could see no reason why formal pre-Confederation divisions should be carried into the new régime. Furthermore, he believed it highly desirable to 'harmonize,' especially in the early years, the two levels of government in the new union.[229]

In the course of the next four years much was accomplished in terms of legislation and administration, as Sandfield attempted to implement those

portions of his Reform programme of 1862-4 that fell within Ontario's jurisdiction. The Free Grant and Homestead Act, passed during the first session
in 1868, was one of his most significant and liberal achievements. Designed
by Sandfield and Richards to counteract the appeal of the American Homestead Act of 1862 on which it was partly based, the act authorized the government to open for free settlement surveyed crown lands north of the then
settled areas that were not especially valuable for pine and minerals. At first
the amount to be granted was 100 acres; shortly this was changed for heads
of families to 200 acres. Title was given only after five years' residence and
with fifteen acres under cultivation; grantees could purchase an additional
100 acres at fifty cents an acre. Pine trees remained with the crown until the
patent was issued, but settlers could cut trees necessary for building, fuel,
fencing, and clearing of the land. Initially the act was very important in opening up to settlement townships in Haliburton, Muskoka, North Hastings,
and Parry Sound.

A supplementary act relating to railways further promoted the homesteading policy. This provided for encouragement and assistance in the construction of lines running northward into the free-grant areas. In 1868 over
46,000 acres were 'located,' and by 1878 the figure for the year was over
274,000; but this level would not again be achieved until well into this century. Settlement proceeded with some rapidity, though whether or not it was
wise is still debatable. Sandfield himself had some doubts. Most of the farming had to be attempted on the rough Canadian Shield, and free grants hurt
areas and companies on the southern fringe still dependent upon sales. Furthermore, lumbering interests argued with considerable force that many
townships suitable only for forestry were being attacked by poor settlers,
some of whom set costly forest fires or were really interested only in pirating
the timber. Sandfield and Richards reassured the lumbermen of their concern, and while Richards substantially increased timber dues, he rightly
pointed out that lumbermen often could clear the land of pine ahead of the
settlers and that the expanding colonization roads and railways would also
help the lumbermen. Indeed, in his 1869 report Richards could claim that
Ontario forests under the lease-hold system were already yielding to the provincial treasury more than forests in both Upper and Lower Canada had
before Confederation. Still, the tension between lumbermen and settlers
would remain.[230] In regard to the latter, Sandfield also promoted immigration
to Ontario by means of a pamphlet widely distributed in Britain and the
appointment of a commissioner of emigration to reside there.

The young province's first premier particularly encouraged its nascent
mining industry. His Gold and Silver Act of 1868 provided for the outright
sale of prospective silver lands (as had been done for gold in 1864) and for
the establishment of Mining Divisions, a licensing system, and staking

procedures. A 'claim,' which followed staking, carried only the right to occupy and to work the ore and was lost if work ceased. Then his General Mining Act of 1869 reformed and consolidated all mining regulations to that date. It abolished all royalties and provided for the establishment, within Mining Divisions, of 'locations' of various sizes that could be purchased outright for one dollar an acre, even if no discoveries, staking, or working had taken place on them. Furthermore, the crown reservation for gold and silver on all new patented land was abolished.[231]

In 1868 two Ontario statutes furthered electoral reform in the direction outlined by Dorion at the time of Sandfield's earlier administration. The Independence of Parliament Act prohibited civil servants and federal ministers from sitting in the assembly, while the Election Act provided that elections would be held on only one day, and that the same day, throughout Ontario. It also increased the number of polling subdivisions, lowered the property qualification for the franchise, and eliminated multiple voting by requiring residence as well as ownership or renting in order to qualify. But the premier was still convinced of the necessary link between property and civic responsibility, and therefore would not go all the way to universal male suffrage.[232]

In many ways Sandfield was less the representative of social Darwinism than were many of his contemporaries; and with respect to Ontario's still rudimentary social welfare institutions, he was far more progressive than most of the Reform opposition. His Prison and Asylum Inspection Act was particularly important, especially since its provision for the establishment of a provincial inspector led to the appointment of J.W. Langmuir, one of Ontario's great early senior civil servants, a fighting reformer, who served until 1882. The inspector was charged with visiting every jail, house of correction, reformatory, and prison at least twice a year, tabling a report in the assembly, and, if necessary, ordering improvements. In 1869 Langmuir's area of responsibility was broadened to include provincially supported hospitals; the impoverished Toronto General Hospital was reorganized with vastly increased public funding. In fact, the usually frugal Sandfield directed much of the growing provincial surplus into penal reform and toward institutions for the unfortunate. Major additions were begun on the Toronto Asylum for the Insane; a new asylum was established in London, and the old Rockwood Asylum near Kingston was obtained from federal authorities. The premier also ordered the construction of the Institute for the Deaf and Dumb at Belleville and the Ontario Institute for the Blind at Brantford.[233] Public charities, he observed, would ultimately have to be paid for by public taxation.

Linked to social legislation was progressive education reform, long blocked by the pre-Confederation paralysis. Usually the premier, Chief Superintendent Ryerson, and M.C. Cameron, the minister through whom Ryerson reported, were of one mind and worked well together, generally in the face of opposition hostility. Nevertheless, on one matter Sandfield acted over Ryerson's objections – objections similarly voiced by the Canadian prime minister. In 1868, with the backing of the opposition, the premier terminated all financial aid to the small denominational colleges throughout the province, including Queen's, Victoria, and Regiopolis, in favour of increased support for the secular University of Toronto. But in 1871, Sandfield, Cameron, and Ryerson finally succeeded together in pushing through major changes in primary and secondary education. Free elementary schooling was becoming general; now schooling was made free everywhere, at both levels, and compulsory in the early years. Standard qualifications for teachers and inspectors were established, municipal rates for secondary schools made essential, and science introduced seriously into the curriculum. Edward Blake, by now the leader of the opposition, bitterly fought the Education bill, particularly its compulsory and centralizing aspects and its alleged trend away from the 'three Rs' as signaled by the provisions relating to science. Blake lost. Also in 1871 Sandfield secured enabling legislation to establish the Ontario School of Agriculture, opened at Guelph in 1874, and a Technical College at Toronto.

Sandfield's ministry, in theory, had to set up Ontario's entire new provincial administration. In fact, of course, those Canadian offices and positions now transferred to the premier's jurisdiction continued initially to function as before. All of this was aided profoundly by the fact of territorial duality in old United Canada. All that happened at first, for example, to the Upper Canadian portion of the old Crown Lands Department was that fisheries, ordnance lands, and Indian Affairs were turned over to federal control. Then, of course, Sandfield's reforms necessitated the opening of new offices and branches in various departments, and the hiring of a small number of new personnel in the field. The overall number of civil servants remained, by later comparisons, astonishingly small. As attorney-general, Sandfield had three assistants, including a clerk; as premier, one could say that he had three more employees under his direction, attached to the Executive Council Office. He thus had six assistants, and he had this same number during his fourth and last year in office as in his first year. In 1870 the number of employees in the Provincial Treasury, excluding E.B. Wood, rose from five to seven. In 1871, in the central bureaucracy of Education, Ryerson had nine employees, up three from 1868. Also in 1871 sixteen persons, including the Clerk of the House, worked directly for the assembly. The Department of Crown Lands had the largest establishment, probably about forty-one in the headquarters staff in 1871, plus perhaps twenty-two land agents and sixteen or fewer timber agents outside. All in all, the civil service may have numbered less than 120 in headquarters and perhaps another 100 or so in the field or at provincial institutions. To this, of course, would also have to be added the judges and staff of the judiciary. In supervising all this, the attorney-general was paid $4000 per annum, over and above his small indemnity as a member, one that varied in relationship to the length of the session. Other ministers were each paid $3200 plus their indemnity.

Sandfield and Wood, the treasurer, administered a provincial expenditure which grew from $1,184,000 in 1868 to $1,817,000 in 1871. Of this, in 1871, more than 25 per cent was spent on social services, prisons, and the reformatory, about 25 per cent on public works and buildings, about 20 per cent on education, and about 5 per cent to support the legislature and to pay its members. Despite the growth in expenditure, the province continued to amass a surplus during the four years of Sandfield's premiership. Income from constitutional transfer payments from Ottawa only increased moderately, but income from provincial sources quickly expanded.[234] Early in 1871 he had the legislature vote $1,500,000 from the surplus into the hands of the Executive Council to be used to assist the northern extension of railways. Despite this grant, the surplus at the end of 1871 was over five million dollars. Ironically, both the turning over of the money for the railway construction – though none of it was ever found to have been misappropriated – and the existence of the huge surplus were held against the premier. He was accused at the same time of crudely overpractising patronage and of being unacceptably parsimonious. The sharply partisan state of politics, and perhaps his self-confessed 'bad habit of joking with a grave face,'[235] prevented Sandfield from ever receiving due credit for his solid careful administration and his very significant reforms.

Moreover, having now embraced the decentralism of their Grit followers, George Brown and his lieutenants extolled the pure theory of 'classical federalism,' and would not tolerate this apologist for the relatively centralized Macdonaldian system of subordinated provinces. Sandfield would have to go. He was, from the beginning, nothing but Sir John A.'s lackey, they cried, and no Reformer at all. This was an unwarranted charge,[236] but the impression it created could be ignored only at the greatest peril. Admittedly, Ontario's first premier was not a theoretical decentralist or a classical federalist. He had, in fact, been in favour of preserving the old legislative union. Yet, under his guidance, Ontario prospered, expanded its power, and became the pivotal province of the federal union. This would probably have been the case no matter who had held the office of premier. Yet, for the Grits, it was not enough. They stridently condemned Sandfield's notion that the two levels of government should be harmonized. Instead, they argued, the federal and provincial spheres should be virtually independent of one another. To their mind, the current premier could not promote Ontario's true destiny.

Sir John A. Macdonald seemed not to be fully aware of Sandfield's tenuous position in Ontario. In fact, however, the prime minister's conception of the Canadian federation could come to fruition only with the political isolation for a few more years of the provincial-rightist Grits; he was thereby dependent upon the success of Sandfield's coalition administration. But the credibility of coalition itself was the key factor in the equation. If Sir John understood this, he made few efforts to confirm it, as his appointment of the discredited Francis Hincks to the federal Finance portfolio, as a 'Reformer,' clearly indicated. By 1871 these failures were to tell on Sandfield's régime in Ontario.

Meanwhile, Sandfield Macdonald, at fifty-eight, was an old, tired, and very sick man. His ill health made worse both his great tendency to independent, unco-ordinated action and his extreme bluntness and awkwardness in personal relations. He often had difficulty relating to his brilliant but splenetic brother, Donald. Moreover, though undoubtedly affectionate, his relationship with his wife, Christine, appeared to be exceedingly formal. On their thirtieth wedding anniversary, in September 1870, he sent her a note which closed, not with an expression of love, but with 'the fervent hope' that she might have continued good health and have 'reason to be content' with her lot.[237] The most revealing comment on the man came from Christine herself. In 1864, during one of Sandfield's short periods of rapprochement with George Brown, Brown had attended a party at the Sandfield's and had occasion to be left alone with Christine and her three oldest daughters. Candidly, they discussed love and marriage and many other subjects of a rather personal nature. Christine, evidently impressed by Brown's openness, confessed to the mellowed editor that her daughters 'never stood in the presence of their father without fear, and never spoke a word to him in confidence in their lives.'[238] It is a sad story, yet Sandfield had been a good provider and, by Victorian standards, an excellent father.

By Victorian standards, he was also by now a rather well-to-do gentleman. On his death his estate was valued at over \$200,000.[239] It had been acquired in the typical way that many small-town lawyers in Upper Canada had put together their estates. Perhaps, however, very few lawyers who had come from such humble beginnings had been so successful. Certainly, being singled out for political office by the old Glengarry patrons in 1841 had given him the initial vital boost. Yet he quickly became, in his own right, a first-class solicitor, dealing especially in land. Successfully buying, selling, mortgaging, and developing properties, while still remaining essentially a solicitor, provided the means whereby a small-town lawyer could accumulate capital and move ahead of his peers. In the town and township of Cornwall alone, between 1847 and 1871, Sandfield was involved in the buying, selling, and mortgaging of over 7000 acres, including major properties in all nine concessions. About 150 personal land transactions were recorded in his name in the Land Registers for the Township of Cornwall. Undoubtedly the contract he and his brothers obtained in 1854, amid the great boom, to build a portion of the Grand Trunk, played a major role in his rise to affluence. He seems also to have been involved in many more ventures with Donald, involving land and lumber developments in the interior of the wedge between the St Lawrence and the Ottawa rivers. Yet as a professional lawyer alone, he stood supreme in Cornwall. This caused him to be sought after by the great businessmen of Montreal for local work. Now, around 1870, he was on the friendliest terms with three of the wealthiest men of that city, Sir Hugh Allan, George Stephen, and E.H. King of the Bank of Montreal; and all three were involved in the Canadian Cotton Manufacturing Company which would soon begin operations in Cornwall.

It was as a successful Victorian patriarch that Sandfield gave his last great party at Ivy Hall on 1 March 1870. The occasion was the dual marriage of his two lovely daughters, Josephine and Louise. After a sickly summer and autumn, he was enjoying a rather good winter. In February the burghers of Cornwall had fêted their favourite son with a banquet attended by 700 guests.[240] Later that month he had been a guest of honour in Ottawa at the great ball in honour of the visit of Prince Arthur, the queen's son; there, with his extra-high old fashioned collar and awkward unbalanced gait, Sandfield had danced the quadrille for hours.[241] Now, Josephine was marrying Jean Langlois, member of parliament for Montmorency, and Louise was marrying an Englishman, Lieutenant J.C. Appleby of the Royal Artillery. Most of the coalition leadership of Canada and many of the business élite of Montreal were present. Cartier, always a favourite with French-speaking Christine, was much in evidence. Sir John A. Macdonald proposed the toast to the brides. The champagne flowed.[242]

In the fall, Sandfield made a rather triumphant tour of the new settlements of his 'free land grant' areas in Muskoka. After travelling by train, stage-coach, and little steamers he slept one night under canvas by the river between Lakes Rosseau and Joseph. In the morning the place was permanently named Port Sandfield.[243] His health was still holding in December 1870, when Josephine presented her father with his first grandson, named Eugene after the Confederate colonel.

Yet not unlike his personal life, Sandfield's political life had been only a qualified success. He understood better than most the nature of the Canadian society of his time. This irascible Glengarrian, this 'outside pillar' of the Catholic church, had long striven politically to reconcile English Canadians with French Canadians, Calvinists from the Peninsula with Jansenists from Quebec City, Torontonians with Montrealers. In the mid-sixties, indeed, he had been unable to teach Reformers the lesson which he had heard many years before from Robert Baldwin, that unless their party was prepared to maintain a unified, if dual, leadership, power would forever 'revert to the old hands' until another series of events 'had taught the party more practical wisdom.'[244] When the seventies opened, however, as the efficient premier of Ontario, he was still rather out of place. Toronto was not his city; Montreal was. The Western Peninsula was not his political home; old 'Central Canada' was. Dynamic and impatient Calvinism was not his religion, but a somewhat secular, easygoing Scottish Catholicism.

In late February 1871 Sandfield decided that, as the political situation seemed to be worsening, an early spring election would be best. The ensuing campaign was not auspicious. Besides all the other matters held against Sandfield, he was now accused of having been in league with Sir John in a design to turn Manitoba, Upper Canadians' rightful hinterland, over to Métis rebels and their priestly French advisers. Edward Blake called on 'the intelligent judgement' of the people, and 'to Him in whom we live and move and have our being.'[245] The *Globe* accused Sandfield of 'a diseased pleasure in ostentatiously parading his utter personal want of principle.'[246] The prime minister himself was away in the American capital involved with the negotiating of the Treaty of Washington, and could be of little help during the campaign in Ontario. At the same time Sandfield, never free from the shadow of sickness, suffered a serious attack of high fever. During most of the campaign he was confined to bed at Ivy Hall.

Nevertheless, the election results on 21 March were inconclusive. Although the Grits under Blake swept the Peninsula, apart from Carling's seat in London, they still did not have a majority. Within the coalition forces, the Conservatives seemed to have suffered more than Sandfield's Reformers, as many Irish, both Green and Orange, had swung toward the Grits. The premier determined to hold on.[247] He postponed meeting the assembly until 7 December. Using Sandfield's own Controverted Elections Act of 1871, a reform measure designed to take electoral disputes away from partisan committees and put them in the courts, the opposition launched several judicial contests. An unwise provision of the act had declared that a seat while contested would have to remain empty. Thus, with several crucial 'government-held' seats technically vacant, Blake carried want-of-confidence motions by a few votes. Sandfield at first refused to consider the votes as valid defeats. But power ebbed away. Wood resigned from the cabinet and crossed the floor. The new Speaker, Sandfield's old Ottawa foe, R.W. Scott, was becoming increasingly friendly with Blake. On 19 December Sandfield and his cabinet resigned. In the assembly the former premier stoutly defended both his actions and the validity of the concept of coalition; he also asked forgiveness for anything he might have said 'offensive to any gentleman opposite.'[248]

Edward Blake then became premier. Although he served for only ten months, until Oliver Mowat replaced him, Blake inaugurated a Grit or Liberal era in Ontario that lasted until 1905, when the Conservative James Whitney (who had studied law in Sandfield's office) was finally able to bring it to an end.

But in December 1871 the first premiership of the new province of Ontario passed into history. It had survived four controversial years, and its accomplishments had been many and substantial. Yet in the following decades no clear consensus emerged concerning the worth of that premiership. In so many ways it was overshadowed by the twenty-four years in which Oliver Mowat reigned supreme (but never with more than 49 per cent of the popular vote), and in some respects Sandfield's régime, largely because of himself, seemed more like a postscript to the past than a preview of the future. Yet in the Ontario of 1867, Sandfield had not been an illogical choice as premier. His régime also suffered by reputation because it expressed a view of federalism divergent from that of most Ontarians. Certainly the federalism which was espoused by Mowat and his two Liberal successors was different from that of Sandfield, and the federalism of Whitney and his Conservatives after 1905 was much closer to that of Mowat than to that of Sandfield. If Ontario's first premier believed it important at least to try to 'harmonize' relations between the two levels of government, his successors considered that to be of no great concern. But Sandfield, who was never under the thumb of John A., did express a view of the constitution, a constitution which he had initially opposed because he thought it too costly and too American, that was much closer to that espoused by many of the Fathers than was the classical federalism of Mowat, Ross, Whitney, and Ferguson.

In many other ways, however, Sandfield was typical of the premiers who were to follow. He opposed interference in what he regarded as Ontario affairs. He resisted the intrusion of federal patronage into provincial politics. He had a vision of Ontario's development northward that ran counter to views of Canadian development to the far northwest. Although concerned about Canada's future, he was watchful lest Ontarians be taxed inordinately and arbitrarily to support weaker provinces.

His government certainly established the institutional foundations for Ontario, or rather it adapted and expanded the surviving provincial aspects of the old Upper Canadian foundations. Sandfield laid the bases, however inadequate, for homesteading, lumbering, and transportation activities in the vast Ottawa-Huron tract, although the crown reserve for pine was re-established in 1880. He also set the pattern for northern mining, though the crown reserve for gold and silver was re-established in 1891 and the sale of locations gradually made more complex. This premiership also produced or provided a basis for the Ontario Agricultural College at Guelph and the future Ryerson Technical Institute in Toronto, along with the provincial institutes for the deaf and blind. He promoted the careers of dedicated senior civil servants such as J.W. Langmuir, Egerton Ryerson, J.G. Hodgins, and Thomas Johnson. Under his administration the system of public education was much enlarged; for better or worse, Mowat and Ross would continue the trend toward provincial centralization, a trend begun by Sandfield and denounced by Blake. Under Sandfield, moreover, the long overdue reform and expansion of Ontario's welfare programme began. It would continue. No *laissez-faire* ideologue, he had no objection to the expansion of what would become known as the positive state. In this his views were closer to those of the pragmatic Mowat than to those of Brown and the more doctrinaire liberals. Conversely, Sandfield opposed the establishment of manhood suffrage divorced from property, whereas Mowat ultimately enacted it. Yet both had spoken against it in the mid-sixties.

Above all, however, Mowat and the other celebrated Ontario premiers who followed him were master political managers. Mowat and others looked to patronage just as Sandfield did, but they practised it more effectively and subtly. Denouncing coalition, they governed by building and nurturing unofficial coalitions. Although Sandfield, after Confederation, believed in formal coalition, he could not control his team effectively. But then so, too, did other later premiers of Ontario who failed to sustain power for long.

In 1872 Sandfield infrequently attended the legislature, where M.C. Cameron was now serving as acting leader of the opposition. In March he was again confined to his bed at Ivy Hall. He learned from his doctors that his heart was so 'displaced and impaired' by previous illnesses that there was no hope for recovery.[249]

On 1 June 1872, at Ivy Hall, John Sandfield Macdonald died, surrounded by his wife, his brothers Donald and Alexander, and many of his children, after receiving the last rites of the church which had previously more often troubled than comforted him.[250] On 4 June the funeral procession, which contained over 2000 vehicles and hundreds of pedestrians, wound its slow way along the canal and north through Cornwall to tiny St Andrew's. There, by the graves of Simon Fraser and other Scottish-Canadian fur traders and explorers, Sandfield was buried in the dress attire of a queen's counsel.[251] In Toronto, where he had never quite felt at home, the coalition's *Mail*, which he had helped to establish, admitted that he had been 'a poor political manager.' Otherwise it was impassioned in its praise for this man who was 'as pure a statesman as ever lived.'[252] The *Globe*, recalling his contribution to Reform, forgave him his recent lapses. Forgetting its erstwhile editorials, Brown's paper lauded 'his personal independence,' noting that 'whatever opinions he held, they were his own, derived from no other man's mind, and they were put into practical operation also after his own fashion.'[253] It was a true verdict on Ontario's first provincial premier – and last of its pre-Confederation government leaders.

NOTES

1 *Quebec Mercury*, 13 Feb. 1863
2 Ibid., 14 and 17 Feb. 1863
3 For more details and documentation on the background, birth, and early life of John Sandfield Macdonald see the author's *John Sandfield Macdonald, 1812-1872* (Toronto 1971) and his 'The Political Career of John Sandfield Macdonald to the Fall of his Administration in March, 1864' (unpublished PHD dissertation, Duke University, 1964). The author would like to express his thanks to Patricia Johnston and Andrea Careless who helped with additional research for this current study.
4 There is some confusion about the actual time and place of the marriage. Family accounts (Public Archives of Canada [PAC], John Sandfield Macdonald-Langlois Papers, Cecily Langlois, 'The Romance of JSM') all assert that John Sandfield and Christine eloped to New York City. Sandfield wrote to Christine on 4 Sept. 1870 on the occasion of their thirtieth anniversary. This would put the date at 4 Sept. 1840. St Andrew's Church Records, however, show a marriage taking place there on 26 Oct. 1840. Church Register B, folio 81, marriage number 16, 1840. St Andrew's West is just north of Cornwall.
5 PAC, John Sandfield Macdonald-Langlois Papers (henceforth J.S. Macdonald Papers), Draper to John Sandfield Macdonald [henceforth JSM] 25 March 1841, confidential
6 Toronto *Examiner*, 11 Aug. 1841
7 Canada, *Journals of the Legislative Assembly, 1841*, 11 Aug. 1841 [henceforth *Journals*]
8 Ibid., 6 Aug. 1841, 302, and 19 Aug. 1841, 38-85; and the *Examiner*, 11 Aug. 1841
9 *Journals, 1841*, 609, and the *Examiner*, 22 Sept. 1841
10 See below, especially 267.
11 *Examiner*, 21 Sept. 1842. The treaty, of course, settled outstanding issues between Britain and the United States, many involving Canada.
12 PAC, McGillivray Papers, Macdonald to McGillivray, 15 Sept. 1842
13 *Journals, 1842*, 14, 66-7
14 J.S. Macdonald Papers, Commission as Lieutenant-Colonel, 7 Nov. 1842
15 *Prospectus of New Weekly Journal to be Published in the Town of Cornwall to be entitled 'The Freeholder.'* A copy of the *Prospectus* is in the possession of the *Standard-Freeholder* of Cornwall. There is nothing in the *Prospectus* linking the paper to Sandfield Macdonald, but it was a recognized fact that he owned it.

16 *Globe*, 16 and 20 July, 7 Aug. 1847

17 Cornwall *Observer*, 18 Jan. 1844

18 *Freeholder*, 12 Sept. 1847

19 Metropolitan Toronto Central Library, Robert Baldwin Papers, JSM to Baldwin, 12 Jan. 1850

20 *Globe*, 9 Oct. 1849

21 Ibid., 9 July and 15 Oct. 1850

22 J.S. Macdonald Papers, McIntyre to JSM, 8 June 1851

23 R.S. Longley, *Sir Francis Hincks* (Toronto 1943), 290-2

24 J.M.S. Careless, *Brown of the Globe*, 2 vols. (Toronto 1959), I, 135

25 Francis Hincks, *Reminiscences of his Public Life* (Montreal 1884), 250-8

26 Ontario Archives, W.L. Mackenzie-Charles Lindsey Papers, JSM to Lindsey, 10 Jan. 1852

27 J.S. Macdonald Papers, JSM to E.J. Barker, 27 Dec. 1851

28 Baldwin Papers, JSM to Baldwin, 31 Jan. 1851

29 J.S. Macdonald Papers, Numerous letters from John Walker and A.M. MacKenzie to JSM during 1852 and 1853; also Peter McGill to JSM, 22 Jan. 1852

30 Ibid., A.M. MacKenzie to JSM, 29 Sept., 12 and 14 Oct. 1852; 19 Feb. and 6 May 1853; and George A. Drew [mill operator] to JSM, 2 June 1853

31 Obituaries of Donald Alexander Macdonald, Montreal *Witness* and Montreal *Star*, 10 June 1896; and *The Parliamentary Companion: 1875* (Ottawa)

32 J.S. Macdonald Papers, John Walker to JSM, 19 and 28 Aug. 1852; and A.M. MacKenzie to JSM, 9 Oct. 1852

33 Cornwall Public Library, J.F. Pringle Papers, Agreement between David Kinneau and Ranald Sandfield Macdonald, 10 Sept. 1846

34 J.S. Macdonald Papers, Donald A. Macdonald to JSM, 8 Aug. 1851

35 *Globe*, 24 Aug. 1852

36 J.S. Macdonald Papers, JSM to E.J. Barker, 27 Dec. 1851

37 Mackenzie-Lindsey Papers, Henry Smith to Charles Lindsey, 2 April 1859

38 J.S. Macdonald Papers, Charles Berger to JSM, 3 May 1853

39 *Le Journal de Quebec*, 10 Mai 1853. It was rumoured that 800 persons attended at a total cost of $1000; J.S. Macdonald Papers, Ranald Sandfield Macdonald to JSM, 11 May 1853. That year parliament increased the Speaker's salary to £800. PAC, Alexander Mackenzie Papers, George Brown to Alexander Mackenzie, 19 June 1853

40 J.S. Macdonald Papers, Donald A. Macdonald to JSM, 5 and 21 March and 5 and 8 April 1853

41 Ibid., Ranald S. Macdonald to JSM, 26 March 1853

42 Ibid., McIntyre to JSM, 18 and 23 March and 22 April 1853

43 Ibid., A.M. MacKenzie to JSM, 30 Aug. and 9 Oct. 1852, and 2, 25, and 31 March 1853

44 Ibid., Walker to JSM, 18 Oct. 1852

45 Ibid., Donald A. Macdonald to JSM, 15 March 1853; similar sentiments expressed 21 March and 5 and 8 April 1853

46 Ibid., JSM to Christine Macdonald, 2 Aug. [1853]; McGillivray Papers, JSM to John MacGillivray, 29 June 1853; *Globe*, 6 June 1872; and Toronto *Mail*, 6 June 1872

47 OA, Charles Clarke Papers, William McDougall to Charles Clarke, 4 April 1854; Montreal *Witness*, 10 June 1896; and *Freeholder* approx. same date 1896 (clipping in Ontario Legislative Library, Chester S. Walters Papers)

48 *Globe*, 24 June 1854

49 *Journals, 1854*, 31

50 *Globe*, 28 June 1854

51 PAC, from clipping located on back of portrait of JSM

52 *Journals, 1854-55*, 75-6, 79

53 *Globe*, 5 June 1856

54 *True Witness*, 27 Oct., 10 Nov., and 8 Dec. 1854; *Globe*, 18 Dec. 1854; J.S. Macdonald Papers, A.M. MacKenzie to JSM, 17 Oct., 11, 24 Nov., 4, 6, 7, 11, 15 Dec. 1854; Ranald S. Macdonald to JSM, 12 Nov. 1854; and Donald A. Macdonald to JSM, 23 Nov. 1854

55 Ibid., Ranald S. Macdonald to JSM, 4 March 1855, and Donald A. Macdonald to JSM, 27 April 1855

56 Ibid., A.M. MacKenzie to JSM, 26 April and 25 Sept. 1856

57 *Globe*, 4 June 1856. Concerning Neilson, Viger, and LaFontaine, note Jacques Monet, *The Last Cannon Shot: A Study of French-Canadian Nationalism, 1837-1850* (Toronto 1969), 79, 204-12, 260, and 395; also William Ormsby, *The Emergence of the Federal Concept in Canada, 1839-1845* (Toronto 1969), 120 and 125

58 Waggaman-Macdonald Papers, in the possession of Mrs Babette Brodie (JSM's great-granddaughter), Alphonsine Dumas to [Christine Macdonald], 11 Feb. 1857; and J.S. Macdonald Papers, Peter McGill to JSM, 10 June 1857

59 *Journals, 1858*, Appendix 28, 'General Election' (Returns from the clerk of the crown in Chancery)

60 PAC, George Brown Papers, T. McNaughton to George Brown, 25 Jan. 1858, private

61 Ibid., Luther Holton to George Brown, 26 Jan. 1858, confidential

62 PAC, John A. Macdonald Papers, JSM to John A. Macdonald, 27 Jan. 1858

63 *Globe*, 20 May 1858

64 Ibid., 18 April 1859

65 JSM to Brown, 14 July 1860, printed in the *London Free Press* [LFP], 19 July 1860

66 The seigneurial dispute is covered in the LFP, 4, 8, 10, and 19 July 1860; also the Toronto *Leader*, 16 April 1859; and the *Globe*, 9 and 10 April 1859.

67 Brown Papers, L.H. Holton to Brown, 15 Sept. 1859

68 Ibid., Holton to Brown, 22 Nov. 1859
69 LFP, 11 and 24 Nov. 1859, and supplement of 18 Nov. 1859
70 Josiah Blackburn Papers, in the possession of W.J. Blackburn, JSM to Black-
    burn, 8 April 1860 (a draft version exists in the J.S. Macdonald Papers.)
71 *Canadian Free Press*, 16 March 1860
72 Blackburn Papers, JSM to Blackburn, 8 April 1860
73 *Globe*, 3 and 5 Jan., and 5 Feb. 1860
74 *Journals, 1861*, 30-2; and LFP, 25 and 28 March 1861
75 *Globe*, 11 April 1861; and LFP, 13 and 16 April 1861
76 LFP, 4 May 1861
77 Ibid., 3 June 1861
78 Ibid., 12 and 26 Aug. 1861
79 Ibid., 13 and 16 July; 10, 12, 14, and 26 Aug. 1861
80 LFP, 3, 9, 20 March; 16 April; 14, 15, 16, and 21 May 1862; and *Journals,
    1862*, 228-9
81 *Globe*, 24 May 1862
82 LFP, 26 May 1862
83 LFP, 28 May 1862
84 *Globe*, 27 May 1862
85 LFP, 30 May 1862
86 LFP, 4, 5, 7, 9, and 10 June 1862; and C.P. Stacey, *Canada and the British Army
    1846-1871* (Toronto 1963), 143
87 *Globe*, 12 June 1862
88 PAC (microfilm), Newcastle Papers, Monck to Newcastle, 30 May 1862, private
89 Ibid., Monck to Newcastle, 10 June 1862
90 Ibid., Newcastle to Monck, 6 and 14 June 1862, private
91 Ibid., 14 June 1862
92 LFP, 21 June (reprints of *Times* editorial of 9 June) and 24 June 1862
93 Newcastle Papers, 11 Aug. 1862, private
94 Newcastle to Monck, 21 Aug. 1862, printed in the *Globe*, 16 March 1863
95 'Memorandum to the Colonial Office,' Minutes of Council, printed in the
    Globe, 16 March 1863
96 PAC, Indian Department, Correspondence, Manitoulin Island, Memorandum
    from the Chief Superintendent, 1862. The author is grateful to Christine Sivell
    for help with this section.
97 *Canada, Indian Treaties and Surrenders from 1680 to 1890* (Ottawa 1905), I,
    235-8; and Canada, *Sessional Papers, 1863*, no 3, 'Report on Measures for
    opening up Manitoulin,' by William Spragge
98 *Quebec Mercury*, 11 and 13 Oct., 1862; and J.S. Macdonald Papers, T.D.
    McGee to JSM, 2 Oct. 1862. The resignation was not formally accepted until
    27 Jan. 1863.
99 Newcastle Papers, Newcastle to Monck, 20 Nov. 1862

100 J.S. Macdonald Papers, Tilley to JSM, 15 Jan. 1863
101 LFP, 11 Aug. 1862; and *Mercury*, 14 and 21 June; 11 and 13 Sept.; and 20 Nov. 1862
102 The details of the arrangement form part of the now-missing portion of the Blackburn Papers. The best account is to be found in a lengthy editorial in the LFP, 21 March 1864.
103 *Mercury*, 20 and 29 Nov., and 2 and 27 Dec. 1862
104 LFP, 20 Nov. 1862
105 *Mercury*, 30 Dec. 1862
106 Ibid., 23 Dec. 1862. His children were: Lilla (now 20), Josephine (18), Louisa (16), Henry (14), Adele (9), and George (2).
107 J.S. Macdonald Papers, JSM to Charles Sumner, 5 Jan. 1863; University of Rochester, W.H. Seward Collection, JSM to Seward, 31 Dec. 1863; Waggaman-Macdonald Papers, clipping from New Orleans paper, mid-1897, obituary of Eugene Waggaman
108 *Mercury*, 8 and 22 Nov., and 13 Dec. 1862
109 Ibid., 1 Jan. 1863
110 Ibid., 10 and 12 Jan.; and LFP, 16 Jan. 1863
111 Mackenzie Papers, Brown to Holton, 5 Jan. 1863
112 *Mercury*, 3 Feb. 1863
113 LFP, 13 Jan. 1863
114 LFP, 4 Feb. 1863; also 7 and 9 Feb. 1863
115 Mackenzie Papers, 12 Feb. 1863
116 *Journals, 1863*, 7-8
117 *Globe*, 26 Feb. and 5 March 1863
118 *Mercury*, 14 and 17 Feb. 1863
119 *Journals, 1863*, 32-41
120 Brown Papers, Holton to Brown, 19 Feb. 1863
121 *Globe*, 5, 6, and 10 March 1863
122 Ibid., 5 Jan. 1863 (probably written by George's brother, Gordon Brown)
123 *Mercury*, 5 March 1863
124 *Globe*, 6 and 11 March 1863
125 *Journals, 1863*, 95
126 Reprinted in the *Globe*, 10 and 11 March 1863
127 Ibid., 10 March 1863
128 Ibid., 13 March 1863
129 Ibid., 14 March 1863; and *Mercury* 12 and 13 March 1863
130 C.B. Sissons, *Egerton Ryerson: His Life and Letters*, 2 vols. (Toronto 1947), II, 481
131 LFP, 16 March 1863
132 *Mercury*, 16 March 1863
133 Sissons, *Ryerson*, II, 481, Ryerson to Hodgins, 16 March 1863

134 *Globe*, 17 and 19 March 1863

135 *Leader*, 16, 17, and 18 March 1863

136 Toronto *Canadian Freeman*, reprinted with comments in the *Globe*, 20 and 21 March 1863

137 *Globe*, 20 March 1863

138 Ibid., 25 March; 3, 6, 15, 17, and 20 April 1863

139 LFP, 8 April 1863

140 *Globe*, 23 April 1863

141 E.R. Cameron, *Memoirs of Ralph Vansittart* (Toronto 1924), 116-17

142 John A. Macdonald Papers, James Patton to John A. Macdonald, 20 April 1863

143 *Globe*, 2, 6, and 8 May 1863; *Mercury*, 2 May 1863; and *Leader*, 2 May 1863

144 LFP, 4 May 1863

145 *Globe*, 2, 4, 5, and 6 May 1863

146 Ibid., 8 May 1863

147 Sissons, *Ryerson*, II, 486, Ryerson to Hodgins, 2 May 1863

148 *Journals, 1863*, 324-5

149 *Globe*, 11 May 1863

150 Brown Papers, Brown to Gordon Brown, 11 May 1863. Note also Quebec *Chronicle*, 29 Aug. 1864, and *Globe*, 18 and 22 Aug. 1863

151 Brown Papers, Brown to Gordon Brown, 11 May 1863

152 *Mercury*, 18 and 20 May 1863

153 *Globe*, 18 and 19 May 1863

154 For an analysis of the dichotomy in comprehension between the 'two majorities' note Gregory Baum, 'Solidarity beyond Nationalism,' excerpts from his Convocation Address to McMaster University, *Globe and Mail*, 16 June 1978; Ramsay Cook, *Canada and the French-Canadian Question* (Toronto 1966), chap. 8, 'The Canadian Dilemma,' 143-67; and Bruce W. Hodgins and Denis Smith, 'Canada and Quebec: Facing the Reality,' *Journal of Canadian Studies*, XII, July 1977, 124-6.

155 PAC (microfilm), John Stevenson Papers, Lewis Wallbridge to John Stevenson, 16 May, 1 June, and 1 July 1863, and JSM to John Stevenson, 16 May 1863

156 PAC, Scott Papers, Scott to John A. Macdonald, 30 May and 11, 12, 24, and 27 June 1863 (copies); and the *Mercury*, 13 and 15 May 1863

157 *Mercury*, 23, 25, 28, and 31 July, and 3, 4, 6, 10 and 11 Aug. 1863

158 *Globe*, 19 June and 6 July 1863

159 Newcastle Papers, Newcastle to Monck, 29 May 1863

160 Ibid., Monck to Newcastle, 8 July 1863

161 *Mercury*, 6 Aug. 1863

162 Ibid., 8 and 10 Sept. 1863

163 Cited by McGee and acknowledged by JSM, *Confederation Debates* (Ottawa 1866), 653; also referred to in Thomas White to George Brown, 23 April 1864, printed in the *Chronicle*, 29 April 1864

164 Newcastle Papers, Newcastle to Monck, 20 June 1863

165 *Journals, 1863*, 22-3

166 *Mercury*, 27 and 28 Aug. 1863

167 Ibid., 13 April, and 5, 9 and 10 Sept. 1863; and Stacey, *Canada and the British Army*, 149-51

168 *Times*, 2 Oct. 1863, reprinted with editorial comments in the *Mercury*, 21 Oct. 1863

169 *Mercury*, 3 Oct. 1863

170 Ibid., 14 Oct. 1863

171 Brown Papers, Brown to Anne Brown, 28 Sept. 1863

172 *Mercury*, 13 Oct. 1863

173 Ibid., 15 Oct. 1863

174 Ibid., 19 Oct. 1863

175 Ibid., 17, 20, 21 Jan., 10 Feb., 4 March, 8 Sept. 1863

176 Newcastle Papers, 2 Feb. 1863, enclosed in Gordon to Newcastle, 2 Feb. 1863

177 J.S. Macdonald Papers, Sandford Fleming to JSM, 2 Oct. 1863

178 Ibid., Charles Tupper to JSM, 21 Dec. 1861

179 Canada, *Sessional Papers, 1864*, #27, 'Documents relating to the Intercolonial'

180 Brown Papers, Holton to Brown, 22 Oct. 1863

181 Mackenzie Papers, Brown to Holton, 23 Oct. 1863, and 19 Jan. 1864; Brown Papers, Holton to Brown, 1 and 21 Nov., 6 and 17 Dec. 1863, and 24 Jan. 1864. The Bank of Upper Canada closed in 1866.

182 Mackenzie Papers, Brown to Holton, 19 and 20 Jan., and 6 Feb. 1863; Brown Papers, Holton to Brown, 24 Jan. 1864

183 John A. Macdonald Papers, C. Alleyn to John A. Macdonald, 29 Dec. 1863; D.F. Jones to John A. Macdonald, 1 Jan. 1864; and James Patton to John A. Macdonald, 5 Feb. 1864

184 *Mercury*, 29 and 30 Jan. 1864

185 John A. Macdonald Papers, Buchanan to John A. Macdonald, 11 Nov. 1864; PAC, Buchanan Papers, Buchanan to JSM, 8 Aug., 5 Oct., and 5 Dec.; wire of 14 Dec. 1863 and 15 Jan. 1864

186 *Mercury*, 8 Sept., 23 Oct., 9, 18, 23, and 28 Dec. 1863, and 1 Feb. 1864; John A. Macdonald Papers, Robert Bell to John A. Macdonald, 29 Dec. 1863; W.F. Powell to Macdonald [two letters, early 1864]; C.V. Brydges to Macdonald, 15 Jan. 1864; John Reid to Macdonald; 10 and 11 Feb. 1864; and Brown Papers, Holton to Brown, 24 Jan. 1864

187 Brown Papers, Brown to Anne Brown, 20 Feb. 1864

188 Ibid., Brown to Anne Brown, 22 Feb. 1864

189 Thomas White to George Brown, 23 April 1864, printed in the *Chronicle*, 29 April 1864

190 Brown Papers, Brown to Anne Brown, 2 March 1864

191 Stacey, *Canada and the British Army*, 49-51 and 237-38; and Robin W. Winks, *Canada and the United States: the Civil War Years* (Baltimore 1960), 118-19, 149-51, and 237-8

192 Seward Collection, Charles S. Ogden to Seward, 13 Nov. 1863, and William McDougall to Seward, 17 Nov. 1863

193 Ibid., JSM to Seward, 31 Dec. 1863

194 *Journals, 1864*, 2-3; and *Mercury*, 19 Feb. 1864

195 W.A. Langton, ed., *Early Days in Upper Canada: Letters of John Langton* (Toronto 1926); Herbert R. Balls, 'John Langton and the Canadian Audit Office,' *Canadian Historical Review*, XXI June 1940, 150-76

196 Norman Ward, *The Public Purse: A Study in Canadian Democracy* (Toronto 1962), 36

197 J.E. Hodgetts, *Pioneer Public Service: An Administrative History of the United Canadas, 1841-1867* (Toronto 1955), 107

198 John A. Macdonald Papers, Brydges to John A. Macdonald, 22 and 24 Feb. 1864

199 Brown Papers, Brown to Anne Brown, 25 Feb. 1864

200 Ibid., Brown to Anne Brown, 1 March 1864

201 J.S. Macdonald Papers, Cartier to Christine Macdonald, 5 March 1864

202 Brown Papers, Brown to Anne Brown, 14 March 1864

203 Ibid., Brown to Anne Brown; *Globe*, 15 March 1864; and *Journals, 1864*, 91-4

204 This is a point emphasized by Professor W.L. Morton in conversations with the author. See his forthcoming biography of Lord Monck. Also note, Elisabeth Batt, *Monck: Governor General, 1861-1868* (Toronto 1976), 79-82

205 P.B. Waite, *The Life and Times of Confederation 1864-67* (Toronto 1962), 41-2, esp. note 20

206 J.S. Macdonald Papers, Dorion to JSM, 21 March 1864

207 LFP, 22 and 23 March 1864

208 This assertion presupposes that Foley would have voted against the government and that G. Sylvain, one of the remaining two rebels of May 1862, was now ready to return to Cartier.

209 LFP, 31 March 1864; *Mercury*, 25 March 1864; Brown Papers, Holton to Brown, 3 April 1864

210 *Journals, 1864*, 223-6

211 *Confederation Debates*, 650-4

212 Ibid., 13-14

213 Ibid., 720-42

214 Ibid., 962

215 Ibid., 962-63, 1008-13, and 1020

313 John Sandfield Macdonald

216 Ibid., 1025
217 Ibid., 1025-7
218 J.S. Macdonald Papers, JSM to A. MacLean, 25 March 1865
219 *Freeholder*, 8 Dec. 1865
220 Ibid., 2, 9, 16, 23, 30 March, and 6 April 1866
221 *Globe*, 14 and 28 July, and 1, 3, 11 Aug. 1866; *Leader*, 11 and 21 July, and
    8 Aug. 1866; Can. Library Assoc., *Parliamentary Debates*, 17 July and 2 Aug.
    1866
222 Brown Papers, Holton to Brown, 16 May and 4 July 1867
223 John A. Macdonald Papers, Macpherson to John A. Macdonald, 27 and
    29 July 1867
224 Brown Papers, Holton to Brown, 10 July 1867
225 J.S. Macdonald Papers, Stisted to JSM, 8 July 1867, and JSM to Stisted, 9 July
    1867
226 *Globe*, 10 July 1867; and John A. Macdonald Papers, John A. Macdonald to
    Gibbs, 11 July 1867
227 *Globe*, 15 and 17 July 1867
228 For greater detail, see the author's *John Sandfield Macdonald*, 89-118.
229 *Leader*, 27 Dec. 1867; Toronto *Daily Telegraph*, 27 Dec. 1867; *Globe*, 27 Dec.
    1867; and the *Canadian Free Press*, 3 Jan. 1868
230 John A. Macdonald Papers, JSM to John A. Macdonald, 5 June 1868; Richard
    S. Lambert and Paul Pross, *Renewing Nature's Wealth* (Toronto 1967), 94-8
    and 117-19; and H.V. Nelles, *The Politics of Development: Forests, Mines and
    Hydro-Electric Power in Ontario, 1849-1941* (Toronto 1974), 44-5. 'No amount
    of agrarian rhetoric,' argues Nelles, 'could transform the wilderness Shield
    into the garden of the freehold farmer' (45).
231 Nelles, *Politics of Development*, 22-4; 31 Vic. c 10 and 32 Vic. c 34; and W.G.
    Miller, 'History of Mining in Ontario,' *Canada and its Provinces* (Toronto
    1914), XVIII, 640-5
232 He believed, for example, that men who had worked to acquire property had
    to be protected from the ill-informed votes of 'bank clerks.' See *Leader*,
    25 Feb. 1868.
233 See Richard B. Splane, *Social Welfare in Ontario: 1791-1893* (Toronto 1965).
234 Ontario, *Sessional Papers, 1868-72*, especially the Public Accounts, 1868-72.
    Note also Splane, *Social Welfare*, and F.F. Schindeler, *Responsible Government
    in Ontario* (Toronto 1969), 3-11 and 40.
235 *Leader*, 7 Jan. 1871
236 In fact, Sir John found him too independent. See John A. Macdonald Papers,
    John A. Macdonald to R. Stevenson, 8 Oct. 1867.
237 J.S. Macdonald Papers, Sandfield to Christine Macdonald, 4 Sept. 1870
238 Brown Papers, Brown to Anne Brown, 23 Feb. 1864
239 J.S. Macdonald Papers, Will of JSM

240 *Leader*, 11 Feb. 1870

241 Ibid., 26 Feb. 1870

242 Ibid., 5 March 1870; C.B. Sissons, ed., *My Dearest Sophie: Letters of Egerton Ryerson to his Daughter* (Toronto 1955), 181 and 186-7

243 Charles Marshall, *The Canadian Dominion* (London 1871), 49-69; Thomas MacMurray, *Free Grant Lands of Canada* (Bracebridge 1871), 82-5; Florence B. Murray, ed., *Muskoka and Haliburton: 1615-1815: Collection of Documents* (Toronto 1963), xcix-cix, 341-3, and 402-6

244 J.S. Macdonald Papers, Robert Baldwin to JSM, 1 Feb. 1848

245 Adam Shortt and Arthur Doughty, eds., *Canada and its Provinces*. XVII: *The Province of Ontario* (Toronto 1914), 120-1

246 *Globe*, 13 March 1871

247 Stevenson Papers, JSM to Stevenson, 24 March 1871; also University of Toronto Library, Special Collections, Tyrrell Papers, JSM to William Tyrrell, 9 and 26 Feb. and 29 March 1871

248 *Globe*, 20 Dec. 1871

249 *Mail*, 3 and 10 June 1872

250 J.S. Macdonald Papers, Christine Macdonald to Josephine Langlois, 7 June 1872

251 *Mail*, 3 and 5 June 1872

252 Ibid., 3 June 1872

253 *Globe*, 3 June 1872

J.M.S. CARELESS

Epilogue

It may be said with all the assurance of the obvious that the pre-Confederation era ended for Ontario in 1867. Yet in a significant sense, and certainly in keeping with the content of this volume, its passing was conclusively marked by Sandfield Macdonald's fall from office in 1871. As Bruce Hodgins has put it in the pages above, Sandfield's years as first premier of the province could be seen more as 'a postscript to the past than a preview of the future.'[1] On his retirement a different era indeed opened in Ontario government, that of the long-lived Liberal régime which remained in power throughout the rest of the century and beyond. The days of successive coalitions and shifting party fronts that extended back to the 1840s were henceforth replaced in provincial politics by a stable, single-party dominance – however shrewdly and diligently enduring leaders like Oliver Mowat still had to work to keep command. In this light, then, Sandfield Macdonald can well be considered as the last of the old, not the first of the new; and the end of his premiership as a suitable place for rounding off this study.

Moreover, historic eras viewed in socio-economic and cultural terms seldom start or finish with the sharp, neat demarcation of some precise political event, such as the enactment of Confederation in 1867. They spread themselves more loosely. Hence the early 1870s, in general, provide quite a reasonable vantage point for a final look at the Ontario community in which the pre-Confederation premiers had played their part. Here also, the census of 1871 offers a ready source of particulars on the province which had now emerged. Drawing upon it even briefly can help one to summarize, by way of a conclusion, the forces of social change that had been at work during the careers of the pre-Confederation leaders, reshaping the life of the ordinary citizen as they had the patterns of government.

At first glance the 1871 census might not suggest any striking change since that of ten years earlier. Ontario's population had risen in rounded numbers from 1,396,000 to 1,620,800.[2] This represented continued but not outstanding demographic growth, indicative as it was of the lesser role of British immigration, the closing of former land frontiers, and the fact that the new lands of the Northwest beyond the lakes had only been incorporated in Canada in 1870. Yet the further fact that population growth was now largely the result of natural increase did indicate one very salient point: the development of a community in which the great majority were Ontario-born; over 1,131,000 in 1871.[3] British ties and sentiments might still be strongly felt in the province, but so was a rising spirit of Anglo-Canadian nationalism. It was not surprising that the opening seventies witnessed the assertive Canada First movement, an effusion of nationalist zeal and optimism mainly focussed in Ontario.

This same community that was so notably becoming 'native,' had by the same token, gained in cultural homogeneity. Ethnic differences, particularly evinced in religious divisions, were still very much present; but they scarcely surged in force and duration to the extent experienced back in the fervent fifties. Moreover, since there were no longer the major ethnic reinforcements of new immigrants, nor sizeable new regions of settlement being opened, the provincial society had acquired a degree of coherence not existent earlier, nor later in the newly expansive twentieth century. High Victorian Ontario had come into being, in many respects a society far closer to equilibrium than that of the strenuous pre-Confederation decades.

The equilibrium was, however, more apparent than real. In particular, class and occupational differences within the community displayed their growing impacts. In the larger towns working-class interests were actively launching an organized labour movement. In 1870, in fact, the contest of capital and labour was exhibited in a struggle over the open or closed shop at the Gurney Foundry in Toronto. The next year the Toronto Trades Assembly was formed. A year after, in 1872, came the celebrated Toronto Printers' Strike, bitterly combatted by newspaper owners headed by George Brown, whose own big *Globe* was a prime target for the union's attack. Yet it led to a significant recognition of union rights, in federal legislation astutely offered by another veteran Ontario political hand, Sir John A. Macdonald, as prime minister of Canada. And if unionism, the Nine Hours agitation, and 'working-man' parliamentary candidates signified the rise of labour group-consciousness in the early seventies, so the structuring of business group interests was signalized by the incorporation of the Canadian Manufacturers' Association in 1871 (derived from meetings in Toronto that went back to 1866) and by the mounting demand among Ontario businessmen for tariff protection – raised indeed in 1870, and soon to be christened 'National Policy' by John A. Macdonald in 1872.[4]

The development of these competing broad interest groups, different from though not necessarily unconnected with the older ethnic and religious elements, was expressive of a more complex, populous, and closed society, where cheap good land had run out and cost factors increasingly favoured larger enterprises against small artisans and proprietors. The results were more evident in the swelling towns in which concentrating numbers brought out strains, differences, and confronting aims. Yet the same process of social change was not beyond perception in the rural areas. Here the rise in land prices, and the problem of how to provide adequately for large farm families in a now populated countryside, had already promoted a drain into the town from adjacent districts that had mounted through the 1860s. Moreover, in areas that proved of lower value, after over-sanguine pioneers had skimmed their original soil reserves, there were movements not of surplus population, but of actual depopulation under way. Thus the census of 1871 revealed declining numbers, for example, in Glengarry, Leeds, Grenville, and Frontenac in Eastern Ontario, in parts of Durham and Northumberland and Peel and York around the centre, and slightly falling or stationary populations in several western districts.[5] A larger set of counties showed considerable increase still. But the manifest evidences of rural population decline by the 1870s were indications of an advancing process of sorting-out and urbanization: signs of a very different world from that of spreading farm frontiers.

One consequence for an Ontario agrarian society that now began to sense itself on the defensive was the growth of the Patrons of Husbandry or Grange movement, which spread rapidly across the province from 1874, to foster mutual support, social and economic co-operation, and general enhancement of the farming life among the people of the countryside. Yet this developed a little later. More notable in 1870-1 was a hopeful exodus from Ontario to break new farms in the Manitoba plains. In any case, however, one should not leave an impression of a generally hard-pressed rural community. Much of it was prospering highly, in the good years for farm markets that extended through the later sixties and until the onset of depression in 1873. Wheat farming was still close to its zenith, but mixed farming and specializing in barley for brewing, dairying, livestock-raising, or fruit and tobacco culture were important and valuable developments in agricultural Ontario. Substantial farms, high yielding through considerable employment of agricultural machinery, were the bright side of the rural picture – if somewhat idealized as the good life and the just reward of honest toil by the society of the day.

Town life looked equally prosperous, if one ignored women sweat-shop workers, vagrant children, and persistent sub-strata of underemployed or dependent poor. Certainly the towns were busy and influential in Ontario. In 1871 it held twelve of the twenty urban places in Canada with over 5000 inhabitants; to five in Quebec and three in the rest of the country.[6] Ottawa (with about 21,000 inhabitants), Hamilton (with 26,000), and Toronto (with some 56,000) had advanced most markedly: the first as the new national capital, the second as a prominent industrial centre, and the third as a regional metropolis. Nor did this urban growth represent the same degree of over-confident expansion that the frantic 1850s boom had produced. After some hard years of readjustment, the later sixties and earlier seventies brought more enduring, broader-based developments in town and city – especially in Toronto.

The provincial metropolis was notably benefitting from a new era of railway expansion as the seventies began; but smaller local lines were now under way, adding new strands to the city's railway net that were of a less costly and more cautious 'narrow gauge' variety. And while Toronto flourished as a regional trade and traffic focus, so its financial outreach was expanding also. In 1867 Toronto interests established the new and vigorous Bank of Commerce that led in a struggle against the predominant power of the Bank of Montreal. In 1871 Toronto banks won a significant success in the federal Banking Act of that year, which essentially ended the favoured position enjoyed earlier by the Bank of Montreal. Significantly, too, Francis Hincks was the minister of finance in the Macdonald government who shaped the new legislation.

Industry also had become a powerful factor in Toronto, and in Ontario urban places generally. Once more the census of 1871 is revealing, in demonstrating sizeable growth in manufacturing output over the 1860s.[7] Flour milling and saw-milling were still by far the province's leading industries, and their production had more than trebled in dollar worth since 1861. Even allowing for depressed times at the start of the sixties, changes in price levels, or census anomalies, this indeed was sizeable. Significant also was the growth in a host of other industries, some of which had been marginal, or even absent, in the census returns of 1861. The clothing industry, for example, now was third in product value in Ontario, whereas it had been of minor importance ten years earlier. Boot-and-shoe factories, foundries and machine shops came close behind; their output had increased in dollar value roughly five times over. The production of agricultural implements now stood at $2,291,000 in annual worth, a more than nine-fold gain. And major industries had been added, such as iron-rail rolling mills, oil refineries, and meat-packing houses, along with continued growth in textile factories, carriage works, furniture plants, and a good deal more. Clearly the industrial revolution was already well in process in Ontario by 1871, for much of it had begun there in the immediately preceding era.

This then, was the province, as the Confederation period ended and the High Victorian years began. It had been all but transformed during the lifetime of the pre-Confederation premiers; and whatever they had done to affect it politically, forces far beyond them had dramatically altered the pioneer world of their youth. The railways, daily newspapers, extensive public schooling were changing social and cultural conditions no less than urban and industrial growth or agrarian stratification. Provincial society had also attained a new level in its cultural amenities and interests – different, at least, from the bleak rawness of settlement days. The theatre was active (though not distinguished) in leading centres; literary, musical, and scientific groups attracted followings. Universities were flourishing, if small and narrowly based on the well-to-do and professional classes. And the age of planned recreation had opened for a more affluent yet more hemmed-in community; from organized sports like the 'national game' of lacrosse to 'picnic trains' out into the summer countryside; or even to the beginning of summer cot-taging northward towards the lake and forest realm – though much of this, such as Muskoka, was still the domain of the onward thrusting lumbermen.

In 1871, of Ontario's pre-Confederation premiers, only Robert Baldwin was long dead, and Sandfield Macdonald nearing the end of his life. William Draper continued to be an imposing adornment of the judiciary, presiding over the Court of Error and Appeal. Francis Hincks, of course, was back in politics in the cabinet of John A. Macdonald. As for the latter, perennial member for Kingston if now ensconced in Ottawa, his sharpest reverse and boldest triumphs yet lay ahead on the national scene. But still within this post-Confederation Canadian prime minister there was inherent the Ontario pre-Confederation leader he had been.

NOTES

1 See above, 303.
2 *Census of Canada, 1870-71*, I (Ottawa 1873), 31
3 Ibid., 364
4 D.G. Creighton, *John A. Macdonald: The Old Chieftain* (Toronto 1955), 120
5 *Census of Canada, 1870-71*, I, 420
6 Ibid., 428
7 Comparisons have been made between the census of 1871 (III, Ottawa 1875, 458-62) and that of 1861 (*Census of the Canadas, 1860-1*, II, Quebec 1864, 226-53), in order to provide the assessment of manufacturing growth presented in this paragraph.

Index

Macdonald's vision of 229-30, 234-5, 239; need for responsible government in 105-6; Ontario's place in 316-17

Canada Act (Constitutional Act of 1791) 29, 32, 34, 38

Canada Atlantic Railway 257

Canada East *see* Quebec

Canada First movement 316

Canada Land Company 100

Canada, United Province of 24, 60, 89, 116, 135, 139, 148, 158, 180, 185-7 *passim*, 193, 197, 205; church-state relations in 160-2, 172, 174-5; defence of 231-2, 265-6, 268-70, 284; demand for representation by population in 175-6, 264, 267-8; effect of American Civil War upon 288-9; establishment of 115; militia 231, 234, 265-71, 273, 289; political development 7-9, 288-9; railway links with Maritimes 164, 167-72, 270-1, 283, 286; responsible government in 130-2

Canada West *see* Ontario

Canadian Cotton Manufacturing Co 301

Canadian Freeman (Toronto) 99, 276

Canadian Manufacturers' Association 316

Canadian volunteers 246

le Canadien (Quebec) 60

Canadiens *see* French Canadians

Carling, Sir John 213, 295, 302

Caron, René-Edouard 60, 61, 66, 67, 70, 71, 74, 259

Cartier, Sir George Etienne 10, 173, 181, 187, 209, 220, 222, 246, 261, 262, 265, 273, 277, 280, 282-5 *passim*, 290, 291, 293, 301; and Militia bill 246, 265, 266, 268

Cartier-John A. Macdonald ministry 79, 246, 261, 263, 268, 284

Cartwright, John S. 36, 39, 40, 41, 45, 49, 50, 51, 55, 78

Cartwright, Sir Richard 187

Cathcart, Lord 62, 65, 66, 68, 70, 129

Cauchon, Joseph 165, 174, 262, 278

Cayley, William 67, 71, 72, 159; budget 63

census returns: 264; (1851) 14, 175; (1861) 14, 318; (1871) 315-18 *passim*

Chandler, Edward Barron 161, 167, 168, 169

Chapman, William 201

Charbonnel, Bishop Armand de 176

Charlottenburgh Township 247

Charlottetown Conference 10, 293

Christie, David 213

church-state relations 18, 160, 172, 174-5

Church of England 18, 19, 30, 32, 37, 49, 58, 59, 72, 73, 125, 139, 199, 228, 238, 253

Church of Ireland 92

Church of Scotland 18, 19, 52, 199, 249, 253

civil service 289, 298-9

Clarke Township 92, 93, 95

Clear Grit-Hincksite coalition 163, 172

Clear Grits 9-11 *passim*, 25, 165, 222, 223, 225, 266, 281-3 *passim*, 285, 288, 291, 295, 299, 300, 302; anti-Catholicism of 160-1, 176, 275; coalition with Hincks 163, 166, 172, 178; emergence of 135; George Brown assumes leadership 158; opposition to Baldwin 139-42, 253, 254; opposition to seigneurial compensation 262; and Reform Convention of 1859 263; and Representation by Population 264, 278-9; split with Hincks 180-1, with Sandfield Macdonald 276-7; support Sandfield Macdonald 267-8

Clergy Reserve Act (1840) 168, 170, 173, 174, 191

Clergy Reserves 19, 30, 37, 98, 115, 139-40, 151, 162, 165, 168, 170, 172, 177, 180-2 *passim*, 228, 253, 256;

papers 172; old-guard 252; party 37, 45, 99; press 178, 192; reaction to 1837 Rebellion 112, 150; sentiment 6; Toryism 26, 71, 76, 110. *See also* British party
Tory-Conservatives 72-4, 115, 117, 124, 125, 127, 129, 134, 135, 140
Tractarian movement 253
Treaty of Washington (1871) 302
Trent Affair 265, 268
True Witness (Montreal) 258
Trust and Loan Co 200, 201, 204, 206
Tupper, Sir Charles 283, 286

Ulster Irish 16-19 *passim*
Ultra-Reformers 41, 42, 53, 120
Union bill 37
Union of British North America *See also* Confederation 226
Union of the Canadas 4-6 *passim*, 10, 15-19 *passim*, 27-9 *passim*, 41, 113, 114, 117, 121, 285; demographic changes 13-15, 21; economic and social changes 13; economic benefits 36; ethnic composition 15, 17-18; expansion and settlement 19; Grit opposition to 263; need for double majority system in 259-60, 273; position of premier in 8; religious groups in 18-19; Tory opposition to 38, 249; Tory split over 36; viewed by Francis Hincks 152, 176; by John A. Macdonald 225-7, 235; by John Sandfield Macdonald 267
Union Parliament 10, 30
'Union with Great Britain' 225
United Empire Loyalists 3, 17, 232
'United Reform party' 119
United States of America 10, 16, 27, 36, 37, 39, 40, 62, 79, 112, 129, 132, 134, 138, 150, 159, 168, 170, 171, 179, 180, 189, 191, 229, 232, 233, 234,

260, 269, 288; anti-Americanism 25, 35, 233; border with 28, 36; and capture of York 95; Civil War 232, 233, 263, 265, 272, 287, 290, 294; Congressional system 139; constitution 39; expansionists 27; financiers 188; frontier 33, 39, 40; Homestead Act (1862) 296; idea of federalism 16; invaders from 97; invasion from 265; machine politics 25, 39; markets 233; mid-west 236; political techniques 233; politicians 233; railway network 233; relations with Great Britain 288-9; Revolution 3, 97; Senate 180; settlers from 33, 98; spoils system 133; sympathizers 112; system of government 135, 233; vessels 170, 171; War of Independence 232
universal suffrage 25, 229, 233
University Act (1849) 136, 256
University bills: 1843 57, 125; 1845 58-9, 61; 1846 66, 67; 'University Spoliation bill' 49
'University question' 18, 19, 71, 73, 78, 175
University of Toronto 126, 136, 175, 228, 298; Senate 136; University College 175
Upper Canada *see* Ontario
Upper Canada Assessment bill 53
Upper Canadian District Councils bill 250
Upper Canadian Reform Convention of 1859 10, 263; of 1867 294
Urquhart, Rev. Hugh 248
Ursuline Convent (Quebec city) 130

Vankoughnet, Philip M. 295
Victoria College 51, 58, 298
Viger, Denis-Benjamin 49, 52-4 *passim*, 60-2 *passim*, 66, 67, 70, 127, 128, 259, 260, 280; first advocate of double